Transpacific Studies

INTERSECTIONS

ASIAN AND PACIFIC AMERICAN
TRANSCULTURAL STUDIES

Russell C. Leong
David K. Yoo
Series Editors

Transpacific Studies

Framing an Emerging Field

Janet Hoskins and Viet Thanh Nguyen, editors

University of Hawai'i Press | Honolulu

Library of Congress Cataloging-in-Publication Data
Transpacific studies : framing an emerging field /
Janet Hoskins and Viet Thanh Nguyen, editors.
     pages cm — (Asian and Pacific American
transcultural studies)
  ISBN 978-0-8248-3994-9 — ISBN 978-0-8248-3998-7
(alk. paper)   1. Asia—Relations.   2. Pacific
Area—Relations.   3. United States–Relations.
4. Interregionalism—Asia.   5. Interregionalism—
Pacific Area.   6. Interregionalism—United States.
I. Hoskins, Janet, editor of compilation.
II. Nguyen, Viet Thanh, 1971- editor of compilation.
III. Series: Intersections (Honolulu, Hawaii)
  DS12.T76 2014
  303.48'25073—dc23
                  2014002196

Printed by Sheridan Books, Inc.

CONTENTS

Part III Transpacific Populations

ACKNOWLEDGMENTS

The idea for a volume of essays discussing the importance of transpacific connections germinated in discussions between the editors in 2007. We sought a way to bridge our fields of Southeast Asian Studies, Asian American Studies, and American Studies, with shared interests in Vietnamese communities in the United States and on the other side of the Pacific. We wanted to develop a more dynamic approach to populations in movement, including new work on diasporic connections and transnational processes that was sensitive to views from Asia and the Pacific. In trying to name this dynamic approach, we settled on the term "transpacific," inspired by Yunte Huang's literary criticism dealing with transpacific spaces in two books: *Transpacific Displacement: Ethnography, Translation and Intertextual Travel in 20th Century American Literature* (2002) and *Transpacific Imaginations: History, Literature, Counterpoetics* (2008). We were also influenced by the impressive range of new research focused on the "Black Atlantic," including Paul Gilroy's *The Black Atlantic: Modernity and Double Consciousness* (1993) and J. Lorand Matory's *Black Atlantic Religion* (2005).

On April 2–3, 2010, we held an international conference at the University of Southern California (USC) titled "Transpacific Studies: Homelands, Diasporas, and the Movement of Populations," hosted by the Center for International Studies. This conference brought together U.S., Asian, and European scholars to examine the phenomenon of transpacific displacement, in order to develop a new research paradigm that would go beyond conventional areas studies and American Studies models. Our intent was to shift the focus from anchored spaces and nations to the movements of people, resources, and materials over the past century. Focusing on these movements, we emphasized the blended identities of people who cross the Pacific, including not only immigrants but dual citizens, "flexible" citizens, refugees, and exiles, all of whom are accompanied by the transitional movement of ideas, languages, and cultural expressions as well as forms of social and economic capital.

For our purposes, shifting focus also involved a reframing of our fields in relation to the transpacific. Like a photograph or a window, a frame puts a border around a subset of reality, allowing it to be seen and understood in a certain way (while also excluding objects not in the frame). While understanding that a transpacific frame requires exclusion, we also believe that such a frame shows how new connections are forged in the "Pacific century," and how modern forms of communication and transport have compressed time and space across this huge body of water. This volume presents a selection from the seventeen papers presented at this conference, with new material added by contributors like J. Francisco Benitez, Weiqiang Lin, and Nancy Lutkehaus, who joined the project after the conference. Since this conference, the term "transpacific" has been appearing in more scholarly work, a sign that other scholars are also finding some use in the term's expansiveness and potential. Thus, it seems appropriate that for this book we label "transpacific studies" as an emerging field.

The book itself would not have been possible without the support of numerous individuals and agencies. The Center for International Studies at USC has provided continuing funding to support our research and publications. We are especially grateful to the Center's Patrick James, Indira Persad, and Erin Barber. USC's Zumberge Interdisciplinary Research Fund sponsored our conference and allowed us to cofound a new Center for Transpacific Studies at USC. The Henry R. Luce Foundation provided us with a generous grant to develop this idea of the transpacific over three years, through seminars, research funding, and fellowships for graduate students. Helena Kolenda was particularly helpful in guiding us through the application for, and administration of, the grant. Thien-Huong Ninh and Jennifer Sibara assisted us greatly in organizing the conference and, afterward, in preparing this volume. At the Center, our colleagues Saori Katada and Carol Wise have proved valuable collaborators in expanding the range of transpacific studies to include international relations and political science. As for the introduction to this volume, Viet Thanh Nguyen presented versions of it to audiences at Hitotsubashi University, Nagoya University, and Tsinghua University. He is grateful to the audiences for the comments and the colleagues who invited him: Mayumo Inoue, Hiromi Ochi, Akitoshi Nagahata, Wang Ning, and Yuan Shu. Lastly, Deborah Grahame-Smith edited the manuscript with a careful eye, while the University of Hawai'i Press, and especially the sponsoring editor Masako Ikeda, have helped to shape the volume in its final stages.

Introduction
Transpacific Studies: Critical Perspectives on an Emerging Field

VIET THANH NGUYEN AND JANET HOSKINS

Transpacific Power and Knowledge

In his book *A Nostalgist's Map of America,* the late poet Agha Shahid Ali writes of his travels in what we might call the simultaneous geographies of landscape and imagination:

> When on Route 80 in Ohio
> I came across an exit
> to Calcutta
> the temptation to write a poem
> led me past the exit
> so I could say
> India always exists
> off the turnpikes
> of America (Ali 1991, "In Search of Evanescence," 41)

India exists in the United States of America, and America, that mythical land, was for a moment imagined to be India. Calcutta marks a spot on the map of the real India, but it also marks a spot of the imagined India that has found its way somehow to Ohio. While the poet did not take the turnpike to see what this imagined India looked like, preserving the sense of the possibility of a real India waiting there, one could say that India did exist because of its claim on the American landscape. Likewise, one could equally conceive of roaming through India and finding bits of the real or the fantastic or the imagined USA in the alleys, streets, and off-roads. The USA there may not be the real USA to an American citizen, but it has a certain materiality to the Indian resident. Ali's poem marks a common enough experience in the relations between "America" and "Asia," two diverse entities whose cultural, economic, and political significance are both attached to particular countries and regions and which also exceed them, existing as imaginative constructions, discourses, and fantasies in the minds of their residents, their expatriates, and their friends and enemies elsewhere. This volume explores a model of "transpacific studies" that can illuminate the traffic in peoples, cultures, capital, and ideas between "America" and "Asia," as well as across the troubled ocean that lends its name to this model. The "Pacific," as many have noted, is as much of a trope and a figure as "America" or "Asia," and no less diverse and contested. This volume is an effort to explore all three tropes in their triangulated relationship to each other and to propose an academic field of study that can think through them simultaneously.

We begin with the idea of the Pacific as a construct that has been relevant to the peoples of Europe and America since the sixteenth century and the beginning of European exploration. The Pacific was important even earlier than this to the Asian and Pacific peoples with whom Europeans and later Americans came into contact via relationships of conquest, commerce, conversion, and collaboration.[1] In the European, American, and Asian imaginations, the idea of the Pacific is inseparable from fantasies of economic expansion and domination, with terms such as the Pacific Basin, the Pacific Rim, and Asia-Pacific having been created to name this strategic zone of contact. All of them have been limited in their own way, and all of them bear connotations of capitalist development.[2] The "transpacific" is the most recent effort at naming this contact zone. While the word itself is not new, it has attained significance recently both through intellectual efforts to theorize it and through state and corporate efforts to deploy it through the proposed Trans-Pacific Partnership (TPP) of twelve countries that border or are in the Pacific: Australia, Brunei, Canada, Chile, Japan, Mexico, Malaysia, New Zealand, Peru, Singapore, Vietnam, and the United States.[3] Like the Asia Pacific Economic Corporation's (APEC's) naming of the Asia Pacific as a space of economic cooperation (and not of conflict or colonization), the TPP signals how the ocean is not only an Asian, Pacific, and North American space of interest, but one for Latin America as well. Underlying the TPP's agreement about the necessity of free markets and transnational corporations for the health of nations, governments, and peoples is an implicit agreement about political, military, and strategic alliances. The agreement may also include a view that the TPP is part of a U.S. effort to contain Chinese influence by building strategic friendships in the Pacific. While the contributors to Arif Dirlik's seminal volume on the Pacific (Dirlik 1998) saw Japan as the contemporary and future competitor to the United States in 1998, the years since then have seen China's remarkable rise and, as a result, the rapid transformation of what transpacific competition and struggle means.

The emergence of a TPP, and the state recognition of such a thing as the transpacific, lends urgency to the work of theorizing the transpacific, which we spell differently from the TPP for three reasons. First, the transpacific gestures at an already existing history and pattern of flows across the Pacific that pre-date the TPP. Second, transpacific signals an inherently critical and oftentimes oppositional approach to the economic and political visions of the partnership. Third, the transpacific gestures at the better-known model of the transatlantic. The difference between a TPP and a transpacific studies evokes the basic differ-ence in the imagination of the Pacific that many academic studies have pointed toward. On the one hand, there is one vision of the Pacific as a space of explora-tion, exploitation, and expansion, advanced by European, American, and Asian powers. On the other hand, there is another vision of the Pacific as a contact zone; its history defined not only by conquest, colonialism, and conflict, but also alternate narratives of translocalism, oppositional localism (Wilson 2000), and oppositional regionalism (Dirlik 1998). From these alternate narratives comes the possibility of collaborations, alliances, and friendships between sub-jugated, minoritized, and marginalized peoples who might fashion a counter-hegemony to the hegemony of the United States, China, Japan, and other regional powers.

This basic bifurcation of visions stems from the root contradictions set into motion by European and American expansion into the Pacific, and informs most of the theories and ideas that we gather under the rubric of the transpacific. These theories and ideas deal with: the movements of peoples under models of dias-pora, transnationalism, translocalism, and cosmopolitanism; the importance of categories such as refugees, immigrants, exiles, tourists, adoptees, war brides, undocumented migrants, trafficked people, laborers, managers, and students; the value of capitalism and labor, the conflict between classes, and the exploita-tion and creation of wealth and inequity; the significance of gender and sexual-ity to the formation of populations, the role of workers, and the imagination of nations and capital; the legacies of imperialism, militarism, and colonization, and the enduring importance of racial and national differences; and last but not least of all for us, the role of intellectuals, academics, universities, and fields of study that consider Asia, America, and the Pacific.

In essence, what these competing visions of the transpacific require is a commitment to one side or the other of a centuries-old problem: the Pacific as an arena of economic development and imperial fantasy or the Pacific as a site of critical engagement with and evaluation of such development and fantasy. In what follows, we lay out some of the key issues and problems around the Pacific and offer some ideas for what a transpacific studies may look like. At the very least, what we hope for is the rise of transpacific studies as a different kind of transpacific partnership, this time between academics on both sides of the Pacific and in the Pacific. Questions about how to study transpacific relations, and their impact on academic fields of study, seem to have been more of a preoccupation for U.S. academics stricken with anxiety about the latent imperialism of U.S. academia. It is our belief, however, that there is an equally urgent need for Asian and Pacific Islander academics to theorize the transpacific and their relationship to it. In the context of the "politics of imagining Asia," as a parallel example, Wang Hui argues that Asian intellectuals cannot (re)imagine Asia without taking into account the history of European intervention in, and construction of, Asia, which has shaped the Asian nationalisms, internationalisms, and revolutions that have produced contemporary Asian nation-states and intellectual formations. Likewise, considering the Pacific, or transpacific relations, without grappling with the way those have been shaped by European and American interventions and intellectual traditions that have influenced Asian thinking and responses would be a mistake.

This is because the idea that Pacific and Asian studies in Asia are immune from the imperial problems of U.S.-based studies is a nostalgic vision. China and Japan are nations with imperial histories in Asia and the Pacific that predate European and American involvement, and they currently have hegemonic, if not outright imperialist, interests in Asia and the Pacific. South Korea, Taiwan, and Singapore are regional powers in Asia and the Pacific, with a vested interest in and track record of exploiting weaker economies and nations. For all of them, academic power is a function of state power, economic power, political power, and military power in similar ways to how academic power in the United States works. With Asian universities on the rise in Asia and the world, the question of how power and knowledge are related is just as critical for Asian academics as it is for American and European ones. Transpacific studies foregrounds this relationship between power and knowledge as applied to the Pacific. As a route and a region between the United States and Asia, the Pacific, both in terms of how it has been imagined and experienced, is central to the problem of how Americans, Asians, and Pacific Islanders know themselves and each other.

Transpacific Worlds and Histories

The study of Asia emerged through the scholarly traditions of "Orientalism," as European scholars looked "east" to what they called the Middle East and Far East. Both of these areas are "west" of the North American continent, but it is nevertheless true that Orientalist visions influenced European and American conceptions of Asia.[4] Before Edward Said's famous critique in 1978, "Orientalism" designated an academic specialization that often celebrated the literary traditions of Asia. Said (1978) argued that European scholars were not representing the Middle East but constructing it as feminine, backward, despotic, and unchanging, in ways that were complicit with colonial domination. Later scholars such as Timothy Mitchell (1988), Gauri Viswanathan (1998a, 1998b), and Ashis Nandy (2010) have shown that Orientalism was a historical process, which not only took different forms when it came to different Asian nations, but also involved an intimate relationship that implicated colonizers as well as the colonized. Going further than Said, Nandy also argues that Orientalist ideas could be a source of resistance to European domination. Just as earlier Orientalists often used positive descriptions of Asian culture to critique their own societies, those deemed Orientals could take negative stereotypes and turn them into positive attributes.

In order to focus on new ways in which Asia is linked to the Americas, however, we need to start with an understanding of how "Asia" itself has been constructed even before the Orientalist tradition. As Martin W. Lewis and Kären Wigen (1997) have shown, "Asia" as a term emerged in classical antiquity when it was used by the Greeks to denote all lands to the east of them, in contrast to Europe to the north and west and Africa to the south. The "myth of continents" was initially constructed as a triangle of land masses arrayed around a body of water, the Mediterranean, that bound them all together through a network of trade. After the new world was "discovered," America was added, so that Victorians could speak of "the four quarters of the world," and later of seven continents (Europe, Asia, Africa, North America, South America, Oceania, and Antarctica, although the three initial continents were in fact part of the same land mass). In effect, the European perspective treated region as a surrogate for religion and culture, demoting huge entities like China and India to "subcontinents." The Pacific is a much larger body of water than the Mediterranean, so for many centuries it was seen primarily as a barrier to exchange, a vast watery expanse that took months to cross. Only a few daring explorers tried to sail from the Americas to Asia, and for most peoples in both Asia and the Americas, it designated a region which was literally "off the map."[5] For many centuries the maritime trade networks that linked the area we now call "Asia" were focused on the Indian Ocean and the South China Sea. "Asian civilizations" interacted through these networks, allowing for the spread of Buddhism, Confucianism, and Taoism across thousands of miles and creating a relatively coherent configuration of cultural flows and the mutual adoption of new beliefs and practices.

A discourse of "Pan-Asianism" emerged during the process of decolonization, as a counter to European imperial domination. Nationalist struggles for self-determination built on western Orientalism to create an idea of "the East" as the inverted mirror image of "the West," opposing mystic spirituality to bureaucratic rationalism and Asian family values and discipline to European decadence, while other abstract, essentialized notions ossified into binary contrasts. Japanese nationalists also developed a vision of "Asia led by Asians," which served in part to camouflage their own imperial designs. As new ideological binaries divided Asia in the twentieth century, World War II gave birth to the idea of "Pacific Asia," a major theater of war operations where American and Japanese visions of Asia conflicted. This idea of Pacific Asia extended into the Cold War era. The Association of Southeast Asian Nations (ASEAN) became the first viable regional organization starting in 1967, and it led in 1989 to APEC, which stressed economic interdependence more than political independence. As an attempt to coordinate regional growth and enhance economic dynamism, APEC redefined regionalism so that "what started as an effort defined mainly in Pacific terms became one in which the Asian element would grow to be the more prominent one" (Acharya 2010, 1010).

This shift from the Pacific to Asia became evident with the dramatic growth of the East Asian economies of Japan, South Korea, Hong Kong, Taiwan, and Singapore in the 1990s. Their rise laid the groundwork for ideas of seemingly exceptional "Asian values" that could lead the coming Pacific century. Drawing on a perceived commonality derived from Confucianism's ethical and theological planes, the proponents of "Asian values" argued that even secular Asian societies were deeply invested in core principles of discipline, thrift, and respect for education and authority. In this century, these proponents tied the idea of a "rising Asia" to the expanding economies of China and India. Instead of speaking of Asia's emancipation from the West in spiritual and moral terms, advocates of a "rising Asia" deploy a language that is predominantly one of commercial expansion and globalization. However, as several chapters in this volume show (Xiang, Lin and Yeoh), this "rising Asia" is increasingly imitating and interacting with the United States and other nations on the opposite side of the Pacific. As Wang Hui (2011, ch. 1) argues, the turn to essentializing notions of culture on the part of some advocates for rising Asian nation-states obscures the heterogeneity of Asian societies and problematically affirms a discourse of nation-states that Asia has inherited from the west.

Recent debates about a resurgent Asia also reveal how much the idea of "Asia" is an emergent reality that is not territorially limited to the Asian side of the Pacific but also resurgent within American public life (see Andaya 2010 and Duara 2010). Prasenjit Duara (2010) argues that the ways in which "regions" and "regionalism" are conceived tends to follow dominant modes of "spatial production" in a particular period of time. The twentieth century was a time when the nation and the idea of national culture was predominant, but in the twenty-first century we may be moving to a period that will emphasize other linkages, connections, and transnational processes. We see the transpacific as one of those "spaces of interaction," which is not itself a "region" (and does not compete with a new notion of Asian interactions) but which does define flows of culture and capital across the ocean. As scholars like Fernand Braudel (1996) could speak of a "Mediterranean world" in the sixteenth century, it is possible that scholars of the twenty-second century will speak of a "transpacific world" that emerged in the twenty-first century around networks of trade, defining flows of both culture and capital across a different body of water.

The most explicit of the arguments in relationship to the Pacific are found in Dirlik's *What Is in a Rim?* (1998), to which this book is something of a sequel. The essayists in Dirlik's book, led by Dirlik himself, take a critical stance on what were the then-dominant terms for discussing the Pacific as a space of capital flows, "Asia-Pacific" or the "Pacific Rim" (Dirlik 1998, Dirlik 1994, 1998; Cumings 1998). The notion of the "Pacific Rim" became a geographic term that anticipated an optimistic future zone of cooperation—a Pacific Rim discourse, as Chris Connery (1994) calls it, of a euphoric regional ideology that focused on rapid economic growth and paid little attention to those who were excluded from or paid the cost of this expansion of transnational commerce. Dirlik (1998) traces the genealogy of "Pacific Rim" to European and American colonial influence and argues that the idea of the Pacific is "a discourse that seeks to construct what is pretended to be its point of departure" (4). This discourse defines the contours of a physical space that it claims only to describe.

Pacific Rim discourse celebrated the "miracles" performed by "tigers" (newly industrialized countries that soared into affluence) and neglected the other countries more appropriately described as "water buffaloes" (still trudging through the mud of rural economies and mired in poverty). By shedding light on these Asian success stories, the concept of the Pacific Rim helped its advocates erase the memory of America's three decades of war in Korea and Indochina, where it fought wars ostensibly to contain Communism but also to advance the development of capitalism in the rest of East and Southeast Asia, notably in Japan and South Korea. Furthermore, the American war in Indochina was supported by Japan, Korea, Thailand, and the Philippines, who provided bases, soldiers, contractors, and supplies for the American war effort. The regional and global significance of this was also evidenced by how the North Vietnamese were supported by China, the Soviet Union, and North Korea, while Laos and Cambodia were eventually dragged into the conflict. The American war in Indochina also left a legacy of violence and displacement for the people of Vietnam, Laos, and Cambodia, many of whom fled across the Pacific to other countries. Through a transpacific framework, we can see how the American war was not simply a military or political event involving a few countries, but was actually part of larger strategies of economic maneuvering in which the future Asian powers of the Pacific Rim played a key part.

The central place of the Pacific in the global imagination and maneuverings of powerful and not-so-powerful nations encourages a reenvisioning of U.S. history. In spite of a dominant Atlantic origin story linking Americans to Britain and the rest of Europe, Asia has influenced American culture very deeply (Cumings 2009). This rhetoric of American and Pacific centuries implicitly praises the economic potential of the United States and powerhouse Asian countries, with cultural potential a distant second and the Pacific Islands largely absent. The economic globalization that is driven by the United States, Europe, and Asia, which is designed to reinforce the economic superiority of already industrialized countries and to suppress the competitive ability of already poor countries, is supplemented by militarism. While the United States, with its overwhelming and potentially self-crippling military budget, is the military enforcer of U.S.-dominated global capitalism, Asian militarism is on the rise as a consequence of an emboldened China and a weakening United States.[6] Thus, even if the "American century" that U.S. force produced may be giving way to a "Pacific century," both are also trademark names labeling the dominant forces of globalization in particular eras. Thus, "transpacific" inevitably carries connotations of economic growth, development, exploitation, and hierarchy, along regional, national, racial, class, and gender lines.

Although the transpacific can be conceived as a complex network of actually realized power and domination among many countries, codified in treaties, organizations, and formal alliances, the latent possibility of opposition, resistance, and counterhegemonic thinking is also to be found, dispersed among many populations and locales. We could look at efforts to build oppositional thinking in the Pacific as well as across the Pacific to other locales. Working from the legacies of scholarship on the Black Atlantic, other scholars have excavated "Afro-Asian intersections" that serve to link both Atlantic and Pacific, as well as black, yellow, and brown peoples. Ho Chi Minh, for example, sought to build anticolonial efforts by forging alliances between Africans and Vietnamese in France between the world wars; W. E. B. DuBois and Richard Wright looked to China and India for inspiration; Africans and South Asians found commonality not in race or national identity, but in commitments to emancipation; some African Americans during World War II were inspired by Japanese rhetoric of anti-imperialism. Afro-Asian revolutionary solidarity was also expressed at the 1955 Bandung Conference, in professions of Third World alliance against colonialism and imperialism, and in efforts to link domestic struggles with international struggles. All of these were inflected by transpacific notions of resistance carried out by minoritized and colonized partners.[7] A transpacific perspective serves as a counterpoint or balance to transatlantic orientations, lending more credence to the role that the Pacific and Asia have played in shaping the United States and Europe.

For Asia, Wang Hui (2011) locates that latent possibility in the history of decolonization and national liberation, whose memories remain even in a "depoliticized" era of Asian nation-states grasping for capitalist power (41). Other latent possibilities reside in what Epeli Hau'ofa (1995) calls "Oceania" and "our sea of islands," his terms for how to reimagine what Europeans called the Pacific, from the points of view of those who live in the islands and the ocean. "The world of Oceania is not small," he writes in defiance of colonial ideas that the islands in the ocean—and their peoples—were inconsequential. "It is huge and growing bigger every day" (Hau'ofa 1995, 89). The voices and perspectives of Pacific peoples foreground campaigns for sovereignty and indigenous rights, and critiques of nuclear testing, environmental destruction, and the imperialist nature of tourism, as in the work of indigenous activists like Haunani-Kay Trask. Tourism in Hawai'i and elsewhere, it should be noted, is no longer a western-dominated phenomenon but increasingly a vehicle for Asian cosmopolitanism in the transpacific, expressive of the rise of Asian capital in internationally powerful and regionally powerful Asian states. Critiques like Wang Hui's of Asia, therefore, need to incorporate an awareness of the Pacific in order to understand how Asian memories of liberation and decolonization may efface efforts by some contemporary Asian peoples to colonize weaker others.

While the peoples of the Pacific bear memories and histories that speak against the "militarized currents" imposed on them, the transpacific legacies of anticolonial wars and intra-Asian wars remain bitter and strong throughout Asia and its diasporas (see Shigematsu and Camacho 2010). The transpacific desires of Europe and the United States led directly to the imposition of colonial authority or the infringement of sovereignty on numerous Asian countries, including incursions into Japan and China, the American colonization of the Philippines, the French colonization of Indochina, and the contemporary "transnational garrison state" extended by the United States through its military bases around the world (Bello 2010, 311). Asian nations were not immune from the impulse to dominate, interfere in, and influence other countries, first their neighbors and increasingly countries further away on the Pacific Rim. Twentieth-century examples include the Japanese colonization of Korea and Manchuria, Japan's occupation of the Philippines and numerous Pacific islands, the South Korean military participation in the United States' Vietnam

War, the Vietnamese invasion of Cambodia in 1978, and the Chinese invasion of Vietnam in 1979. These events illustrate how Asian nations, no matter their victimization by foreign powers, were quite capable of and willing to assume mantles of power as they sought to exercise control over one portion, or even the entirety, of the Pacific. In the last few decades, Asian countries have also tried to extend their influence through trade and investment, as evident in Japanese, Taiwanese, and South Korean firms opening plants in Mexico and developing economic relations with Latin America; China's efforts to expand mining, drilling and trade in Africa; and all the major Asian countries jostling for influence over weaker Asian countries in East and Southeast Asia.

The transpacific is thus defined by deep contemporary and historical conflicts over geography, economy, and political spheres of influence that prevent any one country from claiming moral superiority or insisting, without problem, on centering itself in a transpacific discourse. These conflicts have also produced vast and continuing movements of people between Asian countries, across the Pacific, and between Asia and the Americas that we can examine through concepts of diaspora and transnationalism.

Transpacific Dispersals and (Re)Productions

Even though diaspora and transnationalism deal with dispersed populations across national borders, they are often themselves defined in terms of national or ethnic origins. As a consequence, diasporic and transnational populations can reaffirm problematic nationalist or racial notions, and can also be sources of nationalist fervor rather than postnational openness (see Palumbo-Liu 2007). Nevertheless, diasporic and transnational frameworks are necessary to explore relations among the adopted home, the ethnic homeland, and geographically dispersed coethnics. These relations are sometimes imagined as stemming from or leading to loss, as Agha Shahid Ali (1991) alludes to when he mentions that "cluster of sorrows / that haunt the survivors of Dispersal that country / which has no map" (44). This "country which has no map" is the imaginary cartography of homeland and dispersal that immigrants, refugees, and exiles carry with them in their minds and their souls, but it is not always and only a landscape of loss and sorrow, populated by the most ephemeral of all transpacific migrants, the ghosts that have managed to cross an ocean.[8] These Asian diasporas have also become fused with notions of communities that transcend geographic dispersal, which could provide a perhaps utopian sense of "belonging" without the burdens, limits, and responsibilities of citizenship. The two possible senses of of Asian diasporas as dystopic and utopic demarcate the extreme ends of different ways in which diasporas can be deployed.

Diaspora in its contemporary sense examines the shifting relations between homelands and host nations from the perspective of those who have moved, some voluntarily and many against their will. The scholarly literature has often defined such movements of displaced peoples as the opposite of "indigenous culture," but these two opposed and mutually illuminating concepts have been radically modified by New World settler colonies, the process of colonization, and a globalizing economy in which "indigenous peoples" are most often the most displaced. Furthermore, as Rhacel Parreñas and Lok Siu (2007) argue, diasporas are not simply bilateral phenomenon between two countries. Ethnically defined diasporas are scattered across multiple countries, while single countries host multiple diasporas; a diasporic-oriented studies thus needs to look at the ways diasporas may reaffirm ethnic and nationalist notions of monoculturalism but can also serve as nodes of alliances with other displaced or dispersed peoples.

Transnationalism, on the other hand, encompasses not just the movement of people, but also ideas of citizenship, technology, multinational governance, modes of political organization, differing notions of sovereignty, and market impulses, all combining to shape the contemporary world. While we could speak of "major" transnationalisms that involve the movement of capital or the elite populations that serve it or are served by it, Françoise Lionnet and Shu-mei Shih (2005) draw attention to the phenomenon of "minor" transnationalisms that are composed of minority peoples who move across borders. Rather than focus on the vertical relationship between majority and minority in a given society, they emphasize the horizontal relationships of a minority population across national borders and between minorities within national borders. Like the diasporic model of Parreñas and Siu, minor transnationalism affirms the political possibilities of relationships between disempowered, marginalized, and minoritized peoples.

While many may see diasporic and transnational dispersals as burdens born by displaced persons, we also see them as "spatial resources" capable of exploitation by both the powerful and the less powerful. These spatial resources create international networks for organizing the movements of people and goods in the contemporary world (business networks, religious congregations, communities of readers and of consumers of media in a specific language, etc.). Asians and Pacific Islanders have crossed the seas to become citizens of many countries, while western citizens have gone abroad in Asia for work and study. Asian powers have accrued economic influence in the Pacific Islands and the west, while many Asians have gone to work or settled in other Asian countries, developing diasporic networks in which the United States or European countries are not central nodes. Some of these Asian countries compete with the United States and Europe for influence and profit and deploy various strategies to manage mobile and minority populations. A transpacific framework prevents any easy shift to foregrounding rising Asian countries without considering how they are implicated in problems of power, and how their rise is tied to a complicated history of competition, conflict, and negotiation with the west, with each other, and with their own minorities. Examining the complex web of personal identities, motivated journeys, pilgrimages, returns and remigrations between Asian countries and across the Pacific allows us to envisage a complex new set of relationships that tie one nation to another, and new sets of relationships based on heritage that may be even stronger than those of nation and citizenship.

The transpacific connections that forge diasporas are not simply a matter of subjective identification, however. They emerge in particular social and material conditions that produce, sustain, and perpetuate diasporic formations. The transpacific offers a framework to explore ties between the ethnic homeland, the adopted home of present residence, and "ethnoscapes," or geographically dispersed coalitions of coethnics (see Appadurai 1996). In this sense, the idea of the transpacific is an intellectual and political project as well as an aspect of modern life in the twenty-first century. Calling the twenty-first century the "Pacific century" or the "Asian century" indicates not just a shifting of power but also a change of tactics, with the emphasis less on a single geographic center and more on a complex network of connections. These diasporic connections are not indiscriminately "global" but culturally specific, composed of fragmented, multiple connections emerging from historically particular conditions. Many Asian states now do a great deal to produce and sustain diasporic connections, in order to promote investment, bring in educated technical advisors with homeland ties, and so on. They are following an example perhaps best modeled by Israel (the realization of a diasporic dream of re-creating a homeland as a nation-state) but now common throughout Asia (although less common for Europe). But as diasporas have emerged due to massive migrations, displacements of refugees and re-drawing of national boundaries, they have destabilized notions of sovereignty and autonomy, unsettling the clearer geographies of past centuries. In Arjun Appadurai's (1996) words, "State and nation are at each other's throats, and the hyphen that connects them is now less an icon of conjuncture than an index of disjuncture" (38).

Within the diaspora, it is sometimes easier to feel passionate loyalty and attachment to an imagined homeland that is geographically distant than to reconcile with the imperfect origin that one can eventually revisit. The idea of diaspora's powerful emotional pull lies in its appeal to shared—and imagined—history and experiences, which can be of a positive, celebratory nature or can be constituted by the shared suffering of war, forced migration, and the exploitation of labor, bodies, and sexualities. These common experiences create a sense of "being a people" with deep-reaching roots and destinies outside the time/space of the host nation. Rather than seeing themselves as "ethnic minorities," displaced by suffering, exile, and discrimination, diasporic groups may prefer to see themselves as "transnational subjects" whose affiliations cannot be contained within nation-state boundaries. In Paul Gilroy's (2000) postracial vision, diasporic potential arises from the diasporic place "in between" opposing "camps," which are both nation-states but also rigid ideological, economic, and political forces; "in between," these diasporic populations and their related transnational kin see themselves as possessing greater flexibility in identity than their more nationally, communally, or ethnically bound peers. Thus, the concept of the transpacific not only involves trauma, haunting, and marginalization but also empowerment, enrichment, and expansion.

The celebratory potential of transpacific communities, cultures, and circulations needs to be contrasted, however, with both the histories of conflict and colonization outlined above and with the vulnerability of transpacific populations to cooptation. Minority cultures and identities can become what Inderpal Grewal (2005) calls "lifestyles of empowerment" (16). These lifestyles are based on histories of political struggle against marginalization and persecution that have resulted in the formation of necessary identities, such as "Asian American" or "feminist," that are nevertheless subject to participating in neoliberal and nationalist discourses. U.S. liberal feminism, then, while affirming women's rights, can also use them, inadvertently or deliberately, to reinforce the power of First World nations over others. The classic formulation of this is in Gayatri Spivak's depiction of colonialism as "white men saving brown women from brown men," modulated in this case to include white women (and their diasporic women of color allies) as rescuers of downtrodden women globally (see Shih 2005). The function of transpacific minorities as neoliberal subjects in the west is also apparent, as multiculturalism, diversity, and tolerance, in all their national variations in the west, promote the inclusion of racial and sexual minorities not just to address inequality but to advance the idea of western superiority over darker countries and cultures that are supposedly not so tolerant. In his celebrated treatise on cosmopolitanism, where he argues for the necessity of empathy-building conversation with strangers across different cultures, Kwame Anthony Appiah (2006) notes, rather darkly, that "there are limits to cosmopolitan tolerance. . . . we will not stop with conversation. Toleration requires a concept of the intolerable" (144).

How cosmopolitan societies will respond to noncosmopolitan societies in Appiah's model is left unstated, which is perhaps one sign of how neoliberalism operates: the welcoming hand that is offered to lift up the other can easily turn into the clenched fist if that hand is refused. Racial minorities who function as the "stranger" within western society, and whose acceptance validates western cosmopolitanism, run the risk of being literally domesticated. By focusing only on domestic issues of inequality and inclusion, or by celebrating their status as cultural ambassadors and translators between East and West or North and South, racial minorities in the west obscure the link between their relative privilege as western subjects vis-à-vis the countries that the west dominates. They thus participate in what Gilroy (2006) calls "armored cosmopolitanism," the reworking of the old idea of the white man's burden for a multicultural, neoliberal present in which Asian countries who aspire to global and regional power also participate (60). While most of the discussion on cosmopolitanism and neoliberalism has focused on western majorities as their subjects, minorities and nonwestern majorities also need to be located in these discourses, particularly as countries like China, Japan, Taiwan, and Singapore, as well as their diasporas, all cultivate their own politically complicated versions of Asian cosmopolitanism and neoliberalism.

South Korea provides one example of how a poor country has turned itself into a "subimperial" one whose features include armored cosmopolitanism, neoliberal influence, and diasporic power.[9] This transformation is depicted in Seoul's War Memorial, a museum whose historical narrative shows South Korea being born in agonized struggle from the Korean War, when it was helped by the United States and the United Nations. The culmination of the narrative depicts a strong South Korea that in turn helps defend the freedom of other countries in humanitarian operations. This is a euphemism for war, with the conflict in this case being the Vietnam War in which South Korean forces participated as the United States' strongest ally (and, according to many reports, its cruelest).[10] The so-called humanitarian aid offered by South Korea in Vietnam was, in effect, a reworking of the white man's burden as the yellow man's burden, for South Korea benefited immensely from its participation in American neocolonialism; some historians credit American payments for South Korean troops and American contracts to South Korean corporations as responsible for igniting South Korean's economic development (see Woo 1991).

This development would eventually have further transpacific ramifications with South Korean investment in the United States, where Korean capital has elevated Los Angeles's Koreatown from ethnic ghetto to capitalist enclave. This transformation cannot simply be celebrated, for in Los Angeles we see one of the more spectacular examples of the oppressive side of "Afro-Asian intersections." In a racially divided city where black ghettoes endure, transpacific Asian populations, including but not limited to Koreans, benefit not only from positive images attached to their economic success and cosmopolitan style, but also arguably from the negative "virtue" of not being black. Studies of the transpacific should therefore be conscious about how diasporic populations cannot be considered in isolation, but must be considered in relation to other diasporas and domestic minorities in networks of affiliation and disaffiliation, of alliance and exploitation, of cooperation and conflict.

Lastly, we can consider how the erotic, the romantic, and the heteronormative all play a role in the imagination of countries and peoples competing in and over the Pacific. As Neferti Tadiar says, desire and capitalism are inseparable, and the relations and identities of transpacific nations can be seen as "libidinal economies" where the pursuit of profit is imagined through romantic, erotic, sexual, and gendered ways. Thus, globalization depends on feminized labor to staff low-wage factories, to fulfill domestic work, and to service sexual needs; often, this feminized labor comes from Asia, the Pacific, or Asian diasporic populations (see also Parreñas 2001 and Gerefi 1998). While in the American century it was the United States as a masculine presence that dominated the world, particularly a feminized Asia, in the Asian century it is the stronger Asian powers who seek to appropriate the masculine position, often at the expense of weaker Asian and Pacific countries. Asian cultures and countries themselves participate in different ways in this figurative, cultural, and economic exploitation of labor, from being complicit in the use and export of feminized labor to propagating notions of women as being representatives of a country's pure, national essence. It is because of this that Naoki Sakai and Hyon Joo Yoo argue that a "transpacific imaginary" recognizes a "transpacific complicity" in the imperial struggle for power in the Pacific. They point out how the United States and Japan traded dominant positions in the Pacific after World War II, and how both Japan and the United States helped to justify Japan's postwar role as the assistant to and beneficiary of U.S. hegemony via a deeply a gendered discourse. At the same time, Japan exercises a will to domination in relation to other Asian countries, symbolized for Sakai and Yoo in its treatment of Korean comfort women.[11]

In a variety of discourses—from the academic to the military to the literary to the cinematic to the journalistic—the relationship between colonizer and colonized has been depicted by both east and west as a figurative and literal heterosexual rape, between a masculine west or north and a feminine east or south. If not rape, then this relationship is often seen as a heterosexual and sometimes homosexual romance. While rape is destructive and exploitative, romance is progressive and productive. Both are capable of offspring, the results of miscegenation that can be monstrous or beautiful, standing in as figures for why foreign cultures should never meet or why they should for a more peaceful and prosperous future. The notion of economic wealth as being a part of exploitation or production is always intertwined with rape and romance, and since the economic and the erotic mutually animate each other, queer studies can play a role in disrupting the heteronormative assumptions of transpacific productivity and reproductiveness. Lee Edelman's argument that political discourses are built on a futuristic orientation premised on the inevitability and fetishization of children, reproduction, and the heterosexual family has some resonance for economic discourses of the Pacific. These discourses are predicated on the idea that what Masao Miyoshi calls a "borderless world" for free trade and capitalism will inevitably lead to wealth and riches that can be passed on to future generations (who are both the beneficiaries and the justification for capitalism).

To refuse reproduction and to refuse capitalist production are both queer behaviors in the capitalist worlds of the transpacific. The work that brings together both queer studies and diasporic studies makes evident how diasporas and transnational populations often see themselves not only in capitalist terms of progress and upward mobility but also in terms of the heterosexual reproduction of national cultures. Queer diasporas, then, disrupt the easy transference of romantic, heterosexual metaphors of capital and nations onto the diaspora, and vice versa, such as the marriage of east and west, the inevitability of second generations, the fertile soil of new lands, and so on. Queerness also reconfigures how we understand the mobility of populations. As Nayan Shah argues, the factors that stimulate transnational, border-crossing movements are often considered by scholars to be economic or political in nature. But what would happen if sexual, erotic, or other social factors were considered? Perhaps, he argues, men moved because they were escaping social and sexual constrictions, rather than only or primarily economic limitations. While Shah focuses on the intimate worlds of male migrants and the "stranger intimacy" they formed with other men, such a queer perspective can be extended to women as well. A queer diaspora as an analytic deflates the idea that people were leaving "home," for perhaps they did not consider where they left to be a home for them, as Gayatri Gopinath points out. Transpacific frameworks that include the insights of queer perspectives unsettle many of the economistic, reproductive, nationalist, and culturalist assumptions that power capitalist visions and fantasies of a "Trans-Pacific Partnership," as well as the impulses within academic fields to "settle" into and for disciplinary homes.

Toward a Transpacific Studies

The challenge of transpacific histories and flows means that existing models for studying these topics need to be reconsidered and reconfigured. This is true not only for the west and its universities, but also for Asia and its increasingly powerful and competitive academic complex. In the west, the transpacific has usually been studied under area studies and increasingly in related fields like Asian American studies and American studies, as part of what John Rowe (2012) calls a "scholarly state apparatus" (87). Asian scholars in Asia who also study Asia reasonably look with suspicion on both the western area studies tradition and its debates about the complications of area studies, as well as the nationalist assumptions of U.S.-based Asian American and American studies. But the field questions and methodological problems that U.S.-based scholars have been discussing also have relevance for Asian-based scholars because the academic industrial complex within which U.S. scholars work has trained many Asian scholars and is also being adopted by Asian countries. For these reasons, Asian and Pacific scholars' efforts to distinguish their own work on Asia, the Pacific, and the transpacific, or insurgent calls for Pacific studies, or Asian efforts to study the west, are not immune from some of the issues that have shaped U.S.-based fields and produced American blind spots. Transpacific studies, built on multilateral relationships and staged in multiple countries, allows a reconsideration of dominant U.S.-based fields and emergent or competing Asian- and Pacific-based fields.

The legacies of Orientalism and the critique of the oftentimes compromised position of postcolonial intellectuals provide openings for how to consider the role of transpacific studies and its impact on the fields that study Asia, the Pacific, Europe, or the United States, regardless of where they are based. Scholars in Asia who also study Asia have argued that the United States and Europe should be considered as regions of thought rather than being the centers of universal theory, from where scholars venture from home out into the "field" of Asia (see Harootunian 2002 and C. Lowe 2007). Thus, not only should Europe be provincialized, as Dipesh Chakrabarty (2000) proposes, but the United States as well. "The travels of academic theory in Southeast Asia suggest the provincial nature of American critical theory," Celia Lowe (2007) says. "What might it look like for U.S.-based scholars to proceed as though they do not possess the most significant knowledge about, or all of the solutions to, the world's difficult problems?" (C. Lowe 2007, 133 and 121). The humbling of U.S. area studies is necessary in any post-Orientalist approach to the study of Asia, but if the U.S. university must be located in relation to the history of U.S. power, so do Asian universities need to be located in relation to the histories of Asian power. In a larger frame, Wang Hui (2011) argues that the intellectual and political efforts to imagine a new "Asia" from within Asia can only do so through a critique of the "Europe" that constructed "Asia" in the first place. Such efforts are inevitably intertwined with the how Asian nation-states shape their scholarly apparatuses.

While Wang Hui (2011) bases his concerns in the importance of European thinking about Asia, we argue that American ways of thinking about Asia remain important to Asian intellectuals because of continuing U.S. global dominance and the ongoing influence that the United States has within many Asian countries. Looking at the American example, we find that the problems in how the United States has examined and constructed Asia cannot be contained within Asian studies, but affect U.S. American studies and Asian American studies as well. Both of these fields have some bearing on academic studies of Asians in Asia and American influence in Asia. U.S.-based area studies and American studies came into being to serve the globalization of the United States in the mid-twentieth century. Area studies in the United States began shortly after World War II, when federal funds were allocated to increase American knowledge of world areas to improve the conduct of U.S. policy. Domestically, American studies promoted the idea of American exceptionalism. Cold War politics drove much of these fields' scholarship and program building. The links to national security concerns helped to secure funding, and that funding was later supplemented by governments and foundations in the wealthier Asian nations (Japan, South Korea, Taiwan) as well as diasporic communities within the United States. By the beginning of the twenty-first century, area studies had entered a period of crisis. While some argued that traditional regional boundaries no longer seemed capable of encompassing global phenomena, others defended area studies scholarship as a dynamic, productive, and heterogeneous model that might work best when pairing and comparing insider and outsider knowledge.[12]

Not until the 1990s would American studies in the United States start to pay attention to the issue of U.S. domination in the Pacific as an imperial exercise, a transnational turn that would accelerate dramatically in the aftermath of 9/11. This transnational turn occurred after the multicultural turn in U.S. American studies, which began in earnest with the end of the Cold War. The moment of multicultural dominance in American studies, where the field increasingly focused on questions of race, gender, class, and sexuality within American borders, highlighted internal differences but generally overlooked the United States' role overseas or in foreign countries. The exception was the attention paid to immigration from other countries, and the gradual increase in concepts like diaspora and transnationalism. Asian American studies had always paid attention to immigration, concerned as it was in the 1960s and 1970s with how Asians arrived in the United States and how they transformed themselves into Asian Americans. Asian American studies is an intellectual formation born from the Asian American movement of the 1960s, which was premised on antiracism and anti-imperialism, fueled by the anti-Vietnam War movement and predicated on the radical liberation of racially and class-oppressed populations. The Asian American movement was a reaction against the political order that had given birth to area studies and American studies, and while Asian American studies has sought to be included in American studies, it has had a tense relationship with area studies, particularly Asian studies. This reflects Asian American studies' hesitation in turning toward and across the Pacific.[13]

Asian American studies' historical focus on immigration, with the United States as the destination, meant that Asian American studies was generally reluctant to consider the importance of Asia or countries of origin. Throughout the end of the twentieth century, Asian American studies was focused mostly on issues within American borders. But its concern with immigration meant that it was at least conscious of the role of the United States overseas in the Asian wars that created the conditions of immigration for many populations. Transpacific history was already a structuring factor in the constitution of Asian American populations, but Asian American studies neglected the transpacific nature of these populations because of its imperative to "claim America," in Maxine Hong Kingston's words. Claiming America was a direct reaction to the American tendency to see Asian Americans as perpetual foreigners. This domestic focus meant that Asian American studies was harmonious with American studies in maintaining the importance of national borders and in leaving the dominance of "America" as a categorical definition for American studies uncontested. The critique of American inequality that was fundamental to Asian American studies was, in the end, possibly even complicit with even the most exceptionalist versions of American studies, for what remained affirmed was the importance of perfecting the American democratic project.

But latent within the formation of both Asian American populations and Asian American studies were legacies of warfare and the movement of capital that would be conducive to a transpacific approach, and indeed would necessitate such an approach. Coincident with U.S. wars in Iraq and Afghanistan, Asian American studies increasingly turned its attention overseas. Part of this attention focused on the American wars in Asia that had stimulated Asian emigration and which had provided the initial impetus for Asian American self-formation. Part of the attention went to a transpacific examination of the immigration experience that was as concerned with the sending countries as the receiving ones. Not least of all, some of the attention went to the diasporic and transnational contexts for understanding elements of the Asian American experience, such as the gendered and sexualized dimensions of Asian American cultures, or the popular cultural connections between Asia and Asian America.

Despite these shifts, Asian American studies still finds itself enmeshed in a problem that captured American studies as well in its transnational turn, namely the reliance on an American or Eurocentric point of view. Thus, even as Asian American and American studies stressed the diasporic, the transnational, or the international, and even as they foregrounded American imperialism, both formations tended to rely on European and American theories and centered the United States in relation to Asia or elsewhere. Not least, these studies also often depend on English or European languages, which can distort their objects of study; thus, American and Asian American studies in the United States often means the study of English-speaking and English-writing populations, whose viewpoints may be rather different than immigrants, refugees, exiles, and intellectuals who express themselves in other languages. The result of this reliance on the English language and on American or European theories and perspectives, some critics argued, was to reassert American and Asian American intellectual dominance in the name of criticizing American political, economic, and cultural dominance. Such a contradiction meant that it was possible that the questions and conclusions reached by American and Asian American studies might already be biased or flawed from the beginning by assumptions that placed certain topics or questions out of the intellectual or linguistic frame. Without a transpacific approach, then, even a post–Cold War, anti-imperialist American studies could assert either an intellectual imperialism or an insistence on the United States as the primary object of inquiry. Asian American studies also finds itself in a problematic situation vis-à-vis a latent investment in American nationalism that remains invisible without a transpacific approach.

Critiques from Asia and the Pacific about the limits of U.S.- or European-based perspectives, and the need for perspectives from Asia and the Pacific, therefore have urgency both for their practitioners and those reading from elsewhere. These critiques express a healthy skepticism toward U.S.- or European-based perspectives, from which transpacific studies itself may come. These critiques prioritize Asia as an object of inquiry and as the source of theories and ideas appropriate to such an object, which is inseparable from a wider political project about contesting and controlling the production of knowledge, its location in universities that are a part of nation-states, and the enmeshment of those nation-states in histories of colonialism and capitalism. One such critique is found in Ariel Heryanto's influential essay "Can There Be Southeast Asians in Southeast Asian Studies?" (2007). His essay has wider implications beyond Southeast Asia, and poses a provocative question with mixed answers. Southeast Asian scholars have not been influential in Southeast Asian studies due to the dominance of American and European academics. Western universities, programs, and discourses simply overshadowed Southeast Asian ones, and western discourse became the legitimizing one in a global academic conversation. Heryanto insists that Southeast Asians can study Southeast Asians, and that such a move can be destabilizing to area and Asian studies, with native scholars speaking back to the western scholars, appropriating the knowledge formation of which their population has served primarily as objects rather than subjects.

On the one hand, Heryanto's argument can be extended widely to the issue of whether there can be Asians in Asian studies; on the other hand, his argument can also be used to emphasize the still-subordinated place of Southeast Asians relative not only to Europeans and Americans but to East Asians. In either scenario, the shifting and uneven dynamics of power and knowledge are evident. The rise of prominent Asian scholars from Asia who study Asia is dependent at least partially on the rise of the Asian countries from which they come, China and Japan, and their ability to send students to the west in order, ironically, to become equipped and recognized to study the rest. Economic and political power leads to the ability to claim academic legitimacy, and to contest the terms of academic legitimacy. But competing for academic power and knowledge is hardly a simple matter of saying that it is now possible for Asians to study Asians, as if Asians were a homogenous population. Hence, Heryanto's Southeast Asian focus is key, for it indicates the relative lack of visibility of Southeast Asian studies and scholars even as (East) Asian studies became a necessity with the rise of China and Japan. Southeast Asians must struggle for self-determination in the realm of power and knowledge against both western and East Asian countries with a more developed "scholarly state apparatus."[14] The deployment of theoretical instruments of power-knowledge that are of western origin or influence enforces inequalities within Asian scholarship, since access to this intellectual language is still heavily weighted toward East Asian countries and their universities and scholars.

Recognizing the uneven terrain within Asia, and in regards to Asia and the west, Kuan-Hsing Chen argues for reimagining Asia through what he calls "Asia as method," whereby Asians study Asia and Asians, from Asian locations, and within an Asian context that foregrounds the relations between Asians and Asian countries. Chen argues that "Asia as method" is a decolonizing movement, illuminating how western colonialism has not ended in Asia, but has been succeeded by the neocolonialism of global capitalism in which western countries dominate—particularly the United States—but wherein rising Asian powers and elites enthusiastically participate. Part of the result of U.S. domination is the "Americanization" of the Asian countries, particularly South Korea, Japan, and Taiwan, whose intellectual, political, and military classes are deep under American sway. "Asia as method" also acknowledges the existence of these powerful Asian countries as "subempires" which are themselves intent on competing with each other for regional influence over the weaker countries of Southeast Asia and the Pacific. "Asia as method" provides an alternative to the "politics of imagining Asia" offered by Wang Hui, offering the possibility of an "Asia" that is not beholden to the west. For Asian studies scholars who seek to wrest the meaning of "Asia" away from the west, and to create spaces for less privileged and less translated voices, "Asia as method" has proven inspiring and influential.[15]

"Asia as method" is the Asian counterpart of the radical oppositional method that supposedly animates Asian American studies, which is not surprising, given their intertwined genealogies of origin. "Asia as method" derives from histories of Asian nationalisms and revolutions that were at least partially influenced by European Enlightenment ideas of nation-states and Marxism. Chen, a U.S.-trained scholar of cultural studies, is located at least partially in that European tradition as it was realized in the contemporary United States, which was shaped by domestic insurgencies on the part of American minorities. That same history of domestic insurgency and European ideas about freedom and rights, along with the inspiring example of mid-century Asian revolutions, shaped the Asian American movement and Asian American studies. Despite their shared intellectual and political histories, whether or not "Asia as method" and Asian American studies can be reconciled or partnered through a transpacific approach is an open question, given Asian American studies' relative reluctance to deal with Asia and the silence of "Asia as method" toward Asian Americans or even Asian diasporas. In addition, both Asian American studies and "Asia as method" share some problems. Practicing "Asia as method," like practicing Asian American studies as method, requires operating within and through a western or westernized university that is corporate and instrumental. In this university, knowledge may be critical of power but is also shaped by it as well. In addition, as Asian American studies has based much of its theoretical work on East Asian populations, so does the prioritization of East Asians presumably affect "Asia as method." Even being critical of East Asian "subempires" can inadvertently center East Asians as the primary agents in Asia and the Pacific, including in matters of knowledge production. Lastly, "Asia as method" is the mirror image of "claiming America" that was dominant in Asian American studies. In this case the imperative is to "claim Asia," which is an appropriation of the idea of "Asia" that was created by Europe. As "claiming America" led Asian American studies to neglect international and transnational dimensions that shaped Asian Americans, so does "Asia as method" neglect the heterogeneity of the United States and the west. By doing so, "Asia as method" disregards the internal differences within the United States or other western countries that have led to radical movements of political and intellectual opposition and inadvertently relegates dissident western minorities to a subordinate position both within the west and vis-à-vis the rest.

Prioritizing "Asia as method" and/or Asian American studies both run the risk of continuing to affirm the nation-state, its university, and the discourse of power-knowledge in which "minority" or "dissident" academics and fields are allowed to grow. This is evident in the way that the Pacific has been neglected in both approaches. Within the United States, Pacific Islanders have been sometimes subsumed under, or conjoined with, Asian American studies. This has occurred despite a lack of historical connection to Asian Americans and despite how Pacific Islander studies has sought to identify Asian Americans not necessarily as allies but as a part of settler colonialism in Hawai'i. Meanwhile, in "Asia as method," the Pacific and Pacific Islanders are invisible because of the focus on those same Asian states that from Pacific Islander perspectives were involved in Pacific warfare, tourism, development, and domination. A transpacific approach places Asian American studies and "Asia as method" in relation to each other and Pacific studies; such an approach also provincializes both American studies as area studies, and area studies itself, which should no longer be considered as a universal (western) approach to a foreign object but should instead be treated as a set of regionally based academic fields that share common objects of study.

Perhaps most importantly, however, transpacific studies both critiques and is a part of institutional, academic power and knowledge production. This institutional embeddedness of the transpacific is manifest in how the term also appears in the TPP and all it signifies about the Pacific as a regional manifestation of globalized interests emerging from both Asian and western nation-states. Transpacific studies is not immune from being captured by the logic of capital that is fundamental to the TPP. Transpacific studies within universities can easily become an academic commodity, or, as an administrative unit, can become critically stagnant, rendered into a bureaucratic arm of the TPP, or outstripped by the passage of time and the development of new political and economic forces. Thus, this book is not a call for the institutionalization of "transpacific studies" inasmuch as it is a call for developing transpacific studies as an analytic that can be used to historicize, contextualize, and illuminate the transpacific circulations of peoples, cultures, commodities, and ideas. What is compelling about transpacific studies is not its capacity to be instrumentalized in an institution, but its potential as a set of theories and methods that can help activate those alternative and dissident intellectual currents produced from Enlightenment thought and resistance movements of anticolonial nationalism and minority empowerment. For this reason, we chose to keep "transpacific stud-ies" in lower case letters, to signal its use as a critical vantage point and perspec-tive, rather than as a subdiscipline or department.

Transpacific Theories, Methods, and Cases

What are some of those theories and methods of transpacific studies? As im-plied above, transpacific studies exists at the juncture of area studies, American studies, and Asian American studies, as they are practiced not only in the United States but elsewhere. Area studies and American studies are tradition-ally defined by region, nation, and people, and often take those geographical and ethnic boundaries as parameters limiting intellectual inquiry. The idea of the nation or a place is certainly paramount in their self-definition, but within a framework of mobile populations, ideas, and scholars, tendencies in area studies and American studies to remain fixed within national borders seem outdated. In area studies, this attention to locale has gone hand in hand with a stress on deep knowledge, disciplinary focus, and language acquisition. In contrast, American studies places great emphasis on interdisciplinarity as an expression of how American studies sees itself less as an area studies and more as a type of cultural studies. Asian American studies also stresses interdisci-plinarity and has traditionally assumed America to be its frame and Asian Americans to be its objects, while prioritizing an oppositional method that has been its prime justification. Transpacific studies draws from all three of these approaches while focusing less on the limits of a particular place or a people and stressing the movements of people, culture, capital, or ideas within re-gions and between nations.

Starting from the premise that both sides of the Pacific must be taken into account, as well as the populations, subjectivities, and histories of the ocean in between, transpacific studies acknowledges the importance of American power but stresses the necessity of foregrounding Asia and the Pacific. Hopefully by doing so, transpacific studies can avoid being another imperializing intellectual gesture from the west, wherein an oppositional method also reasserts the dominant subjectivity of western practitioners. The potential certainly exists for such a biased practice of transpacific studies, but the bias is not inherent. Transpacific studies must be conscious of incorporat-ing scholars speaking from different histories, locations, and nations, and any approach that purports to be diasporic, transnational, international, or global must have built into it the possibility of dialogue, contestation, and contra-dictory, material histories. There is urgency, then, for transpacific studies to prioritize Asian and Pacific theories, perspectives, and objects of inquiry. Such prioritization is inseparable from a wider political project about contesting and controlling the production of knowledge, its location in universities that are a part of nation-states, and the enmeshment of those states in colonialism and capitalism.

Today's challenge is to devise institutions that will generate a more complex, subtle knowledge of the world that is multicentered rather than bipolar in perspective. This need for complexity reflects how scholars from every part of the world have come to western universities (as immigrants, refugees, and foreign students), many of them now forming the cutting edge of area studies in the west and in Asia. Thus, world area studies are now domesticated inside the west by the global participation of scholars who take their native regions of cultural difference and experience seriously. At the same time, many western scholars have become partially expatriated by traveling and studying in other countries, which they feel seriously to be home. Global intellectuals from the west and elsewhere move among world regions of cultures and states, but their reputations are built on their knowledge of particular languages, cultures, and histories. Within this framework of mobile populations, ideas, and scholars, current tendencies in area studies and American studies to remain fixed within national borders seem outdated. The study of Asian and Pacific diasporas encourages area studies to examine populations as they move outside of a given nation's borders and encourages American studies, wherever it is based, to turn toward the Pacific as much as the Atlantic.

Not tied to a nation or a people by the name of a field and its genealogy, transpacific studies pays attention to the equally important way that movement defines and shapes cultures, and vice versa. Transpacific studies builds on a "mobilities" perspective or paradigm that examines how social life gains expressions through the movement of people, things, ideas, and institutions across places and nations (see Urry 2005 and Hannan et al. 2006). Rather than seeing globalization as an all powerful force which inexorably determines the fate of cultures caught in its past, or celebrating the "elite nomadism" of a few cosmopolitan globe-trotters, we use transpacific studies to question how such movements are symbolically and materially produced. The circulation of people, ideas, and capital is not simply a mapping of flows but also of the infrastructure, which enables or resists these flows. The celebration of the age of globalization as a time of openness, fluidity, and transnational flows should not blind us to the fact that it is also characterized by new regulations, constraints, and exploitation. Those lower on the social scale provide the "friction" and the resistance to certain global forces that place them more as victims and displaced persons than as cosmopolitans and globe-trotters (see Tsing 2002). The refugee, the domestic laborer migrant, the sweatshop worker may prefer to kick and resist some of these global flows (see Mrazek 2010).

The existence of these less mobile populations and the nations from which they do not move from, or are compelled to flee from, could lead to charges that transpacific studies celebrates prematurely the death or decline of the nation, and fetishizes the idea of flows across the Pacific. Certainly it is the case that nations are not dead or even in real decline. The nation remains both vital and necessary for many even as it is limiting and oppressive. But even though key components of transpacific studies are obviously not about nations, nations and nationalism remain central to transpacific studies. The negotiation in transpacific studies is between the continuing existence and relevance of nations and the movements that cross national boundaries and struggle with the control of nation-states. Transpacific studies proposes that the beginning and ending locations of such movement should both be considered, particularly as they often can be found in segregated fields of study. But while the Americas and Asia comprise two ends of the transpacific, the model is hardly binary, given the importance of these movements across the Pacific and between a variable combination of countries.

Stressing movement in this way could certainly lead to other charges that transpacific studies fetishizes cosmopolitanism and those who can travel, whether they happen to be western or Asian elites. What happens to those who are forced to travel? In the latter instance, transpacific studies focuses on travel in general, not just travel in the sense of a leisurely or capitalistic pursuit. Travel in the broader sense includes forced migration of various degrees of compulsion (such as slaves, indentured laborers, guest-worker programs, economic refugees, adoptees, mail-order brides). Here, "cosmopolitanism" becomes a description of a variety of traveling modes, not just that of the jet-setting elite consumer and capitalist. The migrant worker who must speak two or more languages to survive has cosmopolitan knowledge, of a different type and perhaps greater degree than many First World citizens. Recasting cosmopolitanism to be historically and culturally varied provides new visibility to populations whose travel has not been glamorous or celebrated, like those islanders who explored the Pacific long before Europeans came or those Chinese and Indians who found their way to Southeast Asia, the Philippines, Mexico, Cuba, and many other places before the twentieth century. Transpacific studies emphasizes the importance of crossing the Pacific to so many populations diverse not only in terms of nation, region, language, ethnicity, and religion but also in terms of class and occupation.

But even if this is the case, what about those who cannot travel? Immobilized populations are arguably the ones who suffer the most neglect in forms of study fixated on diaspora, transnationalism, hybridity, and difference. Peasants and the urban poor have little romance of any kind attached to them in these forms of study, despite the possibility that "it is not the immigrant but the ones who stay behind who are the true unvanquished" (Kumar 225). Still, even for those who stay behind, transpacific movements and the circulation of cultures, ideas, and capital remain important. Remittances, to provide just one example, are one way those who are too poor to leave receive benefits from those who have left. Movies and music are other ways by which the popular culture from other countries circulates into regions where the residents are restricted to seeing the world through their television and DVD player. American studies has not been very concerned with remittances, since they leave the United States and go elsewhere, or with the impact of American cultural forms overseas, particularly if they are created by minority populations. Likewise, in reverse, area studies in Asia has neglected the diasporic populations that send remittances home, or that create high-gloss popular cultural artifacts like music videos, movies, and variety shows that are circulated in countries of origin. Transpacific studies foregrounds both the sending and the receiving of these cultures, peoples, capital, and ideas as they disregard national boundaries and as they move in unpredictable ways.[16] Remittances and cultural products, for example, do not move in a binary fashion between the west and Asia, but between Asian countries as well.

Perhaps most importantly, highly mobilized structures of capital, politics, and power that are transpacific, such as the proposed TPP, help to fix poor and disempowered people in their places. The tension between mobility and fixity is at the heart of transpacific studies as both its analytic and its method. What transpacific studies shows is that those with the capacity to move voluntarily, especially in great numbers, with great force, and over global distances—explorers, conquerors, entrepreneurs, capitalists, the armies and navies of powerful countries—have tremendous power over those who cannot move voluntarily. This kind of power also enables the powerful to move commodities and capital, to move other people as labor, and to move ideas. Transpacific studies is not only the study of this kind of empowered and empowering movement that has been crucial to imperialism, colonialism, and capitalism, it is also the expression of a counterimpulse that has sometimes animated those who are fixed to one place or who are forced to move.

This counterimpulse realizes itself in the desire to build coalitions, alliances, and imaginations among the poor, the oppressed, and the disempowered, which would enable them to understand their formation by transpacific histories, to enact their own agency against transpacific forces, and to see themselves as part of transpacific communities. Not least, transpacific studies stresses the fact that academic and intellectual formations are also fixed into place by structures of power. Rigid boundaries of area and discipline help to stabilize academia and create well-demarcated fields of study, but they also hinder academic study from fully understanding those highly mobilized structures of capital, politics, and power. These structures have not only imagined and exploited the transpacific, but have also compartmentalized academic knowledge production in the western university and its westernized counterparts in Asia. In resisting some of these pressures to be contained and fixed in place, transpacific studies is a hopeful intellectual gesture toward a scholarship that can achieve some of the same fluidity as the ocean after which it is named.

The chapters in this volume present a number of different methods and explore a number of ways in which people are linked across the Pacific—through media and culture (Benitez and Sears, Lippit, Lutkehaus), histories of racial divisions and civil war (Kwon, Espiritu), remittances (Thai), multinational corporations (Xiang), migration (Lin and Yeoh, Huang), and imperialism (Rowe). Acknowledging the importance of Asia to a transpacific method, the first three essays in the anthology present transpacific approaches from Asian points of view. Weiqiang Lin and Brenda S. A. Yeoh's "Transpacific Studies: The View from Asia" provides a subtle and nuanced argument for a transpacific studies that resists American-centric approaches and binary models of East and West (which inevitably privilege the latter). Not surprisingly, they argue, Asia is often dispossessed of any true weight in contemporary theorizing of migration. As far as current models are concerned, Asia's lot is to be a perpetual secondary migration space, neither having autonomy or attractive power, nor assuming any centrality in transnational processes. They propose more radical interventions in the way Asia, its subjectivities, and its relations with other Pacific players are being approached. By highlighting not just "ethnic" flows originating in, or returning to, Asia, they argue that expanding the empirical scope of transpacific studies to include, say, "American diasporas" can moderate tendencies to reify ideas about, and dichotomies between, immigrant/receiving societies and emigrant/sending countries. More can be said as well about the similarities, rather than differences, that Asian migrants share with other (especially "white") itinerants. Finally, transpacific connections need to be situated within a larger context of global and supraregional flows. The multiple ways in which Asia has historically been wedded to other regions and economies are indicative of the fact that transpacific linkages constitute only one of *many* transnational orders in the world.

These transnational orders, and the relations between Asia and the United States, were indelibly shaped by the event addressed in Heonik Kwon's "The Transpacific Cold War." He assesses the radically different manifestation of the global Cold War between the transatlantic and the transpacific historical horizon: between Europe's Cold War that was largely a nonviolent "imaginary war" of economic competition and military alliance, and the postcolonial Cold War experienced in the Asia-Pacific that was far from an imaginary war, involving instead vicious civil wars and other exceptional forms of political violence. Transpacific Cold War history, he argues, has to be understood in the context of a particular colonial history experienced in the Asia-Pacific region that involved Asian as well as European imperial powers, and also in relation to the revolutionary anticolonial and postcolonial struggles that permeated the region in the twentieth century. Examining some of the central assumptions in contemporary Cold War historical scholarship and postcolonial historical and cultural studies, the essay objects to the prevailing transatlantic centrality in the interpretation of the global Cold War and questions why contemporary postcolonial scholarship displaces Cold War history from its descriptive and analytical contours. Kwon explores these questions, in part, with illustrations drawn from the history of migration and contemporary social development in southern Vietnam and South Korea, two major sites of global bipolar conflict.

The contemporary conflicts in that region have much to do with the rise of China, and Biao Xiang's "The Pacific Paradox: The Chinese State in Transpacific Interactions" turns our attention to that country. The "Pacific paradox" is Xiang's model for understanding how the Pacific is at once structurally integrated and fundamentally divided. Xiang argues that the Chinese public view is that China *has to* compete with the United States in order to survive, and in order to do that, China *has to* become like the United States in developing capitalism and building up military might. Global capitalism is such that China's economic and social life must be integrated into the world in order to survive and prosper, but at the same time, real geopolitics is such that the United States is inevitably hostile to China regardless of what China does. Tensions between China and the United States do not stem from their differences but their similarities; they are not too far apart, but instead too tightly connected. Xiang also offers a model of "neostatism" for understanding how the Chinese state works. Neostatism emerged as part of, instead of prior to, the Pacific paradox and is a result of the intensification of transpacific exchanges. Neostatism sees the state as the primary and unquestionable *frame* within which society should be organized, and as such the state serves as a central referent in making sense of the world.

The next essays shift to the broad question of how cultures are shaped by transpacific circulation and are themselves constituents of such circulation. In

"Miguel Covarrubias and the Pageant of the Pacific: The Golden Gate International Exposition and the Idea of the Transpacific, 1939–1940," Nancy C. Lutkehaus examines how "The Pageant of the Pacific" was perceived and constructed through a series of murals painted by the Mexican artist Miguel Covarrubias for the San Francisco Exposition in 1939. He developed a way of visually representing the connectedness of societies on either side of the Pacific through illustrated maps, elaborating his earlier fascination with islands like Bali into a utopian canvas of many islands and continents joined by peaceful trade and cooperation. As a dark-skinned "native" of a nation under heavy American influence, he was believed to have natural empathy and "sympathetic understanding of the peoples and lands of the Pacific Basin." Covarrubias's maps were the first ever to put the Pacific Ocean in the middle, with the countries of Asia and the Americas on the sides, so that Europe, Africa, and the Middle East were cut out. This innovation was tied to a "re-orienting" he already saw as imminent with Europe's slide into a "suicidal war," which would push the Pacific area into a more prominent role in global leadership. By late 1941, with the Japanese bombing of Pearl Harbor, his prophetic vision began to be realized.

John Carlos Rowe's "Transpacific Studies and the Cultures of U.S. Imperialism" focuses on the disciplinary role transpacific studies should play in the new American studies with its emphasis on comparative study of the Americas. In this context, he addresses where the many different communities of the Pacific belong in the ongoing study of U.S. imperialism and neoimperialism in this crucial contact zone of the Americas. He locates the efforts by formerly colonized states to achieve cultural, economic, and political sovereignty in their relation to the Pacific region both as a geographical area and as a site for a series of commercial, military, and cultural routes, especially those of the United States. He argues that what Chalmers Johnson has termed the U.S. "empire of bases" needs to be expanded to include specific studies of the Mariana Islands (Guam, Saipan, Tinian, et al.), American Samoa, and other U.S. military bases in the Pacific and Asia that serve the larger colonial purposes of the U.S. military. The U.S. military presence has also had a crucial environmental impact that is a neglected issue in transpacific studies. He discusses some of the infamous cases of nuclear pollution on Pikini (Bikini) Atoll and military construction on Wake Island as examples of the environmental concerns raised by indigenous populations, especially those groups organized to achieve their sovereignty and independence from U.S. spheres of economic, political, and military influence.

J. Francisco Benitez and Laurie J. Sears also take on the question of U.S. imperialism and its impact on academic and cultural formations. In "Passionate Attachments to Area Studies and Asian American Studies: Subjectivity and

Diaspora in the Transpacific," they explore racial subjectivity through a methodology of "critical melancholia," examining the intersection of various forms of social inequality and how these forms have been problematized in area and ethnic studies. Ethnic studies and area studies are both affected by similar "enigmatic signifiers" or traces left by U.S. imperial desires. Both academic fields have had fraught and complex relations with U.S. nation- and empire-building. They ask: How are U.S. area studies changing in the face of these challenges? How has the return of the (repressed) awareness of the United States as an empire affected ethnic studies' long-standing but often forgotten critique of American exceptionalism? How are interdisciplinary and disciplinary methodologies adapting to these changes? Conversations between area studies and ethnic studies are opening up as the diasporic and cosmopolitan routes of travel put more and more subjects in motion, and the insights from each field unsettle the other. To understand how diasporic communities and narrations destabilize the notion of "home" and foreground the "unhomed" or the "multihomed" as conditions of everyday life, they focus on Philippine American author Jessica Hagedorn's and Indonesian author Ayu Utami's novels, whose characters travel back and forth between and within Asian and American imperial formations.

Akira Lippit's "Imaginary Languages in Translation, Imagined National Cinemas" examines transpacific cultural circulation within Asia and, to a lesser extent, between Asia and the west, in order to look at the relationship between nationalism, cinema, and language. On the one hand, strong national cinemas in the Chinas, Japan, and South Korea emerged or resurged at the end of the twentieth century and the beginning of the twenty-first. On the other hand, this resurgence marked the appearance of an Asia and of Asian cinemas no longer formed according to the protocols of the nation, nor entirely apart from the specters of the nation. He argues that national cinemas are always complicit in the forms of nationalism that they sustain and determine. They reflect the nation that they enact, reflections caused by and that cause the appearance of the nation. Nations not only appear in the moments, they are themselves appearances, images. Nations are phantasms, fantastic inventions, or imagined communities, as Benedict Anderson says, which is to say they form and are formed by images. Imagined, imaginary, national cinemas lead to what Lippit calls an imaginational cinema and imaginationalism. These concepts allow him to interrogate the relationship between language and nationalism via cinematic form, where national languages are also imaginary languages. What sort of languages these are, and what happens when these languages that sustain national identities are infiltrated, hybridized, contaminated, or translated, are questions he explores in regards to contemporary East Asian cinema.

The next set of essays look at transpacific populations that move voluntarily or involuntarily across the Pacific. In "Militarized Refuge: A Critical Rereading of Vietnamese Flight to the United States," Yến Lê Espiritu examines the role of the United States in "rescuing" Vietnamese refugees at the end of the Vietnam War. She challenges the "rescue and liberation" narrative of what has been dubbed "the largest humanitarian airlift in history" by exposing the militarized nature of the U.S. refugee resettlement effort. U.S. evacuation efforts were not a slapdash response to an emergency situation that arose in Vietnam in 1975, but rather were part of militarized histories and circuits dating back to 1898. Espiritu traces the most-traveled refugee route via military aircraft—from Vietnam to the Philippines to Guam and then to California, all of which routed the refugees through U.S. military bases—as a critical lens through which to map, both discursively and materially, the transpacific displacement brought about by the legacy of U.S. colonial and military expansion into the Asia Pacific region. She makes two related arguments: the first about military colonialism, which contends that it is the region's (neo)colonial dependence on the United States that turned the Philippines and Guam into the "ideal" receiving centers of U.S. rescuing project; and the second about militarized refuge, which emphasizes the mutually constitutive nature of the concepts "refugees" and "refuge" and shows how both emerge out of, and in turn bolster, U.S. militarism.

The circulation of migrants is at least as varied as the circulation of capital. Hung Cam Thai, in "Special Money in the Vietnamese Diaspora," traces one financial trail between Vietnam and its diasporic populations. He focuses on the relationship between remittances and return visits among low-wage Vietnamese immigrants living in various parts of the diaspora. Remittances have become an institutional dimension of contemporary Vietnamese society, especially in Saigon, where consumption and remittances are the highest in the country. Remittances play a key role in improving the daily lives of family members in the homeland. His article addresses the cultural and moral meanings that surround monetary transactions between those who receive and those who send money across international borders. Money is social in nature and culturally specific, embedded in relations of power, interacting with differences in gender, class, and generations. Money received from inheritances or a wedding, for example, falls in the category of "special money," that is, money that has social and cultural significance in its use. He suggests that remittances in the Vietnamese context are special money, designated for specific purposes and having different meanings for senders and receivers. Thus, when this special money is used beyond the boundaries of its purpose, which overseas Vietnamese often understand only by returning to Vietnam to see how their money is spent, tensions are often created in transnational family ties.

Finally, in the conclusion, we turn to a scholar who pioneered the idea of transpacific studies, and who has crossed borders both autobiographically and as a writer. In "Living Transpacifically," Yunte Huang blends memoir and criticism to recall his years of growing up in China, an experience profoundly shaped by the currents of transpacific flows, cross-cultural exchanges as intangible as radio signals, or as real as blood-soaked pages of pirated foreign books. His narrative leads to Tiananmen Square and then migration to the United States, where he would pen two books on the transpacific. The field of transpacific studies that he named provides a new perspective on the connections and linkages that span an ocean, and tries to both recognize and address inequities in knowledge production between scholars situated in different geographic locations and in different disciplines.

This volume tries to define some of the parameters of this new field of transpacific studies in order to awaken scholars to the shifting tides of the world's greatest ocean, which now unite widely dispersed populations and forge new connections in both the imagination and the material world. In undertaking this enterprise, the editors realize that this volume is far from sufficient in its coverage. Canada, New Zealand, and Australia are all absent, even though they each have transpacific connections. Latin America, with its centuries-long history of what Evelyn Hu-deHart calls the "Spanish Pacific," is only gestured at here. The complexities of the Pacific Islands are not sufficiently reflected in the coverage that is present, and the voices of Pacific Islanders are not represented. The pre-twentieth century histories of the Pacific and the powers and peoples involved in it are in the background of a collection that focuses on the twentieth and twenty-first centuries. In fact, the editing of the volume has been a humbling reminder of how much more the volume undoubtedly excludes rather than includes. At the same time, our awareness of how much more could be and needs to be addressed convinces us of the necessity for continuing work in transpacific studies.

Notes to Introduction: Transpacific Studies: Critical Perspectives on an Emerging Field

1. See Matsuda (2012) for a concise history of the Pacific, including both its island populations and the various ages of exploration, imperialism, and colonialism conducted by Asian, European, and American nations. He offers the useful model of translocalism for understanding the histories of the Pacific.

2. See Dirlik (1998) for a summary of the discourses around the Pacific.

3. See Lim et al. (2012) on the details of the proposed Trans-Pacific Partnership.

4. For more on how European thinkers including Adam Smith, Hegel, and Lenin imagined Asia—from the "starting point of history" to a "progressive Asia" that contrasted with a "backward Europe"—see Wang (2011).

5. See Lutkehaus's essay in this volume for a discussion of how new maps were drawn around the Pacific in the 1930s.

6. See Johnson (2004) for a critique of the United States as an imperial force in the era of globalization.

7. Edwards (2003), Mullen (2004), Prashad (2002), and Von Eschen (1997) elaborate on all these examples.

8. For a particularly affecting account of such ghosts, see Cho (2008).

9. The notion of the subimperial comes from Chen (2010) and is elaborated on in Lee (2009).

10. Notes one American helicopter pilot: "The Koreans had sent out their Tiger teams. They came back with mortar tubes, base plates, and severed VC heads. The Koreans also complained that our gunships had killed some of their men. We came off as a bunch of amateurs compared to the ROKs" (Mason 1982, 198). This American perception of Korean soldiers being as tough or tougher than Americans was not unusual. Vietnamese perception interpreted that toughness differently. The memoirist Le Ly Hayslip (1990) writes: "More dangerous [than the Americans] were the Koreans who now patrolled the American sector. Because a child from our village once walked into their camp and exploded a Viet Cong bomb wired to his body, the Koreans took terrible retribution against the children themselves (whom they saw simply as little Viet Cong). After the incident, some Korean soldiers went to a school, snatched up some boys, threw them into a well, and tossed a grenade in afterward as an example to the others. To the villagers, these Koreans were like the Moroccans [who helped the French]—tougher and meaner than the white soldiers they supported. Like the Japanese of World War II, they seemed to have no conscience and went about their duties as ruthless killing machines. No wonder they found my country a perfect place to ply their terrible trade" (198). As Heonik Kwon (2006) notes, this behavior by South Korean troops was hardly surprising, when their campaign slogans included "kill clean, burn clean, destroy clean," "anything you see is all Vietcong," "children also spy," and "better to make mistakes than to miss" (29).

11. Their focus is limited to the triangular power-sharing arrangements of the United States, Japan, and an aspiring South Korea, whereas the "transpacific imaginary," as first coined by Huang (2002) and dwelt on by Mayer and Kunneman (2009), dealt with China. All these works suggest the possibility that the transpacific extends beyond binary relationships between particular, antagonistic, or collaborative countries, and enrich Sakai and Yoo's (2012) insight into "transpacific complicity," which is certainly more extensive than only the relationship between Japan and the United States.

12. See Miyoshi (1993) and Harootunian (2002) for critiques of area studies, and Szanton (2004) for a defense of area studies.

13. See Lowe (2012) for another perspective on how transpacific concerns are reshaping Asian American studies, and Nguyen (2012) for a more detailed elaboration of the limits of Asian American studies in the international context.

14. Wang's (2011) arguments for reimagining Asia, for example, generally assume that Asia is defined first and foremost through China and Japan, while Sakai and Yoo's (2012) model of the transpacific adds Korea to these two countries.

15. We thank Chih-ming Wang for reminding us of the influence of Chen's work, including the Inter-Asia Cultural Studies project that he spearheaded.

16. Levitt (2007) has argued forcefully that transpacific flows are very important to "those who are left behind," as both sources of income and of circulating cultural inspirations and aspirations (6).

References

Acharya, Amitav. 2010. "Asia Is Not One." *Journal of Asian Studies* 66 (4): 1001–1013.

Ali, Agha Shahid. 1991. *A Nostalgist's Map of America.* New York: W. W. Norton.

Andaya, Barbara. 2010. "Asia Redux: Response to Prasenjit Duara." *Journal of Asian Studies* 66 (4): 1015–1020.

Appadurai, Arjun. 1996. *Modernity at Large: Cultural Dimensions of Globalization.* Minneapolis: University of Minnesota Press.

Appiah, Kwame Anthony. 2006. *Cosmopolitanism: Ethics in a World of Strangers.* New York: W. W. Norton.

Bello, Walden. 2010. "From American Lake to a People's Pacific in the Twenty-First Century." In *Militarized Currents: Toward a Decolonized Future in Asia and the Pacific,* ed. Setsu Shigematsu and Keith Camacho, 309–321. Minneapolis: University of Minnesota Press.

Braudel, Fernand. 1996. *The Mediterranean and the Mediterranean World in the Age of Philip II.* Vols. I and II. Berkeley: University of California Press.

Chakrabarty, Dipesh. 2000. *Provincializing Europe: Post-Colonial Thought and Historical Difference.* Princeton, NJ: Princeton University Press.

Chen, Kuan-hsing. 2010. *Asia as Method: Toward Deimperialization.* Durham, NC: Duke University Press.

Cho, Grace. 2008. *Haunting the Korean Diaspora: Shame, Secrecy, and the Forgotten War.* Minneapolis: University of Minnesota Press.

Chow, Rey. 2002. *The Protestant Ethnic and the Spirit of Capitalism.* New York: Columbia University Press.

Connery, Christopher. 1994. "Pacific Rim Discourse: The United States Global Imaginary in the Late Cold War Years." *Boundary 2* 21 (1): 30–56.

Cumings, Bruce. 1998. "Rimspeak; or, The Discourse of the 'Pacific Rim.'" In *What Is in a Rim? Critical Perspectives on the Pacific Region Idea,* ed. Arif Dirlik, 53–72.

———. 2009. *Dominion from Sea to Sea: Pacific Ascendancy and American Power.* New Haven, CT: Yale University Press.

Dirlik, Arif. 1994. "The Postcolonial Aura: Third World Criticism in the Age of Global Capitalism." *Critical Inquiry* 20: 328–356.

———. 1998. "Introduction: Pacific Contradictions." In *What Is in a Rim? Critical Perspectives on the Pacific Region Idea,* ed. Arif Dirlik, 3–13.

Dirlik, Arif, ed. 1998. *What Is in a Rim? Critical Perspectives on the Pacific Region Idea.* Lanham, MD: Rowman and Littlefield.

Duara, Prasenjit. 2010. "Asia Redux: Conceptualizing a Region for Our Times." *Journal of Asian Studies* 66 (4): 963–983.

Edelman, Lee. 2004. *No Future: Queer Theory and the Death Drive.* Durham, NC: Duke University Press.

Edwards, Brent Hayes. 2003. *The Practice of Diaspora: Literature, Translation, and the Rise of Black Internationalism.* Cambridge, MA: Harvard University Press.

Gerefi, Gary. 1998. "Global Sourcing and Regional Divisions of Labor in the Pacific Rim." In *What Is in a Rim? Critical Perspectives on the Pacific Region Idea,* ed. Arif Dirlik, 143–161. Lanham, MD: Rowman and Littlefield.

Gilroy, Paul. 1993. *The Black Atlantic: Modernity and Double Consciousness.* Cambridge, MA: Harvard University Press.

———. 2000. *Against Race: Imagining Political Culture Beyond the Color Line.* Cambridge, MA: Harvard University Press.

———. 2006. *Postcolonial Melancholia.* New York: Columbia University Press.

Gopinath, Gayatri. 2005. *Impossible Desires: Queer Diasporas and South Asian Public Cultures.* Durham, NC: Duke University Press.

Grewal, Inderpal. 2005. *Transnational America: Feminisms, Diasporas, Neoliberalisms.* Durham, NC: Duke University Press.

Hannan, K., M. Sheller, and J. Urry. 2006. "Mobilities, Immobilities and Moorings." *Mobilities* 1: 1–22.

Harootunian, Harry. 2002. "Postcoloniality's Unconscious/Area Studies' Desire." In *Learning Places: The Afterlives of Area Studies,* ed. Masao Miyoshi and Harry Harootunian. Durham, NC: Duke University Press.

Hau'ofa, Epeli. 1995. "Our Sea of Islands." In *Asia/Pacific as Space of Cultural Production,* ed. Rob Wilson and Arif Dirlik, 86–98. Durham, NC: Duke University Press.

Hayslip, Le Ly, with James Wurts. 1990. *When Heaven and Earth Changed Places.* New York: Plume.

Heryanto, Ariel. 2007. "Can There Be Southeast Asians in Southeast Asian Studies?" In *Southeast Asian Subjects,* ed. Laurie Sears, 75–108. Seattle: University of Washington Press.

Huang, Yunte. 2002. *Transpacific Displacement: Ethnography, Translation, and Intertextual Travel in Twentieth-Century American Literature.* Berkeley: University of California Press.

Hu-DeHart, Evelyn. 2007. "Latin America in Asian-Pacific Perspective." In *Asian Diasporas: New Formations, New Conceptions,* ed. Rhacel Salazar Parreñas and Lok C. D. Siu, 29–62. Stanford, CA: Stanford University Press.

Huntington, Samuel. 2007. *The Clash of Civilizations and the Remaking of World Order.* New York: Simon and Schuster.

Johnson, Chalmers. 2004. *The Sorrows of Empire: Militarism, Secrecy, and the End of the American Republic.* New York: Metropolitan Books.

Kumar, Amitava. 2002. *Bombay London New York.* New York: Routledge.

Kwon, Heonik. 2006. *After the Massacre: Commemoration and Consolation in Ha My and My Lai.* Berkeley: University of California Press.

Lee, Jin-Kyung. 2009. "Surrogate Military, Subimperialism, and Masculinity: South Korea in the Vietnam War, 1965–1973." *positions: east asia cultures critique* 17 (3): 655–682.

Levitt, Peggy. 2007. *God Needs No Passport: Immigrants and the Changing American Religious Landscape.* New York: New Press.

Levitt, Peggy, and Sanjeev Khagram, eds. 2007. *The Transnational Studies Reader: Intersections and Innovations.* New York: Routledge.

Lewis, Martine, and Karen Wigen. 1997. *The Myth of Continents: A Critique of Metageography.* Berkeley: University of California Press.

Lim, C. L., Deborah K. Elms, and Patrick Low, eds. 2012. *The Trans-Pacific Partnership: A Quest for a Twenty-First-Century Trade Agreement.* New York: Cambridge University Press.

Lionnet, Françoise, and Shu-mei Shih. 2005. "Thinking through the Minor, Transnationally." In *Minor Transnationalism,* ed. Françoise Lionnet and Shu-mei Shih, 1–23. Durham, NC: Duke University Press.

Lowe, Celia. 2007. "Recognizing Scholarly Subjects: Collaboration, Area Studies, and the Politics of Nature." In *Knowing Southeast Asian Subjects,* ed. Laurie J. Sears, 109–135. Seattle: University of Washington Press in association with NUS Press Singapore.

Lowe, Lisa. 2012. "The Trans-Pacific Migrant and Area Studies." In *The Trans-Pacific Imagination: Rethinking Boundary, Culture and Society,* ed. Naoki Sakai and Hyon Joo Yoo, 61–74. River Edge, NJ: World Scientific Publishing.

Mason, Robert. 1982. *Chickenhawk.* New York: Viking Press.

Matsuda, Matt. 2012. *Pacific Worlds: A History of Seas, Peoples, and Cultures.* New York: Cambridge University Press.

Mayer, Ruth, and Vanessa Künnemann, eds. 2009. *Trans-Pacific Interactions: The United States and China, 1880–1950.* New York: Palgrave Macmillan.

Mitchell, Timothy. 1988. *Colonising Egypt.* Berkeley: University of California Press.

Miyoshi, Masao. 1993. "A Borderless World: From Colonialism to Transnationalism and the Decline of the Nation-State." *Critical Inquiry* 19: 726–751.

Mrazek, Rudolf. 2010. "Floating. No Gears Shifting." In *Journal of Asian Studies* 66 (4): 1021–1025.

Mullen, Bill. 2004. *Afro-Orientalism.* Minneapolis: University of Minnesota Press.

Nandy, Ashis. 2010. *Bonfire of Creeds: The Essential Ashis Nandy.* Oxford: Oxford University Press.

———. 2005. *Exiled at Home.* New Delhi: Oxford University Press India.

Nguyen, Viet Thanh. 2012. "Refugee Memories and Asian American Critique." *positions: asia critique* 20 (3): 911–942.

Palumbo-Liu, David. 2007. "Asian Diasporas, and Yet . . ." In *Asian Diasporas: New Formations, New Conceptions,* ed. Rhacel Salazar Parreñas and Lok C. D. Siu, 279–284. Stanford, CA: Stanford University Press.

Parreñas, Rhacel Salazar. 2001. *Servants of Empire: Women, Migration, and Domestic Work.* Stanford, CA: Stanford University Press.

Parreñas, Rhacel Salazar, and Lok C. D. Siu, eds. 2007. *Asian Diasporas: New Formations, New Conceptions.* Stanford, CA: Stanford University Press.

Prashad, Vijay. 2002. *Everybody Was Kung Fu Fighting: Afro-Asian Connections and the Myth of Cultural Purity.* Boston: Beacon Press.

Rowe, John C. 2012. *The Cultural Politics of the New American Studies.* Cambridge, UK: Open Humanities Press.

Said, Edward. 1978. *Orientalism.* New York: Random House.

Sakai, Naoki, and Hyon Joo Yoo. 2012. "Introduction: The Trans-Pacific Imagination— Rethinking Boundary, Culture and Society." In *The Trans-Pacific Imagination: Rethinking Boundary, Culture and Society,* ed. Naoki Sakai and Hyon Joo Yoo, 1–44. River Edge, NJ: World Scientific Publishing.

Shah, Nayan. 2012. *Stranger Intimacy: Contesting Race, Sexuality and the Law in the North American West.* Berkeley: University of California Press.

Shigematsu, Setsu, and Keith Camacho. 2010. "Militarized Currents, Decolonizing Futures." In *Militarized Currents: Toward a Decolonized Future in Asia and the Pacific,* ed. by Setsu Shigematsu and Keith Camacho, xv–xiviii. Minneapolis: University of Minnesota Press.

Shih, Shu-mei. 2005. "Toward an Ethics of Transnational Encounters: Or, 'When' Does A 'Chinese' Woman Become a 'Feminist'?" In *Minor Transnationalism,* ed. Françoise Lionnet and Shu-mei Shih, 73–108. Durham, NC: Duke University Press, 2005.

Spivak, Gayatri Chakravorty. 1994. "Can the Subaltern Speak?" In *Colonial Discourse and Post-Colonial Theory,* ed. Patrick Williams and Laura Chrisman, 66–111. New York: Columbia University Press.

Szanton, David L. 2004. "Introduction: The Origin, Nature, and Challenges of Area Studies in the United States." In *The Politics of Knowledge: Area Studies and the Disciplines,* ed. David L. Szanton, 1–33. Berkeley: University of California Press.

Tadiar, Neferti Xina M. 1998. "Sexual Economies in the Asia-Pacific Community." In *What Is in a Rim? Critical Perspectives on the Pacific Region Idea,* ed. Dirlik, 219–248.

Trask, Haunani-Kay. 1999. *From a Native Daughter: Colonialism and Sovereignty in Hawai'i.* Honolulu: University of Hawai'i Press.

Tsing, Anna. 2002. *Friction: An Ethnography of Global Connection.* Princeton, NJ: Princeton University Press.

Urry, J. 2005. "The Complexities of the Global." *Theory, Culture and Society* 22 (5): 235–254.

Viswanathan, Gauri. 1998a. *Masks of Conquest: Literary Study and British Rule in India.* New Delhi: Oxford University Press India.

———. 1998b. *Outside the Fold: Conversion, Modernity and Belief.* Princeton, NJ: Princeton University Press.

Von Eschen, Penny. 1997. *Race against Empire: Black Americans and Anticolonialism, 1937–1957.* Ithaca, NY: Cornell University Press.

Wang Hui. 2011. *The Politics of Imagining Asia.* ed. Theodore Huters. Cambridge, MA: Harvard University Press.

Wilson, Rob. 2000. *Reimagining the American Pacific: From South Pacific to Bamboo Ridge and Beyond.* Durham, NC: Duke University Press.

Woo, Jung-En. 1991. *Race to the Swift: State and Finance in Korean Industrialization.* New York: Columbia University Press.

Part I

Theories of the Transpacific

1

Transpacific Studies
The View from Asia

WEIQIANG LIN AND BRENDA S. A. YEOH

Like many ideas in the last half century, transnationalism is a conceptual innovation whose beginnings can in many ways be traced to the United States. We do not just refer to the manner in which the idea arose as a brainchild of American scholarship (see Basch et al. 1994 and Glick Schiller et al. 1995 for some pioneering work), but also how the term invokes very particular U.S.-centric understandings, assumptions, and worldviews about globalization and migration.[1] Undeniably, this is a provocative charge. But our intention is neither to make light of the contributions of this literature in describing a distinct form of migrant adaptation (Portes et al. 1999), nor to belittle what other, *non-*American authors have said about contemporary social networks spanning across different countries. Rather, we wish to highlight how interpretations of transnationalism—as a mode of "global" living—often coalesce around a thinly veiled subtext that, on the one hand, celebrates the unraveling of territorial thinking, and, on the other, appears wary of the "threats" that this liberal form of border-transcendence may pose to the national integrity of "immigrant" societies like America's. Such an eagerness to delineate the opportunities, challenges, and remedies entailed in transnationalism, we argue, betrays an anxiety and a particular asymmetric understanding of the same. In assuming hegemonic vantage points and perspectives, this vein of work not only gives rise to several blind spots and elisions, but also heightens the risk of "colonizing" knowledges about migrants, their places of origin, and their mobilities.

The formulation of a new "transpacific" research paradigm and regional construct bounded by a littoral rim dominated by America on one side arguably sets itself up for very similar dangers and pitfalls. In forcing the West Coast of the American continent(s) into contact with the Eastern seaboard of Asia—and thus constituting the "trans" in transpacific—it is easy to turn this project into one about narrating a contrived and tendentious transoceanic story, if not a new colonial discourse imbued with its own idea(l)s about U.S. supremacy, natural leadership, and Orientalism. As Wilson (2000, 570) precociously notes, the desire to conjure a national identity founded on (extra)territorial expansion has long "haunted American culture from the era of Manifest Destiny and the movement westward across continental vastness, via frontier settlement and Indian dispossession, towards the 'illimitable' Asian markets of the Pacific Ocean." To teleologically envisage the Pacific Basin as an integral whole, and possibly an extended sphere of U.S. influence, without realizing how it serves American beliefs, agendas, and geopolitics thus risks exactly feeding this U.S. appetite for frontier-making and geographical imagination. To this end, the result may well resemble that found in transnationalism research, whereby while some places and flows are deemed to be natural and legitimate, others are rendered penetrative and problematic.

This cautionary note however is not meant to deter the formulation of a more progressive transpacific optic, as this volume is interested in. Pursuing such an agenda, in fact, allows for some timely revisions to attendant efforts today to spotlight the Pacific Rim (again) as a realm in portentous—or dangerous— "rising" (Wilkins 2010). In seeking to question and destabilize these elitist viewpoints, our contribution to this volume seeks to explore new, and counter-hegemonic, ways of appreciating the putative region and its relational dynamics. By focusing specifically on the migratory aspect of transpacific connectivities, we draw parallels and lessons from transnationalism studies to demonstrate how alternative articulations of flows surrounding the Pacific are possible *and* desirable. In particular, we seek to lend a fresh impetus to those perspectives that challenge the discursive centrality of America, and, to a lesser extent, Canada, Australia, and New Zealand, in troubling their place as the ultimate destinations in all transnational journeying in the Pacific. In this regard, we take advantage of our positionality as "Asian geographers in Asia" to rethink these transpacific geographies and mobilities. Short of completely sidelining the United States, we take a middle-ground approach to identify avenues through which we can rethink transpacific migration as a diverse and multifaceted affair. Following some critical reviews of the current literature in three discrete areas—transnational spatialities, migrant subjectivities, and the centrality of the transpacific world in mobile processes—we offer a few proposals on how each of these can be recentered and reconceptualized in more productive ways.

The "Pacific" in Transpacific Migration

Notwithstanding their long history, transnational mobilities in the Pacific region have gained prominence in recent decades with the increasing awareness that Asia is fast becoming a major source of "immigrants" to the United States and other "traditional" receiving societies along the Rim (Ip et al. 2006). In the year 2011, for instance, the U.S. Census Bureau reports that Asians had accounted for almost 29 percent of foreign-born persons in America, dramatically up from just 5.0 percent in 1960. Of the Asian-born, the Chinese constitute the largest group at 19.3 percent, followed by migrants from India (16.1 percent), the Philippines (15.7 percent), Vietnam (10.9 percent) and Korea (9.4 percent). Albeit outpaced by Latin American immigration, the Asian share of U.S. foreign-born population is still more than twice that of those from European countries (Gryn and Gambino 2012). Closer to the Pacific coastline, this trend gets even more pronounced, with California and Washington each seeing over a third (35.1 and 39.0 percent respectively) of their foreign-born residents comprising Asian ethnics in 2009 (Greico and Trevelyan 2010)—particularly those from East Asia (11.4 and 14.5 percent of total foreign-born) and Southeast Asia (15.0 and 16.7 percent). This same situation is replicated further north in Canada. As Ley (1999, 3) reveals, by the late 1990s, as many as 80 percent of new immigrants to British Columbia had originated in Asia, led by China, Hong Kong, Taiwan, and more recently India and the Philippines; comparatively, British contribution to the province had dwindled to a paltry 2 percent. For these Rim societies therefore, the unprecedented rate at which Asian migrants are "penetrating" their borders also seems to augur a new era of active dialogue between the two sides. More than that, it appears to indicate a shift in the center of gravity in the world, from the Atlantic to the Pacific Basin.

So widespread has this view been that, since the 1980s, save a brief pause in the late 1990s, the 21st century has frequently been touted as the "Pacific century" (Linder 1986). This is an era, they say, that is characterized by a "confluence of trade, technology, telecommunications and training" that has had the effect of bringing together "Asia, Australia and the American continents in a swell of economic, political, and cultural interplay that no one power can control" (McCord 1991, 1). It is here, too, that the rise of "Asia" and (hence) the "Pacific Rim" would become a permanent fixture in any discussion about the world's future developmental trajectory—reinterpreted now as being fraught with realigned opportunities as well as new structural dynamics and challenges for the entire world. Corresponding to these formulations, migrations across the ocean are, without exception, expected to play an increasingly significant role too, not just in numerical terms, but also in abetting the very process of Pacific regionalization and integration. Being now populated by skilled professionals and unskilled labor alike, these mobilities are seen to be both responses to and embodied vehicles of the accelerating exchanges in trade, politics, and other fields of cooperation between the East and the West (Koehn and Yin 2002).

What it portends is not simply a matter of geographical shift, but the forging of new relationships and forms of geopolitical management.

Yet, not everyone is fully persuaded about the transformative power and structural coherence of these integrative forces. Some scholars argue that the "Pacific Rim" is foremost an invented concept and model, and is only of interest because it represents a convenient geographical language that is readily intelligible and highly symbolic of the geopolitical zeitgeist of the day (Harris 1989). For them, to reduce the complexity of world development to a few superficial indicators such as rising gross domestic products or robust migratory exchanges in specific pockets of the world bestows the project with a little too much simplicity. Not only does it unhelpfully gloss over the enormous social heterogeneity and contradictions within the region, it also effaces the lines of relations and power hierarchies that are responsible for producing particular transnational realities and outcomes in the first place (Palat 1993; Findlay 2001). Indeed, in its articulation, it is (too) often the "Pacific" that is to be submitted under the narrative of "Euro-American capitalism," such that the former—including its significant swath of Asian "hinterland"—invariably plays a subservient role to the latter (Dirlik 1998). In endorsing the use of spatial terms that rigidly bifurcate the Pacific Basin into two distinct spheres of East versus West, a certain segmentarity has also been introduced, "opposed in a binary machine, arranged in the State apparatuses, overcoded by an abstract machine as the sketch of a World Order" (Deleuze and Parnet 2007, 131).

This is not the place to go into further expositions on the various critiques relating to the discursive and historical constructions of the Asia-Pacific (see Chapter 2 in this volume). But suffice to say, the way the region has been constructed, talked about, and put into motion has traditionally been an asymmetric and imperialist affair, not usually given to fully grasping the true dynamism and complexity of its subject. As Eperjesi (2005, 4) puts it succinctly, the idea of the Pacific Rim, or more accurately *America's* Pacific Rim, is foremost "a regional, or regionalizing, myth," which mostly harbors the concerns and exclusive viewpoints of its epistemological owners. Its significance not only hinges upon its validation by U.S. strategists and planners, but also finds value in its likeliness to suit, or threaten, America's politico-economic agendas and grand visions for the world (Berger and Borer 1997). Such tendencies to privilege the metropole's position, we argue, similarly affect present discourses about migrations *across the Pacific*. In fact, the latter inhabits a more extensive "problem space" that gets watched by several Western states (including America), because of the implications that it holds for them as potential "host" countries. In this sense, what is supposedly a shared, and *transpacific,* universe of mutual alliance and exchange is also paradoxically unilateral and hegemonic in imagination and exercise. What gets silenced in the process ineluctably are the many subaltern viewpoints that are waiting to be uncovered from a different locus and positionality. In the following sections, we turn to unpick three such counter-possibilities through the prism of transnationalism research. Through a careful analysis on this literature, we hope to contribute to an alternative transpacific agenda that is more fluid, balanced, and circumspect.

Transpacific Spatialities

While not directly allied with any overt transpacific agenda, cross-border itinerancies spanning the Pacific Ocean—especially those undertaken by Asians—have received increasing attention in the academy in recent years. Owing in part to this growing visibility, they now constitute some of the most thoroughly investigated phenomena in the transnationalism literature, rivaling research on Latin American and Caribbean migrations in both incidence and prominence (Rogers 2004). Commensurable with the interest it has garnered, this body of work additionally distinguishes itself in its analytical approach. As opposed to treating migration as neutral statistical events, it has sought to reestablish Pacific movements as agency-filled and geographically specific processes. Much of this has been the result of some careful interrogations on how Asia and America (often extending to Canada) now constitute a mutually reinforcing dyad that motivates particular transnational journeys. To a lesser extent, Australia and New Zealand have also been noted to play an increasingly important supporting role in absorbing Asian migrants, who, because of chain migration or resource constraints, were unwilling or unable to journey to North America. As we shall see, this framing has led to a few idiosyncratic research habits and tendencies. Not least, it has regularized particular ways of understanding Pacific worlds, and how they interact and converse with each other.

Early research on transnational activities in the Asia-Pacific region arguably began with a curiosity about how East Asian migrant communities residing in the Western world related to their "original" homelands across the Pacific. A case in point concerns the recrudescent interest in Chinatowns in North American cities in the late 1980s, when scholars projected them not only as hearths of "overseas" Chinese culture, but also as transnational bases for Chinese migrants to orchestrate their entrepreneurial expansions (Li 2009; Chinn 1989). For instance, the "Sinicization" of Monterey Park, a suburb in Los Angeles, has been interpreted as the result of, not just cultural preferences, but large infusions of capital from Asia to local businesses, which boosted home financing and ownership in the area (Fong 1994). Extending this view beyond the confines of ethnic neighborhoods, Wong (1998, 85) more elaborately argues that recent Chinese migrants to the U.S. West Coast "differ significantly from the old settlers in that many are highly educated professionals and affluent businessmen who operate on a global stage." These footloose travelers, he posits, lead lives that involve a frequent need to commute over long distances, as they seek to "travel, live, and work in different parts of the world [in search of] opportunities in the global village" (Wong 1998, 87). In this context, they are seen to *require* an enlarged habitus, of which America is only part, where they can dwell and operate from; transpacific mobility in turn serves as a means for them to achieve these expansionary goals and to combat the inherent disadvantages of being fixed in one place.

Ong's (1999) flexible citizenship thesis further substantiates this view when it attributes the transnationalizing tendencies among East Asian migrants to a "cultural logic" of pragmatism and adaptability. In broadening the outlook to include a wide range of middle-class interests, her work outlines the various citizenship-based strategies that Chinese managers, technocrats, and professionals use to enhance their social mobility and facilitate their capital accumulation projects across space (see also Mitchell 1995). Not only does becoming dual citizens of multiple countries, preferably on both sides of the Pacific, help them gain access to a greater selection of national markets, it also empowers them to "take advantage of political and economic conditions in different parts of the world" (Ong 1999, 113). Noting the expediency of such bridge-building efforts, some scholars propose that transnationalism is conceivably an avenue for these migrants to attain *non*pecuniary benefits as much as pecuniary ones. In partaking "the best of both worlds," these "flexible citizens" may seek two or more citizenships to afford themselves the option to enjoy a "better" standard of living (Wong 1997) and/or education (for their children) (Ong 1993) in the West, while concomitantly retaining the ability to participate in the "Asian boom" back home. Seen in this light, their transnational projects across the Pacific are also spatial manifestations of a new mode of "global" living that strives for locational flexibility through a surfeit of residency rights. Such arrangements are especially well-exemplified by Hong Kong and Taiwanese "astronaut" families, which consist of mothers and children who relocate to Canadian and U.S. cities to take advantage of "superior" social and educational amenities there, while breadwinning fathers make the transpacific shuttle back (and forth) to capitalize on business opportunities in Pacific Asia (Yeoh et al. 2005).

Recent scholarship further adds to this idea of simultaneity when it sketches out how these transnational strategies are articulated in *time* as much as they are in space. By switching to a dual-focus, Chinese transnationalisms are now no longer studied for only the relations they lay up between places, but also for how they are undertaken at timely intervals to maximize the benefits of straddling between two opposite Pacific worlds. Often enrolling the entire household in these migratory projects, (school-going) children are frequently seen to be the "trigger" of many of the initial uprootings from Asia to English-speaking Pacific Rim countries, as families seek to acquire more "valuable" education credentials for their children (Waters 2006). Following this preliminary move, future possibilities such as the return of these "overseas-educated" children to Asia for employment and (eventually) the reuniting of the transnationally "split" family in the West upon citizenship acquisition can then be contemplated. Ley and Kobayashi (2005) aptly coin this as a chain of "transnational sojourns" involving repeated circulations with ever more movements ahead to coincide with the shifting motivations of the migrant family. More explicitly about its successive nature, Kobayashi and Preston (2007) point out that key life-course transitions, such as schooling and retirement, are often the impetus for (re)mobility and transnationalism among East Asian families, even as these seek to smooth out the disruptions that life's contingencies bring. In short, the Asia-Pacific is a region too unevenly endowed to permanently settle in one place; but, with the right legal credentials, it can be a very navigable terrain with designated waypoints to shuttle between.

Analogous transpacific configurations have been observed outside the East Asian context as well. In Southeast Asia, the end of European colonialism half a century ago has seen a simultaneous rise in indigenous nationalism in many constituent states, leading to a disruption of the region's internal racial balance. Ensuing discrimination against "nonnative" groups that had migrated to Southeast Asia in colonial times has in turn resulted in their remigration, or even expulsion, to third countries in recent decades. In Vietnam, Laos, and Cambodia, for instance, the Indochina wars of the 1970s created large numbers of refugees, notably among minority groups such as the Viet Hoa and the Hmong, who fled to Australia, Canada, and the United States to escape the (geo)political upheavals in these Asian states (Haines 1996; Coughlan 1992). These migrants would in turn constitute a major source of remittance income for these countries in the ensuing years, contributing, especially in the case of Vietnam, to their stabilization and present development (Pfau and Giang 2010). In a similar (but milder) case, Malaysian-Chinese have been noted to resettle "abroad" too in response to the Malaysian government's unfair economic treatment of descendants of former migrant communities under the bumiputra[2] laws, generating a "second-wave diaspora" of ethnic Chinese from Malaysia to Australasia and North America (Cartier 2003). Yet again, this does not mean that Malaysian migrants cease connections with their country of birth upon their departure. On the contrary, many continue to share a bond with their ancestors' first-adopted "homeland," viewing themselves as not just economically but also emotionally tied to the country. Evidently, identified in these examples are further complexities in the circulations around the Pacific, incorporating not just pragmatic considerations, but also political, historical, and nostalgic influences.

Scripted into these intricate storylines is the view that the transpacific constitutes a variegated time-space fraught with disparities, risks, constraints, memories, and opportunities for migrants from Asia. This understanding perhaps bears much truth. However, simultaneously implicated within these fluid cartographies is another hidden geography that is arguably more static and problematic (Lin and Yeoh 2011). In reinforcing how particular mobile outcomes correspond with particular places along the Pacific Rim, a second map of *fixed* localities and *fixed* ethnic personalities has furtively been drawn up and reified. To this extent, a predictable pattern purported of all transpacific journeying has emerged, with its starting point invariably on the Western side of the Pacific, and its receiving end on its other coast. While tempered by what are indicatively termed as "return" flows in recent years, Asian nations continue to assume the role of (historical) originator and source of motivation for all such mobilities, just as Western countries along the Rim figure as the favored destination, extended habitus, and/or place of desire for many of the migrants. Consequently, most, if not all, research interested in "Pacific crossings" has also focused overwhelmingly on the mobile intentions and practices among East and Southeast Asians, who are seen to be found on the "flightier" side of the Ocean. Notwithstanding the recurrent nature of their circuitous movements, the dichotomous distinctions between immigration/emigration, destinations/origins, and receiving/sending countries, in this way, remain resiliently valid and intact. More crucially, they continue to structure how the directionalities and spatialities of transpacific mobilities are to be apprehended and expressed, implicitly invoking a binary pitting East against West.

This rigidified interpretation can in part be traced to the asymmetrical outlook that the transnationalism literature has thus far tended to adopt. While much attention has recently been paid to the human agencies patent within migration conduct today, we argue that many studies continue to be encumbered by sets of Western-centric questions and state-based ideals—where are the "immigrants" from; why do "they" come "here"; what do "they" do after they arrive; why do they "return"; what transnational practices do "they" enact—that permit only a limited range of migratory possibilities and geographical imaginations. What a new transpacific agenda must therefore seek to avoid is the overdependence on a single preponderant logic that sidelines other trajectories and alternative thought in Pacific migrations. Indeed, it may be prudent to start looking for, or documenting more of, the mobilities of "forgotten" migrants who do not fit easily into current models. These may include the itineraries of transnational migrants who transit between Asia and Latin America while bypassing North America (McKeown 2004), or those who may have a different conception of "home" and "return" in the Pacific than what their ethnicity presumes (see Tsuda 2003), or even (non-Asian) American job seekers who look to the Pacific for employment (Chiou 2010), reversing the conventional direction of flow. More than an academic attempt to amass new case studies, this contrasting framework can lend a new voice to challenge predictable, and static, understandings about transpacific mobilities, wrestling the same from their current subordination to the viewpoints and assumptions of America and other Western countries.

In many ways, our proposed agenda draws inspiration from Beaverstock's (2005) work on British transnational managerial elites circulating between London, New York, and other cities, in which he treats them as independent agents who undertake *disparate* journeys around the globe as part of their career demands. Not willing to conflate their mobilities with any particular routes or predetermined pathways, his research offers a lucid example of how migrant flows can be better known for their inherent unpredictability, spontaneity, and inclination to develop into diverse circuits and relations, even within the same cultural group. Adopting an approach that unpresumptuously follows where *individuals* go and how different spaces uniquely fold onto each other (Crang et al. 2003), we suggest, can precisely help to establish a methodological orientation that pays due attention to the diverse transpacific possibilities that characterize the region. Alternatively put, the stance we are promoting is one that espouses a more open-ended and cosmopolitan research paradigm, which actively seeks out and experiments with new trajectories and configurations of travel while not losing sight of global capitalistic forces. Not only would such a maneuver help to avoid the limitation of transpacific studies to a few overrehearsed examples of "Asian" transnational migration *to* Western states, it can also aid in the rescripting of transpacific mobilities into a livelier and more dynamic anthology of spaces, flows, and relations.

Transpacific Subjectivities

The propensity to focus on the transnational pathways and morphologies of Asian migrations is not the only conceptual limitation deserving of scrutiny. If there has been a lack of criticality in the way transpacific migrations are spatially plotted, there exists an even greater dearth of sensitivity toward the kinds of *identities* that are being created out of these same mobilities. Not unlike the way Asian American studies adopts a nationalistic posture in its explications of "immigration" and "acculturation" experiences in the United States (Lowe 1998), transnationalism research seems to have engaged in a very similar act of constructing international "Others" out of Pacific Rim migrants. By construing them as, first, "immigrants" whose mobilities inevitably contradict Western notions of "white" nationalism in many receiving societies, these nomads have been counted exterior to the "destination" countries in which they have "landed," and an unnatural branch of those states. To be sure, scholars have gained a better understanding, through this research, of how globalization is giving birth to new categories of migrants and sojourners from Asia and other sending regions in the Pacific. But given that many of these interpretations remain preoccupied with the receiving nation's perspectives, they have inadvertently enabled new rounds of boundary-drawing and discursive production.

Returning to Ong's thesis on middle-class Chinese transnationalism can give us some clues as to how some of the most prominent streams in transpacific migrations today have been characterized. At a perfunctory glance, it would appear that the old image of the ethnic settler permanently cloistered away in an enclave with fellow countrymen has lost part of its appeal. What replaces it, however, is a narrative that is unfortunately just as exclusionary. Specifically, there is an overt tendency now to caricature these migrants as opportunistic and calculating denizens, who strategically plot to profit from the newly liberalized immigration regimes in the West, while laboring to "fall . . . prey to as few responsibilities as possible" (Miller 2002, 231). Applying these newfound agencies to middle-class Chinese from East and Southeast Asia, Ong (1999, 19) writes that "those most able to benefit from their participation in global capitalism" are the same who "celebrate flexibility and mobility," and who are able to (re)fashion themselves "as the multiple-passport holder; the multicultural manager with 'flexible capital'; the 'astronaut' shuttling across borders on business; 'parachute kids' who can be dropped off in another country by parents on the trans-Pacific commute." While Ong has prefaced that these formations are to be treated as cultural inventions born out of late capitalism, it is not clear if subsequent work has taken a similarly constructivist approach, rather than presume the phenomenological reality of these "Chinese" tendencies. Worrisomely, by conflating contemporary Asian mobilities with certain personas such as "astronauts," "parachute kids," and "transient returnees," transpacific movements have become marked not by the shifting dynamics between migrants and nation-states, but an "inflexible" application of particular subjectivities, techniques, and cultural logics (Lin 2012).

Going beyond the middle-class context, a different, but equally unsettling, set of sociopolitical issues arises in the case of lower-class migrants undertaking the same transoceanic journey. Gerry Pratt's work on Filipino domestic workers migrating to Canada via the Live-in Caregiver program is exactly one example of how the scholarship has alternatively sought to (re)write a more poignant story for *poorer* migrants, including how they have been enrolled and exploited within transpacific circuits. As she asserts, the Filipino diaspora is far from an incidental outcome, but "a product of global uneven development, the [postcolonial] labor export policy of the Philippines' government . . . , and the demand in industrial nations for migrant women to provide low-wage service work . . . that many resident women no longer . . . perform" (Pratt 2007, 124). In contrast to the strategic "flexible citizen," these migrants occupy a transnational space not of their own choosing, but one purportedly created by their difficult circumstances in Asia; restrictive legal provisions in host nations necessitating their separation from their families; and their acceptance of an impoverished and sometimes impermanent existence devoid of rights (Mattingly 2001). While Asian migration has over the last decades become more skilled in character (due to stricter qualification criteria), those who suffer such constraints are seen to share the same plight as the chorus of similarly marooned Latin American laborers who, too, inhabit the lower rungs of the North American economy. In swinging to the other end of the spectrum, these lower-class migrants take on a character role starkly oppositional to the "exploitative strategists," playing now the part of the "exploited victim," for whom agency proves to be elusive.

While useful in highlighting the very divergent experiences extant within transpacific flows, these twin perspectives introduce a certain extremity to our appreciation of those who are actually "on the move" in the Pacific. Their unflattering portrayal of Asian migrants as either the targets of global victimization or the exploiters of Western societies without meaning to integrate dually confirms Favell's (2003) observation about the propensity of transnationalism research to reify the "ethnic" temperaments of particular mobile persons, who, in this case, are either too intrusive or too helpless. By doubting their capacity to act as emotionally or economically "viable" citizens, these migrants are given the dubious honor of serving as a "source of insight into processes of social and cultural change in modern Western societies," wrought by migratory pressures and global labor restructuring (Favell 2003, 400). In our view, what warrants attention is precisely this unspoken assumption that the transnational ties and precarious incorporation of these migrants somehow render them problematic subjects in particular states, seeing that their full domestication and assimilation may be unattainable. Setting the focus squarely on how "they" have been imag(in)ed, subjectified, and set apart instead, we suggest that being cognizant of the potential areas of conceptual rigidity, and even stereotype, that may still be lurking in academia is perhaps a more productive stance to take. This endeavor to (re)understand these migrants in fairer and more positive terms is also what we advocate for future transpacific research.

Exactly demonstrating such a sensitivity, Ho (2002) turns to the New Zealand context to challenge the "myth" that "astronaut" strategies are a widespread custom and disposition among middle-class Asian migrants in the country. What she discovers, on the contrary, is that those who staunchly pursue such projects actually constitute only a small minority in New Zealand. In a similar vein, Ip (2000, cited in Bartley and Spoonley 2008, 66) takes issue with how Chinese transnationals have been unfairly demonized in some literatures. Specifically, she cites as problematic "the over-simplified and reactionary characterisation of these migrants as 'disloyal' or as cynical manipulators of bureaucratic systems, who employ their 'astronaut strategy in order to exploit . . . social and environmental resources [of the destination country] for their own gain." Not convinced that their mobilities amount to tactical acts of system abuse, she argues that the circulatory movements of these Pacific-crossers are perhaps a more benign and universal phenomenon, having more to do with their middle-class status than with their cultural background or ethnicity. Finally, turning to the working class context, Yeoh and Soco (2014) likewise repudiate overly negative understandings of transpacific migrants from Asia. In their case, instead of reiterating the widespread exclusion of Filipino domestic workers in the sociopolitical life of many countries, their work recovers at least one aspect of these women's agency while in transit. Specifically, the authors find that a process of learning and self-improvement can take place for these lower-class migrants quite intensively in the course of their sojourns, as contact zones and cultural exchanges multiply and their perspectives are being renewed. In this sense, they are also not completely victimized, but retain a certain degree of autonomy for bettering their lives.

Capturing the essence of these arguments, Kothari's (2008) study on Bangladeshi and Senegalese migrant traders in Spain and the "cosmopolitan" identities they assume is perhaps able to address a more deep-seated issue that we have been grappling with as well. As she rightly points out, there seems to be an unproductive consistency with which "migrants of color" are repeatedly being portrayed as moving for economic gain alone, while the search for enrichment, adventure, and experience is often reserved for Euro-American expatriate travelers. Given that a significant part of current transpacific research revolves around middle-class mobilities, which should entail greater latitude for exploration and self-fulfillment, it seems puzzling that Asian migrancies are still being singled out and framed in highly pragmatic ways—either in terms of capital accumulation or economic necessity. A more tangible sense of this incongruence is given by examining the transnational mobilities of "white migrants."[3]

Expressly, it is telling how their itinerancies are often vested with a contrasting gloss of "normality" and "legitimacy," when juxtaposed with Asian mobilities. Earlier, we have seen in Beaverstock's (2005) work how British transnational elites regularly engage in "globetrotting" missions between London, New York, and Asia-Pacific cities as part of their employment, often with the (familiar) intention of accumulating valuable cultural capital as they progress through places. While little is said about the kinds of strategic residency rights that these expatriates acquire, this is a form of intercontinental circulation that presumably also involves a certain degree of calculation and life-course planning, not unlike Asian "flexible citizens." In another instance, Conradson and Latham (2005) harmlessly refer to New Zealanders' migrations to South East England, and later their return, as mundane acts of getting "on" and "off" the "jobs escalator." For these professionals, working "overseas" is curiously seen to be a perfectly rational—rather than "strategic"—motion, through which they can explore ideas of creative individualism and self-actualization for their personal profit (Findlay et al. 2008).

Ostensibly, a situation arises presently where the migratory activities of white "flexible citizens" are readily sanctioned and applauded, while the mobilities of transnational Asians are deemed to be "threatening" and "problematic." Clearly, an uneven set of scales has been applied here, when almost identical acts of *human* mobility are evaluated so differently. Attributing this to the dominance of receiving/Western societies' perspectives, this analysis compels some significant revisions to the way we think about and approach transpacific migrants from Asia and "ethnic" regions. Not least, it warrants recognition that these mobile persons neither have a single (and unfavorable) identity, nor do they bear a fundamental difference from other migrants when it boils down to their motivations and behaviors. A key prerequisite to recalibrating current perceptions is thus to tune in more to the *similarities* between migrants of different "diasporic" origins, and how they are stitched conterminously into a single Pacific/global domain (Ang 2007). Suggestively, it is by refocusing on such cross-cutting human aspirations for mobility and universal vulnerabilities that transpacific connections can be appreciated for their role in forging an integrated—rather than divided—Asia-Pacific. Only by safeguarding our theories from the colored lenses of ethnic strangeness can our vision of the same be truly lightened, and remain untainted by perennial suspicions of the "Other."

(Re)centering the Pacific

This leads on to our final analysis concerning the frequent projection of transpacific movements in almost epochal terms (cf. Ong and Nonini 1997). While this has in many ways increased the visibility of Asian transnational migration and given it greater conceptual weight, we argue that it has also allowed America and other Western states such as Canada, Australia, and New Zealand to take center-stage once again, permitting them to pose as the destinations of "new" migrations, the "new" stage for social change, and the "new" locus for policy review. Given these tendencies, it is not surprising then that so little has been written about how transpacific formations matter to other centers of knowledge in the Pacific region—whether they are indeed "new" and/or "revolutionary" to them. In fact, it seems appropriate to us to question if the transnationalism literature has sometimes read like an imperial anthology of area studies, targeted at "solving" how migrant activities in the "Near East," the Caribbean, and, now, Asia may impact the Euro-American metropole. Objecting to the resultant act of problematizing "Other" spaces and thereby "peripheralizing" them, this section seeks to rethink how these same spaces can be more accurately interpreted as copartners and coevals in transnational processes. Specifically, we wish to trouble America's long-standing position as the de facto "immigration" center of the world through which all migratory flows must be routed, proposing in its place a new optic that firmly restores the Pacific as a shared space of diverse traffics.

Such an agenda is immediately pregnant with the potential of distancing Asia from its former role as a chronic dependent of the West in migration. Notwithstanding the fact that the literature has recently paid increasing attention to how return flows are enrolling the latter now as part of a system of structural circulation, we contend that greater weight can be accorded to the region's position as an *autonomous* stakeholder in Pacific mobilities in itself. In this regard, a few studies on the changing complexion of rapidly globalizing cities in East and Southeast Asia can offer some guidance. While not explicitly alluding to the concept of the transpacific per se, Farrer (2010, 1225), for instance, investigates how a group of (white) European and American expatriates are emplaced in the Chinese city of Shanghai, constituting a "new ethnic commercial diaspora" not unlike that of the Chinese in the West. Turning to Singapore, Yeoh and Khoo (1998), in contrast, look to the experiences of *women* expatriates and "trailing spouses" living in the city-state for a different perspective of how Asia's social landscapes have been reconfigured by transnational flows. In their study, they not only particularize the various contact zones and communal spaces that have emerged in Singapore as a result of these gendered mobilities, but also detail the ways in which the lives of the expatriate women are far from smooth sailing, but riddled with negotiations and uneven incorporation at work and at home. These paradigms unequivocally alert us to the far-reaching impacts of transpacific, and other modes of, mobilities on different locales, exceeding the conventional focus on America and other "traditional" receiving societies.

The salience of Pacific Asia in migration stories becomes even more apparent when one considers the intensity of *intraregional* flows (Hugo 2004). Paying heed to this growing concentration of mobilities along (only) the western coast of the Pacific does not just redirect our attention away from the archetypal "flexible citizen," it also enables new appreciations of transpacific crossings as only one of *many* regional orders that Asia participates in. On one level, fixating on these other morphologies may seem to be overstepping the empirical boundaries of this volume, but we argue that, even (or especially) in accounts that presume the arrival of the Pacific century, it is paramount to keep in perspective the *marginality* of Asia-U.S. traffic in certain circumstances. Indeed, historical accounts abound with regards to the presence of itineraries skirting only the West Pacific, long before European colonialism appeared in the seventeenth century. While Chinese traders had begun plying maritime routes between South China and Nanhai (Southeast Asia) as early as the sixth century BC, important trade and migratory links between the two sides had become firmly established by the fifteenth century (Wang 1992). Similarly in contemporary times, there has been a reconsolidation of intraregional economic integration between the modern states of East and Southeast Asia, this time owing to current rounds of global market segmentation (Yeoh and Lin 2013). While high-performance economies and aging societies like Singapore, Japan, and Taiwan face chronic manpower shortages and are in constant need of fresh infusions of migrant labor, countries such as China and Indonesia are found with surplus populations of underemployed workers who are able to plug this gap (Wong 2011). Consequently, there has also been an explosion of migratory exchanges—from temporary contract workers and domestic workers to international students and skilled professionals—who are now moving in response to this intraregional discrepancy. Beyond the ties that Asia shares with the United States, there thus exist other mobile regimes and histories within the Asian region, testifying to its longtime position as an independent migration space.

In addition, another striking feature of migration processes within Asia has been its increasing penchant and ability to set its own rules for the regulation of population flows. While this is obviously nothing new, underscoring these emergent managerial efforts to harness, speed up, and sometimes even stall the proceedings of transnational mobilities in this part of the world can help trouble current assumptions that such modern techniques of control are solely the prerogative and concern of Western nation-states (Hiebert et al. 2003). To be sure, scholars have written extensively about the ways in which mobility is very much a tool and a window through which contemporary Asian governments tackle various demographic and developmental problems at home (Hugo 2004). Where it pertains to enhancing the foreign exchange position of the nation, countries like the Philippines, Indonesia, and Vietnam actively facilitate the *out*-migration of (more of) their citizens to other parts of Asia, the Middle East, and Europe in the hope of benefiting from the remittance trade (Hugo and Stahl 2004); on the competition for global talent and skilled labor, rapidly developing economies such as China have been mobilizing various institutions and governmental arms to attract talent and promote the homecoming of their diasporic citizens to help jump-start their own industrial growth (Zweig 2006); and in yet more nimble ways, global cities from Singapore to Hong Kong have devised exclusionary employment and admission procedures for certain classes of migrants, adopting a use-and-discard attitude toward "unskilled" workers who are from the start meant to be transient contributors to the city (Yeoh 2006).

This brief overview on the remarkable growth of migration in, from, and *of* Asia is not meant to be a critique of its state interventions (although this is important), but rather a recognition of the different practices of demographic control in Asia, as well as the impact of these on the future outlook of Pacific mobilities. Taking a multicentered approach, we propose that transnational flows, including those traversing the Pacific Ocean, do not (or perhaps never) just revolve around a structural center in the United States, but are constituted through a motley blend of multisited policies, restrictions, and facilitations that increasingly implicate the Asian world. As Xiang's (2007) example of the highly diffuse South Asian labor system in the information technology sector is able to make clear, transnational streams are far from linear trajectories, being rather the dynamic product of a concoction of divergent governmental regimes, actions by private institutions and agencies, and other place- and industry-specific practices spanning across numerous centers. As opposed to fixating on any single country's migration "appeal" (or "repulsion") therefore, we posit that more attention needs to be paid to the manner in which *multiple* sites are concatenated in highly specific and inconsistent ways into chains of complicit spaces in the Pacific realm and beyond. In particular, a new emphasis on the *central* role that Asia is playing in setting Pacific worlds in motion is now exigent. If anything, it can afford a more holistic understanding of the relationships that the former shares with other coplayers in the Pacific, as well as of its active involvement in folding together diverse parts of the world.

In refusing to think of Asia as a passive fixture to be aligned with certain hegemonic transnational interests of the West, our vision of a forward-looking transpacific agenda thus entails constantly viewing transpacific mobilities and flows through the prism of "other" nodes, processes, and spatial contexts. We have intimated above that Asia—indubitably a vital half of what makes up the transpacific—makes a perfect candidate for engaging in such juxtapositions, not least for its coming of age as a migration powerhouse and its recent salience to globalizing processes. While not discounting the fact that significant (transpacific) exchanges do still occur between the region and the United States, the myriad of alternative paradigms that an Asian perspective can inform—of other migratory configurations—demonstrates the multifariousness with which Pacific worlds are stitched into the "global." These connections are not only capable of encroaching landward, from East and Southeast Asia to the Indian subcontinent and Europe—and, not to forget, seaward to the much-neglected South America—they are also mediated through a variety of mobilities that include expatriates, students, temporary contract workers, marriage migrants, and other more irregular travelers. In view of this immense diversity, the import of transpacific flows must always be considered against this wider backdrop of *manifold* Pacific stories. In this way, the temptation to paint the transpacific hastily in strokes that signal exceptionalism and revolutionary times can also be resisted.

Conclusions

In this chapter, we began by contemplating the need to be cautious about advancing any "new" transpacific research paradigm. As several authors have contended, the epistemological clipping together of two sides of the Pacific has less to do with any essential basis than with the imperial desire of the United States and its allies to naturalize a particular way of mapping and organizing the world (Eperjesi 2005; Wilson 2000). Not willing to wholly dismiss the validity (and reality) of transpacific connections, however, this chapter has sought to imagine a reformed, balanced, and more flexible model of the "Pacific Rim," by exploring new and counterhegemonic ways of thinking about the region and its relational dynamics in all directions. Short of making any positive identification of what shape this reformulation might take, we have chosen to discuss some of the weaknesses and possible areas of oversight in previous renderings of the transpacific. In so doing, a spotlight was placed on empirical studies looking at the various forms of transnational migrations taking place around the Pacific Ocean. In particular, we have focused on the transoceanic passages emanating out of Asia, a region which has also gathered much interest in recent years.

Albeit only a mnemonic device, focusing on the migratory aspect of the transpacific has arguably afforded us a unique insight into a root problem, namely that different locales along the Pacific Rim have been inequitably esteemed in the literature. This epistemic asymmetry not only signals the struggle ahead to reacquaint ourselves with the region on a more even plane, but also testifies to the complicity of (some branches of) academia in forwarding a skewed understanding of the same. Specifically, by interrogating three different aspects of transpacific mobilities, we repeatedly found "Asia"—as a heterogeneous entity comprising not just China, but also diverse players like Japan, Taiwan, Vietnam, Indonesia, and Singapore—to be cast as the constant concern and affliction of its counterpart on the other side of the Pacific Ocean. Concerning its place within transpacific networks, it inevitably plays the role of a "sending society," a source of "emigration," and the "origin" of all (problematic) transnational journeying (Lin and Yeoh 2011); in terms of the people it disseminates, it is unflatteringly the ethnic hearth for either "opportunistic" or "victimized" denizens who migrate for the purpose of bettering their lives "abroad," without necessarily taking on their civic responsibilities in their receiving societies (Miller 2002). Not surprisingly, Asia is also often dispossessed of any true autonomy in contemporary theorizings of migration in spite of its putative fearsome rise. As far as current models are concerned, its story has been one to be told from the exclusive vantage point of the West, which inexorably translates it into a contentious space to be analyzed, solved, and contained.

This profound proclivity to pander to a leery and lopsided portrayal of Asia—whether due to theoretical bias or empirical choice—is to us a key impediment to any real appreciation of the transpacific. Throughout this essay, we have reiterated the need to undertake more radical interventions in the way Asia, in all its diversity and relations with other Pacific players, is being approached. First, it may be gainful to start reconstituting the "forgotten" webs of relations that just as vitally make up the transpacific world. By highlighting not just "ethnic" flows originating in, or returning to, "sending countries" such as China, Malaysia, and Vietnam, expanding the empirical scope of transpacific studies to include, say, "American diasporas" can moderate tendencies to reify ideas about, and dichotomies between immigrant/receiving societies and emigrant/sending countries. Closely related, more can be said about the similarities, rather than differences, that Asian migrants share with other (especially "white") itinerants. By viewing their movements and motivations as corresponding *variants,* and not deviants of, other mobilities, the prejudicial treatment of these subjects as exploitative "flexible citizens" or economically driven lower classes can also be avoided. Finally, transpacific connections need to be situated within a larger context of global and supraregional flows. The multiplicitous ways in which Asian countries—from Japan to Indonesia, through China—have historically been yoked together and wedded to other regions and economies are already indicative of the fact that transpacific linkages constitute only one of *many* transnational orders in the world. Rather than fixating on a single configuration, it is expedient to accent how different "constellations" of flows and other "centers" of mobilities are capable of interacting with each other, producing possibilities that exceed simple oscillations across America's Pacific.

Left deliberately open-ended, these reorientations hopefully constitute crucial starting points to the development of a more progressive transpacific agenda. They not only shun the frequent temptation to frame Pacific worlds in predictable and hierarchical ways, but also actively pursue the production of other postcolonial and counterhegemonic knowledges from (oft-neglected) *Asian* perspectives. In thus disrupting the usual sequence of priority given to (first) East and (then) West Pacific, our intention is to affirmatively dispel any notion that the two sides of the Pacific Rim should form diametric opposites of each other, with one playing the role of an epistemic authority over the "Other." Much preferring to treat them *both* as masters of Pacific fortunes in their own right, our desire is to see a research agenda that can learn to look upon the great traffic of people, resources, and materials in the present "Pacific century" with not so much anxiety and suspicion but a greater appreciation of its potentials and futures for cooperation.

Notes to Chapter 1: Transpacific Studies: The View from Asia

1. While transnationalism has been used to refer to all kinds of economic, political, cultural, and social forms of organization across national boundaries, this chapter's usage is only limited to that of migration, as a social morphology and cultural practice.

2. *Bumiputra* is translated as "son of the soil" and in the Malaysian context refers to the Malays.

3. "White migrant," while seemingly a fusion of two incompatible words, is deliberately used here to unsettle the usual tendencies to equate "migrants" with "ethnic" persons.

References

Ang, Ien. 2007. "Together-in-Difference: Beyond Diaspora, into Hybridity." *Asian Studies Review* 27 (2): 141–154.

Bartley, Allen, and Paul Spoonley. 2008. "Intergenerational Transnationalism: 1.5 Generation Asian Migrants in New Zealand." *International Migration* 46 (4): 63–84.

Basch, Linda, Nina Glick Schiller, and Cristina Szanton-Blanc. 1994. *Nations Unbound: Transnational Projects, Postcolonial Predicaments, and Deterritorialized Nation.* Langhorne, PA: Gordon and Breach.

Beaverstock, Jonathan. 2005. "Transnational Elites in the City: British Highly-Skilled Inter-Company Transferees in New York City's Financial District." *Journal of Ethnic and Migration Studies* 31 (2): 245–268.

Berger, Mark, and Douglas Borer. 1997. "Introduction: The Rise of East Asia: Critical Visions of the Pacific Century." In *The Rise of East Asia: Critical Visions of the Pacific Century*, ed. Mark Berger and Douglas Borer, 1–33. London: Routledge.

Cartier, Carolyn L. 2003. "Diaspora and Social Restructuring in Postcolonial Malaysia." In *The Chinese Diaspora: Space, Place, Mobility and Identity*, ed. Laurence J. C. Ma and Carolyn L. Cartier, 69–96. Lanham, MD: Rowman and Littlefield.

Chinn, Thomas. 1989. *Bridging the Pacific: San Francisco Chinatown and Its People*. San Francisco: Chinese Historical Society of America.

Chiou, Pauline. 2010 "Asia: Help Wanted." *CNN Business 360*. http://business.blogs. cnn.com/2010/09/09/asia-help-wanted (accessed 28 October 2010).

Conradson, David, and Alan Latham. 2005. "Escalator London? A Case Study of New Zealand Tertiary Educated Migrants in a Global City." *Journal of Contemporary European Studies* 13 (2): 159–172.

Coughlan, James E. 1992. "Patterns of Settlement in Australia of Indochinese Refugees." In *Asians in Australia: The Dynamics of Migration and Settlement*, ed. Christine Inglis, S. Gunasekaran, Gerard Sullivan, and Chung-Tong Wu, 73–115. Singapore: Institute of Southeast Asia.

Crang, Philip, Claire Dwyer, and Peter Jackson. 2003. "Transnationalism and the Spaces of Commodity Culture." *Progress in Human Geography* 27 (4): 438–456.

Deleuze, Gilles, and Claire Parnet. 2007. *Dialogues II*. New York: Columbia University Press.

Dirlik, Arif. 1998. "Introduction: Pacific Contradictions." In *What Is in a Rim? Critical Perspectives on the Pacific Region Idea*, ed. Arif Dirlik, 3–13. Lanham, MD: Rowman and Littlefield.

Eperjesi, John. 2005. *The Imperialist Imaginary: Visions of Asia and the Pacific in American Culture*. Hanover, NH: Dartmouth College Press.

Farrer, James. 2010. " 'New Shanghailanders' or 'New Shanghainese': Western Expatriates' Narratives of Emplacement in Shanghai." *Journal of Ethnic and Migration Studies* 36 (8): 1211–1228.

Favell, Adrian. 2003. "Games without Frontiers? Questioning the Transnational Social Power of Migrants in Europe." *Archives Européennes de Sociologie* 44 (3): 106–136.

Findlay, Allan. 2001. "International Migration and Globalisation." In *International Migration into the 21st Century*, ed. Muhammed Abu B. Saddique and Reginald Thomas Appleyard, 126–152. Cheltenham, UK: Elgar.

Findlay, Allan, Colin Mason, Richard Harrison, Donald Houston, and David McCollum. 2008. "Getting off the Escalator? Scots Out-Migration from a Global City Region." *Environment and Planning A* 40: 2169–2185.

Fong, Timothy. 1994. *The First Suburban Chinatown: The Remaking of Monterey Park, California*. Philadelphia: Temple University Press.

Glick Schiller, Nina, Linda Basch, and Cristina Szanton-Blanc. 1995. "From Immigrant to Transmigrant: Theorizing Transnational Migration." *Anthropological Quarterly* 68 (1): 48–63.

Grieco, Elizabeth, and Edward Trevelyan. 2010. "Place of Birth of the Foreign-Born Population: 2009." *American Community Survey Briefs.* http://www.census.gov /prod/2010pubs/acsbr09-15.pdf (accessed July 21, 2011).

Gryn, Thomas, and Christine Gambino. "The Foreign Born From Asia: 2011." American Community Survey Briefs. https://www.census.gov/prod/2012pubs/acsbr11-06 .pdf (accessed February 5, 2014).

Haines, David W., ed. 1996. *Refugees in America in the 1990s: A Reference Handbook.* Westport, CT: Greenwood Press.

Harris, Nigel. 1989. "Review Article: The Pacific Rim." *Journal of Development Studies* 25 (3): 408–416.

Hiebert, Daniel, Jock Collins, and Paul Spoonley. 2003. "Uneven Globalization: Neoliberal Regimes, Immigration and Multiculturalism in Australia, Canada and New Zealand." Research on Immigration and Integration in the Metropolis Working Paper Series, no. 03–05.

Ho, Elsie Seckyee. 2002. "Multi-Local Residence, Transnational Networks: Chinese 'Astronauts' Families in New Zealand." *Asian and Pacific Migration Journal* 11 (1): 145–164.

Hugo, Graeme. 2004. "International Migration in the Asia-Pacific Region: Emerging Trends and Issues." In *International Migration: Prospects and Policies in a Global Market,* ed. Douglas S. Massey and J. Edward Taylor, 77–103. Oxford: Oxford University Press.

Hugo, Graeme, and Charles Stahl. 2004. "Labor Export Strategies in Asia." In *International Migration: Prospects and Policies in a Global Market,* ed. Douglas S. Massey and J. Edward Taylor, 174–200.

Ip, David, Raymond Hibbins, and Wing Hong Chui. 2006. "Transnationalism and Chinese Migration." In *Experiences of Transnational Chinese Migrants in the Asia-Pacific,* ed. David Ip, Raymond Hibbins, and Wing Hong Chui, 1–16. New York: Nova Science Publishers.

Kobayashi, Audrey, and Valerie Preston. 2007. "Transnationalism through the Life Course: Hong Kong Immigrants in Canada." *Asia Pacific Viewpoint* 48 (2): 151–167.

Koehn, Peter, and Xiao-huang Yin, eds. 2002. *The Expanding Roles of Chinese Americans in U.S.-China Relations: Transnational Networks and Trans-Pacific Interactions.* Armonk, NY: M. E. Sharpe.

Kothari, Uma. 2008. "Global Peddlers and Local Networks: Migrant Cosmopolitanisms." *Environment and Planning D* 26: 500–516.

Ley, David. 1999. "Myths and Meanings of Immigration and the Metropolis." *Canadian Geographers* 43 (1): 2–19.

———. 2003. "Seeking *Homo Economicus:* The Canadian State and the Strange Story of the Business Immigration Program." *Annals of the Association of American Geographers* 93 (2): 426–441.

Ley, David, and Audrey Kobayashi. 2005. "Back to Hong Kong: Return Migration or Transnational Sojourn." *Global Networks* 5 (2): 111–127.

Li, Wei. 2009. *Ethnoburb: The New Ethnic Community in Urban America.* Honolulu: University of Hawai'i Press.

Lin, Weiqiang. 2012. "Beyond Flexible Citizenship: Towards a Study of Many Chinese Transnationalisms." Geoforum 43 (1): 137–146.

Lin, Weiqiang, and Brenda S. A. Yeoh. 2011. "Questioning the 'Field in Motion': Emerging Concepts, Research Practices and the Geographical Imagination in Asian Migration Studies." *cultural geographies* 18 (1): 125–131.

Linder, Staffan Burenstam. 1986. *The Pacific Century: Economic and Political Consequences of Asian-Pacific Dynamism.* Stanford, CA: Stanford University Press.

Lowe, Lisa. 1998. "The International within the National: American Studies and Asian American Critiques." *Cultural Critique* 40: 29–47.

Massey, Douglas S., and J. Edward Taylor, eds. *International Migration: Prospects and Policies in a Global Market.* Oxford: Oxford University Press.

Mattingly, Doreen J. 2001. "The Home and the World: Domestic Service and International Networks of Caring Labor." *Annals of the Association of American Geographers* 91 (2): 370–386.

McCord, William. 1991. *The Dawn of the Pacific Century: Implications for Three Worlds of Development.* New Brunswick, NJ: Transaction Publishers.

McKeown, Adam. 2004. "Global Migration, 1846–1940." *Journal of World History* 15 (2): 155–189.

Miller, Toby. 2002. "Cultural Citizenship." In *Handbook of Citizenship Studies,* ed. Engin F. Isin and Bryan S. Turner, 231–243. London; Thousand Oaks, CA: Sage.

Mitchell, Katharyne. 1995. "Flexible Circulation in the Pacific Rim: Capitalisms in Cultural Context." *Economic Geography* 71 (4): 364–382.

Ong, Aihwa. 1993. "On the Edge of Empires: Flexible Citizenship among Chinese in Diaspora." *positions* 1 (3): 745–778.

———. 1999. *Flexible Citizenship: The Cultural Logics of Transnationality.* Durham, NC: Duke University Press.

Ong, Aihwa, and Donald Nonini. 1997. *Ungrounded Empires: The Cultural Politics of Modern Chinese Transnationalism.* New York: Routledge.

Palat, Ravi A. 1993. "Introduction: The Making and Unmaking of Pacific-Asia." In *Pacific-Asia and the Future of the World-System,* ed. Ravi A. Palat, 3–20. Westport, CT: Greenwood Press.

Pfau, D. Wade, and Giang Thanh Long. 2010. "The Growing Role of International Remittances in the Vietnamese Economy: Evidence from Vietnam (Household) Living Standard Surveys." In *Global Movements in the Asia Pacific,* eds. Pookong Kee and Hidetaka Yoshimatsu, 225–247. Singapore: World Scientific Publishing.

Portes, Alejandro, Luis E. Guarnizo, and Patricia Landolt. 1999. "The Study of Transnationalism: Pitfalls and Promise of an Emergent Research Field." *Ethnic and Racial Studies* 22 (2): 217–236.

Pratt, Geraldine. 2005. "From Migrant to Immigrant: Domestic Workers Settle in Vancouver, Canada." In *A Companion to Feminist Geography,* ed. Lise Nelson and Joni Seager, 123–137. Malden, MA: Blackwell.

Rogers, Alisdair. 2004. "A European Space for Transnationalism?" In *Transnational Spaces,* ed. Peter Jackson, Philip Crang, and Claire Dwyer, 164–182. London: Routledge.

Tsuda, Takeyuki. 2003. *Strangers in the Ethnic Homeland: Japanese Brazilian Return Migration in Transnational Perspective.* New York: Columbia University Press.

Wang, Gung Wu. 1992. *Community and Nation: China, Southeast Asia and Australia.* St Leonards, NSW: Allen and Unwin.

Waters, Johanna L. 2006. "Emergent Geographies of International Education and Social Exclusion." *Antipode* 38 (5): 1046–1058.

Wilkins, Thomas. 2010. "The New 'Pacific Century' and the Rise of China: An International Relations Perspective." *Australian Journal of International Affairs* 64 (4): 381–405.

Wilson, Rob. 2000. "Imagining 'Asia-Pacific': Forgetting Politics and Colonialism in the Magical Waters of the Pacific. An Americanist Critique." *Cultural Studies* 14 (3–4): 562–592.

Wong, Bernard. 1998. *Ethnicity and Entrepreneurship: The New Chinese Immigrants in the San Francisco Bay Area.* Boston: Allyn and Bacon.

Wong, Lloyd. 1997. "Globalization and Transnational Migration: A Study of Recent Chinese Capitalist Migration from the Asian Pacific to Canada." *International Sociology* 12 (3): 329–351.

Wong, Tai-Chee. 2011. "International and Intra-National Migrations: Human Mobility in Pacific Asian Cities in the Globalization Age." In *Asian Cities, Migrant Labor, and Contested Spaces,* ed. Tai-Chee Wong and Jonathan Rigg, 27–44. London: Routledge.

Xiang, Biao. 2007. *Global "Body Shopping": An Indian Labor System in the Information Technology Industry.* Princeton, NJ: Princeton University Press.

Yeoh, Brenda S. A. 2006. "Bifurcated Labour: The Unequal Incorporation of Transmigrants in Singapore." *Tijdschrift voor economische en sociale geografie* 97 (2): 26–37.

Yeoh, Brenda S. A., Shirlena Huang, and Theodora Lam. 2005. "Transnationalizing the 'Asian' Family: Imaginaries, Intimacies and Strategic Intents." *Global Networks* 5 (4): 307–316.

Yeoh, Brenda S. A., and Louisa-May Khoo. 1998. "Home, Work and Community: Skilled International Migration and Expatriate Women in Singapore." *International Migration* 36 (2): 159–186.

Yeoh, Brenda S. A., and Weiqiang Lin. 2013. "Chinese Migration to Singapore: Discourses and Discontents in a Globalizing Nation-State." *Asian and Pacific Migration Journal* 22 (1): 31–54.

Yeoh, Brenda S. A., and Maria Andrea Soco. 2014. "The Cosmopolis and the Migrant Domestic Worker." Cultural Geographies In-Press. doi: 10.1177/1474474014520899.

Zweig, David. 2006. "Learning to Compete: China's Efforts to Encourage 'Reverse Brain Drain.'" In *Competing for Global Talent,* ed. Christiane Kuptsch and Eng Fong Pang, 187–214. Geneva: Institute for Labour Studies.

2

The Transpacific Cold War

HEONIK KWON

In his recent book, *Dominion from Sea to Sea: Pacific Ascendancy and American Power,* the historian Bruce Cumings proposes a new way to look at the progression of modern U.S. history (Cumings 2009). Drawing a history of migration with a broad brush (from Europe to North America, from North America's eastern to western coastline, and from Pacific Asia to California) and also attending to major world events and global economic trends since the nineteenth century, Cumings argues that a shift in perspective has taken place in America's view of the world and of its place in the world since roughly the time of World War II. Before WWII, the United States saw itself primarily from a transatlantic perspective, grounding its cultural identity in the formative history of migration from the Old World and in the related idea of the modern American civilization as having a European origin. After the war, however, a new perspective arose on the horizon forcefully, which Cumings calls a Pacificist or transpacific perspective. The existence of this perspective actually long predates the time of WWII, according to Cumings, who offers a fascinating account of the early Asian labor migration to Hawaii and California in this light. However, America's transpacific perspective on its place in the world changed from a relatively marginal status to one of major standing (to the level at which it can compete with the traditionally predominant transatlantic perspective) in the mid-twentieth century and, since then, has undergone continuous empowerment. In this respect, Cumings discusses, among other topics, the resurgence of Japan as an economic power in the 1960s and 1970s and the rise of China as an economic and political superpower in more recent years.

Dominion from Sea to Sea looks at the rise of America's global power both in the context of the nation's domestic history, particularly its westward expansion from the Atlantic to the Pacific coast, and in the expansion of its cultural and political relations in the international sphere from its old historical ties to Europe to its relatively new interest in the Asia-Pacific region. In doing so, it defines the American power as a unique historical entity, compared to European powers, with both transatlantic and transpacific horizons being constitutive elements in its making. Depicting America's modern economic and political power as having two wings of historical identity, the work intends to challenge the prevailing transatlantic focus in the existing scholarship of America's political and cultural history. It also highlights the significance of the international and transnational histories in the transpacific horizon in the United States' ascendency to global power.

The United States' rise to global power is associated, in conventional historical knowledge, particularly with the end of the WWII and the onset of the Cold War. The United States is unique among the Western powers as having fought WWII both in the European and the Asian theatres; its rise over the other Western powers is inseparable from this historical experience as well as from its leadership in the subsequent era in the confrontation with the Soviet power. Early Cold War history, in fact, looms large in the background of *Dominion from Sea to Sea*. Cumings is primarily known as an authority on the Asian Cold War, with emphasis on the history of the Korean War. It is fair to conclude, therefore, that Cumings's attention to the transpacific historical horizon and perspective, in critical relation to the transatlantic historical and cultural perspective, grows out of his long-held interest in Cold War history in the Asia-Pacific context.

How concretely, then, does the experience of the Cold War relate to the shifting dynamics between the transatlantic and transpacific historical perspectives? Are there specific issues in understanding the global Cold War that are distinct to the transpacific historical horizon? Does transpacific studies need to be based on a unique understanding of the global Cold War in distinction to the experience of the Cold War along the transatlantic trajectory? This chapter intends to reflect on these questions as a way of clarifying the descriptive and analytical parameters of transpacific studies. Focusing on the history of the early Cold War, it first asks what conceptual challenges this history poses to transpacific historical and social studies. The discussion concentrates on the contrasting experience of the global Cold War, which is particularly pronounced when we compare early Cold War history between the post-WWII European context, on the one hand, and, on the other, how the nations and communities in the Asia-Pacific experienced the epoch as part of turbulent decolonization, which often involved vicious civil wars and other exceptional forms of political violence. Noting that Cold War history in the Asia-Pacific region has a distinct postcolonial dimension, this chapter then considers how transpacific studies may relate to the contemporary scholarship of postcolonial histories and postcolonial cultural criticism, asking what merits and limits the existing postcolonial studies has in store for advancing a historically grounded understanding of the transpacific.

Duplicity in Cold War History

In the southeastern region of the Korean Peninsula, there is a village that was once known as the region's *moskoba* (Moscow)—the wartime reference for a communist stronghold. Each year, people originally from this village return to their homeland in order to join a ceremony held on behalf of the family and village ancestors. On these periodic occasions, the relatives from distant places are pleased to meet each other and exchange news—but not always so.

When a man cautiously suggested to his lineage elders in November 2005 that the family might consider repairing a neglected ancestral tomb, this broke the harmony of the family meal held after the ancestral rite. One elder left the room in fury, and other elders remained silent throughout the ceremonial meal. The man who proposed the idea of tomb renovation was the adopted son of the person buried in the neglected tomb, having been selected as such in his childhood by the family elders for a ritual purpose, whereas the elder who was offended by the idea happened to be a close relative of the entombed person. The last had been a prominent anticolonial communist activist before he died at a young age without a male heir; the elder's children were among the several dozen village youths who left the village together with the retreating communist army in the chaos of the Korean War (1950–1953). The elder believed that this catastrophe in village history and family continuity could have been avoided if the ancestor buried in the neglected tomb had not brought the seeds of "red ideology" to the village in the first place. Beautifying that particular ancestral tomb was unacceptable to this elder, who believed that some of his close kinsmen had lost, because of the ancestor, the social basis on which they could be properly remembered as family ancestors after their death.[1]

The morality of ancestor worship is as strong in Vietnamese cultural tradition as in Korean. These two countries also share the common historical experience of being important sites and symbols in Asia for American leadership in the global struggle against the threat of international communism (Lee 1995, 11–16). Since the end of the 1980s, when the Vietnamese political leadership initiated a general economic reform and regulated political liberalization in the country, there has been a strong revival of ancestral rituals in Vietnamese villages. These rituals were previously discouraged by the state hierarchy which regarded them as backward customs incompatible with the modern secular, revolutionary society (Malarney 2003, 234–242).

In the communities of southern and central regions (what was South Vietnam during the Vietnam War, 1961–1975), a notable aspect of this social development has been the introduction to the ancestral ritual realm of the identities previously excluded from public memory. The memorabilia of the former South Vietnamese soldiers and other hitherto socially stigmatized or marginalized historical identities became increasingly visible in the domestic and communal ritual space. Before the reform, the Vietnamese public ritual space was exclusively for the memory of the fallen revolutionary combatants from the Vietnam War. It is now increasingly becoming open to the memories of the dead from both sides of the war and is therefore in conflict with the state-controlled public institution of commemoration, where one sees no records of deaths from what the Vietnamese call *bên kia* ("the other side" or the side of the enemy) (Kwon 2006, 161–164).

These communal developments and conflicts are common in societies where people experienced the Cold War in forms other than the "long peace"—the idiom with which the historian John Lewis Gaddis characterizes the international environment in the second half of the twentieth century, partly in contrast to the war-torn decades of the first half (Gaddis 1987). Gaddis believes that the bipolar structure of the world order, despite the many anomalies and negative effects it generated, contributed to containing an overt armed confrontation among industrial powers. As Walter LaFeber notes, however, this view of the Cold War speaks a half-truth of global bipolar political history (LaFeber 1992, 13–14). The view represents the dominant Western (and also the Soviet) experience of the Cold War as an "imaginary war" (Kaldor 1990), referring to the politics of competitively preparing for war in the hope of avoiding an actual outbreak of war, whereas identifying the second half of the twentieth century as an exceptionally long period of international peace would be hardly intelligible to much of the rest of the world. The Cold War era resulted in 40 million human casualties in different parts of the world, as LaFeber (1992, 13) mentions; how to reconcile this exceptionally violent historical reality with the predominant Western perception of an exceptionally long peace is a crucial question for grasping the meaning of the global Cold War. According to Cumings (1999, 51), it is necessary to balance the dominant "balance of power" conception of the Cold War, on which the idea of the long peace is based, with the reality of the "balance of terror" experienced in the wider world.

The Cold War was a global conflict. Yet, this does not mean that the conflict was experienced on the same terms all over the world. One way to think about the Cold War's encompassing but variable political realities is implicated in its name. The Cold War is both the general reference for the global bipolar conflict and the representation of this conflict from a particular regional point of view. Societies variously endured the political history of the Cold War as an imaginary war or as other than imaginary, with or without large-scale violence and human suffering. Cold War politics permeated developed and underdeveloped societies, Western and non-Western states, and colonial powers and decolonizing nations: it was a truly global reality in this sense. However, the historical experience and the collective memory of the Cold War have aspects of radical divergence between the West and the postcolonial world. The differing experiences of the Cold War as a long peace and as a total war may not be considered within a single framework, unless this framework is formulated in such a way that it may accommodate the experiential contraries and deal with the semantic contradiction embedded in the idea of the Cold War. The duplicity of the Cold War as an imaginary war and as a nonimaginary total war, in the context of the early Cold War, is most pronounced in the comparative historical trajectories of post-WWII Europe and the postwar Asia-Pacific. From the perspective of modern U.S. history, the duplicity can be understood in terms of a radical divergence in the politics of the Cold War between the transatlantic and the transpacific geographical horizons.

The Postcolonial Cold War

The transpacific Cold War experience is distinct to the transatlantic Cold War experience largely because of the fact that the bipolar political conflicts in the Asia-Pacific region advanced as part of decolonization, which was not necessarily the case in the European theatre of the global Cold War. In order to understand the specificity of the transpacific Cold War in distinction to its transatlantic counterpart, therefore, it is necessary first to come to terms with the concurrence and overlapping of decolonization and political bipolarization on this historical horizon.

The anthropologist Ann Stoler approaches colonial historiography in an innovative way. According to Stoler (1995, 1997), the colonial rule suffered from the inherent and irreconcilable self-contradiction between the rhetorical inclusion of the colonial subjects in the metropolitan sovereignty and the political imperative to exclude them from the rights of citizenship in the polity. Stoler calls this structural contradiction "the tensions of empire"—"the tension between a form of domination predicated on both incorporation and distancing at one and the same time"—and she illustrates these contradictions and tensions with the legal debates and moral confusions about the status of racially mixed children (parented by a European man and an indigenous woman) in the Dutch East Indies and French Indochina (Stoler 1995, 143). The legal and political status of "mixed-bloods" was a highly contentious issue for colonial administrations, according to Stoler, because it threatened to destabilize the biopolitical foundation of the colonial rule, which, based on a rigid hierarchical ordering of racial and cultural roots, linked "domestic arrangements to the public order, family to the state, sex to subversion, and national essence to racial type" (Stoler 1995, 130).

Tensions of empire were equally critical in the history of the ensuing Cold War era. The two countries Stoler focuses on, Indonesia and Vietnam, proclaimed political independence in 1945, and both of them experienced violent bipolarization of political forces in their postcolonial eras. A large territory of Indonesia was devastated by the radical anticommunist terror campaigns waged amidst a political crisis in 1965–1966, resulting in an estimated 1 million human casualties. Observers note how the legacy of extreme political violence from this era continues to haunt Balinese lives today (Dwyer and Santikarma 2003; Robinson 1995). Genealogical history in southern and central regions of Vietnam, as briefly mentioned above, is crowded with a history of radical political disunity, relating to the bifurcated mobilization to the Vietnam War whose force of destruction reached its apex in the second half of the 1960s (Kwon 2006).

In both theatres of destruction, the violence against individuals who were believed to harbor subversive political ideas took on, and was justified by, the essentialist idioms of differences, and it often targeted the collective social units to which these individuals belonged. If a person had consanguine ties with someone considered as ideologically impure, that person could be classified as a subversive individual in the light of kinship or other communal ties and punished as such. Families who had a politically impure ancestral heritage may have a politically contrary genealogical history, especially with the background of a civil war. If not, they might try to escape from the status of a politically damned family by actively joining the very political campaigns that made them suffer in the first place. The histories of these families can also illuminate the tensions of empire—the novel imperial order of the Cold War era.

The bipolarization of social forces reached a critical point in Pacific Asia in the postcolonial era; nevertheless, it had a deeper root in colonial histories. Melvyn Leffler observes that the Russian revolution of 1917 was not a particularly impelling event for most Americans until the 1940s. According to Leffler, "Most Americans were more concerned with Bolshevism at home [domestic Communism and other forms of radicalism] than with Bolshevism abroad" (Leffler 1994, 15). In the colonial world, however, the Russian Revolution had a formative impact on intellectual discourses and political imaginations from the 1920s. Hue-Tam Ho Tai describes how Vietnamese intellectuals, impressed by events in Russia, began to imagine different roads to freedom and independence during this period, and other historians of Vietnam write similarly that the Vietnamese struggle for freedom, contrary to how this is portrayed in the official history in contemporary Vietnam, took on bifurcated visions of their postcolonial future; some believing in liberal ideals while others followed the Russian example (Tai 1992, 57–87; also Pelley 2002, 3). In Indonesia, the charismatic leadership of Sukarno, the unchallenged hero of the anticolonial independence war, managed to contain the conflicts between left-wing and right-wing nationalist forces until the crisis of 1965, when some army groups, supported by the U.S. administration, launched the "holy war of cleansing communism from the national body politic" (Robinson 1995, 300; see also Dwyer and Santikarma 2003, 295). In these contexts, foreign interventions and geopolitical tensions distorted and radicalized the existing ideological color line between the "reds" and non-reds, the formation of which was nevertheless rooted in the pursuit of a world without the injustice and the contradictions of the colonial color line.

The racial and ideological color lines coexisted for much of the twentieth century across territories, making various collusions and sometimes becoming practically indistinguishable (Borstelmann 2001). The Vietnam War magnified their connectedness on the home front of the United States, where civil society was bitterly divided on questions of racial inequality amidst the mounting crisis and debacle in the distant overseas theater of containment of communism. Jeff Woods shows how the radical segregationist polemicists in the American South, like the apartheid regime in South Africa, went against the advocacy of racial integration, propagating that the latter was an act of collusion with communist ideology or even a concerted communist-directed agitation (Woods 2004). According to Mary Dudziak, U.S. administrations from Truman to Johnson were preoccupied with "the Negro problem," believing that the unresolved domestic problems of racial segregation and inequality were America's "Achilles' heel," which seriously undermined America's leadership of the world in the global struggle against communism (Dudziak 2000, 29). The question of racial inequality in general and the segregationist force in America's South in particular became a "Cold War liability" for the Kennedy and Johnson administrations (Westad 2005, 135). If Dudziak focuses on the impact of the domestic racial issue on American foreign policy making, Woods examines how the international politics of anticommunism affected the horizon of racial conflicts in mid-twentieth-century America. Against this background, Douglas Field rightly concludes that the containment of racial conflicts and that of communism are two sides of the same coin in modern American history, despite the fact that they are often treated as separate subjects in existing literature (Field 2005, 88).

If questions of racial segregation are imagined in terms of the idioms of the Cold War, the questions of ideological difference can be translated to biological or racial terms. The tragic civilian killings during the Vietnam War were caused, to a large degree, by the collapse of the two color lines into the mystified image of a generic ideological enemy (Olson and Roberts 1998, 11–16; Kwon 2006, 52–53). The expression *hạt giống đỏ*, meaning "red seed" or "communist born and bred," originally referred to the orphaned children of southern revolutionaries who were brought to North Vietnam during the war and educated by the North Vietnamese authority at *trường học sinh miền nam* ("schools for students from the South"). Today, the expression is used sometimes to refer to the children of high-ranking party cadres privileged in terms of education and career prospects. During the war, however, the expression was also employed in the political campaigns of former South Vietnam to uproot communism from communal lives. In this context, *hạt giống đỏ* implies that uprooting communism from society requires eliminating not only the "plants" of individual suspects, but also the "seeds" of their social, genealogical origins. Civil-war-generation Koreans are familiar with similar expressions such as "red blood line" (Yun 2003, 214–222). For people whose genealogical backgrounds include ancestors once classified as communist subversives, sympathizers of communism, or defectors to the communist north, "red blood line" is a terrifying idea associated with the memory of summary killings and mass murder, with the experience of social stigma for the surviving families, and with the restriction of civil rights for their members. The idea materialized in the public records system, which displayed profiles of such families and individuals with red-colored lines and circles. The massive anticommunist violence unleashed in Bali and elsewhere in Indonesia in 1965 was based partly on "the logic of associative guilt and the need for collective retribution," which aimed to destroy the ideological enemies within the society "down to the roots" (Robinson 1995, 294, 300).

In these historical contexts, it was possible for individuals to be labeled "red" just because they belonged to a specific social group, and to experience something accordingly akin to extreme racial discrimination in society even if they had the same color skin as everyone else. If racial colors were ideological constructs, not biological conditions (Wade 2002), political ideologies, in turn, could take on biological and racial imagery in the history of the twentieth century. Although racial and ideological color lines overlapped in many ways during the past century, it is important to note that the two forms of division nevertheless had different dimensions. Bipolar politics took particularly violent forms in the decolonizing world, but this should not obscure the fact that it affected societies across the old colonial color line. The ideological color line was distinctive in that its formation encompassed the traditional boundaries of racial and cultural hierarchies.

After WWII, the United States staged vigorous campaigns in Europe to "win the battle for the hearts and minds of Western Europeans" (Ryan 2005, 51). In Austria after May 1945, for instance, the U.S. occupation authority ran an elaborate, if not always successful, public relations program, aiming to educate the local population about the dangers of harboring sympathy for communist ideals and about the superiority of American liberal ideals, manifested in their thriving material and popular cultures (Wagnleitner 1989). The campaigns stressed America's material cultural superiority in terms of "People's Capitalism" and defined the latter as against "the wretched socialism of the Soviet, concealing behind its barbed wire and its low living standards, slave labor, and cruel restrictions on personal freedom" (Hixson 1997, 134). In parts of postwar southern Europe, the possibility that the Communist Party might take over political power was real, and this prospect triggered the announcement of the Truman Doctrine in 1947, which some observers consider the official beginning of the Cold War (Osgood 1970). In 1951, the French politician Cavaillet campaigned in favor of the law of amnesty—the initiative debated in the French parliament to pardon former Nazi collaborators of the Vichy regime. This initiative was necessary because, as Jacques Derrida recalls, "to repair the national unity meant to re-arm with all available forces in a combat which would continue, this time in a time of peace, or of a war called cold" (Derrida 2001, 40). A similar "geopolitics of forgiveness" was practiced in other postwar European states and elsewhere in emerging postcolonial nation-states (Derrida 2001, 30; Duggan 1995; Mazower 2000). For the latter, the amnesty concerned collaborators with the colonial regimes, and these acts of forgiveness, often conducted against the expectations and wishes of the population, weakened the moral legitimacy of the states and distorted subsequent political developments. The new bipolar color line encompassed societies previously divided by the traditional colonial color line, partly replacing the latter in significance and partly further complicating it. If the Cold War was a global conflict, it merits this characterization probably in the sense that it was a common human experience of a division of humanity across the racially and culturally divided world.

To sum up, we can say that it is misleading to think of the Cold War as a unitary historical reality. The Cold War took diverse forms across diverse territories, and the idea that it was an "imaginary war" between blocs of states along a clearly defined border speaks of a particular form and experience of the global conflict. Relating the events of mass violence and mass death to the history of the Cold War may make the idea of the Cold War appear somewhat odd and contradictory; yet, I argue that confronting this semantic contradiction is a necessary step toward understanding the Cold War in a genuinely global perspective; that is, the Cold War as a globally shared but, at once, locally distinct experience.

The problem, however, is that the imaginary war, being an expression of a locally specific Cold War experience, claims to be a defining paradigm for the global Cold War.[2] This confusion of historical particularity with universal history, according to Dipesh Chakrabarty, displaces a particular thought about history from its place of origin and empowers it as a universal currency of thought whose relevance is supposed to encompass all places (Chakrabarty 2000).

Centering the Periphery

In his seminal book *Provincializing Europe,* Chakrabarty confronts a set of critical issues in the cultural history of colonialism. Focusing on the literature of Bengali nationalism under British rule, Chakrabarty probes into the tortuous terrain of political thought in colonial society, in which the pursuit of the vision for a liberated modern polity brings those who pursue the ideal to a confinement within the very system of ideas and values from which they struggle to be free. Calling this situation "the politics of historicism," he explores how the colonization of indigenous thought by historicism is as significant in the historiography of colonialism as the exploitation of indigenous labor and resources. Chakrabarty advocates "getting beyond Eurocentric histories" and emphasizes the need to dislocate the universal, linear, and evolutionist conception of time that, in his view, constitutes the core of these histories (Chakrabarty 2000, 6–11).

For the purpose above, Chakrabarty introduces the Bengali idea of nationhood, and contrasts it with the formulations of national identity developed in early European political thought of the eighteenth and nineteenth centuries. The latter were grounded in the rise of the bourgeoisie as a distinctive social category, from which came John Locke's idea of fraternity among property-holding individuals as the foundation of modern democratic polity. According to Chakrabarty, the Lockean notion of national brotherhood as a contractual relationship among autonomous, self-interested individuals does not extend to the idea of brotherhood advanced by the early Bengali nationalist intellectuals under British rule. He describes how Bengali understanding of political brotherhood is anchored in a traditional notion of patrilineage called *kula,* which situates a person's identity in a vertical line of male descent and under the unchallenged sanctity of patriarchal authority. The Lockean idea of the nation as a brotherhood of men assumes that the constitutive elements of this fraternity are freed from the paternal authority through their possession of private property: "Fraternity in the Lockean schema was predicated on the emergence of private property and the political death of parental/paternal authority" (Chakrabarty 2000, 217). By contrast, according to Chakrabary (2000, 217–218), "[Private property] was never stipulated as a requirement in Bengali nationalist thought that the political authority of the father be destroyed before the brothers' compact could come into being . . . Fraternity in Bengali nationalism was thought of as representing a natural rather than contractual solidarity of brotherhood. European bourgeois assumptions regarding autonomous personhood based on self-interest, contract, and private property were subordinated in Bengal to this idea of 'natural' brotherhood."

In this widely acclaimed, exciting project to pluralize modern history and related efforts to "provincialize" European experience and thought of political modernity, Chakrabarty also includes a discussion of religious symbols. He shows how the Bengali vision of the postcolonial nation-state was partly constituted by traditional cultural imaginaries about ancestors (and other important religious entities such the Hindu goddess Lakshmi). Presenting a pluralistic picture of political modernity, Chakrabarty simultaneously intends to free the diversity in the project of modernity from the historicist tendency to order the differences in social formation according to an evolutionary temporal scheme, in which the diversity is translated to the stages in the hierarchical ladder of historical progression, representing "Indians, Africans, and other 'rude' nations" as lacking the property of modernity and consigning them "to an imaginary waiting room of history" (Chakrabarty 2000, 8).

Chakrabarty considers Locke and Marx as two sublime intellectual examples of European historicism, and he introduces Heidegger as a counterexample in Western thought and a radical alternative to the paradigm of global historical time. Focusing sharply on the literature about the origins of modern nationalist ideology, Partha Chatterjee similarly confronts what he considers the tendency in existing theories of nationalism to understate the differences between nationalist imaginations in European history and the forms of anti-colonial nationalism in Asia and Africa (Chatterjee 1993). Challenging Benedict Anderson's classic work on the subject of "linguistic nationalism," which focuses on the role of printing technology and mass literacy in disseminating the political ideas of national liberation, he highlights the "spiritual" domains of nationalism rather than the "material" culture of nationalism such as the technology of printing (Anderson 1991 [1983]).

The above scholars confront the tortuous logic of decolonization: postcolonial modernity was envisioned in the colonies in terms of the political modernity learned from Europe; this makes resistance to colonial domination an act of emulating the dominator rather than an authentic creative act. They propose that the project to "provincialize" European heritage of political modernity is a necessary step for pluralizing modernity, which is in turn an indispensable step for the decolonization of the imagination. Making one's own political history distinct from the theoretical premise of historical development in European thought, in other words, is an act of obtaining freedom from colonialism in thought.

The idea of postcolonial experience suggested by the above scholars projects the historical epoch from the end of WWII to the present as an uninterrupted struggle to be free from the cultural and mental effects of colonialism, after these countries were freed from the formal institutional grid of colonial subjugation between the 1950s and the 1960s. This conceptual scheme does not allow room for consideration of the momentous shift in global power relations from colonial to bipolar in nature during the period, nor for the resultant complication in nation-building in the postcolonial world. The scheme is oblivious to the radical political bipolarization of postcolonial processes and treats the questions of right and left primarily in terms of an intellectual exercise, having no relevance to the structure of social life and the contours of collective identity.

In this presentation of the colonial history and postcolonial historical process, the idea of fraternity is presented either in the scheme of Western individualism or in that of indigenous collective kinship ideology. There are no traces of the human kinship and brotherhood that were brought to bear in fratricidal war during the global Cold War, nor stories of their contemporary struggle to move beyond the violent history of extreme right and left antithesis. The bifurcation of Lockean and Marxian historicisms is rendered as forces external to the unity and authenticity of indigenous lineage and fraternity, whereas it was in this domain of intimate relatedness, as mentioned earlier, that people experienced the clash between militant visions of right and left in forms of naked force of violence and systemic political coercion. The exclusion of Cold War history from postcolonial historical processes also involves the exclusion from analysis of the immense complications in the decolonization of Asian and African nations caused by the U.S. and Soviet interventions in the process, while the latter pursued respectively, in the words of Arne Westad, their ambitions for "the empire of liberty" or "the empire of justice" (Westad 2005, 8–72). Conceptualizing the Cold War merely in terms of external constraints against seemingly autonomous postcolonial struggles contradicts the fact that nationalist struggles in the postcolonial world were in fact constitutive of the development of the patterns of superpower competition. It is true that postcolonial developments (such as those in Vietnam) were entangled in the escalating polarization of global politics; yet, the Cold War as a global conflict developed in the way we understand now precisely because there were sustained, formidable challenges from the decolonizing nations, including the Vietnamese, to the imposed hegemonic designs of global modernity.

The externalization of bipolar history from colonial and postcolonial history not only distorts the theoretical contours of postcolonial criticism, it also results in a misrepresentation of the main object of the critique. In Chakrabarty's otherwise forceful rendering of European ideas of political modernity and their historical particularity, there are no traces of a modern Europe as we know it; that is, the Europe that, after experiencing a catastrophic war, was divided into mutually hostile forces in an undeclared ideological war. His depiction of Europe's political modernity focuses on its traditional, imperial past with no consideration of its recent history of political fragmentation and bifurcation. Europe in the second half of the twentieth century was not the same entity as the Europe we know from colonial history, and the transition from one to the other coincided with some of the most violent events experienced in Asia and Africa. Whereas decolonization and political bipolarization were concurrent processes in much of the non-Western world and the violent postcolonial struggles took place within the context of the Cold War, the scholarship of postcolonial criticism relegates the bipolar history to an analytical void. As a result, it fails to place in proper historical context both its critical aim of cultural decolonization and the main object of its cultural criticism—European political modernity.

Chakrabarty introduces "translation" as the principal element of postcolonial criticism. According to him, understanding Bengali history is not simply to stage it according to the developmental logic of European historicism. Rather, it requires attending to the indigenous logic and language of development, and, on this basis, engaging critically with the differences between this local language and the theoretical, universalizing language of European origin (Chakrabarty 2000, 17). Homi Bhabha also presents "translation" as a key word for the postcolonial intellectual project (Bhabha 1994, 172–173). Like Chakrabarty, Bhabha conceptualizes translation as a communicative process between local histories and the universality-claiming theoretical language from European modernity. Furthermore, Bhabha associates the practice of cultural translation with what he calls "the transnational dimension," by which he refers to the condition of "migration, diaspora, displacement, relocation," conceptualized in contrast to the "natural(ized), unifying discourse of 'nation', 'peoples', or authentic 'folk' tradition, those embedded myths of culture's particularity" (Bhabha 1994, 172). These transnational conditions and "translational" practices constitute "the location of culture" in the globalizing contemporaneous time, according to Bhabha, and, as such, they call for the relocation of the culture concept from a set of taken-for-granted values to the process of mixing different sets of normative values. A transnational social life, he concludes, is a translational cultural life.

Several observers have identified an overt textualism in the above-illustrated trend in postcolonial theory and an excessive reliance on the metaphor of translation (San Juan, Jr. 1998, 27–30, 265–267). For the purpose of our discussion, the problem with the theoretical posturing lies, rather than in relegating movements across bounded cultural entities to translations, in understanding these movements merely across the border that I called earlier the colonial color line, without taking into consideration the intertwining of this border with a new ideologically constituted frontier in the bipolarizing postcolonial history.

Christina Klein argues that the transnational migrations of the past century were intimately connected to the geopolitics of the Cold War, and she explores how their connectedness partly took the form of transcending racial and cultural differences through an invention of particular kinship practices (Klein 2005). Focusing on the policy documents and middlebrow mass-educational materials of the mid-twentieth-century United States, Klein traces in this light how the adoption of orphaned children from the troubled regions of Asia developed into a powerful geopolitical practice. Advancing the political objective to contain communism globally, she argues, U.S. policymakers were worried that America's leadership in this moral crusade lacked a positive substantive quality. Anticommunism was not an ideology with an authentic vision; liberal individualism or benevolent capitalism were hard to sell to the Asian populations who associated such ideologies with European colonialism. Against those Asians who were wary of Western imperialism and those Americans who were wary of expensive overseas commitment, a way had to be found to mobilize these unconnected groups of people to a common struggle against communism. One of the solutions was the idiom of kinship, according to Klein, which rendered the problem of America's political obligation to Asia as a problem of family (Klein 2005, 37). With this background, the prominent U.S. educational media began to disseminate the extension of kinship relations as a prime civic obligation of Americans in the global struggle against communism.

In the 1950s, American families were encouraged to adopt homeless children in Calcutta and Bombay, the abandoned "GI babies" in Japan, the refugees from communist East Germany, and war orphans in Korea. The media propagated the idea that these hungry children of the world were more dangerous to the United States than the atom bomb; that, unless they were brought into the paternal care of the benign American power, they would become "the most powerful weapon in the hands of the communists" (Klein 2005, 47–48). Klein's careful analysis of this post-WWII baby-boom era presents the practice of adoptive kinship as a two-way process of learning: the American "parents" learned about the misery and inhumanity caused by communism in the wide world, and the adopted Asian "children" learned about "the material abundance and personal generosity that the free world offered" (Klein 2005, 50). The political ethos of paternal love, according to Klein, was meant to distinguish America's Cold War civilizing mission from the imperial practice of European nations, as well as to mobilize the American public toward the aggressive battle against communism by letting them participate in this geopolitical activity in their familiar, intimate domains of family norms and religious charity. Through this development of Cold War kinship, Klein (2005, 37) concludes that the horizon of transnational ties and mass immigration began to change dramatically in American society, which had restricted immigration from Asia on racial grounds since 1875.

If Chakrabarty is oblivious to the fragmented, broken mid-twentieth-century Europe in his depiction of European political modernity, Bhabha's understanding of human diaspora and cultural dislocation is equally oblivious to the aforementioned history of mass human displacement during the construction of the bipolar world. Large-scale human displacement was common in the mid-twentieth century, and it took place not only in Asia, but also in large parts of Europe under the circumstances, which, although they all vary locally, are broadly related to the onslaught of the Cold War conflict. In the Soviet Union, entire populations of several ethnic groups were forcibly relocated from one end to the other of the Eurasian continent. A large population of East and Central Europe moved to the West, and some of these immigrant communities have exercised considerable influence, after the fall of the Berlin Wall, on political developments in their native countries. In the decolonizing world, the anachronistic attempts of some Western European nations to reclaim their colonial territories under the pretext of fighting communism generated a whirlwind of social crisis, in which displacement became a generalized experience of the population. The dislocation of human lives was exacerbated in the ensuing era when nationalist struggles evolved to full-scale civil wars with prolific international intervention.

The transnational migrants of the past century often brought troubling questions of political identity from one home to another rather than bringing themselves out of the enclosed boundary of the political community to a translational cultural space. Gisèle Bousquet describes how the Parisian Vietnamese community in the 1980s was divided between the pro-Hanoi and anticommunist factions (Bousquet 1991). Rooted in the history of political and military conflicts in their homeland, these factional divisions were constitutive of the identity of the overseas Vietnamese, cross-cutting their awareness of being an ethnic minority in France. The generation of immigrants who arrived in France before 1975 tended to be sympathetic to the unified Vietnam and defined themselves as "liberals," whereas these people appeared as "communists" to some of the new immigrants who arrived in France after 1975 as war refugees (Bousquet 1991, 6). Political division affected family relations and kin networks among the Parisian Vietnamese. It was not uncommon for the members of a family to support different factions, and kinsmen who had contrary political views avoided one another (Bousquet 1991, 104–105). Bousquet goes on to describe how bipolar politics within the Parisian Vietnamese community affected the community's ethnic identity in relation to wider French society.

Sonia Ryang's study of Koreans in Japan demonstrates similar predicaments of a minority community seized both by racial discrimination and political polarization (Ryang 1997). The Korean community in Japan is divided into the pro-North Korea group and the anti-North Korea group, which maintains close ties with South Korea. This dichotomous loyalty is strong with the older generation, whereas their children, particularly those from the pro-North Korea group, are torn between familial obligation to share their parents' loyalty and their individual needs to integrate into Japanese society, which is generally hostile to North Korea. Ryang is at pains to draw an optimistic picture for these children, beyond the double grid of the racial inequality of colonial origin and the political bifurcation of the postcolonial era.

Postcolonial history and bipolar history can cross-cut a traditional village as well a migrant community. I began reading about Cold War history when, while trying to write about a village in central Vietnam, I realized that I could not write the village history without contextualizing it in global history. My historical research led me to learn about North Africa as well as the history of French colonialism in Indochina, after I learned from the villagers about their wartime experience and memory of colonial conscripts from Algeria and Morocco. It came to involve a political history of South Korea as well as the foreign politics of the United States, as I learned that the village had lost many lives to the pacification activity during the Vietnam War undertaken by America's close East Asian ally in the transnational struggle against communism. The village history project also led me to learn about WWII in Europe, when some elderly villagers told me about their experience there. These villagers were among the thousands of Vietnamese conscripted by the French colonial authority in the 1930s to work in a munitions factory in Marseille, and some of them later fought against the Germans as part of the French Resistance. Having contributed to France's economy and having shared in its humiliation of foreign occupation, these laborer-soldiers were shipped back to Vietnam soon after WWII was over. Most of the returnees perished in the ensuing chaos of war between the French and the Vietnamese resistance forces, and the survivors later had problems with the Vietnamese revolutionary authority because of their past "collaboration" with imperial France. Many of their children later joined the revolutionary forces when the conflict escalated and took the form of a war against America. Meanwhile, some of the few laborer-soldiers who managed to stay in France after WWII turned into what Bousquet might call "pro-Hanoi" activists and, alongside French activists, campaigned against the Vietnam War.

The village's modern history implicated a world history, and the transition from the colonial to the bipolar order was central to the village's global historical experience. Other examples introduced above show the complicated intertwining of colonial and bipolar history in the postcolonial experience of dislocation and transmigration. Why, then, is bipolar history excluded from postcolonial historical criticism? How should we make sense of the removal of this history in the contemporary critique of imperial culture, the state, nationalism, and political modernity, all of which are unthinkable, from the perspective of the present, without considering the dislocation of global power from Europe after WWII? What is this thing called the postcolonial process, if it is not anchored in the transformation of the global order from an imperial to a bipolar form, through which we have come to inhabit the so-called globalizing world?

In a recent collective essay, Bhabha, Chakrabarty, and others raise this question: "The twilight of Transition, rather than the dawn of millennial transformation, marks the questions of our times: Do we live in a post-Cold War world *tout court,* or in the long shadow of that disastrous postwar experience of superpower collusion and competition that deformed the development of the rest of the world?" (Pollock et al. 2000, 580). In order to explore this important question, one can no longer keep bipolar history as a voiceless subaltern under the preeminence of postcolonial discourses. There is another more fundamental issue at stake in the disengagement of postcolonial theory with bipolar history. As stated in the above quotation, postcolonial theorists tend to view the Cold War merely as the affairs of the balance of power; that is, according to the paradigm of the imaginary war. This view is problematic in at least two ways. First, it excludes the dynamics of decolonization from the constitution and development of the bipolar global order. Second, the paradigm of the imaginary war marginalizes the experience of the bipolar conflict in large parts of the decolonizing world as a civil war or other forms of organized violence. The uncritical acceptance of this paradigm constitutes a most critical problem in contemporary postcolonial discourse.

Conclusion

Why is the reality of bipolar history excluded from the project of postcolonial historical criticism? The answer is because this project, while aiming to free historical thought on political modernity from the grip of European political thought, approaches Cold War modernity, the flip side of postcolonial modernity, from a predominantly Eurocentric perspective of this historical process. The above discussion raised one key issue in understanding Cold War history in comparative terms: the cross-cutting dimensions of colonial history and bipolar history that I expressed as two color lines. The twentieth century's two intermingled color lines are problems for all sides of the color divides, and I believe that any vision of an alternative future where human beings and societies are not color-bound has to deal with both forms of ideological polarity.

For the purpose of clarifying the research arenas and conceptual parameters of transpacific studies, therefore, I believe that close attention to the fusion and fission of these two color lines is necessary. It is through such attention that transpacific studies will be able to engage critically with the existing historical scholarship and literary tradition centered on the transatlantic horizon, as well as with the limitations in the critical postcolonial historical and literary scholarship that intend to challenge the transatlantic centeredness. If postcolonial studies and Cold War studies are thematically interrelated in the Asia-Pacific, it is necessary to think of a way to bring these two fields of inquiry into a more intimate, constructive dialogue. It is also necessary to question why the existing Cold War studies and the existing postcolonial studies have ignored each other and how they have managed to do so by ignoring the historical terrain in which questions of postcolonial social development and issues of global political bipolarization are inseparably fused together. If the rise of the transpacific perspective is a product of the turbulent modern history that communities in the Asia-Pacific region underwent during and after WWII, as Cumings argues, it is evident that the research arena of transpacific studies is grounded in the history of the postcolonial Cold War. The distinctive merit of this research genre, therefore, should partly lay in its capacity to consider the postcolonial history and the political process of the Cold War as mutually constitutive historical processes.

Notes to Chapter 2: The Transpacific Cold War

The ethnographic research for this chapter was supported by the British Academy and the Academy of Korean Studies (AKS-2010-DZZ-3104). I thank these institutions for their generous support and Janet Hoskins and Viet Nguyen for their insightful comments.

1. The villagers did reach an agreement after considerable controversy and successfully refurbished the ancestor's grave in April 2008.

2. Tony Judt writes with reference to John Lewis Gaddis's depiction of Cold War history: "[This] way of narrating cold war history reflects the same provincialism. John Lewis Gaddis has written a history of America's cold war: as seen from America, as experienced in America, and told in a way most agreeable to many American readers. As a result, this is a book whose silences are especially suggestive. The 'third world' in particular comes up short" (Judt 2008, 371).

References

Anderson, Benedict. 1991 [1983]. *Imagined Communities: Reflections on the Origin and Spread of Nationalism*. London: Verso.

Bhabha, Homi. 1994. *The Location of Culture*. New York: Routledge.

Borstelmann, Thomas. 2001. *The Cold War and the Color Line: American Race Relations in the Global Arena*. Cambridge, MA: Harvard University Press.

Bousquet, Gisèle. 1991. *Behind the Bamboo Hedge: The Impact of Homeland Politics in the Parisian Vietnamese Community*. Ann Arbor: University of Michigan Press.

Chakrabarty, Dipesh. 2000. *Provincializing Europe: Post-Colonial Thought and Historical Difference*. Princeton, NJ: Princeton University Press.

Chatterjee, Partha. 1993. *The Nation and Its Fragments: Colonial and Post-Colonial Histories*. Princeton, NJ: Princeton University Press.

Cumings, Bruce. 1999. *Parallax Visions: Making Sense of American–East Asian Relations at the End of the Century*. Durham, NC: Duke University Press.

———. 2009. *Dominion from Sea to Sea: Pacific Ascendancy and American Power*. New Haven, CT: Yale University Press.

Derrida, Jacques. 2001. *On Cosmopolitanism and Forgiveness*. New York: Routledge.

Dudziak, Mary L. 2000. *Cold War Civil Rights: Race and the Image of American Democracy*. Princeton, NJ: Princeton University Press.

Duggan, Christopher. 1995. "Italy in the Cold War Years and the Legacy of Fascism." In *Italy in the Cold War: Politics, Culture, and Society, 1948–58*, ed. Christopher Duggan and Christopher Wagstaff, 1–24. Oxford: Berg.

Dwyer, Leslie, and Degung Santikarma. 2003. "When the World Turned to Chaos: 1965 and Its Aftermath in Bali, Indonesia." In *The Specter of Genocide: Mass Murder in Historical Perspective*, ed. Robert Gellately and Ben Kiernan, 289–306. Cambridge, UK: Cambridge University Press.

Field, Douglas. 2005. "Passing as a Cold War Novel: Anxiety and Assimilation in James Baldwin's *Giovanni's Room*." In *American Cold War Culture*, ed. Douglas Field, 88–105. Edinburgh: Edinburgh University Press.

Gaddis, John L. 1987. *The Long Peace: Inquiries into the History of the Cold War*. New York: Oxford University Press.

Hixson, Walter L. 1997. *Parting the Curtain: Propaganda, Culture, and the Cold War, 1945–1961*. New York: St. Martin's.

Judt, Tony. 2008. *Reappraisals: Reflections on the Forgotten Twentieth Century*. New York: Penguin.

Kaldor, Mary. 1990. *The Imaginary War: Interpretation of the East–West Conflict.* Oxford: Blackwell.

Klein, Christina. 2003. *Cold War Orientalism: Asia in the Middlebrow Imagination, 1945–1961.* Berkeley: University of California Press.

Kwon, Heonik. 2006. *After the Massacre: Commemoration and Consolation in Ha My and My Lai.* Berkeley: University of California Press.

LaFeber, Walter. 1992. "An End to Which Cold War?" In *The End of the Cold War: Its Meaning and Implications,* ed. Michael J. Hogan, 13–20. New York: Cambridge University Press.

Lee, Steven H. 1995. *Outposts of Empire: Korea, Vietnam, and the Origins of the Cold War in Asia, 1949–1954.* Liverpool, UK: Liverpool University Press.

Leffler, Melvyn P. 1994. *The Specter of Communism: The United States and the Origins of the Cold War, 1917–1953.* New York: Hill and Wang.

Malarney, Shaun K. 2003. "Return to the Past? The Dynamics of Contemporary and Ritual Transformation." In *Postwar Vietnam: Dynamics of a Transforming Society,* ed. Hy V. Luong, 225–256. New York: Rowman and Littlefield.

Mazower, Mark. 2000. "Three Forms of Political Justice: Greece, 1944–1945." In *After the War Was Over: Reconstructing the Family, Nation, and State in Greece, 1943–1960,* 24–41. Princeton, NJ: Princeton University Press.

Olson, James S., and Randy Roberts. 1998. *My Lai: A Brief History with Documents.* Boston: Bedford Books.

Osgood, Robert E. 1970. *America and the World: From the Truman Doctrine to Vietnam.* Baltimore, MD: Johns Hopkins University Press.

Pelley, Patricia. 2002. *Post-Colonial Vietnam: New Histories of the National Past.* Durham, NC: Duke University Press.

Pollock, Sheldon, Homi Bhabha, Carol Breckenridge, and Dipesh Chakrabarty. 2000. "Cosmopolitanisms." *Public Culture* 12 (3): 577–589.

Robinson, Geoffrey. 1995. *The Dark Side of Paradise: Political Violence in Bali.* Ithaca, NY: Cornell University Press.

Ryan, David. 2005. "Mapping Containment: The Cultural Construction of the Cold War." In *American Cold War Culture,* ed. Douglas Field, 50–68. Edinburgh: Edinburgh University Press.

Ryang, Sonia. 1997. *North Koreans in Japan: Language, Ideology and Identity.* Boulder, CO: Westview.

San Juan, E., Jr. 1998. *Beyond Postcolonial Theory.* New York: St. Martin's Press.

Stoler, Ann Laura. 1995. "Mixed-Bloods and the Cultural Politics of European Identity in Colonial Southeast Asia." In *The Decolonization of Imagination: Culture, Knowledge and Power,* ed. Jan Nederveen Pieterse and Bhikhu Parekh, 128–148. London: Zed Books.

———. 1997. "Sexual Affronts and Racial Frontiers: European Identities and the Cultural Politics of Exclusion in Colonial Southeast Asia." In *Tensions of Empire: Colonial Cultures in a Bourgeois World,* ed. Frederick Cooper and Ann Laura Stoler, 198–237. Berkeley: University of California Press.

Tai, Hue-Tam Ho. 1992. *Radicalism and the Origins of Vietnamese Revolution.* Cambridge, MA: Harvard University Press.

Wade, Peter. 2002. *Race, Nature, and Culture.* London: Pluto Press.

Wagnleitner, Reinhold. 1989. "The Irony of American Culture Abroad: Austria and the Cold War." In *Recasting America: Culture and Politics in the Age of Cold War,* ed. L. May, 285–302. Chicago: University of Chicago Press.

Westad, Odd Arne. 2005. *The Global Cold War.* Cambridge, UK: Cambridge University Press.

Woods, Jeff. 2004. *Black Struggle, Red Scare: Segregation and Anti-Communism in the South, 1948–1968.* Baton Rouge: Louisiana State University Press.

Yun, Taik-Lim. 2003. *Red Village: A History* [in Korean]. Seoul: Historical Criticism Press.

3

The Pacific Paradox
The Chinese State in Transpacific Interactions

BIAO XIANG

The vast western Pacific has in recent centuries constantly brought shame and suffering to our continent, but today, on the treacherous ocean, enormous wealth seems surging with an irresistible appeal . . . The western Pacific is becoming the new stage of the world economy. Fate is presenting us with yet another golden opportunity. After centuries' silence, with a long pent-up hunger and thirst, the coastal region, the Chinese Gold Coast, is the first to hurl itself into the Pacific (Su and Wang 1988).[1]

This was how the television documentary series *River Elegy* (*He Shang*), aired in China in 1988 as a climax of the "cultural fever" of the 1980s, portrayed the Pacific. Critical scholars on the other side of the Pacific may see this narrative as part of the dominant American perception about the Pacific. Arif Dirlik and Rob Wilson, for example, have made the powerful case that the discourses of the "Pacific Rim" and the "Asia-Pacific community" represent a triumph of capitalist teleology and the neoliberal hegemony (Dirlik 1998; Wilson and Dirlik 1996; Wilson 2002). Under such discourses the historical, social and cultural specificities across the Pacific Ocean, from Qingdao to Fukuoka to Fiji to San Francisco, were erased to make a homogenous and empty space of capitalist economic development. But for the audience of millions who were watching the six-part documentary in China, such a narrative of the Pacific was liberating, progressive, and conveyed hope and courage for change. It might have represented a false consciousness, but a very empowering consciousness nevertheless. Such an imagination about the Pacific was a locally situated critique of the conditions in China of that time, and not a replica of the dominant global discourse.

At the same time as *River Elegy* set off an intellectual fanfare across China, some scholars and policy makers started questioning the celebratory Pacific discourse. He Xin, one of the most controversial intellectuals closely related to some factions in the central leadership in China, urged the Chinese government to move attention away from the Pacific Ocean. He stressed that this ocean was "an American lake," and a Pacific-oriented China would be too vulnerable to American domination. China should instead ally with Russia and central Asia to consolidate the hinterland and develop the land-based counter-Pacific space.[2] His call was never fully accepted; on the contrary, China's economic integration and social connections across the Pacific became ever intensified, as evidenced by the neologisms of "G2" and "Chimerica."[3] But He Xin's suspicion about the Pacific nevertheless became widely shared in the 1990s. An article in the Chinese version of the *Financial Times* describes China's Pacific concern in this way: "As China's economic gravity lies in the southeast coast, and Taiwan looms large in Beijing's mind, the widely open door in the Southeast [to the Pacific] is a concern for Beijing, and it is also the priority for China's military exercises . . . China-U.S. competition over the Pacific is inevitable" (Wang Yaping 2009).

A comparison between a number of dramatic events that took place in the early 1990s and in the 2000s casts in sharp relief the shift in China's perception of the Pacific. The world should remember well how Chinese students enthusiastically welcomed Western media, especially CNN and other U.S.-based agencies, to report the 1989 student movement. "Take [videos]! Take [videos]! Let the world know!" we heard students urging foreign journalists. Western media was a trustworthy voice for justice. Exactly ten years later, a new batch of students went to the street again, this time to protest the North Atlantic Treaty Organization (NATO) bombing of the Chinese embassy in Belgrade. The same Western media, especially American media, had now become a subject of suspicion, criticism, and even hatred. Western media would never understand how the Chinese felt, the students believed, and even worse, they may deliberately distort facts. Take another example. China applied to host the 2000 Olympics in 1993 with the slogan "The world gives China a chance and China will give the world a surprise." The desire to embrace the world and to be recognized by the powerful was obvious. But that desire was not materialized. By 2008 when China finally hosted the Olympics, China indeed impressed the world, but with a rather different message. The tensions surrounding the Olympic torch relay were as important as the largely harmonious games itself. Nyiri, Zhang and Varrall (2010) documented how Chinese students in Australia were genuinely outraged by the demonstrations in various major cities in the West aimed at disrupting the torch relay, which the students saw as Western humiliation of China before the Olympics. The bestseller *Unhappy China* (Song et al. 2009) concluded that the students protest worldwide marked a new, much more confrontational, relationship between Chinese youth and the West, and especially the United States.

The suspicion about the Pacific among the Chinese urban public and policy makers was deepened at precisely the same time as transpacific connections became closer. Zhao Suisheng (1997, 730) suggested that the increasing familiarity with the West, and subsequent "de-romanticization" in the 1990s was crucial in the development of the new nationalistic sentiment. Chinese youth become more, rather than less, assertive when they gain wider exposure to the West. All the authors of *China Can Say No* (Song et al. 1996), which is widely regarded as the first major nonofficial "anti-West" manifesto in China's postreform era, emphasized how they had been deeply influenced by the United States, only to have become disillusioned in the 1990s (see also Fewsmith 2008, 160). The book was appealing precisely because it provides personal accounts of how the authors woke up from their earlier faith in "total Westernization" as China's future.

This chapter wishes to demonstrate that the socioeconomic integration across the Pacific on one hand, and the political, ideational, and military tensions on the other, are not contradictory. They are deeply intertwined and mutually enhancing. The Pacific is at once structurally integrated and fundamentally divided. I call this the "Pacific paradox." A well-known saying among the Chinese diplomats goes: "The China-U.S. relation can't be much better, can't be much worse." The Pacific paradox generates perpetual tensions as well as provides structural stability.

Where does this "Pacific paradox" come from? Instead of focusing on trade and geopolitics as most existing literature does, this chapter addresses the question by delving into the domain of perception and imagination on the China side. I ask: Why do the Chinese public see societal exchange across the Pacific desirable and at the same time state-centric tension inevitable? And why does the public not believe the former will override the latter, or the latter curtail the former?

The resurgence of Chinese nationalism looks like an obvious answer. Academic literature and public commentary have commonly argued that the Chinese party-state encourages nationalism as a basis for its political legitimacy at a time when communist doctrine is fading away. The construction of "new anti-American icons or nationalist hatred" is often seen as "a convenient practice used by the party-state for diverting nationalist attention away from targeting the regime" (Shen 2007, 249). The communist regime waves the "nationalist flag" when its "red flag" is no longer red (Shen 2007). Although nationalism certainly plays a role in the emergence of the Pacific paradox, it still begs the question of what makes the current nationalistic sentiment in China hold deep political suspicion about the West and a strong faith in economic integration? I contend that nationalism as conventionally understood—a sentimental attachment and ideological commitment to one's nation as defined by common race, history, territory, and culture—provides at best a partial explanation. Pride in the Chinese historical heritage, emphasis on essential Chineseness, and the belief in intrinsic differences between the Chinese and Americans, which is fundamental to conventional nationalism, do not figure prominently in the current popular imagination of transpacific relations. Rather, the public view holds that China *has to* compete with the United States in order to survive, and in order to do that, China *has to* become like the United States, for instance by developing capitalism and building up military might. The Pacific in which we live thus looks very different from the one portrayed by Marshall Sahlins (1994), where incommensurable "cosmologies of capitalism" coexisted and collided. Hawai'i is now part of the United States. China consciously and actively participates in the game of capitalist geopolitics. This is the only game left. It is believed that global capitalism is such that China's economic and social life must be integrated into the world in order to survive and prosper, but at the same time, real geopolitics is such that the United States is inevitably hostile to China regardless of what China does. Cross-Pacific tensions do not stem from the fact that China and America are too different, but from the fact that they are too similar; not because the two are too far apart, but because they are tightly connected.

The *River Elegy* is highly significant because it indicates the climactic end of a culturalism that had dominated the Chinese public intellectual thinking from the May Fourth Movement in 1919. The May Fourth Movement was regarded as such an epochal event because it marked the beginning of the abandonment of earlier efforts to rebuild the Chinese civilization by adopting Western technologies and then modern institutions ("Chinese as base, Western as tool") and instead advocated that China had no choice but to fundamentally rework its core value systems. The May Fourth Movement was referred to as the "New Culture Movement" because it was fundamentally a cultural, ideological, and spiritual revolution. As a continuation of the May Fourth Movement spirit, *River Elegy* urged China to rid itself of the thousand-year-old "Yellow" civilization (represented by the Yellow River) and to plunge into the "Blue" civilization (the Pacific Ocean). The conservative counternarrative in the 1990s was equally culturalistic. The sometimes self-orientalizing neo-Confucianism, for instance, attributed the success of East Asian capitalism to cultural ethos, and therefore presented traditional Chinese culture as a basis instead of an obstacle of modernity. These culturalistic interpretations had lost public appeal in China by the 1990s. Samuel Huntington's theory of a clash of civilizations (1993), which could have been hugely popular earlier, was seen as a mask for a so-called clash of realpolitik (see Wang Hui and Zhang Tianwei 1994). One of the first important articles on soft power in China, authored by Wang Huning, who was then a professor in political science at Fudan University and is now a top party ideologist, argued that soft power was nothing but a reflection of hard, crude power (Wang Huning 1994). The recent revival of popular Confucianism should not be seen as a continuation of the 1980 neo-Confucianism because, while neo-Confucianism aimed to formulate a grand historical narrative alternative to the usual Western version, popular Confucianism teaches individuals to lead a meaningful and ethical private life when liberal capitalism is the only way of existence. If neo-Confucianism imagined globalization as a film festival where every society is encouraged to claim its unique value based on its own culture and tradition, the popular imagination in the 2000s in China sees the world as the Olympic games where one can participate only by following the rules, and can win only by being recognized by the common standards.

Thus, culture and civilization are marginalized, and interstate competition dominates the public imagination. If we call this nationalism, it is a nationalism based on blunt geopolitical calculations instead of cultural heritage or historical mythology. It is defined by (potentially confrontational) relations with others instead of articulation about the self, which stress the importance of the state on the top instead of shared solidarity from below. For the lack of a better term, I tentatively call such a sentiment "neostatism." Neostatism sees the state as the primary and unquestionable *frame* within which society should be organized, and as such the state serves as the central referent in making sense of the world. Neostatism is manifested as a *perspective* instead a substantive ideology. Unlike popular nationalism, neostatism hardly evokes the desire to die for one's nation, the archetypical nationalist sentiment (see Anderson 1991; Kellas 1991), nor does it intrinsically imply anti-Americanism (cf. Fewsmith 2008, 140–162).[4] Neostatism also differs from more "substantive" statism. For statism, "sovereignty is vested not in the people but in the national state, and that all individuals and associations exist only to enhance the power, the prestige, and the well-being of the state. The concept of statism . . . repudiates individualism and exalts the nation as an organic body headed by the Supreme Leader and nurtured by unity, force, and discipline" (Plano 1973). In contrast, neostatism in China emerges alongside decollectivization, privatization, and the triumph of individualism. The Singaporean diplomat and influential commentator Kishore Mahbubani (2003 [1998]) noted the cultural comfort between China and the United States due to their common flexibility, pragmatism, and individualism, which is much greater than that between Japan and the United States, as one of major paradoxes in Asia-Pacific security (172). Furthermore, neostatism does not believe in supreme leaders, nor does it advocate state's disciplining of its population. It instead emphasizes a state's capacity to deal with international uncertainties. Neostatism is not directly related to the billiard ball model in realist international relations thinking that regards the state as the given and privileged unit of analysis. For neostatism, the state is not only a rational actor but also a source of meaning, honor, and dignity. The state is not a pre-given, but should be constructed. As a public perception instead of a scholarly analytical approach, neostatism is a sentiment resulting from complex historical experiences.

This chapter does not suggest that Chinese neostatism causes the Pacific paradox. Firstly, the Pacific paradox is fundamentally interactive. What the U.S. government does and what the U.S. public thinks are more consequential than their Chinese counterparts simply because of the economic and military might of the United States. Secondly, the Pacific paradox as a structural condition is by definition multifaceted, and public perception is only a small part of it. Finally and most importantly, neostatism emerged as part of, instead of prior to, the Pacific paradox. As I demonstrate below, neostatism is itself a result of the intensification of transpacific exchanges. As such, neostatism is important to our understanding of the Pacific paradox not as its cause but as a lens that reveals the cultural logic that underpins the paradox. In her piercing analyses, Aihwa Ong (1999) discerned two seemingly contradictory cultural logics in the transpacific mobility and capitalism. Ong suggests, on a macro level, overseas Chinese operate as an intermediary "contrast category" of Chinese modernity in a structural position between the mainland Chinese and the non-Chinese foreigners who embody Western modernity (Ong 1999, 43). In this sense overseas Chinese, especially the transpacific subjects, help China seek its own development without being subjugated to the West. On a micro—the individual and household—level, economic calculations supersede national allegiance. For instance, passports for transpacific migrants have become "less and less attestations of citizenship, let alone of loyalty to a protective nation-state, than of claims to participate in labor markets. The truth claims of the state that are enshrined in the passport are gradually being replaced by its counterfeit use in response to the claims of global capitalism" (Ong 1999, 2). Such an odd entanglement between essentialist culturalism and relentless instrumentalism, as depicted by Ong, is certainly an important thrust along which transpacific interactions unfold. But this chapter wishes to stress that transpacific subjects, and the Chinese public in general, are not merely examples of benefit-maximizing *homo economicus* or essentialist believers in "culture." Real geopolitics looms large in the public transpacific imagination, just as it does for scholarly analysis on transpacific relations. Neostatism helps us understand how the "state" plays a central role in the meaning making process. While the rules of games are supposed to be universal, the meanings of the games diverge widely across the Pacific.

Neostatism as a perspective of public imagination is by definition an elusive subject, what Jean and John Comaroff call "an awkward scale." Such a subject—simultaneously subjective and objective, macro and micro, constituted and constitutive—resists simple identification of its location, contour, causes and effects. They thus call for "a radical expansion of the horizons of ethnographic methodology, for a method simultaneously inductive and deductive, empirical and imaginative" (Comaroff and Comaroff 2003, 147). This is the analytical strategy of this chapter as well. Yet it is important to recognize that neostatism is not a rootless, shapeless, and floating sentiment. It is historically conditioned and socially constructed. In what follows I first examine how the state becomes a primary "frame" in the public imagination of the world order. The Chinese state's framing effects partly resulted from the historical development of modern China, and are also shaped by interactions with the United States in the 1990s. I then provide an ethnographic account of how the Chinese state positions itself as a "stage" when interacting with international, especially transpacific, flows and connections. It is through such concrete "staging" strategies that the state's framing effects are enacted and reinforced. My treatment of the framing effects is largely historical and macro, based on documentary studies and my first-hand observations as a student at Peking University from 1990 to 1998. My discussion of the staging strategy draws on my field research on the Chinese state's engagement with overseas Chinese professionals (2004–2007). Collectively the chapter constitutes a historical sociological analysis of a particular way of imagining the global order that emerges from transpacific interactions.

The State as a Frame

In order to constantly frame the public perceptions, the state should have at least two properties in its people's imagination. Firstly, the state should be taken as a total and all-encompassing entity, and secondly the state should be seen as neutral; that is, not explicitly representing a particular ideology. The two properties are interrelated. When the state is imagined as all-encompassing and all-accommodating, it becomes an organizing frame instead of an embodiment of particular ideologies; conversely, only when the state is seen as "empty" of ideological stance can it serve as an effective frame. The first of the two properties, namely a totalizing sovereignty, has been widely documented as part of traditional Chinese political perception. In official as well as vernacular Chinese expressions, the concept of *guojia* simultaneously means state, nation, country, government, and even the Communist Party (Xiang 2010). Chinese nationalism has long been characterized by its "strong state complex" (Zheng 1999; Zhao 1996). I would like to stress that the totalizing perception should not be seen as a static cultural heritage, rather it is formed through specific historical experiences and should be considered in relation to the second property, namely the imagined state capacity of distancing itself from an explicit ideological stance. In thinking through the historical specificities of the Chinese public imaginations about the state, I find Li Zehou's (1986) framework revealing. Li argued that modern Chinese politics and ideologies were dominated by tensions between the themes of enlightenment and of salvation. Enlightenment means cultural awakening, self reformation, and pursuits of grand ethical ends such as liberty, equality, and justice. The theme of salvation concerns the survival of China as an entity in face of internal fragmentation and external threats. The theme of enlightenment regards the state as a tool for realizing larger ideals, while the focus on salvation sees a strong and unified state itself as the end. Li argues that Chinese intellectuals have oscillated between the two extremes throughout the modern era. One of the earliest manifestations of statism, the Young China Association and the school of "Warring State Strategies" (*zhanguoce pai*), emerged after the 1911 Revolution because of the disillusion about revolutionary ideals and newly felt urgency about the integrity of China. The resistance against Japanese invasion in the 1930s was another moment when the concern of salvation overrode that of enlightenment. The establishment of the communist China and especially the Cultural Revolution can be interpreted as a return to the theme of enlightenment. The state was seen as a means of universal socialist revolution. The China–U.S. relation was construed as clear-cut ideological confrontation between two historical forces instead of interstate relations.

The state became "frame-like" again after the Cultural Revolution, and especially after 1989. This was firstly because the Chinese state adopted an apparently apolitical, pragmatic developmental strategy. As epitomized by Deng Xiaoping's famous "white cat, black cat" theory, narrowly defined economic development have become the top priority, and major reforms of the political system and ideological debates are steadfastly avoided. It is hoped that social conflicts can be resolved through economic growth and through nonpolitical, technical procedures. With regard to political slogans, the "four cardinal principles" that set black and white distinctions between rights and wrongs, have been replaced by "scientific development" and "harmonious society," which contain no substantive and specific judgment. The dissociation of the state from ideology was dramatically demonstrated by He Xin's declaration in 2009 that China was at a critical threshold: "We either rely on statism that upholds the supremacy of safeguarding the interests of the Chinese nation to unify national consciousness or we will eventually fall into the vicious cycle of national turmoil and fragmentation in the ambiguity and debates of political ideologies!" (He 2009). In a time in which Marxism has lost ground as a popular ideology, socialism has failed to fulfill its promises, and liberal capitalism has caused considerable human costs and anxieties, the only faith left seems to be the faith in the state as an abstract frame that can hold China together.

A less dramatic, but far more influential, thought that contributed to neo-statism is the thesis on state capacity. Introduced in *China's State Capacity Report* by Wang Shaoguang and Hu Angang in 1991 (formally published in China in 1993), "state capacity" soon became a keyword among Chinese intellectuals and policy makers. The thesis made a strong case that state performance in promoting economic development and delivering social welfare is not necessarily related to the nature of the regime. A democratic state without strong capacity can be as problematic as an authoritarian regime. The emphasis on technical and institutional capacity instead of political and ideological concerns fits the mainstream post-1989 thinking well, which does not tolerate any political debate and which has seen intellectuals become disillusioned with grand ideological discussions. Furthermore, the fact that Wang Shaoguang and Hu Angang (1993 [1991]) developed the argument in the United States, and first publicized the idea at a workshop in Princeton University, attracted even more attention in China to the argument. The voices from across the Pacific lent additional authority to the argument not so much because the Chinese public believe that ideas from the other side of the Pacific are always wiser, but because Chinese intellectuals after 1989 were eager to gain more nuanced understandings about the West. The Tiananmen Square tragedy in China and the depression in post-Soviet Russia made it clear that an overnight transformation into liberal democracy was not as feasible or desirable as previously wished. The simple dichotomy of liberalism versus authoritarianism could no longer address the more complex questions of the time. The thesis of state capacity was originally concerned with internal problems, especially regarding the fiscal income, but after 1997 Asian financial crisis the concept was widely used in discussing the state's capability in dealing with the global economy and, by extension, China's position in the world (see Wang Hui 2008, 137). The Communist Party repeatedly cited the financial crisis to highlight the leadership's sophistication in navigating through highly complex global financial turmoil, and to remind the public that a strong state is absolutely indispensable for China to survive global capitalism.

The shift of focus in the public perception of the state from internal affairs to external relations, and from an ideological stance to practical capacity, is nicely captured by a popular saying. Playing with Mao's famous statement that "Only socialism can save China" (Mao 1957), it goes:

Only capitalism can save China in 1899 [referring to experiments with capitalist reforms in the late Qing]

Only socialism can save China in 1949 [referring to the establishment of the People's Republic of China]

Only China can save socialism in 1989 [referring to the fall of the Berlin Wall and subsequent collapse of the Soviet Union, which left China as the only major socialist power in the world. This line was an official expression of the party-state at that time.]

Only China can save capitalism in 2009 [referring to the global financial crisis that started in 2008]

It is meant to be a humorous exaggeration that only China can save global capitalism. But the point is also serious: the Chinese state's capacity in mobilizing and coordinating financial and other resources in the world's most populous and fastest-growing economy has made China indispensable for stabilizing the world economy. It took merely six weeks for the Chinese government to put in place its ambitious stimulus package to fight the crisis. In addition, the Central Committee of the Communist Party issued an internal document to all local governments and banks in November 2008 urging the whole nation to spend more. As a result, bank lending increased by 15 percent in 2009 as compared to 2008. Note that it was the party, instead of the central government, that issued the order. This is firstly because banks are supposedly autonomous institutions and local governments are also supposed to be responsible for their budgets, and thus interference from the central government would be inappropriate. Communications between party organs are in theory not governmental interference. But more importantly, "suggestions" from the Central Committee carry much more weight than governmental circulars. The Chinese public hardly see it as ironic that the Communist Party of China worked hard to save American capitalism. Communism and capitalism are no longer relevant; at stake are the interests of China as organized and represented by the state. The party's action would not only protect China's economic interest, but also used the crisis as an opportunity to enhance the Chinese state's position in the world economy.

The state became frame-like also in the process whereby China deepens its interactions with the West, especially the United States. In this process neo-statism directly intertwines with the Pacific paradox. The Chinese public, especially the younger population, were largely pro-America up to the 1990s.

The world awareness of the Chinese public in fact became narrower and more U.S.-centric with the end the Cold War. Less attention was given to Europe, Africa, and Latin America. Students of the 1989 movement erected the giant Chinese Statue of Liberty (*Ziyou Nushen* or "Goddess of Liberty" in Chinese) in the middle of the Tiananmen Square as their central symbol. But this did not last long. The U.S. opposition to China's hosting of the 2000 Olympics in 1993 was the first downward-turning point. Fewsmith (2008, 221) identified the Chinese reaction as historically extraordinary "because it was the first time since 1949 that elite politics, bureaucratic interests, intellectual opinion, and broader (but still urban) public opinion came together." The cross-Strait crisis in 1995 triggered by a visit to the United States by Taiwan's president Lee Teng-hui turned out to be far more serious. While Chinese intellectuals often privately welcome U.S. criticisms of China's human rights record and lack of rule of law, they tend to see the United States' ambiguity regarding the cross-Strait relations as a deliberate policy aimed at containing China. For China, its reunification with Taiwan would be the ultimate symbol of reclaiming its rightful place in the world after a century's international humiliation, and the United States' blocking of this path is hurtful. The U.S. role in the cross-Strait tensions left many pro-U.S. intellectuals disappointed and disillusioned. The book *China Can Say No* (Song et al. 1996) was to a great extent an expression of such feelings.

Despite Beijing's tough stance in the 1995 cross-Strait showdown, China continued deepening its engagement with the United States in security dialogue, economic cooperation, and societal exchange. Jiang Zemin's pro-U.S. stance during his presidency (1989–2002) remains one of his most controversial legacies today. Then came the NATO bombing of the Chinese embassy in Belgrade in 1999. University students, both in China and overseas, took to the streets swiftly. "Shock! Outrage! Protest!," cried the headline of the popular *Beijing Youth Daily*. "Waking up in the dark midnight, I heard wolves laughing on the other side of the world," read a poem by a young professor at Beijing University (Wang Dong 1999). The state leadership by contrast reacted surprisingly slowly. Western media at the time saw this as a sign of a weak and possibly divided leadership, but with hindsight it may be more accurately interpreted as a result of the leadership's genuine shock and difficult situation, given Jiang's pro-U.S. stance. After the bombing Jiang's close adviser Liu Ji, a preeminent pro-U.S. ideologist, was removed from the position of deputy president of the Social Science Academy. This was widely seen as Jiang accommodating the growing hostility towards the United States. Most Chinese remain unconvinced by the explanations provided by NATO and the White House. This is not so much because of the lack of credible information or technical improbability of the "mistake"; it is more a reflection of the general suspicion about Western powers that struggle to dominate the politically multipolar world.

One of the most powerful revelations of the peculiarly complex tensions in the Pacific paradox was the comment by a senior Chinese diplomat on the bombing. He was stationed in the Chinese embassy in Washington when the bombing took place; I asked him what he thought the truth of the matter was. His answer: "We have to say that Clinton didn't know [about the plan of bombing] even if he did know. Otherwise it meant the United States declared war on China. What can China do if China insists that the United States declared war?" Thus, what exactly happened did not matter much. In any case, China had to avoid an outright conflict regardless of what the United States actually did. There is perhaps no absolute truth anyway, except the structural conditions under which truth is made, pronounced, apprehended, debated, and applied in actions. The actual meaning of the "truth" is determined by interstate relations. Some may see Beijing's arguments with Washington on technicalities and on the principles of sovereignty merely diplomatic gestures. The real business is to build a strong Chinese state. Without a strong state as the frame, all rhetoric and gestures are empty.

The State as a Stage

The state becomes a frame in the public perception not merely because of historical memories and dramatic international events. Concrete actions, policies, and performance are needed in order for the state to be imagined into a frame (for anthropological discussions on the importance of everyday encounters in the symbolic construction of states, see Gupta 1995; Mitchell 1991; Mitchell 1999; and others). This section moves from historical narrative to an ethnographic examination of how the Chinese state positions itself in engaging with one of the most significant transpacific groups, namely overseas Chinese professionals (OCPs), and particularly how the state's framing effects are reinforced by facilitating transnational connections. The state's outreach to the Chinese diaspora in the reform era is well documented (see Wang Gungwu 1985; Nyiri 2002; Thuno 2001; Barabantseva 2005). Two recent trends are discernable in the state's interaction with a priority group, namely the OCPs, especially those who emigrated after the Cultural Revolution as students. First, instead of reaching out to existing communities, the state actively seeks to influence the *formation* of the transnational groups from the beginning. Second, culturalist and racially based discourses on "Chineseness" become a less important common ground, and pragmatic calculation, especially on economic benefit, is prioritized. Yet this does not mean that the Chinese state has become more interventionist. "Government set the stage, business run the opera"—this is the central method adopted by the Overseas Chinese Affairs Office (OCAO) of the State Council in working with OCPs. According to this method, the state should stay back and create conducive conditions for businesses to develop and benefit from vibrant transnational connections. "Business" primarily means commercial enterprises, but also include other nonstate actors such as research and development institutions. Being a stage on the ground provides a concrete basis for the state's becoming a frame in people's mind.

In order to act as a stage, the state needs first to create new social spaces for spontaneous mobility. The Chinese state has considerably liberalized regulation over outmigration. Students were, in the words of *River Elegy*, among the first who hurled themselves into the Pacific. From 1978 to 2012 more than 2.6 million students left China to study overseas, including 400,000 in 2012 alone, over 465 times the 1978 figure (860). The United States is by far the most popular destination. Nearly 200,000 students from China were enrolled in tertiary learning institutions in the United States in the year of 2011–2012, compared to 65,000 in the United Kingdom, 25,000 in Canada, and 23,000 in Australia, the other three leading destinations. In the United States, students from China accounted for 25.4% of all foreign students, and outnumber by a wide margin the second largest nationality group (India, which accounted for 13.1%). Furthermore, the number of high school students from China in the United States increased by more than 10 times since 2005, creating new momentum for future growth. (The Ministry of Education, cited in Zhongguo Jiaoyu Zaixian 2013)

Originally, the student migration was directly organized and monitored by the state. Students had to return on completion of their study. Those who had jobs in China already were subject to stricter regulation. They had to return on time or apply for approval from their employers in China to extend their stay overseas, otherwise they would be punished both financially and politically. The policy was changed in the early 1990s, and those who stayed overseas without permission could pay compensation to the employer and terminate the employment relationship as a normal arrangement, in contradistinction to the fact that this was previously recorded as a violation of rules. New policies also allow returnees to quit their jobs in the public sector if they prefer to work in private or foreign-owned enterprises. The liberalized official policy is summarized in the "Twelve-Characters Approach," the twelve characters in Chinese being *zhi chi liu xue, gu li hui guo, lai qu zi you*, meaning "support study overseas, encourage returns, guarantee freedom of movement." In the late 1990s the central government called OCPs to *weiguo fuwu* (serve the motherland). Compared to the earlier slogan of *huiguo fuwu* (return and serve the motherland), the new notion indicated that staying overseas is just as patriotic as physically return-ing. In sum, OCPs were no longer sojourners dispatched by the government and tied to state institutions; they were independent migrants who seek to maximize their own benefits following the logic of flexible transnational accumulation.

At the same time regulations over mobility have been liberalized—the state sets the stage—by promulgating policies, initiating programs, and orga-nizing events—to facilitate transnational interactions. First, the state has de-vised numerous policies to encourage overseas Chinese to return to China to work either temporarily or permanently. Following an index provided by the Ministry of Education (MoE 2004), I collected 180 government policies issued during the period from 1986 to 2003, including eight general policies issued by the State Council, 90 general policies by local government, 34 regarding indus-trial parks exclusively for returned overseas students, 7 on education for return-ees' children, 27 on personnel policy, nationality, household registration, and even marriage of returnees, and 14 on customs regulations. Indeed, since so many ministries promulgated favorable policies on their own, the MoE decided to issue special ID cards for selected OCPs that enable them to enjoy all benefits provided by different ministries, from buying cars to sending children to kin-dergartens. In sharp contrast to the earlier policies stating that graduates would be punished if they did not return to China or to their previous work units, in most cases returnees are entitled to these benefits regardless where they work.

Apart from promulgating policies, the government has also taken actions to fund programs aimed at encouraging transnational connections. The Chun-hui Plan, which was launched in 1996, supports OCPs' short-term visits for the purposes of academic exchange, the provision of training, and joint supervision of PhD students. The Cheung Kong Scholar Program, jointly funded by the Hong Kong-based company Cheung Kong Holdings, the Lee KC Foundation, and the MoE, has recruited leading researchers in strategic areas since 1998. The program sponsors OCPs to work in China for three years, on an annual stipend of $15,000. Other initiatives include the Distinguished Young Scholars Program set up by the National Science Foundation, and the One Hundred Talent Pro-gram of the Chinese Academy of Sciences (for a more detailed overview of these programs, see Cao 2008 and Xiang 2011).

The most typical examples of the state's "staging" strategy are the large-scale conventions that bring together OCPs, China-based employers, and in-ternational investors to facilitate recruitment, collaboration, and technology transfer and commercialization. The Guangzhou Overseas Students Fair which started in 1998 was the first such convention. It was an initiative of the Guangzhou municipal government and is jointly organized by the ministries of education, personnel, and science and technology. The fair takes place annually during the Christmas break to cater to the schedule of most OCPs, and attracts more than 200,000 participants each year. The Guangzhou fair is known for its scale, generous funding (it used to cover the full expenditure of travel and accommodation), and openness (it welcomes anyone who has studied or worked overseas). A middle-ranking officer at the OCAO called the Guangzhou fair a "Rome gathering," a term whose origin I cannot identify (possibly it has something to do with Catholic masses that are open to everyone), and commented that its main functions are "creating momentum" (*zaoshi*) and "forming influence" (*zaocheng yinxiang*). In other words, serving as a good stage is what such conventions aim at.

Quite a few local governments started emulating Guangzhou in the early 2000s. But few could allocate as much funding as Guangzhou; they instead developed much more focused working methods. One of these was organized by the OCAO and three provincial governments in northeast China in June 2004, with the lengthy, impressive title of "Convention for Cooperation and Exchange among Overseas Chinese Enterprises in Scientific and Technological Innovation." When I landed in the host city Changchun, I was immediately enthralled by the festive atmosphere. In the sky flew colorful balloons, on the ground lay carefully arranged flowers. The main road from the airport to downtown Changchun was densely dotted by banners of different shapes: the vertical, narrow ones hung on lampposts and the horizontal ones covering the sides of flyovers; huge billboards were erected in strategic places such as roundabouts or in the middle of squares. "Northeast Rejuvenation, Win–Win Cooperation" (*dongbei zhenxing, yingying hezuo*) was the key slogan highlighted in the banners and billboards. The inclusion of "Win–Win" was novel. Official discourse about overseas Chinese in China has long been dominated by notions like patriotism and contributions (to the development of homeland), and overseas Chinese are typically depicted as "wandering sons" (*youzi*) who yearn for mother's hug. But "Win–Win Cooperation" clearly puts the motherland and OCPs in the position of a mutually beneficial, equal partnership.

The convention started with a gala banquet for 500 guests. In the middle of the hall, at a table twice the size of the others, sat almost all the top leaders of the province, a deputy minister of the OCAO, and a couple of OCP representatives. As an observer I was placed on a peripheral table with drivers, bodyguards, reporters, and photographers. The real business started the next day. At numerous concurrent panels, OCPs presented their technological innovations, highlighted market potential, and projected astonishing profits for investors. Mr. Yang, a middle-ranking official in the OCAO in charge of OCP affairs, told me that this part of the convention was modeled on the investment seminars organized by venture capitalists in Silicon Valley. At the same time, local firms and institutes, including government departments, set up stalls in the hall to recruit employees and collaborative partners for the projects they had in mind. Official hierarchy was temporarily suspended for these Silicon Valley days. Middle-ranking officials roamed around, sneaked into seminar rooms in the middle of presentations, sat down and observed quietly.

The convention was concluded on the fourth day with a grand ceremony of signing agreements between OCPs and China-based institutions. After a few selected OCP representatives and local companies reported how much they had achieved at the meeting, officials from OCAO and the provinces then made brief speeches to confirm that the convention had been a great success. Officials from Beijing retreated. Local officials stood on the stage in line, wine glasses in hand, overseeing batches of OCPs and local companies coming on stage to sign agreements. A press conference followed immediately. Detailed information about the achievements of the convention—in terms of the number of contracts signed and the amount of investment committed—was readily available in printed material. Given that almost all the business deals had been signed just minutes earlier, the outcomes of the convention were obviously ensured even before it started. A large part of the convention was indeed literally "staged."

Such a "staging" strategy seems to work. Although many OCP participants agreed that such conventions are to some extent only "shows," they maintained that such activities are necessary and beneficial to them. Ms. Hua, who runs a number of trading companies in both the United States and Hungary, was one such participant. She was purchasing a certain type of stone for construction projects, which had nothing to do with high technology. She had sealed a deal with the seller in northeast China, but decided to sign the agreement at the convention when she learned about it by chance. For Ms. Hua, the convention gave great publicity and legitimacy to the project, and she expected that this would "make things easier in dealing with government."

The conventions are at once commercial, technological, political, and theatrical. Political rituals and business calculations enhance and legitimize each other. It is through endorsing and even encouraging these uncompromisingly pragmatic business endeavors that the state projects itself as progressive, scientific, forward-looking, and capable of delivering concrete achievements. The political rituals were not so much meant to remind the participants of the role of the state, but were primarily used to raise morale, create a serious yet festive atmosphere, and, as one official put it, "to show that we take the OCPs seriously and want to treat them well." Most OCP participants seemed to enjoy the rituals, seizing every opportunity to take photos, and shake hands and exchange name cards with officials. On the stage set by the state, it seems, that transpacific connections driven by market calculation generate feelings of honor and pride. On a different occasion, a returned OCP who obtained his PhD in Australia and who had worked in the United Kingdom before, told the press that he considered an article published by his team in *Science*—a landmark achievement—as a gift to the Communist Party for its birthday on July 1 (Cao 2008, 341). It is by being made such a ritualistic and fictive gift that the article acquires its social significance. By acting as a stage, the state not only facilitates flows and connections, but also becomes itself a central reference point from which the flows and connections acquire meanings.

Discussion

The notion of "Asia-Pacific," Rob Wilson (2002) suggested, represents "a de facto way of overriding problems and bypassing political tensions without resolving them in such a market-driven forum" (244–245). The Pacific paradox shows that market forces are even more dominant now than when the notion of Asia-Pacific was first proposed. But political tensions are not simply bypassed; they are entrenched and in many ways escalated at the very same time. The hegemonic, market-oriented Pacific vision is not simply imposed by the United States. Multiple actors actively contribute to such an imagination, and China is certainly no less enthusiastic than the United States. Transpacific neoliberalism, if there is such a thing, should be understood as a highly complex articulation of diverse local experiences and perceptions instead of a doctrine invented and imposed by the United States. Attention to such nuanced entanglements is crucial to understanding transpacific relations. But voluntary participation in the same game does not imply the game *means* the same thing to all the participants. For China, joining the globally integrated market serves as the most realistic path leading to its rightful position in the world. It is believed that China as a late comer and weaker player needs a strong state when engaging with the world economy, and the capacity to do so has become a main basis for the legitimacy of the state. Interstate political tensions are not only part of the Pacific engagement, but are also what makes the engagement meaningful. The Pacific paradox analytically resembles the postcolonial paradox whereby colonies adopted the European model of nation-states in order to free themselves from European domination. While postcolonial states sought independence by becoming self-sufficient and even through self-imposed isolation, the Pacific paradox requires one to assert one's political identity and autonomy through deep economic integration with others. The Pacific paradox is therefore doubly paradoxical.

Complicating the image of Chinese transpacific subjects as examples of *homo economicus*, I call attention to the articulation of meaning—senses of honor, justice, recognition, and history—in people's global imagination. Yet moving away from the culturalist narrative that is common in studies of the Chinese diaspora and transnationalism, this chapter stresses the symbolic importance of realpolitik in the public imagination. The Chinese public are more aware of realpolitik because their interactions with the world, especially the West, have become more intimate. Given its emphasis on the symbolic effects of the state, this chapter differs from political economy analyses of states' roles in globalization (e.g., Sassen 2010). Apart from being a skillful and powerful political actor, the Chinese state is also a frame and a stage that together condition social consciousness, strategies, and practices.

The Pacific paradox is not a stable condition. Transpacific economic integration may wane, and political tensions may fluctuate. What the Pacific paradox indicates is a complex structure of engagement, a mode whereby economic imperatives, geopolitical calculations, and meaning-making processes are deeply intertwined. From the Chinese point of view, the hostile environment that China faces does not result from intrinsically evil intentions of the West but is determined by the global structure. Unlike the Atlantic crossings where believers in progressive capitalism on both sides of the Atlantic echoed each other and formed transnational alliance in promoting common ideals and policies (Rodgers 1998), and even less like the transatlantic relations after World War II that stressed principles, norms, and values, the transpacific relation is driven by pragmatism. Indeed, the Chinese public tends to discuss international affairs in a much less moralizing tone than their U.S. counterparts do. The Pacific paradox, because of its pragmatism, ambiguity, and multifacetedness, opens up new space for intellectual interventions and political debates.

Notes to Chapter 3: The Pacific Paradox

1. I thank my friend David Kelly for his help with the translation of this paragraph.

2. This was proposed first in He's letter to the top leadership at the end of 1988; parts were published afterward in various news media. Also see He (1995).

3. According to Wikipedia (2014a), the notion of G-2 (Group of Two) was originally coined by the economist Fred Bergsten in 2005, and soon gained wider currency among foreign policy experts. G-2 suggests that China and the United States are deeply intertwined in their strategic interests, and should work out solutions to global problems together. The term Chimerica was invented by historian Niall Ferguson and economist Moritz Schularick in late 2006. Chimerica points to the symbiotic economic relationship between the two countries that was based on saving by the Chinese and overspending by Americans (Wikipedia 2014b). Both G-2 and Chimerica (*zhongmeiguo*) have attracted much attention in China, especially in 2009 in the wake of the

financial crisis. They are seen as signs of both China's economic success and China's danger of losing autonomy in strategic areas.

4. In his excellent book on changes in the Chinese intellectual landscape since 1989, Fewsmith (2008) uses the term "neostatism" to mean a general school of thought that stresses state capacity and the desire for a strong state (140–162). Fewsmith regards neostatism as compatible with "popular nationalism" and the New Left for three reasons: its anti-Americanism ("there is a common nationalism directed primarily against the United States, both in terms of its presumed desire to control China internationally and in terms of the American model of liberal democracy and neoclassical economics"); its concern with social justice; and its populist orientation (133). But Fewsmith never gives a clear definition of what exactly constitutes neostatism.

References

Anderson, Benedict. 1991. *Imagined Communities*. London: Verso Books.

Barabantseva, Elena. 2005. "Trans-Nationalising Chineseness: Trans-Nationalising Chineseness: Overseas Chinese Policies of the PRC's Central Government." *ASIEN* 96: 7–28.

Cao Cong. 2008. "China's Brain Drain at the High End: Why Government Policies Have Failed to Attract First-Rate Academics to Return." *Asian Population Studies* 4 (3): 331–345.

Comaroff, Jean, and John Comaroff. 2003. "Ethnography on an Awkward Scale: Postcolonial Anthropology and the Violence of Abstraction." *Ethnography* 4 (2): 147–179.

Dirlik, Arif. 1998. *What Is in A Rim?: Critical Perspectives on the Pacific Region Idea*. Lanham, Md.: Rowman & Littlefield.

Fewsmith, Joseph. 2008. *China since Tiananmen*. New York: Cambridge University Press.

Gupta, Akhil. 1995. "Blurred Boundaries: The Discourse of Corruption, the Culture of Politics, and the Imagined State." *American Ethnologist* 22 (2): 375–402.

He Xin. 1995. "1992 Nian Gei Xiaoping Tongzhi Guanyu Zhongmei Guanxi de Xin" [A Letter to Comrade Deng Xiaoping on Sino-US Relations in 1992.] In *He Xin Zhengzhi Jingji Lunji* [*He Xin's Essays on Politics and Economy*], ed. He Xin and Zhengzhi Jingji LunJi, 185–196. Harbin: Heilongjiang Education Press.

———. 2009. "Lun Zhengzhi Guojia Zhuyi" [On Political Statism.] Post on *He Xin Luntan* [*He Xin Forum*]. August 31. http://www.caogen.com/blog/index.aspx?ID=32 (accessed October 21, 2010).

Huntington, Samuel. 1993. "The Clash of Civilizations?" *Foreign Affairs*. 72 (3): 22–49.

Kellas, James. 1991. *The Politics of Nationalism and Ethnicity*. London: Macmillan.

Li Zehou. 1987. "Qimeng yu Jiuwang de Shuangchong Bianzuo" [Double Variation of Enlightenment and Salvation.] In *Zhongguo Jindai Sixiang Shi* [*History of Modern Chinese Thought*], 7–50. Beijing: Oriental Press.

Mahbubani, Kishore. 2003 [1998]. "Seven Paradoxes on Asia-Pacific Security." In *Can Asians Think?: Understanding the Divide between East and West*, 168–174. Singapore: Marshall Cavendish.

Mao Zedong. 1957. "On the Correct Handling of Contradictions among the People." *People's Daily*, June 19.

Ministry of Education. 2004. *Liuxue Gongzuo Wenjian Huibian [Compilation of Policies Regarding Studying Overseas]*. Beijing: Ministry of Education (unpublished document).

Mitchell, Timothy. 1991. "The Limits of the State: Beyond Statist Approaches and Their Critics." *American Political Science Review* 85 (1): 77–96.

———. 1999. "Society, Economy, and the State Effect." In *State/Culture: State-Formation after the Cultural Turn*, ed. George Steinmetz, 76–97. Ithaca, NY: Cornell University Press.

Nyiri, Pal. 2002. "From Class Enemies to Patriots: Overseas Chinese and Emigration Policy and Discourse in the People's Republic of China." In *Globalizing Chinese Migration: Trends in Europe and Asia*, ed. Pal Nyiri and Igor Saveliev, 208–241. Aldershot, UK: Ashgate Publishing.

Nyiri, Pal, Zhang, Juan and Varrall, Merriden. 2010. "China's Cosmopolitan Nationalists: Heroes' and 'Traitors' of the 2008 Olympics." *The China Journal*, No. 63: 25–55.

Ong, Aihwa. 1999. *Flexible Citizenship: The Cultural Logics of Transnationality*. Durham, NC: Duke University Press.

Plano, Jack C. 1973. "Statism." In *Political Science Dictionary*, ed. Jack C. Plano. New York: Dryden Press.

Rodgers, Daniel T. 1998. *Atlantic Crossings: Social Politics in a Progressive Age*. Cambridge, MA: Harvard University Press.

Sahlins, Marshall. 1994. "Cosmologies of Capitalism: The Trans-Pacific Sector of 'the World System.'" In *Culture/Power/ History: A Reader in Contemporary Social Theory*, ed. Nicholas B. Dirks, Geoff Eley, and Sherry B. Ortner, 414–416. Princeton, NJ: Princeton University Press.

Sassen, Saskia. 2010. *Territory, Authority, Rights: From Medieval to Global Assemblages*. Princeton, NJ: Princeton University Press.

Shen, Simon. 2007. "'Holding Nationalist Flags against Red Flags'—Anti-American Icons in Contemporary China and Their Reconstruction by the Public (1999–2003)." *East Asia* 24: 229–250.

Song Qiang, Huang Jisu, Song Xiaojun, Wang Xiaodong, and Liu Yang. 2009. *Zhongguo Bu Gaoxing: Dashidai, Damubiao Ji Women de Neiyou Waihuan [Unhappy China: The Great Time, Grand Vision and Our Challenges]*. Nanjing: Jiangsu People's Press.

Song Qiang, Zhang Zangzang, Qiao Bian, and Gu Qingsheng. 1996. *Zhongguo Keyi Shuobu: Lengzhan Hou de Zhengzhi yu Qinggan Jueze [China Can Say No: Political and Emotional Choices in the Post Cold-War Era]*. Beijing: Chinese Industry and Commerce Association Press.

Su Xiaokang, and Wang Luxiang. 1988. "Xin Jiyuan" [The New Epoch]. In *He Shang [River Elegy]*. Beijing: China Books and Journals Press. (page missing).

Thuno, Mette. 2001. "Reaching Out and Incorporating Chinese Overseas: The Trans-Territorial Scope of the PRC by the End of the 20th Century." *China Quarterly* 168: 910–929.

Wang Dong. 1999. "Heiye" ["The Black Night"]. *Beijing Daxue Xiaokan* [*Peking University News*]. (date and page missing).

Wang Gungwu. 1985. "External China as a New Policy Arena." *Pacific Affairs* 58 (1): 28–43.

Wang Hui and Zhang Tianwei. 1994. "Wenhua Pipan Lilun yu Dangdai Zhongguo Minzu Zhuyi Wenti" [Theories of Cultural Critique and Issues of Contemporary Chinese Nationalism]. *Zhanlue Yu Guanli* [*Strategy and Management*] 5 (4): 17–20.

Wang Huning. 1994. "Wenhua Kuozhang yu Wenhua Zhuquan: Dui Zhuquan Guannain de Tiaozhan" [Cultural Expansion and Cultural Sovereignty: The Challenge to the Idea of Sovereignty]. *Fudan Daxue Xuebao (Sheke ban)* [*Fudan University Journal* (Social Science edition)], November 3. (page missing).

Wang Shaoguang. 2010. Personal conversation with the author. Oxford, October 21.

Wang Shaoguang and Hu Angang. 1993 [1991]. Zhongguo Guojia Nengli Baogao [*China's State Capacity Report*]. Liaoning: People's Publishing House.

Wang Yaping. 2009. "Zhongguo Zouxiang Haiyanghua" [China's Path towards Oceanization]. *Financial Times* [Chinese online version], December 23. http://www.ftchinese.com/story/001030441. (accessed February 10, 2014).

Wikipedia. 2014a. "Group of Two." http://en.wikipedia.org/wiki/Group_of_Two. (accessed February 9, 2014).

Wikipedia. 2014b. "Chimerica." http://en.wikipedia.org/wiki/Chimerica. (accessed February 9, 2014).

Wilson, Rob. 2002. "Imagining 'Asia-Pacific' Today: Forgetting Colonialism in the Magical Free Markets of the American Pacific." In *Learning Places*, ed. Masao Miyoshi and Harry D. Harootunian, 231–260. Durham, NC: Duke University Press.

Wilson, Rob, and Arif Dirlik, eds. 1996. *Asia/Pacific as Space of Cultural Production*. Durham, NC: Duke University Press.

Xiang, Biao. 2010. "Putongren de Guojia Lilun" [Guojia: A Common People's Theory of the State in Contemporary China]. *Kaifang Shidai* [*Open Times*] October: 117–132.

———. 2011. "A Ritual Economy of 'Talent': China and Overseas Chinese Professionals." *Journal of Ethnic and Migration Studies* 37 (5): 821–838.

Zhao Suisheng. 1997. "Chinese Intellectuals' Quest for National Greatness and Nationalistic Writing in the 1990s." *China Quarterly* 152: 725–745.

Zheng Yongnian. 1999. *Discovering Chinese Nationalism in China: Modernization, Identity and International Relations*. Cambridge, UK: Cambridge University Press.

Zhongguo Jiaoyu Zaixian [China Education On-Line] 2013. 2013 *Nian Chuguo Liuxue Xushi Baogao* [*Report on Trends in Studying Overseas 2013*]. www.eol.cn/html/lx/baogao2013/page1.shtml. (accessed February 9, 2014).

Part II

Transpacific Cultures

4

Miguel Covarrubias and the Pageant of the Pacific

The Golden Gate International Exposition and the Idea of the Transpacific, 1939–1940

NANCY C. LUTKEHAUS

"As I have said many times, the United States is and always will be a Pacific nation."[1] President Obama made this remark in Thailand, just days after his reelection to a second term as president of the United States in November of 2012. Obama was on his way to Cambodia to meet with leaders of the Association of South East Asian Nations (ASEAN). He went on to say: "as the fastest-growing region in the world, the Asia Pacific will shape so much of our security and prosperity in the century ahead . . . And that's why I've made restoring American engagement in this region a top priority as President."[2]

While it is apparent to many people that the United States' current desire to maintain good relations with the ASEAN nations is greatly motivated by our concern about the rising dominance of China in the Pacific, I want to turn our attention to an earlier moment in the history of the United States, a moment prior to our engagement in Vietnam and World War II; another moment when we began to see ourselves as a "Pacific nation." It was also a moment in the history of the United States when the idea of the nation's transpacific connections was made manifest.

The event in San Francisco where this idea was made manifest—the Golden Gate International Exposition—occurred in 1939 on Treasure Island, a man-made entity dredged up from the bay especially for the fair. The theme of the exposition was the "Pageant of the Pacific," coupled with the idea of "Peace and Pacific Unity." One of the most visually captivating ways in which the idea of transpacific connections was made materially manifest was a series of six murals painted by the Mexican artist Miguel Covarrubias on display in Pacific House, the thematic centerpiece of the exposition.

Miguel Covarrubias in front of one of the "Pageant of the Pacific" murals, 1939. Golden Gate International Exposition, Treasure Island, San Francisco. Unknown photographer. Courtesy of Harry Ransom Humanities Research Center, University of Texas at Austin.

The six murals—each of which was actually a large illustrated map of the Pacific—were titled: *The Fauna and Flora of the Pacific; Native Means of Transportation in the Pacific Area; Arts and Artifacts of the Pacific; Economy of the Pacific; Native Dwellings of the Pacific Area;* and *Peoples of the Pacific.* Only one of the original six murals—*The Fauna and Flora of the Pacific*—is still on public display today, where it can be seen at the De Young Museum in San Francisco.

There are two main points I elaborate here. First of all, I want to introduce Miguel Covarrubias to scholars of the transpacific who are not already familiar with him and his work because I think this artist, self-taught anthropologist, and Mexican intellectual made several important contributions to our present-day notion of the transpacific. Moreover, I think it is significant to the intellectual history of the idea of the transpacific that Covarrubias was Latin American rather than Anglo-American or Asian American; in other words, race and country of origin played a role in the development of this idea, but perhaps in ways that we have not always thought about it.

Second, I want to discuss the Golden Gate International Exposition as a specific type of cultural formation—one that scholars of imperialism have identified as characteristic of the late nineteenth- and early twentieth-century West—and describe the role it played in the development not only of the idea of the transpacific but also of the idea of the United States as a Pacific nation, the historical precursor to President Obama's statement.[3]

There had been two previous twentieth-century California expositions, both held in 1916—the Panama-Pacific International Exposition in San Francisco and the Panama-California Exposition in San Diego—that had celebrated the United States completing the construction of the Panama Canal. Both expositions, as the historian Robert Rydell (1984) has argued, had conveyed a social evolutionary message that celebrated the dominance of Anglo-Saxon North America—epitomized in the technological acumen exemplified by the canal—over its southern Latin American neighbors and the nation's Hispanic past. The completion of the canal signified a joining not only of the Atlantic and the Pacific Oceans but of the east and the west coasts of the United States and more rapid transportation—hence trade and communication—between Europe, the United States, and the Far East.

In a similar manner, the Golden Gate International Exposition also celebrated U.S. technical prowess, this time with regard to the completion of both the Golden Gate and the San Francisco–Oakland Bay Bridges. Even more importantly, it also foreshadowed the future dominance of U.S. aeronautical prowess, as it introduced the possibility of transpacific passenger flights—perhaps the original meaning of the term "transpacific"—that Pan American Airlines was soon to embark on with its *China Clipper* planes that were scheduled to depart in the future from the airport that would replace the Golden Gate Exposition on Treasure Island.

Thus, one of the interests of the businessmen, politicians, and professionals who comprised the Golden Gate Corporation was to promote the idea of San Francisco as the "Gateway to the Pacific," both by sea and by air.[4] The exposition's celebration of transpacific commerce and communication represents one of the earliest attempts in the twentieth century by North Americans to articulate an explicit notion of a transpacific world. However, Covarrubias's Pageant of the Pacific murals express a different meaning about transpacific connections, one that suggests a lengthy history of cultural connections between peoples on both sides of the Pacific and up and down the Americas. The murals are the only attempt I know of to visually present a set of ideas about the interconnectedness of the peoples and cultures of the Pacific Rim.

Finally, taking into consideration what scholars of imperialism such as Rydell (1984) and Paul Greenhalgh (1988) have written about the racist agendas and imperialist functions of world's fairs and universal expositions of the nineteenth and early twentieth centuries, I want to suggest that the Golden Gate Exposition represents a transitional form different from the earlier fairs that

Poster for the 1939 Golden Gate International
Exposition, San Francisco.

preceded it or, at the very least, a more complex cultural artifact than other
earlier fairs in the United States and Europe. The change in form, I argue, reflects larger social changes at work in the United States and Europe on the eve
of World War II.[5]

Miguel Covarrubias (1904–1957): "El Chamaco" = "The Kid"

But why was Miguel Covarrubias—an artist from Mexico—asked to paint the
Pacific House murals? Although never considered to be as great an artist as his
fellow Mexican modernists, Covarrubias was one of a number of early
twentieth-century Mexican artists that included some of Mexico's most noted
muralists—individuals a generation older than he such as Diego Rivera (1886–
1954), José Clemente Orozco (1883–1949), David Alfaro-Siquieros (1896–1974),
Rufino Tamayo (1899–1991) and Frida Kahlo (1907–1954),—who were known in
the United States by individuals interested in modern art.[6] In fact, his fellow artists gave Covarrubias the nickname "El Chamaco"—"The Kid"—and the name
stuck with him the rest of his life.[7]

The answer to the question "Why Covarrubias?" begins in 1923 when Covarrubias was just nineteen.[8] At this time he left Mexico City—where he had a job in the Mexican government's Division of Communication drawing maps—to travel to New York City. A talented caricaturist, he had been awarded a modest scholarship by the Mexican government to study art abroad.

Covarrubias in New York City

To be seen through so easily by a boy of twenty, and by a Mexican, a national of a country that we have been patronizing for a century or two, an outlander and a heathen, was a bitter but corrective pill.[9]

The American artist Ralph Barton (1891–1931) wrote these words about Miguel Covarrubias in 1925 in response to the publication of Covarrubias's first collection of caricatures called *The Prince of Wales and Other Famous Americans* (1925). Even if Barton was saying these things in jest—and, as a fellow caricaturist with a similar sense of humor to Covarrubias perhaps he was—his comments shed light on the prejudices that many mainstream Americans felt—and expressed—about Mexicans and other Latin Americans during the 1920s. But pure jealousy probably lay at the base of Barton's remarks because Covarrubias had quickly made a name for himself through the caricatures and other illustrations that he did for the *New Yorker, Vogue,* and *Vanity Fair.* The editor of *Vanity Fair,* Frank Crowninshield, was especially taken with Covarrubias's drawings and used his work extensively during the 1920s and 1930s.

However, in part because of racist sentiments such as those expressed by Barton, Covarrubias had found himself drawn to burgeoning 1920s jazz scene in Harlem, which he documented through sketches, caricatures, and, eventually, illustrations for books by Langston Hughes, Zora Neal Hurston, and W. C. Handy. Hughes complemented Covarrubias, saying, "I think [the jacket cover illustration] the best pictorial interpretation of my *Weary Blues* that I have ever seen . . . You are the only artist I know whose Negro things have a 'Blues' touch about them" (Williams 1994, 40).

For his part, Covarrubias felt a strong affinity for the music and gaiety he experienced at the clubs and other venues he frequented in Harlem and thought that he fit in more easily with the black Americans in Harlem than with many of the posh celebrities and other influential white people he hobnobbed with off and on Broadway. Some of his now better-known drawings of African Americans dancing and performing in Harlem were featured in *Vanity Fair* and published as a collection as *Negro Drawings* (1927). It was the first time that pictures of black Americans had been published in a mass-circulation magazine that reached a predominantly white readership. The article and book helped to popularize the Harlem Renaissance and inspired a growing number of middle- and upper-class white Manhattanites to venture up to Harlem.[10]

Covarrubias and Island of Bali

In the early 1930s Covarrubias had married the American dancer, Rosa Cowen. Rosa, whose father was Scottish and mother Mexican, had been born and raised in Los Angeles. When she became a professional dancer in New York City she changed her name to Rosa Rolando as she felt it was a more exotic stage name, and more attuned to her dark complexion. The newlyweds had spent part of their honeymoon in Bali, Covarrubias's first experience with an island culture in the Pacific. Enthralled by the Balinese people and their rich artistic culture,

Miguel Covarrubias, 1939. *Clark Gable vs. Edward, Prince of Wales.* "Impossible Interview, No. 12," 1932. Published in *Vanity Fair*, November, 1932. Courtesy of Harry Ransom Humanities Research Center, University of Texas at Austin.

he applied for and received a Guggenheim fellowship to study Balinese culture and the couple returned to Bali in 1933.

Covarrubias made extensive sketches and paintings of the Balinese, many of which were included in his book *Island of Bali,* the study of Balinese culture he published in 1937.[11] The book was a popular success. It was so popular that it engendered a small fad in New York City for all things Balinese, including women's garments fashioned out of material that looked like Balinese batik.

Just as significant was the fact that Covarrubias—harking back to his earlier training as a mapmaker—had drawn a detailed map of Bali that was included in the front and back inside covers of his book.

The time that Covarrubias and his wife spent in Indonesia—both on their honeymoon and in 1933—was formative for him in terms of helping him to

Miguel Covarrubias, n.d. *Harlem Dancers.* Courtesy of Harry Ransom Humanities Research Center, University of Texas at Austin.

Fabric Design: Bali prints by Miguel Covarrubias, ca. 1937. Franklin Simon's Fifth Avenue, New York store window display. Unknown photographer, 1937. Prints and Photograph Division, Library of Congress.

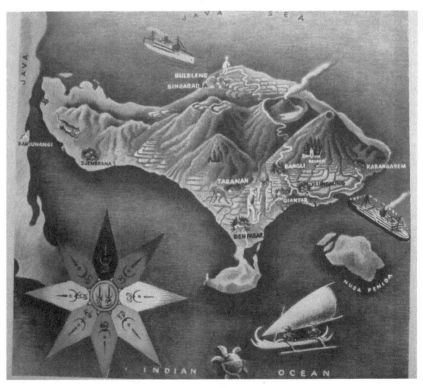

Miguel Covarrubias, 1937. Map of Bali from Covarrubias's book *Island of Bali*. New York: Alfred Knopf, 1937. Courtesy of Harry Ransom Humanities Research Center, University of Texas at Austin.

develop his understanding of the interconnectedness of cultures around the Pacific Rim. For in addition to spending time traveling throughout Java and Bali, the Covarrubiases also took time to travel through mainland Southeast Asia and parts of China.

While Miguel wrote notes and drew numerous sketches during their travels, Rosa took photographs. Together this data—both written and visual—provided an experiential underpinning to the work he was eventually to do on the Pacific murals.

Pre-Columbian Mexico, Archaeology, and the Ideology of *Indigenismo*

Miguel and his fellow Mexican artists—Diego Rivera and the other muralists as well as individuals such as painter Roberto Montenegro and Mexican intellectuals such as Moisés Sáenz and Dr. Atl[12]—were products of the Mexican Revolution. As such, they eschewed the influence of the colonial past and the decades—indeed centuries—of Spanish hegemony in all dimensions of Mexican culture and ways of life. They began to champion "the people"—in particular, the peasants or *campesinos*—praising them as the producers of truly authentic indigenous Mexican art. They eagerly purchased folk art at local markets throughout the country and displayed it in their sophisticated urban homes in Mexico City alongside modern art painted by one another, as well as expatriate Europeans such as Wolfgang Paalen who were fleeing the rising tide of fascism in Germany, Austria, France, and Italy in the 1930s and 1940s.[13] Equally important, they searched for the roots of a true Mexican identity in the archaic artifacts that were beginning to be found with more and more frequency at Aztec, Olmec, and Mayan archaeological sites in Mexico and Central America. Covarrubias, for example, published articles about the archaic archaeological findings at Tlatilco, a site in Mexico City (Covarrubias 1943). Eventually he also published two now classic volumes, *Indian Art of Mexico and Central America* (1957) and *The Eagle, the Jaguar and the Serpent: Indian Art of the Americas* (1954).

Both Mexican artists and expatriates were enthusiastic collectors of these tangible vestiges of the pre-Columbian past in Mexico. One of the expatriates who became very knowledgeable about both Mexican folk art and pre-Columbian objects was an Austrian count by the name of René d'Harnoncourt. He and Covarrubias first became friends in Mexico City but continued their friendship in the United States, where d'Harnoncourt had become director of the U.S. Department of the Interior's Indian Arts and Crafts Board. In this capacity, d'Harnoncourt was charged with organizing a pavilion at the Golden

Gate International Exposition that would highlight American Indian arts and crafts. He was also influential in convincing Covarrubias that he should accept the offer to paint the Pageant of the Pacific murals.[14]

To do so meant that Covarrubias had to interrupt a second ethnographic research project he had begun with Guggenheim funds, this time closer to home. He wanted to study the indigenous cultures living in the Isthmus of Mexico, that narrow part of the country where the Atlantic and the Pacific Oceans almost met, and where some of the most vibrant indigenous cultures were still thriving in centers such as Oaxaca and the rural communities surrounding Veracruz. Although he did postpone this research to paint the Pageant of the Pacific murals, he later carried out his research in the Tehuantepec region, publishing his findings in the book *Mexico South: The Peoples of the Isthmus of Tehuantepec* (1962).

The Golden Gate International Exposition: "The Pageant of the Pacific" and "Pacific Unity" Style

Blending Mayan, Incan, Malayan and Cambodian architecture, the walls of the Magic City arose on Treasure Island.[15]

The Golden Gate International Exposition could never have succeeded without the support of the Federal Works Progress Administration (WPA). The WPA supported three monumental construction projects in the Bay Area: the Golden Gate and San Francisco–Oakland Bay Bridges and the construction of an entire island, the aforementioned Treasure Island, as the site for the fair. Franklin Delano Roosevelt, having been impressed with the number of jobs generated by the two previous fairs in California, saw international expositions as a means not only of stimulating the economy—a large number of workers were needed to construct the fair's pavilions, pools, and monumental statues, as were architects, artists, and accountants—but also of generating pride in the country and its technological achievements and optimism in a brighter future for the nation as a whole.

The theme for the fair was "The Pageant of the Pacific" and as the quote above suggests, the fair's designers drew on the monumental architecture of the archaic cultures found around the Pacific Rim to create such iconic structures at the fair as "The Elephant Pyramids" and a monumental statue of a female figure named Pacifica that towered over fairgoers.

A new art style, labeled "Pacific Unity," was developed by the fair's architects and artists—men such as Bernard Maybeck and William G. Merchant, who had designed the Beaux-Arts buildings at the Panama-Pacific Interna-

Postcard of the Elephant Pyramids, Golden Gate International
Exposition, Treasure Island, San Francisco, 1939.

tional Exposition of 1915, as well younger artists such as Timothy Pflueger and
Ralph Stackpole[16]—that, in addition to Stackpole's *Pacifica*, was exemplified by
other huge sculptures such as a Chinese musician playing a horn, an Alaskan
boy spearing a fish, and a Polynesian woman holding bananas that were scattered over the fairgrounds.[17] The style was a blend of 1930s art moderne with
design elements from cultures around the Pacific. An observer, Helen Phillips,
described the style as "weighty, compressed, and full of energy." "The artists,"
she continued, "created an aspect of refined primitivism; if you don't look too

closely, you might think that the sculptures had just been unearthed from some archaeological dig." While *Time* magazine derided the style as "stage design fakery," others viewed it more generously, saying, "You go to World's Fairs to have fun," and the fourteen-foot cubist-inspired Elephant Towers did just that "with considerable ziptarara-boom-de-ay about it."[18]

The fair itself was originally the idea of a group of well-connected businessmen and professionals in San Francisco who viewed it as a means of promoting the city and its role as the gateway to the Pacific. In order to do so they decided to focus the theme of the fair on the cultures of the Pacific, thus intro-

Postcard of Ralph Stackpole's statue *Pacifica*. Golden Gate International Exposition, Treasure Island, San Francisco, 1939.

ducing people in the United States to many new peoples and traditions in the region that they might never seen before or knew very little about. More importantly, they stressed the idea of transpacific connections—especially since transpacific voyages would depart from the airport that was to be built on Treasure Island after the fair ended.

As Europe was on the brink of war, the fair's promoters also wanted to stress the notion of peace and the unity of mankind. The centerpiece of the fair, both physically and ideologically, was to be a building called Pacific House where entertainment such as dances and musical performances from countries throughout the Pacific Rim would be held and where people could learn about the interconnections among the nations in this vast region.

Pacific House: A Center for the Pacific in San Francisco

Dr. Ray Lyman Wilbur, a San Francisco physician and former president of Stanford University as well as secretary of the interior under Herbert Hoover, had been chosen to serve as the president of Pacific House. He explained that not only was Pacific House the theme building of the Golden Gate International Exposition, it was also "a group of people who would like to see still more goodwill and trade throughout the Pacific Area." He and the other members of Pacific House had intended that it would continue after the exposition and become a center for the Pacific in San Francisco.[19]

The architect William G. Merchant designed the building, which was situated on an island surrounded by a large lagoon. Pedestrians approached Pacific House by an arched bridge reminiscent of China or Japan. Monumental, yet simple in design, it had a wall of vertical windows that looked out onto the lagoon and an indoor pond with replicas of whales that cavorted and spouted water! Surrounding the Pacific House were a collection of pavilions dedicated to individual countries—Japan, the Philippines, the Dutch East Indies, New Zealand, Australia, French Indochina, and Hawai'i. Underscoring the fair's theme of Pacific Unity nearby was the Latin American Court with pavilions representing Mexico, Costa Rica, Panama, Guatemala, Ecuador, Peru, Colombia, and Chile. As the art historian Eugen Neuhaus remarked, "these pavilions were combined in one picturesque aggregate which reflects the ancient architectural heritage of those countries" (Neuhaus 1939, 35).

The Pageant of the Pacific murals Covarrubias was commissioned to paint covered the interior walls of Pacific House and were an important aspect of its educational agenda. In his forward to an edition of lithographic reproductions of the murals made available for sale to the public in 1940, Pacific House

Postcard of Pacific House, Golden Gate International Exposition, Treasure Island, San Francisco, 1939.

president Wilbur expressed the hope that "friendship and understanding between the nations of this vital area could be the residual benefit from the masses of people attracted to the Exposition."[20]

The Pageant of the Pacific Maps as Mass Media

> You have a unique style and a great fund of knowledge which will enable you to dramatize the educational purposes we have in mind. We are thrilled you have accepted this commission.[21]

Echoing the above words of the exposition's director, Paul Youtz, Wilbur added, "recognizing that murals are a most effective medium for mass education, Pacific House commissioned Miguel Covarrubias to execute in murals on its walls the sweeping and colorful Pageant of the Pacific." The idea that the murals—and in this particular case, murals that were maps—were an effective medium for mass education was predicated on the fact that images rather than words were believed to be the best means through which "the masses" could be educated about the geography, economics, and cultures of the Pacific Rim since images could convey information without the constraint of language; pictures, that is, were believed to be a universal language understood by all.

Although Covarrubias, unlike Diego Rivera and other modern Mexican artists, had not painted large-scale murals before, his work was known to a considerable number of Americans, especially individuals such as the men who made up the governing body of the exposition and Pacific House, through the paintings and drawings he had published on the cover of *Vanity Fair*, and in the *New Yorker* and *Vogue*. The map he had drawn for his book about Bali had also been published in an article on Bali that had appeared in *Vanity Fair*, thus demonstrating his ability to create an accurate yet accessible and visually appealing map. The distinctive elements of his map of Bali were the small images of people, canoes, plants, and animals that he had decorated it with, making the geography and topology of the island come alive with local color and activities.

More specifically, Wilbur pointed out that Covarrubias was selected to paint the murals because:

He was . . . the one who could make visual the idea of the Pacific area, not only with the imagination and skill of a great artist, but with an understanding of the verities and needs all people held in common. He was seen as an ethnologist and anthropologist, subtle and sensitive to the unrecorded past of unknown peoples, with a humorous, penetrating perspicacity of contemporaneous life, and with a wide knowledge of the governmental forms and trade relations of the moving forces that bind people together or sever their relations.[22]

However, it was not just Covarrubias's unique combination of skill as an artist as well as his experience and knowledge gained as an ethnologist and anthropologist that made him an ideal choice in Wilbur and his compatriots' minds. According to Wilbur, Covarrubias's racial identity also gave him "a sympathetic understanding of the peoples and lands of the Pacific Basin."[23] Voicing a not uncommon—and racist—sentiment of the time, that some races had closer affinity toward one another than others, based on such superficial traits as skin color, hair type, or physiognomy, and so on, Wilbur implied that because Covarrubias was Mexican rather than, for example, Anglo, he therefore had greater understanding of the other darker-skinned peoples of the Pacific Basin.

Covarrubias's initial hesitation to take on the project had nothing to do with an objection to Wilbur's sentiments, but rather with the timing of the project since it would conflict with his ethnographic research in Southern Mexico. However, his old friend and former minister of education in Mexico, Moisés Sáenz, reminded him that the murals gave Covarrubias an opportunity to promulgate his ideas about the unity of the cultures of the Pacific and their importance to the Americas, saying that the maps would be "an educational depiction of sociological truth through art." As his biographer noted, "Miguel conceived of them as six mini-lessons in anthropology" (Williams 1994, 101). Implicit in the murals is Covarrubias's theory of a radical form of cultural diffusion. Inspired by the anthropological publications of Franz Boas, especially *Primitive Art* based heavily on Boas's field work with Northwest Coast Indians, Covarrubias believed that there were transpacific connections between archaic cultures on both sides of the Bering Straits and that people had diffused southward from Alaska into Mexico, Central America, and finally, South America. His evidence for this radical diffusion was stylistic design elements found in objects as far apart as the Northwest Coast and Central Mexico (Covarrubias 1943; Usabiaga 2012, 97).[24]

Moreover, when the lithographs of the murals were published Covarrubias wrote a short text that accompanied them, saying that "With the advent of air transportation the Extreme Orient is only a few days away from America; consequently, the need for a better understanding of the Pacific Area is becoming more and more imperative . . . particularly since the Old World has embarked into savage, suicidal wars that will leave it maimed, if not destroyed, to convalesce for many years to come."[25] He hoped, like the fair's organizers, that peace and unity would prevail throughout the New World and the Pacific Area.

Covarrubias's Maps: A New Orientation for the Pacific[26]

Rather than any mysterious racial affinities, Covarrubias's notion of cultural similarities throughout the Pacific Basin was instead based on empirical evidence: his travels and his archaeological and ethnographic research as well as the research of other anthropologists and geographers with whom he consulted. Also, perhaps not surprisingly, Covarrubias first job as a teenager in Mexico City was as a map draftsman in the government's Department of Communication. Aware of the limits of his own knowledge of anthropology and archaeology, he consulted with anthropologists Alfred Kroeber and Walter Goldschmidt at the University of California, Berkeley, and Erna Gunther at the University of Washington, a specialist on the Indians of the Northwest Coast.

Covarrubias also worked with the geographer Carl Sauer at University of California, Berkeley, on the design of the map of the Pacific Basin that he would use for all six of the murals. Sauer suggested that Covarrubias use the van der Grinten projection for the map, a type of map projection that is neither equal-area nor conformal but rather projects the earth onto a circle.[27] Covarrubias's maps became the first ever to represent the Pacific Basin with the Pacific Ocean

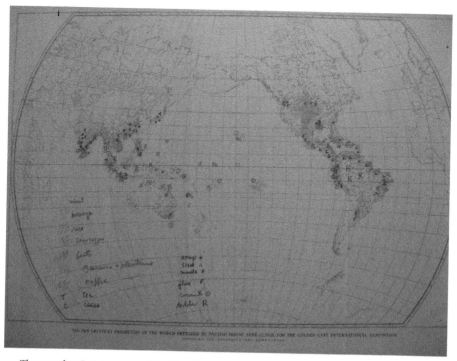

The van der Grinten map of the Pacific Basin. Courtesy of Harry Ransom Humanities Research Center, University of Texas at Austin.

in the center and the countries of Asia, Southeast Asia, and North and South America along the left and right edges.

Two of the six murals were nine feet by thirteen feet and the other four were fifteen by twenty-four. Rather than the usual fresco technique used for murals of wet plaster and paint, Covarrubias invented a new technique that used a flat duco lacquer with a nitrocellulose base. He diluted this medium with lacquer thinner and added pure dry pigment to it instead of using the usual watercolor on plaster. He then applied this combination to Masonite panels that were mounted on the walls. Thus each brush stroke embedded particles of pigment into the lacquer. When the mural dried it was hard and water-resistant and the color was sealed inside a clean, clear shield. The technique worked, creating a permanent washable surface. Faced with a daunting task, he was assisted in the painting of the murals by his long-time friend and fellow artist, Antonio Ruiz (also known as "El Corcito"—"the little Corzo," because of his resemblance to the popular Mexican bullfighter, Manuel Corzo) and two younger apprentices.

Wilbur and the other members of the Pacific House were delighted with the murals:

If, at this moment, you might walk into Pacific House on Treasure Island you would understand at one glance how well [Covarrubias] succeeded with his difficult commission. An all-pervading sense of beauty would be your first impression. The whole interior of the building seems almost bathed in the luminous blues and greens that Covarrubias lavished on his huge panels. Arrested and drawn to them, you would note the myriad tiny figures, each one actually a studied portrait, as they swirl in graceful, decorative designs over the colorful surfaces.[28]

Covarrubias made dozens of sketches for the "myriad of tiny figures" on each map, conducting extensive research on every culture he portrayed, including details concerning the material culture, housing types, modes of transportation, styles of art and architecture, environment, and economy. As Adriana Williams observed, "In typical Covarrubias style the people's mural used representational characters such as the agrarian revolutionary Emiliano Zapata outfitted in a familiar *charro* costume for Mexico and, for North America, a plump East Coast business executive with a cigar in his mouth and a voluptuous Hollywood starlet in a bathing suit and goggles" (Williams 1994, 102).

Miguel Covarrubias, 1939. "Pageant of the Pacific" mural titled *The Fauna and Flora of the Pacific*. Originally displayed in Pacific House, Golden Gate International Exposition. Now on display at the DeYoung Museum, San Francisco. Photograph by the author.

Miguel Covarrubias, 1939. Sketch of figures for the *Peoples of the Pacific* map, one of six "Pageant of the Pacific" murals by Covarrubias for Pacific House. Golden Gate International Exposition, Treasure Island, San Francisco. Courtesy of Harry Ransom Humanities Research Center, University of Texas at Austin.

Art critics and historians were also impressed with the murals. In his book *Modern Mexican Painters,* MacKinley Helm exclaimed that "Covarrubias has just about summed up his special interests and proficiencies as a plastic artist with these murals."[29] And Eugen Neuhaus, in *The Art of Treasure Island,* found the total effect of the murals to be "gay, even exhilarating, full of fascinating information that is often quaintly humorous."[30]

Wilbur, in his concluding comments that accompanied the portfolio-sized collection of lithographs of the maps, said:

like thousands before you [who had seen the murals at Pacific House], you would wish, fervently, that there might be reproductions that you could take home with you . . . If your job is making information stay in students' heads . . . if you wish to give your children a true understanding of the world they are growing up in . . . if you yourself want an over-all view of the vital area in which you live . . . you will most certainly want these beautiful reproductions. They make education amusing and learning fun.[31]

The Fate of the Murals Today

Ironically, just as the idea of an interconnected Pacific Basin was being promoted by the Golden Gate International Exposition, it was on the brink of being sabotaged by the Japanese, ushering in a period of one of the most vituperative racist reactions the United States had seen in its decision to incarcerate its Japanese-American citizens. Both the display of the murals and the idea of an interconnected transpacific world were ruptured by the onset of World War II. The murals were removed from their location on Treasure Island after the Japanese attack on Pearl Harbor and sent to New York City where they were on display for several years at the American Museum of Natural History before they were put into storage. And Pacific House was dismantled when it was decided to reconfigure the exposition grounds and buildings into a military base.

As we have seen, the murals had a second life after the exposition when they were reproduced as lithographs and reduced in size to a portfolio set of maps that people could purchase for their own enjoyment. Eighteen years after having been shipped across country to New York City, five of the six murals made their way back to San Francisco, where they were on display in the Ferry Building for many years. One of the murals, *Art and Styles of the Pacific,* has disappeared. At present *The Fauna and Flora of the Pacific*—the largest of the six murals—is the only mural that is still on display. It can be seen in San Francisco in the De Young Museum's Art of the Americas section where it pays homage to Covarrubias and his Mexican origins.

Conclusion

Following Edward Said in *Culture and Imperialism* (1993) and Rick López (2010) in his study of nation formation and Mexican modernism, I am interested in understanding the particular ways in which diverse cultural formations have emerged and articulated, or interlinked, with one another. In the case at hand, this means the ways in which twentieth-century U.S. and Mexican intellectuals—including scholars, artists, professionals, and writers—began to craft a new idea of transpacific connections through the artifact and experience that was the 1939 Golden Gate International Exposition. In particular, although the idea of the "Pageant of the Pacific" that was promulgated as the theme of the exposition and made manifest in Pacific House and its murals was at heart one that still promoted the hegemony of American economic, technological, and social superiority, I argue that the images of transpacific connections that Miguel Covarrubias depicted in the six murals that he painted for Pacific House actually helped to make explicit new ideas about the interconnections between the indigenous peoples of what we now call the Pacific Rim.

The British art historian Paul Greenhalgh has written about world's fairs and expositions as ephemeral worlds:

> The empire displays at exhibitions fulfilled a role which has been persistently underplayed or romanticized since the demise of the tradition . . . Nevertheless, it is an aspect that not only improves our vision of them as events but which also increases our understanding of Western culture as a whole during the period. The coming together of contradictory values at the exhibitions, whereby positive notions of progress were buttressed against organized oppression and exploitation, says much about the plural morality in operation throughout European culture at the time. Ultimately, as with a vast number of cultural artifacts, it must be concluded that the exhibitions embodied neither good nor evil in any simple sense but were a complex mixture of both. (79)

Of course, the irony of the 1939 Golden Gate International Exposition was that it has all but disappeared from memory in large part because its utopian theme of Pacific Unity was ripped asunder by real events. Although the vision of an ever-increasing connection between Asia and the United States was stillborn because of the Japanese attack on Pearl Harbor in December of 1941—rupturing the utopian idea of Pacific Unity that the exposition had envisioned—ironically, the ensuing Pacific theatre of World War II did introduce a huge number of Americans to the peoples of the Pacific first hand, and thus forever altered the distance between Pacific Island societies and the United States and ushered in a new understanding of the interconnections within the "Transpacific" region.

Notes to Chapter 4: Miguel Covarrubias and the Pageant of the Pacific

1. President Obama quoted in White House (2012).

2. Ibid. See also the "A Pacific Nation" chapter in Borthwick (2007) for a short history of Obama's engagement with the Asia-Pacific region since he took office in 2009.

3. One might argue that there were important earlier precursors to the Golden Gate International Exposition that promulgated the idea of the United States as a Pacific nation. For example, no one was more enthusiastic about the vastness and importance of the Pacific Ocean and the transpacific world than Melville. See Rowe in this volume.

4. For more information about the organization of the exposition see "Hard Times, High Visions: Golden Gate International Exposition." http://bancroft.berkeley.edu /Exhibits/Looking/hardtimes.html (accessed January 30, 2014).

5. Both Covarrubias and his fellow Mexican muralist Diego Rivera were especially aware of the specter of fascism at this time. Cf. note 8 below.

6. Covarrubias was asked to curate the section on modern Mexican art for an exhibition titled "Twenty Centuries of Mexican Art" that opened at the Museum of Modern Art in New York City in 1940. See *Twenty Centuries of Mexican Art*. New York: Museum of Modern Art.

7. For more details about the life of Covarrubias see Williams (1994).

8. Rivera, who shared many of Covarrubias's interests—intellectual, political, and sensual—also had a commission for a mural at the exposition, a work that became known as *Pan-American Unity*. It is presently on display at San Francisco City College.

9. Barton (1925). Quoted in Reaves (2004), 63.

10. Today Covarrubias's drawings strike some viewers as verging on racial stereotypes, but as Reaves (2004, 72) points out, "in the 1920s an audience attuned to the demeaning racist imagery of minstrelsy and the 'Darktown Comics,' saw Covarrubias's drawings as celebratory." Confirming his legacy as a promoter of African American cultures in 2011, the California African American Museum in Los Angeles had an exhibition of Covarrubias's drawings titled "The African Diaspora in the Art of Miguel Covarrubias: Driven by Color, Shaped by Cultures."

11. The book also included an album of black and white photographs of the Balinese people, the landscape, rituals, as well as everyday life taken by Rosa Covarrubias. She proved to be a talented photographer and Covarrubias used many of her photos later on as models for his own paintings.

12. See López (2010) and Oles (1993), among others, for details on the role that Mexican artists and other intellectuals played in postrevolutionary Mexico in the cultural renaissance that took place there beginning in the 1920s and 1930s through the 1940s. Covarrubias's interest in Mexican archaeology can be seen in his publication for the experimental magazine *Dyn* (1940) as well as the books he wrote on the subject of pre-Columbian art in Mexico, such as *Indian Art of Mexico and Central America* (1957).

13. For more about Paalen and his circle of expatriate artists and intellectuals and his publication of the art journal *Dyn* see Leddy and Conwell (2012) and Ades et. al. (2012).

14. See Lutkehaus (2011).

15. Text from a pamphlet advertising the Golden Gate International Exposition. Miguel Covarrubias Collection, Harry Ransom Center, University of Texas at Austin.

16. For more about the art and architecture of the exposition see Neuhaus (1939).

17. The sculptures were made of cast stone rather than plaster. Many of the sculptures no longer exist, but some of them are in storage on Treasure Island and another six were restored in 1994 and are at the time of writing on view there outside of Building One. Digitized photographs of many of the statues can be seen on the San Francisco Public Library's website (www.sfpl.org) for their collection pertaining to the Golden Gate International Exposition (G.G.I.E.): Polynesian Woman [Photo ID Number: AAK -0335]; Pacifica [Photo ID Number: AAK-0329]; Alaskan Boy Spearing a Fish [Photo ID Number: AAK-0326]; and the Chinese Musician [Photo ID Number: AAK-0259]. See also "Pacific Unity Sculptures." http://www.atlasobscura.com/places/pacific-unity -sculptures (accessed January 30, 2014).

18. "Treasure Island Celebrates 50th Anniversary of the Golden Gate International Exposition." February 1989. *Heritage Newsletter.* 17 (1): 1–2.

19. Wilbur (1940).

20. Ibid.

21. Paul Youtz, quoted in Williams (1994), 342 n. 55.

22. Wilbur (1940).

23. Ibid.

24. Thus, he did not ascribe to the idea that Pacific Islanders originated in South America, as the Norwegian explorer Thor Hyerdahl did a decade or so later; rather, he did believe that the affinities between the cultures of the Pacific Basin that were related to ancient migrations of peoples across the Bering Straits.

25. Covarrubias (1940).

26. Other maps made by Covarrubias subsequent to his Pageant of the Pacific murals included a popular map titled "Covarrubias's America," a map of the state of Florida published in *Life* magazine, and a map of the popular arts in Mexico painted as a mural in the Museo Nacional de Artes e Industrias Populares in Mexico City. See Ybarra-Frausto (1987) for more details.

27. The van der Grinten projection of the world was made familiar, even famous, when *National Geographic* adopted it as their logo.

28. Wilbur (1940).

29. Helm (1941), 195.

30. Neuhaus (1939), 35.

31. Wilbur (1940).

References

Ades, Dawn, Rita Eder, and Graciela Speranza, eds. 2012. *Surrealism in Latin America: Vivsimo Muerto.* Los Angeles: Getty Research Institute.

Barton, Ralph. 1925. "It Is to Laugh." *New York Herald Tribune,* October 25.

Borthwick, Mark. 2007. *Pacific Century: The Emergence of the Modern Asia Pacific,* 3rd ed. Boulder, CO: Westview Press.

Covarrubias, Miguel. 1925. *The Prince of Wales and Other Famous Americans.* New York: Knopf.

———. 1927. *Negro Drawings.* Introduction by Frank Crowninshield. New York: Knopf.

———. 1937. *Island of Bali.* New York: Knopf.

———. 1940. Pamphlet accompanying lithographs of the "Pageant of the Pacific" murals. Miguel Covarrubias Collection, Harry Ransom Center, University of Texas at Austin.

———. 1943. "Tlatilco: Archaic Mexican Art and Culture." *Dyn* 4–5: 40–46.

———. 1946. *Mexico South: The Isthmus of Tehuantepec.* New York: Knopf.

———. 1954. *The Eagle, the Jaguar and the Serpent. Indian Art of the Americas: North America, Alaska, Canada, the United States.* New York: Knopf.

Covarrubias, Miguel. 1957. *Indian Art of Mexico and Central America.* New York: Knopf.

Cox, Beverly J., and Denna Jones Anderson. 1985. *Miguel Covarrubias Caricatures.* Catalogue for the National Portrait Gallery. Washington, DC: Smithsonian Institution.

de Maria y Campos, Alfonso. 2007. "Esplendor del Pacifico." In *Miguel Covarrubias en Mexico y San Francisco,* 9–29. Mexico City: Instituto Nacional de Antropologia e Historia, Museum Nacional de Antropologia.

Greenhalgh, Paul. 1988. *Ephemeral Vistas: The Expositions Universelles, Great Exhibitions and World's Fairs, 1851–1939.* Manchester, UK: Manchester University Press.

Heinzelman, Kurt, ed., *The Covarrubias Circle: Nickolas Muray's Collection of Twentieth Century Mexican Art.* Austin, TX: University of Texas Press.

Helm, MacKinley. 1941. *Modern Mexican Painters.* New York: Harper Brothers.

Instituto Nacional de Antropología e Historia y Museum Nacional de Antropología. 2007. *Miguel Covarrubias en Mexico y San Francisco.* Mexico City: Instituto Nacional de Antropología e Historia.

James, Jack, and Earle Weller. 1941. *The Magic City, Treasure Island, 1939–1940: The Story of the Golden Gate International Exposition.* San Francisco: Pisani Printing and Publishing Company.

Leddy, Annette, and Donna Conwell. 2012. *Farewell to Surrealism: The Dyn Circle in Mexico.* Los Angeles: Getty Research Institute.

López, Rick A. 2010. *Crafting Mexico: Intellectuals, Artisans and the State after the Revolution.* Durham, NC: Duke University Press.

Lutkehaus, Nancy. 2011. "René d'Harnoncourt and the 20th Century Display of Indigenous Art in America." *Collections: A Journal for Museum and Archives Professionals* 7 (4): 426–427.

Museum of Modern Art. 1940. *Twenty Centuries of Mexican Art.* New York: Museum of Modern Art.

Neuhaus, Eugen. 1939. *The Art of Treasure Island.* Berkeley: University of California Press.

Oles, James. 1993. *South of the Border: Mexico in the American Imagination, 1914–1947.* Washington, DC: Smithsonian Institution Press.

Reaves, Wendy Wick. 2004. "Miguel Covarrubias and the Vogue for Things Mexican." In *The Covarrubias Circle: Nickolas Muray's Collection of Twentieth Century Mexican Art,* ed. Kurt Heinzelman, 63–82. Austin: University of Texas Press.

Rydell, Robert. 1984. *All the World's a Fair: Visions of Empire at American International Expositions, 1876–1916.* Chicago: University of Chicago Press.

Said, Edward. 1993. *Culture and Imperialism.* New York: Knopf.

Usabiaga, Daniel Garza. 2012. "Anthropology in the Journals *Dyn* and *El hijo pródigo:* A Comparative Analysis of Surrealist Inspiration." In *Surrealism in Latin America: Vivísimo Muerto,* ed. Dawn Ades, Rita Eder, and Graciela Speranza, 95–110. Los Angeles: Getty Research Institute.

White House, Office of the Press Secretary. 2012. "Remarks by President Obama and Prime Minister Shinawatra in a Joint Press Conference" [Press release]. 18 November. http://www.whitehouse.gov/the-press-office/2012/11/18/remarks-president-obama-and-prime-minister-shinawatra-joint-press-confer (accessed January 30, 2014).

Wilbur, Ray Lyman. 1940. Pamphlet accompanying lithographs of the "Pageant of the Pacific" murals. Miguel Covarrubias Collection, Harry Ransom Center, University of Texas at Austin.

Williams, Adriana. 1994. *Covarrubias.* Austin: University of Texas Press.

Ybarra-Frausto, Tomas. 1987. "'El Chamaco' y sus mapas: Miguel Covarrubias Cartografo." In *Miguel Covarrubias: Homenaje,* 118–127. Mexico City: El Centro Cultural de Arte Contemporáneo.

5

Transpacific Studies and the Cultures of U.S. Imperialism

JOHN CARLOS ROWE

We have entered a new stage of scholarship of what was previously designated "the Pacific Rim," even though the precise boundaries of the region remain as contested as ever. In my view, this new stage can be characterized as predominantly postcolonial, in which interests revolve around efforts by formerly colonized states to achieve cultural, economic, and political sovereignty in their relation to the Pacific region both as a geographical site and as a series of commercial, military, and cultural routes. Despite the familiar criticism of postcolonial studies as "presentist," we know that the best work in postcolonial studies never forgets the imperial legacies so many have worked to overcome. The academic field itself is tied profoundly to these anticolonial struggles, even when it is critical of specific postcolonial state formations in which the imperial heritage is still operative.

Area studies specialists in the Pacific have done very substantial work on the diverse indigenous communities of this vast oceanic and insular region, as well as its contact zones with other oceans and seas and their bordering communities. Their archive is too vast to be summarized here, although I will try to include relevant scholars in what follows, but I want to acknowledge from the beginning that Pacific studies is usually postcolonial in its outlook. In many cases, scholarly studies of the Pacific are closely connected with political and civil rights movements led by native peoples in demographically and territorially small communities, further "minoritized" by the global interests of First World powers, like the United States, People's Republic of China, Japan, and Russia. The recent turn in Pacific studies toward the affirmation of indigenous and other local communities strengthened by their histories of resisting imperialism is evident in such collections as *Inside Out: Literature, Cultural Politics and the New Pacific* (Hereniko et al. 2012) and *Militarized Currents: Toward a Decolonized Future in Asia and the Pacific* (Camacho et al. 2010). Rob Wilson's

Reimagining the American Pacific: From "South Pacific" to Bamboo Ridge and Beyond (2000) focuses on both the imperial realities and postcolonial utopia other scholars identify with the "new Pacific," and such work is complemented by Keith Camacho's recent *Cultures of Commemoration: The Politics of War, Memory and History in the Mariana Islands* (2010). Scholar-activist poets like the Chamoru writer Craig Santos Perez have contributed to coalitions of political and cultural activists with poetry like his *From Unincorporated Territory* (2010) and spoken-word performances on Guahan (Guam) and elsewhere in the Pacific, Asia, and the United States.

These scholars are just a few of the many working today at the intersections of Asian, Pacific, postcolonial, and Asian American studies and who remain attentive to the continuing effects of global imperialism in these regions. I cannot pretend to possess their expertise or to command these large, overlapping fields, but I do think much of their work has been marginalized in American studies, even the new American studies I strongly advocate for its hemispheric scope, its attention to the consequences of imperialist expansion, its respect for cultural and linguistic diversity, and its concern with transcultural and transnational relations. My effort in this essay, then, is to identify some of the ways in which the new American studies might more positively address the issues raised by the new Pacific and Asian studies. I recognize that my approach risks an incorporation of the work of such area studies of the Pacific into an enveloping American studies, which might itself be understood as cultural imperialism. But I think this risk is itself worthwhile if it will help us distinguish cultural inclusiveness and attention from neoimperialist appropriation. My goal, then, is to find ways for the new Pacific studies to influence the new American studies, as well as to identify some common concerns.

The editors of this volume and the other contributors offer their own interpretations of the term "Transpacific" as a replacement of the older, now outmoded "Pacific Rim," but I want to offer my own understanding of how the term changes the scholarly study of U.S. imperialism. In addition to treating reductively a complex series of regions and routes in the Pacific, the term "Pacific Rim" employed a visual metaphor suggesting an emphasis of the "horizon" of East Asia. The Pacific Ocean and its diverse island cultures signified as means of transport—way stations in the journey between West and East. Unquestionably European and U.S. relations with East Asia were shaped by an Orientalism specific to Japan, Korea, and China, as well as to the border regions in South and Southeast Asia. Of course, there is a great deal of work still to be done to understand and challenge such Orientalism, but we must also recognize that the central attention paid to its critique in Asian studies has often resulted in another, unintentional Orientalist effect: the neglect of the multiple imperialist activities that have reshaped the Pacific island communities from nations in Europe, Asia, and the United States.

Edward Said's (1978) adaptation of the European term for the Middle East is today overused and not entirely appropriate either to East Asia or the Pacific (1–3). My intention is not to debate terminology, but instead call attention to the insular communities otherwise overlooked as we cast our gaze toward that distant horizon of the Pacific Rim. The Transpacific perspective would bring into view these different human and natural communities by first addressing the multiple colonial inscriptions of them, treating both the hybridized postcolonial societies and recovering their indigenous or migratory histories. We should not abandon too hastily this critical study of colonialism in the Pacific, because many of its communities are so shaped by these different colonial influences as to be no longer recuperable in their traditional or indigenous forms. To be sure, independence and sovereignty movements throughout the Pacific suggest diverse agency on the part of the Pacific's traditional inhabitants, but in many cases such political activism is still engaged with oppressive colonial and neocolonial practices, often ignored by the wider world.

New postcolonial scholarship in the Transpacific area will thus be concerned primarily with a continuation of the work initiated by the Asian and African nations meeting at the Bandung Conference in Indonesia in 1955. That celebrated post–World War II gathering of so-called non-aligned nations recalled longer legacies of anticolonial struggles, including the Pan-African congresses of the early twentieth century, in order to pursue postcolonial goals independent of the Big Three's one-sided declaration of "decolonization." Indeed, Great Britain, the Soviet Union, and the United States had barely announced the project of decolonization before they began to divide up the world again according to their own neoimperial ambitions. Sixty-five years after the Yalta and Potsdam conferences in which this postwar redistribution began, scholars have so thoroughly criticized such imperialism as to warrant new directions more in keeping with the agencies of the peoples once struggling as subalterns under colonial and neocolonial domination.

Valuable as I consider this new scholarship, I also am convinced we must continue to study the still operative legacies of imperialism and neoimperialism in the Pacific. Unlike the Atlantic, which at least since Paul Gilroy's *The Black Atlantic* (1993) has been reinterpreted in terms of several counternarratives to the dominant North Atlantic narrative, the Pacific has remained relatively under theorized in terms of the imperial narrative. First, the "Transpacific" region is far more difficult to conceptualize than the Atlantic, because of the Pacific's immensity both in size and complex borders. Does the Pacific "end" at the Coral Sea's and Tasman Sea's borders with the Indian Ocean, thus excluding Australia from consideration, but retaining New Zealand? Are there "primary" Transpacific routes, such as those defining the conventional "Pacific Rim" of Japan, Korea, and China by way of economic relations to the west coasts of the United States and Canada? How should we consider the North Pacific routes of Asian peoples who historically migrated by sea, Bering land bridge, or a combination of both to North America millennia before European contact, thus connecting however distantly in historical terms indigenous peoples on both sides of the Pacific? Second, such examples of the complex borders involved in any study of the Pacific region are rendered even more differential when we consider the remappings produced by imperial contestation among European, Asian, and Creole nationalists from the Western Hemisphere from the seventeenth-century voyages of global exploration to eighteenth- and early nineteenth-century colonization efforts in Asia and the Pacific to twentieth-century independence movements in the region.

The reconceptualization of the Atlantic as a series of flows and circulations, rather than as a specific geography or region, has been made explicit in recent years by cultural geographers interested in maritime "contact zones." Martin Lewis and Kären Wigen argue in *The Myth of Continents: A Critique of Metageography* (1997) that the "Continental" model for understanding the different regions of the globe has tended to reify geopolitical boundaries and neglected "the complex webs of capital and commodity exchange" that become visible when we think in terms of "oceans and bays," rather than "continents" or "cultural blocs" (1–25). Since 1998, they have conducted a multidisciplinary research project at Duke called "Oceans Connect: Culture, Capital, and Commodity Flows across Basins."[1] Interestingly, their own argument in *The Myth of Continents* tends to rely heavily on the Atlantic, even though Lewis began his career with a scholarly study of Luzon in the Philippines and Wigen is a specialist in Japan.

In many respects, the idea of theorizing regions in oceanic terms finds its most interesting applicability in the Pacific, where so many different insular communities have traditionally defined themselves and been defined by outside forces, often imperialist, in terms of the economic, cultural, political, military, and other flows they facilitate. Indeed, oceanic thinking encourages connections between indigenous and imperial contacts in ways that I think might avoid some of the potential binaries we risk in postcolonial work that tends to forget its anticolonial origins. Although I disagree with several of Lewis and Wigen's claims in *The Myth of Continents* and in some of the work that has come out of the Oceans Connect project, I want to draw on the broad conception of "oceanic" thinking to explain how my own work on Euro-American imperialism in the Pacific may have continuing relevance to Transpacific scholarship.

My interests in Transpacific studies focus on the rise of the United States as an imperial power in its nineteenth-century contestation with other European powers in the Pacific. Trained as a literary and cultural historian, I am interested most in how U.S. imperialism was understood culturally between the War of 1812 and the Spanish–American (1898) and Philippine–American (1899–1902) Wars. All of my previous work on U.S. neoimperialism in the post–World War II period, which has focused on the cultural responses to the Vietnam War (Rowe and Berg 1991) and to post-9/11 military missions in Iraq and Afghanistan (Rowe 2011), follows my initial interest in U.S. imperialism in the formative years of the U.S. nation in *Literary Culture and U.S. Imperialism: From the Revolution to World War II* (Rowe 2000).

I understand nineteenth-century U.S. expansion in and across the Pacific in terms of the expanded notion of "Manifest Destiny" elaborated by Richard Drinnon in *Facing West: The Metaphysics of Indian-Hating and Empire-Building* (1980), which remains one of the key works in American studies to articulate the relationship between "internal" and "external" colonialism (268–274). Drinnon is particularly persuasive in his critical account of Henry Adams, the well-connected American historian who seems to have little to do with the Pacific, but who actually has much to say about the proper path of U.S. expansion across the Pacific with the primary goal of gaining a U.S. "foothold in Asia," as he termed it in a letter to his brother, Brooks Adams, on November 3, 1901. Every student who has read *The Education of Henry Adams* (1973 [1907]) knows how deeply invested in European culture and politics Henry Adams was. His famous meditation on the steps of the Church of Santa Maria di Ara Coeli (a Christian church built on the foundation of an ancient Roman temple) traces all modern history back to classical Rome. Despite Adams's famous declaration of confusion and despair in not understanding what that history meant, his Eurocentrism is unavoidable and urgent: "Rome was actual; it was England; it was going to be America" (91).

But ancient Rome had not expanded across the Pacific as England had done in the eighteenth and nineteenth centuries with the United States following, annexing extensive territory from the Philippines to Hawai'i, American Samoa, and Guam in the late nineteenth and early twentieth centuries. Henry Adams was by no means naive or just old-fashioned. His close relationship with Secretary of State John Hay, Adams's close friend and neighbor (they occupied two "semi-detached mansions" designed by the famed architect Henry Hobson Richardson, located just across the street from the White House, where today's Hay-Adams Hotel stands) put him in direct, daily conversations with the architect of U.S. foreign policy in the Pacific and Asia in the late nineteenth and early twentieth centuries. There is little question that Adams understood profoundly the importance of the Pacific Rim to what he considered the British and U.S. inheritance of the Roman legacy: an imperial destiny, after all (Rowe 2000, 165–176).

Traditional scholars of Henry Adams had little to say about his travels to the South Pacific and Japan in 1890–1891 with his close friend, the artist John La Farge, except to comment on Adams's "flight" from the tragedy of his wife, Marion Hooper Adams's suicide in 1885. But the trip that produced Adams's odd, privately printed volume, *Memoirs of Maura Taaroa, Last Queen of Tahiti* (1893) and La Farge's exquisitely illustrated and Orientalist *An Artist's Letters from Japan* (1897) was more than just some junket for wealthy Americans, but part of the developing U.S. foreign policy narrative that would lead through Tahiti to Japan and to the colonial wars in Vietnam so many years later. Adams's memoir is a "fictionalized autobiography" that betrays his deeply ethnocentric assumptions about Pacific "primitivism" and the need for the enlightenment Anglo-American civilization would bring.[2] With its anxieties about mixed race genealogies, its reliance on European "heritage" and "values," Adams's family history is a small, but important, testament to the Pacific's role in U.S. expansionism in the period culminating in the Spanish–American and Philippine–American Wars.

What John Hay advocated was "free-trade" and his brand of modern U.S. imperialism depended on the argument that all foreign policy decisions should be shaped by free-trade ideology. Nearly a century before Hay formulated U.S. foreign policy in these terms, Captain David Porter attempted to annex the Marquesas Islands—he would have renamed them the "Washington Islands"—for the United States while he cruised the Pacific attempting to harass British shipping during the War of 1812. His effort was nearly our first extraterritorial annexation by legal fiat, had it not been that President Madison and other government officials missed his dispatch because they were fleeing a White House set on fire by British forces. What Porter wanted in the Marquesas was only nominally a "naval station," a "foothold" in Polynesia, or even trade with the local Happars and Taipi tribal peoples. He wanted most of all some symbolic status in the ongoing struggle of the European and Russian powers for colonial influence in the Transpacific region, already imagining that the next great stage of colonial contestation would be Asia. Melville's *Typee, a Peep at Polynesian Life* (1846) is a wonderful nineteenth-century account of how Porter's Marquesan misadventures are linked with European colonialism and U.S. colonialism at home. Many have read Melville's novel as an allegory of the fugitive-slave narrative and still others have interpreted it as a thinly disguised criticism of U.S. policies toward Native Americans.[3]

Less frequently remarked upon is Melville's connection of the Marquesas with the growing U.S. involvement in the Hawai'ian islands in the 1840s, a subject Mark Twain would take up more vigorously in his concluding sections of *Roughing It* (1872), as the United States meddled more directly in the colonial instabilities and internal politics of Hawai'i as it moved toward annexation of the islands. I won't recount here the complex use Melville makes in *Typee* of Captain Cook's fate—both his death and the much-rumored fate of his body—in order to offer what seems to me a very profound indictment of how the United States would follow and improve upon the "cultural" arguments used to justify British colonialism, except to note that this transformation of "traditional" imperialism (exemplified by the British) into "neoimperialism" (exemplified by the United States) is extremely evident in the nineteenth-century Transpacific and yet still relatively understudied. Reenacted in several nineteenth-century theatrical productions, Cook's death was quickly mytholo-gized in Great Britain and the United States as a "tragic" encounter between the "modern" explorer and the "primitive" native, even though the most likely ex-planation of Cook's death is his ignorance of Hawai'ian cultural and religious practices (Hough 341–355, 362–371).

In *Island World: A History of Hawai'i and the United States* (2008), Gary Okihiro provides a counternarrative, in which the Hawai'ian influences on the shaping of the U.S. nation are given priority. In many respects, Okihiro pro-vides a theoretical model for further studies of the Transpacific, insofar as he reads the continental United States from the perspectives of the maritime and Pacific islands, stressing the impact the latter have had on the U.S. nation. Re-covering the history of how Hawai'ian immigrants lived in nineteenth-century California, fought in the Civil War, served as sailors on nineteenth-century New England whalers and commercial vessels, Okihiro emphasizes what Sara Johnson (2012) terms the "transcolonial imagination" at the height of Western nationalism. We should not forget, however, that the history Okihiro recounts cannot be separated from its imperial entanglements. Hawai'ians traveled more widely in the United States as American economic, political, and religious interests in the islands grew; the dialectical relationship must be understood to avoid a simple interpretation of the evils of Western imperialism and the vic-timization of Pacific islanders.

The annexation of the Hawai'ian islands by the United States in 1898 was motivated in part by the desire to control commercial routes that would serve, among other far-flung enterprises, the ill-fated Klondike Gold Rush. In *China Men* (1980), Maxine Kingston links "The Great Grandfather of the Sandalwood Mountains" with "Alaska China Men," reminding us that the geographically disparate ventures of sugar-cane and pineapple agribusiness in Hawai'i and the Yukon Gold Rush are not only linked by way of Chinese workers, but also by the logic of U.S. neoimperialism (121–149, 159–162). Much as Kingston condemns the mistreatment of Chinese immigrants during the period of Chinese exclusion, she also recognizes the complicity of these same Chinese workers in the sorts of racial marginalization that would condemn Native Americans and African Americans to subaltern positions, subject not only to economic and social exploitation but often to social death and outright murder. Witnessing executions of Native Americans in Dawson on Douglas Island, Chinese miners were expelled from the Yukon by the judgment of the miner's meetings, then rowed out by local Native Americans to a ship in the harbor, where the Captain of the ship promised to "take them home," only to have them agree: " 'Yes, . . . Take us home . . . to Douglas Island,' " where they would ignore their exploitation, their conflicts with other racialized and excluded minorities, Native Americans, and still look, as their fathers had hunted in the Sierra, for the yellow metal that makes men crazy, to paraphrase Nick Black Elk (Kingston 1980, 161).

Kingston's fictional reconstruction of Chinese immigration to the United States complicates further Okihiro's efforts to recognize Hawai'ian contributions to U.S. nationalism and modernity. Oppressed by the Manchu dynasty in China, worked as virtual slaves by colonial agribusiness in Hawai'i, legally excluded from citizenship and basic civil liberties in the United States, nineteenth-century Chinese immigrants also contributed importantly to U.S. modernization, whose expansionist logic also rendered these Chinese immigrants legally invisible and economically poor. The history of Hawai'i is one important example of how our study of the Transpacific often involves multiple imperialisms and thus several distinctly exploited groups.

Three other issues in Transpacific studies are of both historical and continuing relevance when viewed in terms of the cultural history of U.S. imperialism. The Philippine–American War is still neglected in American studies, despite wonderful new work on Philippine-American writers and culture from Bulosan to Hagedorn. Students do not even know we fought such a war against republican insurgents encouraged by the U.S. defeat of the Spanish empire. Philippine scholars like Dylan Rodriguez (2009) and Susan Harris (2011) have done remarkable work, but American studies continues to pay only the vaguest lip service to this unrecognized war and the "postcolonial" situation of the Philippines from the capture of Aguinaldo to the exile of the Marcoses. The extent to which the Philippines remain a U.S. client state is still neglected in scholarly debates. In the U.S. health care industry alone, Philippine immigrants, many with medical degrees from Philippine universities, are denied certification, forced to retake courses of study in U.S. institutions, and often relegated to positions of part-time "home care" givers with far more expertise than their U.S. equivalents. Today's Philippine-American health care workers are in many respects the late-modern heirs of the Piñoy agricultural workers whose exploitation

Carlos Bulosan famously criticizes in *America Is in the Heart* (1973 [1946]). Public debates in the United States regarding immigration reform hardly ever address these crises facing middle-class, well-educated Philippine immigrants, reinforcing the impression that "immigration issues" revolve around unskilled laborers from Mexico, Central America, and China.

What Chalmers Johnson (2004) has termed the U.S. "empire of bases" needs to be expanded to include specific studies of the Mariana Islands (Guam, Saipan, Tinian, et al.), American Samoa, and other U.S. military bases in the Pacific and Asia that serve the larger colonial purposes Johnson understands by the legal, territorial, and social boundaries established by the U.S. military (151–186). U.S. military zones surrounding U.S. bases in Japan, for example, are outside Japanese jurisdiction and governed by the U.S. military command through its Military Police and Judge Adjutant General's authority. Workers in bars, restaurants, houses of prostitution, and other enterprises flourishing on the edges of U.S. military bases are thus protected not by Japanese law, but by U.S. military law. Immigrants to Japan who often work in such poorly paid, easily exploited jobs are thus doubly mistreated in this shadow economy and have little recourse in the U.S. military legal system, which certainly favors its own personnel and English-language fluency (C. Johnson 2004, 137–143). Many of these migrant workers in the sex and entertainment industries come from other Pacific regions, such as the Philippines, and can thus be legally and economically marginalized both by the Japanese and U.S. governments. In addition, some immigrants are often caught between the cultural and social conventions of the host country and the U.S. military (Parreñas 2008).

The long history of different colonial conflicts in the Pacific has usually included U.S. participation from Porter's excursion in the Marquesas during the War of 1812 to the present, despite our tendency to think of U.S. neoimperialism as a recent phenomenon, developed primarily in the aftermath of the Cold War. Saipan was the principal airbase for the air force bombers that targeted Japanese cities during World War II, and the *Enola Gay* took off from Tinian Island on August 6, 1945, on its mission to drop the atomic bomb on Hiroshima at the end of the war, as would the other B-29, *Bockscar*, which three days later dropped an atomic bomb on Nagasaki. Guam became a U.S. territory at the end of the Spanish–American War, was occupied by the Japanese in 1914, then again during World War II until U.S. troops reoccupied the island in 1944 after fierce fighting.

Following the Gilbert and Marshall Islands campaign during World War II (1944), the U.S. military established a large military base on Wake Island (Enen-kio) in the Marshall Islands. Atomic testing on the island of Bikini

(Pikinni) Atoll in the Marshall Islands from 1946–1958 contaminated the atoll with Cesium-123. In 1979, the Republic of the Marshall Islands (RMI) achieved its independence from the United States, operating from 1979 to 1986 under a "Compact of Free Association" with the United States and then ratified in 1990 as an independent republic by the United Nations (UN). Nevertheless, the U.S. military still occupies Wake Island, despite the RMI's claim to it. And despite international appeals for clean-up of the toxic waste on Bikini Atoll, the United States has done nothing to repair the environmental and human damage left from the detonation of twenty-three nuclear devices on the atoll. In addition to the U.S. military base on Wake Island, the United States maintains a missile-testing range on Kwajalein Atoll within sovereign RMI territory.

The Transpacific can thus not be imagined apart from this long, continuing use of the Pacific islands by diverse imperial interests, which stretch from Spanish, Portuguese, French, English, and Dutch ventures in the region from the seventeenth to the end of the nineteenth century and include German, Japanese, and United States claims in the later nineteenth to first half of the twentieth centuries. More careful scholarly accounts would include contested claims by South American nations to Pacific islands, such as Chile's military occupation of Juan Fernandez and Ecuador's annexation of the Galápagos Islands in 1832 (subsequently donating them to the UN as a World Heritage Site). Modern nations, territories, protectorates, and other geopolitical designations in the Pacific may in many cases have achieved "postcolonial" status of various kinds, but the legacies of imperial definition are profound and not easily dismissed. From the Spanish, English, French, and other imperial "names" given to islands often with their own indigenous names to economies and political processes deeply dependent on their previous colonial rulers, many islands in the Pacific are the means of broader military and commercial ventures across the Pacific, rather than ends in themselves.

I have only briefly alluded to the much more complex history of U.S. annexation of the Hawai'ian Islands and U.S. involvement in modern Philippine politics, in part to stress how these smaller, usually forgotten insular ventures are part of that larger history in which the United States has been involved since its inception. When considered merely as discrete entities, small, under-populated islands like the Marshall Islands hardly deserve our attention in the already crowded liberal arts curriculum. But when understood as crucial parts in the larger movement of the United States across the Pacific to gain a "foothold in Asia," these neglected areas gain significance not only in the study of U.S. imperialism but also in terms of their own struggles for cultural identity and geopolitical sovereignty. There is historical continuity linking the Plains

Wars in the late nineteenth century with the U.S. role in the Philippine–American War and the Taping Rebellion and Boxer Rebellion in China, as Drinnon (1980, 250–258) has pointed out. Of course, if we equate the indigenous revolts of the Lakota Sioux (among others) with those of Aguinaldo in the Philippines or Hung Hsu-Ch'üan (1812/13–1864), the Christian mystic who led the Taiping Rebellion, we will repeat the racist rhetoric of U.S. troops who called Philippine insurgents "Indians" in the Philippine–American War.

But the connections established by U.S. imperialism have had real consequences on colonized and postcolonial communities across the Pacific. The U.S. decision to use nuclear weapons to defeat the Japanese in World War II not only is related to later atomic testing in the Marshall Islands in our Cold War struggle for military supremacy over the Soviet Union, but it connects perversely the Marianas (to which Guam and Saipan belong) with the Marshall Islands' Bikini/Pikinni Atoll. Environmental damage from military testing or just occupation also gives the inhabitants on these islands common cause to protest and work toward reform, reparation, and environmental restoration. European, Asian, and U.S. imperialist ventures in the Pacific not only provide a shared history of oppression and desire for postcolonial independence, but they have created shared conditions that can enable such coordinated, transnational organization for reform. Thus local struggles against U.S. military imperialism in Japan and the Korean Peninsula inevitably are connected with similar efforts in the Philippines and the smaller Pacific island republics hosting U.S. military bases.

Such coalitions of "non-aligned nations" were the goals of the Bandung Conference and remain worthy purposes in today's inequitable processes of globalization. Understanding the specific complaints and thus histories of colonized and occupied communities across the Pacific should include our broader interpretation of how such imperial and neoimperial practices have contributed to the long history of European, Asian, and U.S. expansionism. As I have suggested in this essay, there is a direct historical line connecting U.S. involvement in the Taiping Rebellion, the Boxer Rebellion, the Chinese Exclusion Acts, the Spanish–American and Philippine–American Wars, the Portsmouth (New Hampshire) Treaty concluding the Russo–Japanese War, World War I, World War II, the postwar Occupation of Japan, the Korean War, support of the French in the Indochina Wars, the Vietnam War, our invasion of and ongoing military presence in Iraq, and our current occupation of Afghanistan and deep involvement in Pakistan's politics and military campaigns against dissidents. When connected with this larger history, the people and ecosystems of the Pacific islands become visible and relevant, as do their challenges to such alternative forms of imperialism as operation of foreign military bases in their territory, often with questionable or archaic rights of access.

Indeed, the general issue of how and when the U.S. government acquired leases to land and facilities for military uses needs to be studied in detail. From Guantanamo in Cuba to Clark Air Base and the U.S. Naval Station in Subic Bay in the Philippines, U.S. military installations have been contested and challenged by local political leaders. In the Philippines, the nearly century-old U.S. military bases were closed in 1991, although U.S. efforts to establish new military bases have led to U.S. political interference between the Philippine government and the dissident Moro Islamic Liberation Front (MILF). Since 2006, rumors have circulated that the United States has been in negotiations with the MILF to trade rights to military bases in territory it controls in exchange for help in concluding a favorable peace treaty with the Philippine government (Scarpello 2006). Not until the U.S. military base at Guantanamo Bay, Cuba, was used for "terrorist detainees"—in order to avoid Geneva Convention provisions requiring legal due process for such prisoners of war, if held within the United States—did the American public pay much attention to this long-established lease agreement between the United States and Cuban governments. The lease is traceable back to U.S. efforts in the late nineteenth century to acquire a naval base in the Caribbean to control shipping in the region in anticipation of the construction of the Panama Canal. Rejected by the Haitian government in its efforts to lease, buy, or simply "annex" Môle St. Nicolas, the large natural harbor on the northwest coast of Haiti, the United States looked to Cuba for a military base in the Caribbean.

In 2009, six Uighur men who were held in Guantanamo as Chinese dissidents, charged along with other Uighurs in terrorist acts in China, were sent by the Obama administration to the tiny island nation of Palau, composed of 200 islands (only 10 of which are inhabited) about 400 miles southeast of the Philippines. Other Uighur detainees in Guantanamo have balked at being relocated to Palau, but the Obama administration paid Palau $200 million to house these six detainees (Magistad 2010). Viewed by most Americans as simply another instance of how difficult it would be to relocate the Guantanamo detainees, the removal of the Uighurs to Palau is by no means an exceptional path of migration between the Caribbean and Pacific. Nineteenth-century Chinese immigrants, often drawn from those who had already worked in Hawai'i, were imported to work as virtual slaves on the uninhabited "guano islands" of the Caribbean. The rich deposits of bird guano were a valuable fertilizer in the nineteenth century, but the labor and life on these islands for imported Chinese laborers were at the very limits of human existence. In short, migrations and diasporas from the Caribbean to the Pacific are stark reminders of the consequences of Euro-American imperialism in the Western Hemisphere and the Pacific.

Finally, the comparative cultural, political, and legal study of Maori (New Zealand), Aboriginal peoples and Torres Straits' Islanders (Australia), and North American Native Americans needs to be included in any theorization of Transpacific studies and our continuing work on the consequences of modern imperialism. Considered in "oceanic," rather than "continental," terms, indigenous rights in New Zealand, Australia, and North America are closely related not only by respective appeals to legal precedents but also by shared indigenous arguments regarding their original rights to land ownership. In the United States, the 1831 decision *Cherokee Nation v. Georgia* of the John Marshall Supreme Court declared Native American tribes to constitute "domestic dependent nations." In the earlier Supreme Court decision in *Johnson v. McIntosh* (1823), the Court attempted to solve the problem of who owned the land by declaring native peoples mere "occupants" replaced by European "ownership" established by conquest and use, effectively converting indigenous "'owners of discovered lands into tenants on those lands'" (Lindsay Robertson quoted in Calloway 2008, 268).

In Australia, the British used the legal doctrine of *terra nullius*—literally Latin for "no land"—to contend that the Aboriginal inhabitants of the Continent did not own the land because they did not enclose it and thus use it productively, despite evidence that different Aboriginal communities traditionally granted each other seasonal access to their lands for purposes of hunting and gathering. Indeed, many Aboriginal leaders assumed that British settlers who requested land for farming and grazing were merely doing so on such unpaid lease arrangements, rather than actually settling permanently on Aboriginal lands. *Terra nullius* prevailed as a legal doctrine until 1992, when the celebrated Eddie Mabo case, first brought in the 1950s against the Australian government, was finally settled in favor of Mabo, who had in the meantime died. Even that case depended on establishing very clear indigenous claims to enclosed property, thus affirming the British principle of land ownership, because Mabo was a Murray Islander in the Torres Straits Islands, where islanders had for millennia enclosed land. In fact, Mabo's legal suit was based on the enclosure of his kitchen garden, but it did at least establish the concept of indigenous enclosure, even if the larger issue that different land uses than European enclosure might establish "property rights" was ignored in the final decision. Nevertheless, the Mabo victory in 1992 effectively overturned *terra nullius,* although not before more than two centuries' devastation of Australian aboriginal cultures, including the forced removal of Aboriginals and Torres Strait Islanders from their traditional homelands and the imprisonment of many in remote internment camps, often on inhospitable islands, like Flinders Island in the Bass Straits (between Tasmania and Australia), or the concerted efforts to exterminate Aboriginals as the Tasmanians did in the so-called "Black War" of the 1830s (Reynolds 2000, 186–189). *Terra nullius* probably influenced John Marshall as he framed his Supreme Court decisions in the 1820s and 1830s regarding Native American land rights; North American legal precedents and treaties justifying indigenous removal certainly influenced subsequent Australian decisions regarding the civil, economic, and legal rights of Aboriginal peoples and Torres Strait Islanders. Yet Australia barely figures in most U.S. university curricula and is rarely discussed in American studies scholarship, except as a distant analogy or comparison state.

There are, of course, countless other, equally complex indigenous rights issues to be studied in "Transpacific" terms, including not just the many different insular peoples of the Pacific but also indigenous peoples of Japan, China, Korea, Tibet, Nepal, Mongolia, and other regions in Asia with historical, legal, or just "universal" ties to the indigenous rights of those living in Canada and the Americas. Indeed, those six Uighurs languishing now on Palau and their comrades on Guantanamo are examples of indigenous rights dissidents cast far and wide across the Pacific and the Western Hemisphere as a consequence of the displacements of Euro-American imperialism. In particular, then, "Transpacific studies" should include centrally "indigenous" rights; just how we read the rights and cultural issues of the indigenous peoples "in the way" of European and U.S. imperialism will tell the real story of our research in the coming years.

The differences among indigenous peoples in the Pacific region should also remind us that "oceans disconnect" even more than they "connect." Thinking in oceanic, rather than continental, terms should also encourage us to articulate social, political, environmental, and human differences sustained by the *separation* of land masses by the oceans. Lewis and Wigen are thus not entirely correct to stress the "contact zones" of the world's oceans while ignoring the ineluctable fact that oceans disconnect in ways that produce dramatically different ecosystems. In *Following the Equator* (1897), Twain notes how the Australian platypus "was never in the Ark" and makes hash of Darwinian theories of evolution (105). Its status as a monotreme (neither fish nor fowl!) threw nineteenth-century European natural science into such disarray that some naturalists insisted the platypus must be a "hoax," not a real animal. Scientific efforts to study *Ornithorhyncus anatinus* almost drove the shy creature to extinction in the nineteenth century, as the wry Twain himself acknowledges when he notes that while in New Zealand his host "gave me an ornithorhyncus, and I am taming it," a considerable challenge even for this great satirist (301)!

Some scholars might argue that in the era of air travel, satellites, and such related technologies as the Internet, "oceanic" thinking, whether focused on contacts in maritime flows or on the differences such distances between communities create, is archaic and easily overcome. But when considered in ecocultural terms, oceanic thinking also stresses our profound dependence on the health of oceans, the different global environments those maritime zones nurture, and common debt we have to the entire system of natural differences that is the true source of productivity, wealth, and health. We live in an era in which overfishing and climate change have threatened immediately the health of our oceans. The Fijian government at the last Summit on Climate Change in Copenhagen argued that the rising level of the Pacific threatened the very existence of its nation. In 2009, the Alliance of Small Island States (AOSIS) joined the Least Developed Countries (LDCs) Group to create a coalition of some eighty countries advocating that the UN set a limit of 1.5° centigrade global temperature increase per year—a limit so far ignored by most First World, highly industrialized nations. AOSIS includes such small island states as the Seychelles Islands in the Indian Ocean and the Marianas and the Fiji Islands in the Pacific. Yet the history and contemporary global concerns of these island states hardly figure in liberal education, except as the conventional "Pacific Rim" that has traditionally designated one-way globalization and the seemingly ceaseless upward spiral of capitalist need. One way to resist such a limited conception of the Pacific is to understand the many different ways the communities of the Pacific have affirmed their own cultural, political, and economic identities, and a related critical part of that counternarrative is our scholarly articulation of the ongoing European, Asian, and U.S. imperialism in the Transpacific region.

In conclusion, we should not assume that the disappearance of overt institutions and practices of imperial domination from the Pacific leaves us simply with postcolonial struggles for sovereignty and cultural self-representation. Decolonization is still an activist agenda, which depends on alliances among globally situated activists. Commercial exploitation of minerals and other natural resources on the Pacific seabed threatens not only the Pacific islands but the continental mainlands. The legacies of imperialism are historically long and culturally deep; they are as visible in the tattooing practices of Samoan Christians as they are in the tourism of Waikiki Beach and the Uighurs wandering a bit bewildered on the shores of Palau. Imperialism, indigeneity, and migration/diaspora all must be read together in their layered simultaneity; they are the currents of the Transpacific region.

Notes to Chapter 5: Transpacific Studies and the Cultures of U.S. Imperialism

1. The Oceans Connect project is part of the Center for International Studies at Duke University.

2. Although technically an autobiography, it is printed under Adams's authorship, as if he were the Western anthropologist recording the "testimony" of his native informant.

3. See Rowe (2000, 77–96).

References

Adams, Henry. 1893. *Memoirs of Marau Taaroa, Last Queen of Tahiti.* Washington, DC: Privately printed.

———. 1973 [1907]. *The Education of Henry Adams,* ed. Ernest Samuels and Jayne N. Samuels. Boston: Houghton Mifflin.

Brickhouse, Anna. 2004. *Transamerican Literary Relations and the Nineteenth-Century Public Sphere.* New York: Cambridge University Press.

Bulosan, Carlos. 1973. *America Is in the Heart.* Seattle: University of Washington Press.

Calloway, Colin G. 2008. *First Peoples: A Documentary Survey of American Indian History.* 3rd ed. Boston: Bedford/St. Martin's.

Camacho, Keith L. 2010. *Cultures of Commemoration: The Politics of War, Memory and History in the Mariana Islands.* Honolulu: University of Hawai'i Press.

Camacho, Keith L., Cynthia Enloe, and Setsu Shigematsu, eds. 2010. *Militarized Currents: Toward a Decolonized Future in Asia and the Pacific.* Minneapolis: University of Minnesota Press.

Drinnon, Richard. 1980. *Facing West: The Metaphysics of Indian-Hating and Empire-Building.* Minneapolis: University of Minnesota Press.

Gilroy, Paul. 1993 *The Black Atlantic: Modernity and Double Consciousness.* Cambridge, MA: Harvard University Press.

Harris, Susan K. 2011. *God's Arbiters: Americans and the Philippines, 1898–1902.* New York: Oxford University Press.

Hereniko, Vilson, Rob Wilson, and Patricia Grace, eds. 2012. *Inside Out: Literature, Cultural Politics and the New Pacific.* London: Rowman and Littlefield.

Hough, Richard. 1997. *Captain James Cook: A Biography.* New York: W. W. Norton.

Johnson, Chalmers. 2004. *The Sorrows of Empire: Militarism, Secrecy, and the End of the Republic.* New York: Henry Holt.

Johnson, Sara. 2012. *The Fear of French Negroes: Migration, Struggle and the Transcolonial Imagination in the Age of Revolution.* Berkeley: University of California Press.

Kingston, Maxine Hong. 1980. *China Men.* New York: Random House.

La Farge, John. 1897. *An Artist's Letters from Japan.* New York: Century.

Lewis, Martin, and Kären Wigen. 1997. *The Myth of Continents: A Critique of Meta-geography.* Berkeley: University of California Press.

Magistad, Mary Kay. 2010. "Life in Palau after Guantanamo." *PRI's The World,* 10 March.

Okihiro, Gary Y. 2008. *Island World: A History of Hawai'i and the United States.* Berkeley: University of California Press.

Parreñas, Rhacel. 2008. *The Force of Domesticity: Filipina Migrants and Globalization.* New York: New York University Press.

Perez, Craig Santos. 2010. *From Unincorporated Territory [Saina].* Richmond, CA: Omnidawn Publishing.

Reynolds, Henry. 2000. *Why Weren't We Told? A Personal Search for the Truth about Our History.* Ringwood, Victoria: Penguin Books Australia.

Rodriguez, Dylan. 2009. *Suspended Apocalypse: White Supremacy, Genocide, and the Filipino Condition.* Minneapolis: University of Minnesota Press.

Rowe, John Carlos. 2000. *Literary Culture and U.S. Imperialism: From the Revolution to World War II.* New York: Oxford University Press.

———. 2011. *The Cultural Politics of the New American Studies.* London: Open Humanities Press.

Rowe, John Carlos, and Rick Berg, eds. 1991. *The Vietnam War and American Culture.* New York: Columbia University Press.

Said, Edward. 1978. *Orientalism.* New York: Random House.

Scarpello, Fabio. 2006. "US, Philippines Weigh New Military Marriage." *Asia Times Online,* 23 December. http://www.atimes.com/atimes/Southeast_Asia/HH23Ae01.html (accessed January 29, 2014).

Twain, Mark. 1897. *Following the Equator: A Journey around the World.* Hartford, CT: American Publishing Company.

Wilson, Rob. 2000. *Reimagining the American Pacific: From "South Pacific" to Bamboo Ridge and Beyond.* Durham, NC: Duke University Press.

6

Passionate Attachments to Area Studies and Asian American Studies

Subjectivity and Diaspora in the Transpacific

J. FRANCISCO BENITEZ AND LAURIE J. SEARS

This essay links ideas of race and gender with the changing fields of Southeast Asian studies and American ethnic studies, as fields situated between the rise of scholarship from the region and the growing interest of Southeast Asian-American students and activists in their diasporic histories. We suggest that intersectionality—the systemic conjunction of various forms of social inequality—particularly in racialized gender and gendered racialization, requires a critical interpretive strategy that maintains the critique of conditions of imperial and national subjection while foregrounding the limits of subject formation in knowledge production. Gendered bodies are also marginalized bodies and both women and men suffer "intrusive intimacies" in the form of sexual transgressions in the novels we discuss below. Focusing on the field of representations and equal recognition tactically requires the subordination of one kind of representation over another in the need to mobilize a community against oppression or marginalization. Thus Kimberlé Crenshaw (1989) points out that the debates over racism often obstruct the critique of sexism. Engaging in a war of positions requires attention to particular institutions and social fields whose boundaries are in fact porous and often intersect. Chela Sandoval's (2000) notion of U.S. Third World feminism provides a guide for how differential consciousness, "a cruising, migrant, improvisational mode of subjectivity," of those deemed to lack the cultural capital of the nation-state overlaps with what she calls the "oppositional consciousness" of anticolonial liberation movements (180).[1] Such consciousness calls for collaborative and hybrid thought beyond the confines of the nation-state. We propose to explore racial subjectivity through a methodology of "critical melancholia," which allows us to examine the intersection of various forms of social inequality and how these forms have been problematized in area and ethnic studies.

Critical Melancholia and Race in the Transpacific

In *The Melancholy of Race* (2000), Anne Anlin Cheng asks: "Is there any *getting over* race?" Cheng questions why psychoanalysis and philosophy consider a notion of mourning that successfully kills off the lost object as normative, and melancholia that keeps the lost object alive as pathological. In this light, we read Cheng as suggesting there is no getting over race, and Freud's idea of "working through" does not/cannot work through race without positing a privileged white nonpathological norm. Thus an attitude of critical melancholia is perhaps the most realistic option for thinking about race, gender, and privilege in the twenty-first century (Cheng 2000).[2] As a complement to Cheng's ideas on the failure of "working through" to carve out new possibilities for racial, ethnic, and gendered subjects who move across and within the transpacific, Jean Laplanche has expanded upon Freud's idea of deferred action—James Strachey's Standard Edition translation—or "afterwardsness" (G. *Nachträglichkeit*) as Laplanche himself prefers to translate it. Messages given in early childhood by caregivers/motherers/punishers leave a trace, what Lacanians call an "enigmatic signifier." These messages implant ideas, and these ideas—"intrusive intimacies" in Laplanche's terms (1999)—must be retranslated in new ways before anyone can "work through" race, gender, or other forms of subaltern identity and marginalization.

Racial melancholia would necessarily be the awareness of the open secret of racial difference that cannot and ought not to be surmounted. Melancholia has a similar structure to modernity's subject in so far as it opens up a contradiction of the split subject always in process/on trial without apparent foundation or essence. Racial melancholia becomes our awareness of the liminality of racialized bodies to the normative structures that constitute hierarchies and social maps in various locations. Always othering bodies to the norm, racialization fixes meaning only in relation to this often unmarked norm. The melancholia keeps the need for commemoration ongoing, insists on tarrying with the negative rather than providing us with the moment of retranslation or transformation. It foregrounds our passionate attachments to the affirmative powers of culture while insisting on the utopic impulse of our desires to get beyond that which we cannot work through and the conditions of our subjection that make our subjectivity even possible (Butler 1997, ch. 3). It is, we suggest, the condition through which racialized bodies and persons must negotiate and live within imperial formations, discussed below. What do these questions of psychoanalysis, melancholia, and subjectivity bring to debates over area studies and American ethnic studies? Scholars and subjects of area studies and Asian American studies are not marginal to questions of psychoanalysis and imperial formations. They are rather at the heart of them. We suggest that Lisa Lowe's call in *Immigrant Acts* (1996) to understand the heterogeneity, hybridity, and multiplicity of Asian America can best be understood when articulated with studies such as Malaysian historian Sumit Mandal's interrogation of racialization in Malaysia (Lowe 1996, ch. 3; Mandal 2004). In the complex struggles over and against national subjection and belonging, ethnonationalist racisms moving from Southeast Asian and into Asian American discourses on race often reconfigure differences, thus erasing distinctions between Ilocano and Cebuano, Javanese and Sundanese, or Chinese and Singaporean. Such ethnic biases, reconfigurations, and erasures have much to offer when studied together. American ethnic studies and area studies are entwined because of the overlapping time of their emergence as scholarly discourses, and both are affected by similar "enigmatic signifiers" or traces left by U.S. imperial desires. Both came into focus and scholarly prominence at the same moment of the 1960s, in the imperial context of the Euro-American Cold War and the hot wars of Vietnam, Cambodia, and Laos—a time period that also saw the rise of new movements around feminist, ethnic, racial, and sexual identities. Both scholarly discourses emerged out of the ferment of these new imperial formations, and both included places and peoples to be studied as marginal and/or exotic, often as objects, only sometimes as subjects. While area studies was a government response to the pressures of the Cold War and thus directed by the state, ethnic studies arose out of activist struggles for academic recognition and inclusion. Both academic fields have had fraught and complex relations with U.S. nation- and empire-building.

How are U.S. area studies changing in the face of these challenges? How has the return of the (repressed) awareness of the United States as an empire affected ethnic studies' long-standing but often forgotten critique of American exceptionalism? How are interdisciplinary and disciplinary methodologies adapting to these changes? Conversations between area studies and ethnic studies are opening up as the diasporic and cosmopolitan routes of travel put more and more subjects in motion, and the insights from each field unsettle the other. To understand how diasporic communities and narrations destabilize the notion of "home" and foreground the "unhomed" or the "multihomed" as conditions of everyday life, we use literary texts from Southeast Asia and Asian America to open up and display these melancholic wounds. Examples from Filipino American author Jessica Hagedorn's and Indonesian author Ayu Utami's novels present characters who travel back and forth between and within Asian and American imperial formations. The novels suggest that individual subjectivity and identity can fade and alter in particular gendered and racial formations, as people move or are pushed into the diasporic trajectories of postcolonial imperial fields. One such field is the "transpacific," whose outlines and possibilities this essay traces.

Can the "Transpacific" Encompass Area and Ethic Studies?

Like the idea of the "transpacific," transnational studies that cross conventional area studies' arbitrary borders, and especially the separation of area studies and Asian American studies, are interdisciplinary and timely, but they might also call scholars of area studies and Asian American studies away from situated knowledges and their potential political commitments to local fields of struggle.[3] Clearly juridical formations like passports, global taxation, and the like, maintain the bounded seriality that can be counted, stored, and retrieved, in Benedict Anderson's terms. Thus, while Masao Miyoshi (1998, 1996) argues that from the point of view of global capitalism, transnationalism erodes the sovereignty and the efficacy of the institutions and narratives of nation-states, Linda Basch and her colleagues (2000) argue that from the point of view of transmigrants and their social practices and labor, the transmigrants have to negotiate within the power structures of the various nation-states and take part in multiple nation-building projects across the borders of social fields. From this view, transnationalism may actually reinforce these structures as state apparatuses by calling for the laborers that follow flows of capital. The pathways and networks of these flows become the necessary conditions of labor's own productivity and mobility within empire. Transnationalism in this case shades off into diasporic communities in which migrants dwell "with a difference."[4] Implicit in this argument is the transmigrants' need for community and identity in order to function in the multiple social fields that they inhabit. The affective relations upon which sociality depends turn the "nation" into a floating signifier—a signifier with contingent attachments—for a communal formation whose signified shifts and changes. Thus, as the subjectivities constructed in Southeast Asian and Asian American narratives lose their attachments rooted to place, those same subjectivities, and the different forces that hold them together at different times, are effaced in different ways. What do they gain in the process of forming new subjectivities and attachments? Do some only fade into spaces of postcolonial melancholia, like Hagedorn's Rizalina discussed below? What questions about the ethics of sociality and community do they foreground? What social and critical practices do they engender? What kinds of postfoundational and postessentialist hermeneutics are available to scholars in the face of urgent political demands? How do our own academic enclosures within the global imperial field make our productions of knowledge of service to what Pierre Bourdieu and Loïc Wacquant have called the "cunning of imperialist reason" (1999)? What sort of transnational collaborations can remain attuned to emergent social forces and blocs whose interactions are producing new intellectual constellations today?

Cosmopolitan routes of travel that have imperial provenances and that we pass through as scholars, transmigrants, refugees, or tourists refigure acts of "knowing" in postcolonial and feminist studies of Southeast Asia. The study of what happens to people who are in motion in the transpacific will tell us much about the future directions of the field. Not only because subjects of Southeast Asian studies are moving as fast as those who study them, but also because current conditions require continuous reassessments of hermeneutical assumptions about the "subject" and subjectivity. Identity formations are continually changing as the subjects and the objects of Southeast Asian studies are caught between global and local governmentalities and conflicting subject positions. Our vision of travel and collaboration would take the elite doubled-vision of Benedict Anderson's (1998) specter (or demon) of comparisons and turn it back on itself, highlighting the haunted visions of those left behind, as well as providing the doubled vision for those nonelites who travel (2). Thus rather than elites who have been to Europe and begin to see their lives in the region haunted by their European experiences, mothers who leave the Philippines to seek work in Mainland Southeast Asia, Europe, or the Middle East are haunted by visions of their children and families left behind even as they take care of other people's children elsewhere. Such haunting visions from elsewhere, "intrusive intimacies" that persist after travel and displacement, resist full deterritorialization. They affectively reterritorialize mobile subjects into diasporic communities and transnational social fields—an old dilemma given new urgency and intensity with contemporary imperial infrastructures of transportation, communication, and finance. We suggest that a critical melancholic method that recognizes the contradictions and strategic essentialisms of raced and gendered identities can uncover the ruptures in these flows of people and stories. It can also interrupt how people and stories accrue value and privilege in the nodes of power and knowledge differentially organized in an imperial field.

The essays in the edited volume *Knowing Southeast Asian Subjects* (Sears 2007) focused on the different kinds of questions being asked by scholars from Southeast Asia as they published more of their work in English and as their concerns entered the debates of Southeast Asian studies as a field.[5] The intention of the book was to put the idea of "knowing Southeast Asia" in flux. The authors of those essays wanted to know what it meant to claim to "know" Southeast Asia, especially for those who live and work outside the region. Rey Chow (2006) succinctly captured the book's dilemma: "Can 'knowledge' that is derived from the same kinds of bases as war put an end to the violence of warfare, or is such knowledge not simply warfare's accomplice, destined to destroy rather than preserve the forms of lives at which it aims its focus?" (41). Ariel Heryanto's contribution asked: "Can there be Southeast Asians in Southeast Asian Studies?" Can knowledge formations clear a space for subjects that have been objectified? Can scholars foreground the forces of knowledge and power production without simply reaffirming old modes of objectification? What happens to these modes of objectification when they manifest themselves situationally? Can, in the words of Audre Lorde, the master's tools dismantle the master's house?

As Sumit Mandal argued in Kuala Lumpur in August of 2007 on a panel discussing "Knowing Southeast Asian Subjects":

> In the work that I do, undoing race, I feel that so much of scholarship produced within the country is steeped in the language of the state (colonial and independent). Even the oppositional political efforts work within this language and thereby affirm it. Put simply there is no thoroughgoing, consistent and critical discussion of race as the subject is wrapped up in the political interests of the ethnic parties of the ruling coalition and opposition through the unspoken (publicly) othering of Malays. Little serious thought is put into building a new or different research agenda, based on changing global and local contexts—at least not in the study of identity, race, ethnicity, and cultural diversity. On the other hand a new agenda is growing significantly abroad, led by Malaysians and others . . . Let it not be area studies alone, and the narrow confines of U.S. debates, that set the agenda but an attempt to theorise and build on a shared space of inquiry globally.

Questions of establishing a credible historical record in places like post–New Order Indonesia, questions of organizing by women, by workers, by artists, by religious groups and others to confront societal problems, looking for ways of organizing knowledge outside of Euro-American categories and away from political centers, and questioning the scholarship produced on Southeast Asia by Euro-American scholars—these are topics of vital interest to intellectuals in Southeast Asia as well as in Asian America and the transpacific.

These observations are now being addressed in studies of imperial formations where the discussion of cosmopolitan travel under conditions of changing hierarchies mentioned above are pertinent.[6] Ann Stoler and Carole

McGranahan (2007) define the term thus: "Imperial formations are polities of dislocation, processes of dispersion, appropriation, and displacement. They are dependent both on moving categories and populations" (8). Another definition of the imperial field comes from the collaborations of Francisco Benitez and Ileana Rodriguez-Silva, a scholar of Latin American histories. The notion of the imperial field supplements imperial formations by highlighting the networks of value exchange and production as well as the practices and agencies of those inhabiting empire. The military bases that protect global trade—what Indonesia's Soekarno (1955) called the "life-line of colonialism" and the "main artery of imperialism"—and the implicit threat of state violence are constitutive of the imperial apparatus that maintains the field. Here an imperial field combines the idea of imperial formations with Foucaultian ideas of governmentality and its related ideas of "cultivation of the self" or "technologies of the self" as modes by which value is produced, extracted, and accumulated through the proximities and relations that delimit and constitute the imperial field. Cultivation of the self is a process of self-disciplining one's behavior to fit with government policies and priorities without actual government intervention. The imperial field combines this idea of cultivation of the self with actual military threat and its accompanying infrastructure. While still maintaining an awareness of the complex and differential concentration of power, attention to the field deemphasizes the old center–periphery frame that privileges metropolitan centers, and instead alerts us to flows and movements rather than just to sites.

Another intervention we would make expands the notion of imperial formations beyond the critique of U.S. exceptionalism and includes the study of the classed, raced, and gendered relations in postcolonial and neocolonial regimes in Southeast Asia today. These regimes emerged as nation-states modeled on colonial governments after World War II, and they defined the borders of the new nations as coterminous with the older borders of the colonial states. These regimes inherit the colonial and imperial state's need to manage the circulation of force, commodities, and capital and to regulate the diverse races and ethnicities within, and flowing through, their porous borders—not only toward the transpacific, but also toward a trans-Indian Ocean exchange, a remnant of both colonial and precolonial worlds. Thus studies of imperial formations and fields would allow us to see these nations as imperial states, not only in terms of their genealogies, but also in terms of their internal arrangements and their long history of sensitivity to trends in global trade. Southeast Asian polities have had a pattern of rising in wealth and importance inverse to that of the land-based silk route of global trade. Southeast Asia was also a site of important transpacific nodes under the Spanish and U.S. empires. Studies of imperial formations also allow us to ponder the shifting arrangements of the contemporary imperial terrain that for many in Southeast Asia—south of China and east of India—suggest that the United States is being eclipsed by China and India. Taking seriously attachments to communities of identity and politics while keeping in mind the violences required in imperial formations keeps us sensitive to the exigencies of lived experience and to the knowledge/power coupling. These are the conditions under which people live within imperial formations as part of their everyday life.

This same problem has been stated in Southeast Asian studies as Euro-American scholars talk of the erosion of national borders in response to flows of capital and people across the boundaries of nation-states. Regional Southeast Asia scholars focus on the oppressions of governments whose violence looms large in the lives of its citizens. This was particularly true in New Order Indonesia (1966–1998). But these studies of national postcolonial oppressions have only entered Southeast Asian studies through scholars working mainly in Indonesia and the Philippines. Regional scholars of Burma, Malaysia, Thailand, and Vietnam cannot easily write of government abuses and internal racisms. What links studies of imperial formations with Asian American studies as it has developed in the United States over the past decades is a particular focus on questions of race and the politics of empire. What troubles these links is the tension between local tactics and terrains of engagement with the global strategies of resistances to Southeast Asia's varied imperial formations. This arises partly because constructions of subjectivity have different genealogies. As an effect of a particular structure, subjectivity has both universal aspirations and specific provenances.

The field of Asian American studies itself has been decentered by deconstructive postcolonial theories and the influx of Southeast Asian Americans into the scholarly debates of Asian America. Speaking of Kandice Chuh (2003), Shirley Geok-lin Lim and her colleagues (2006) note, "Her [Chuh's] project formulates a postsubject theory for Asian American studies; that is, what happens when we radically query the stability of unitary identity in imagining the 'Asian American'? . . . The emphasis on difference rather than on identity allows for a new discursive space in which, while no subject is unnatural, no subject is naturalized either; that is, where the constructedness of subjects rather than their representations is analyzed" (4).[7] In contrast to this "subjectless signifier," Lim and her colleagues would like to construe Asian American as a "multiplier signifier": "attributed with political, social, and cultural value particularly by U.S. institutional forces such as state and federal governments, legal, educational, and cultural systems and organizations, capitalist apparatuses like banks and corporations and so forth, whose significance in a literary and critical domain is at once capable of incorporating fresh immigrant subjectivities as well as recuperating historical multilingual texts" (Lim et al. 2006, 4–5). Do Asian American studies and critiques provide multiple subjectivities or a subjectless signifier? What is at stake in this debate and how might we adjudicate? Subjectivity in this light would be about both representation and construction, for one cannot have one without the other, and both representation and construction can be a precipitate of agency. What Crenshaw (1989) has called "demarginalizing the intersections of race and sex" argues against the simplistic acceptance and construction of a coherent unitary legal persona that possesses stable representable attributes upon which juridical decisions and evaluations can be grounded. Are these questions pertinent to Southeast Asian texts (Laplanche 1999, 260–65)?

Conversations between area studies and ethnic studies like Asian American studies have opened up as the diasporic and cosmopolitan routes of travel put more and more subjects in motion and the insights from each field invigorate the other. To illustrate such intersections, we address literary works that highlight the diasporic and cosmopolitan travels of Asian American studies while maintaining the situated knowledges of Southeast Asian studies. *Dream Jungle* (2003) and *Dogeaters* (1990) by Jessica Hagedorn and *Saman* (1998) and *Larung* (2001) by Ayu Utami highlight the ways in which such novels focus on new kinds of subjectivities and the gendered state of postcolonial melancholia. In *Dream Jungle,* a novel about the making of the film *Apocalypse Now* in the Philippines in the late 1970s mixed with the story of the lost Tasaday tribe discovered in the Philippines during the Marcos years, Hagedorn weaves a story filled with characters who move fluidly in the Philippines, and between the United States and the Philippines. Hagedorn also provides us with a sketch of the structure within which subject positions and standpoints are produced and power relations are queried. In Utami's works, questions of class and gender follow the lives of four elite Indonesian women who speak in a fluid intersubjective way as their stories and voices move between Jakarta and New York City. The women subvert male voices and actions as they work to silence patriarchy in the spaces of the transpacific.

Filipinas in Transpacific and U.S. Imperial Fields

The novels we look at below offer "situated testimonies" of life in the Philippines, the United States, and Indonesia in the late twentieth century and use the paradigm of the transpacific as a site of diaspora and mobility written under the sign of the gendered and racialized melancholic states discussed in the introduction to this essay.[8] At the end of Jessica Hagedorn's novel *Dream Jungle,* a novel that takes place almost entirely in the Philippines, both heroines Rizalina and Paz Marlowe wind up living in the United States, isolated and disillusioned. Diaspora here must be seen as a kind of double consciousness, a position from which to critique state and nation formations rather than a mythology that hails a specific "ethnic" community into existence and maintains it as a social formation. As a kind of consciousness that understands racialized marginality within the state apparatus, mobile subjects must contend with the repressive and ideological state apparatuses of subjection that position them in ways that provide differential access to mobility and recognition. The debate in Asian American studies about the gains and losses of a transnational or diasporic frame as opposed to one focused on U.S.-centered rights activism often hides or marginalizes the imperial reach of the United States. A focus on the analysis of imperial formations ought not bypass or preclude local engagements. Such analyses provide a larger terrain of cognitive mapping while still demanding political engagement. As an example of this, Hagedorn's *Dream Jungle* juxtaposes two apparently disconnected events that happened in the Philippines under Marcos: the discovery of a supposedly untouched Stone Age tribe and the filming of Francis Ford Coppola's classic film, *Apocalypse Now*. Hagedorn attempts a sketch of the milieu as well as demanding a conceptual mapping of the situatedness of characters and subjects who must find their way through the imperial formations of the transpacific. These two events are in fact extremely mass-mediated and speak to the transpacific links between the United States and the Philippines. *Apocalypse Now* was, of course, a blockbuster Hollywood film, but the discovery of the Tasaday tribe in Mindanao was also a *National Geographic* mass-mediated event that later became the center of an academic debate about hoaxes and "truth."

Rizalina, the main female character in *Dream Jungle*, is a subaltern heroine who works as a maid for Zamora, the main male character. Zamora Lopez de Legazpi shuttles back and forth between the Philippines and America but he is neither filled with nostalgia nor ambivalent about his choices. He chooses the "dream jungle" where he found the gentle Tasaday whom he loves more than his family. Paz Marlowe is the diasporic subject, shuttling back and forth between the Philippines and her Filipino/American world. Caught between nostalgia and melancholia—Paz Marlowe can never find a place to call home. The novel invokes the discovery of the Tasaday and the filming of *Apocalypse Now* as historical events. In *Dream Jungle*, Hagedorn takes clearly recognizable historical personages and renames them much as she did in her earlier novel *Dogeaters*. In *Dogeaters*, Hagedorn plays with the distinction between reality and fiction and with narrator credibility. Famously, *Dogeaters* undercuts narrative authority by writing through multiple narrators who critique each other's testimonies and points of view. Paying attention to the epigraphs and her deployment of paratexts within the novel opens up other consequences of the transpacific relation.

In addition to Hagedorn's explicit and powerful satire of the Marcos years and "consumerist neocolonialism,"[9] *Dogeaters* also provides oblique critiques of Philippine racializations and the ambivalent relationship of Filipino Americans to the Philippines. Thus the section entitled "Jungle Chronicle" has a quote from Jean Mallat from 1846 speaking about the position of "Negritoes" as domestics. The following section entitled "Mister Heartbreak" introduces Joey Sands, the half-black Filipino protagonist, and the mistreated janitor Pedro the Igorot. Mallat's quote clarifies Joey's claim that his employer Andres Alacran (from the Spanish for "scorpion") is contradictory when Andres states "a little black is good for the soul" despite treating "Pedro like a slave" (Hagedorn 1990, 34). American black is thus of a different value than Philippine indigenous "black" in a U.S.-dominated imperial field. Mallat's quote in turn precedes the description of Joey Sands's mother and the role of his "uncle" in prostitution and drugs, linking nightlife, consumption, neocolonial tourism, gender, class, and racialization—the presumed variables that engendered Joey himself. The *Dogeaters* narrative ends with a suggestion of Joey Sands committing himself to future radical action. Then Hagedorn disrupts narratorial authority and multiplies the voices of the novel. Her epilogue is a blasphemous prayer ("Kundiman") that distills the complex and hybrid cultural history of the Philippines to which Filipino Americans are also heirs. Suturing these pastiche parts of, and narratorial positions in, the novel requires that readers work to navigate the multiple positions and voices and, in so doing, they themselves become woven into a web of interlocution much like the manner in which gossip or *tsismis* works formally and diegetically within Hagedorn's novels. Rumor does not only cast suspicion on official narratives, it also sends us on a quest for truth even as it implicates us in the complex webs of storytelling and situated historicity.[10]

The technique of evoking historical people, documents, and events in both *Dogeaters* and *Dream Jungle* reminds us of a roman à clef—taking actual personages and only slightly veiling their identity in a fictional account. In such a technique, once we know the key; that is, the historical events that form the bases of the story—for example, Zamora Lopez de Legazpi can only be a shallowly fictionalized version of the very real Manuel Manda Elizalde, the man who actually orchestrated the discovery of the Tasaday in 1971, and Pierce, the great director of *Napalm Sunset* in *Dream Jungle*, is a lightly disguised Francis Ford Coppola—we are tempted to read the text simplistically as a thinly veiled allegory. The reader is then coerced to scour Hagedorn's source material, tallying her deviations from "historical truth," from "reality," seeking the kernel of truth that is the novel's secret, certain of finding the latent meaning that the manifest text hides only through an ironic disavowal. In fact Hagedorn herself in interviews about the book is quite open about the inspiration that Elizalde and Coppola provided her. These historical referents then become taken as the subject and the content treated in the novel.

This was, we confess, our own most immediate response—to go looking for as much information as we possibly could about the Tasaday, the event of their discovery and their transformation into a phenomenon of academic controversy. There is no space here to discuss this interesting and complex case. Suffice it to say that Hagedorn clearly wishes to allude to the entire case that we can only gesture to as the Tasaday complex. The "Gentle Tasaday," as they were termed in the 1970s, were believed to have been a hunting and gathering tribe that lived in caves and did not know agriculture. They were reported to live as humans did during the Stone Age. American media, particularly *National Geographic,* circulated and popularized stories and fantasies of the Tasaday—they did not know the word for "war," for example—to provide a picture of what life must have been like in the past. They were touted as a figure of our lost innocence, of a peaceful Edenic existence, found in the middle of the Cold War and toward the end of the Vietnam War. In order to "save" the Tasaday from the contamination of modernity's technologization, of modernity's fallen state, Elizalde and Marcos closed off access to the Tasaday. In this act of what Renato Rosaldo might call imperialist nostalgia, the Tasaday were saved from the ravages of modernization, supposedly to remain in a "pristine" condition of innocence and primitivism throughout the dictatorship. We signal the historical context of the production of the Tasaday images because, by the mid-1980s, after the fall of Marcos, anthropologists visited the Tasaday and proclaimed them an elaborate hoax concocted by Elizalde and possibly by Marcos (Hemley 2003). Disturbing to many of those who followed the case was not so much that Elizalde and Marcos would perpetuate a hoax, but that they could be so successful at it!

Consequently, these mass-mediated images and stories of the "Gentle Tasaday" and their successful dissemination have been the object of much genealogical work. Jean Paul Dumont, for example, argues that it is less important whether they were an authentic Neolithic tribe than that the public was eager to use the encounter with this tribe to project lost hopes and desires, to produce a late twentieth-century version of Orientalism. For Dumont (1988), the United States needs to reclaim the image of the jungle as a safe space after the ravages of America's wars in Vietnam, Cambodia, and Laos, and the Marcos government's need to project an image of an essentially peaceful Philippines in the face of an ongoing communist rural and urban armed struggle, provided the value of and need for the Tasaday as an "ethnographic sign." The Tasaday, called by another anthropologist the "paleo-hippies of the 70's," were consumed in other words in the light of the needs of the late twentieth century. In Hagedorn's work, both the Tasaday and *Apocalypse Now* are shown to be events mediated by the needs and structures of new imperialism. The mass mediation of these events in fact brings us up against Hagedorn's own use of them. Like some reviewers of the book, we at first saw in Hagedorn's techniques the presentation of a central anxiety about the nature of historical truth. In fact Hagedorn in many ways goes even further than this. The more we sought to ground the novel in its source material, in the "real" case of the Tasaday, for example, the more we felt that Hagedorn had been laughing at us all along. For *Dream Jungle* does not truly employ the roman à clef, but at best only a pseudo-roman à clef—where one expects to find the key to interpretation to the novel, instead one finds juxtapositions, gaps and gutters, openings between and within images, and excessive descriptions that must be sutured.

In fact, both the Tasaday and *Apocalypse Now* appear in Jean Baudrillard's *Simulacra and Simulation* (1994) precisely as expressions of mass-mediated hyperreality. In many ways like Baudrillard, Hagedorn asks us to reconsider our fixations on truth, on authenticity, on the real. She asks, like Baudrillard, what happens when the material, the images and narratives we use to construct our identities, are in fact revealed to have themselves been simulations, simulacra, mere representations, fakes—or at least material for Freudian dreamwork, a jungle of dreams. Using a style that is filled with descriptive excess in an almost baroque manner, she evacuates our capacity to prioritize between latent and manifest content, between the secret kernel of truth and the unfolding of truth's structuration and staging. Identifying Zamora as Elizalde does not get the reader very far in interpreting the novel. Fidelity to the "real" source is not Hagedorn's primary concern. Instead the "real" becomes an ever-receding horizon we desire but cannot capture. The materiality of the historical referent echoes throughout the novel, but this echo occurs only through displacement or condensation, through Freud's dreamwork. What we are left with are images, images that resist full incorporation into discourses of power even as they seem to abet and constitute them. These images ask us to foreground the codes we use to read and yet, like all images, only offer us a remainder that keep us wanting more. At the same time, Hagedorn is cognizant of the seductive qualities of the jungle as material for dreaming.

The opening section of the novel is an excerpt from Antonio Pigafetta's eyewitness account of Magellan's interrupted journey around the world and ostensible discovery of the Philippines. The section she picks is the one in which Pigafetta describes a group of islanders as thieves. In a section called "Discovery and Conquest" and as a frame for Zamora's encounter with the Taobo, as the Tasaday are called in the novel, one is tempted to ask who is the thief and what has been stolen? The easy imperialist answer sees Pigafetta and the Europeans who call the islanders thieves as the ultimate thieves. Spanish colonization, the original transpacific network of the Manila Galleon, connected the seventeenth- and eighteenth-century trade among Spain, Mexico, the Philippines, and China as a base of Spain's imperial formation. Spain's imperial trans-Pacific and trans-Atlantic trade completed global trade routes. Capital's grasp of the world then becomes fulfilled, in a Laplanchian movement of afterwardsness, by Zamora's discovery of the Taobo. Yet even this direct interpretation is muddied by Hagedorn. By taking images of the Philippines and suturing us into them in the novel, Hagedorn opens herself up to a critique that she is just like Coppola, like Zamora, and like Pigafetta, taking images and using them for her own purposes. The jungle for her, like the Philippines, is a resource for production and for the reproduction of images whose value and significance is a question of *mētis*, practical knowledge, and a struggle against an imperial panopticon of regulation and management.[11]

Unlike Baudrillard who focuses in his text on what happens when the old binaries' grounds have been undercut by the proliferation of images and representations and the negative no longer holds its power of reversal, Hagedorn foregrounds questions of situatedness and asks about the parameters of practices of survival by those living within and through empire. She articulates readers within an imperial field and asks about the gains and losses of boundary-making and border-crossing practices. The kernel of truth hidden in the novel is in the search for these connections and transgressions between "reality" and fiction. The very process of searching uncovers the tissue of connections and the necessary links readers must construct in order to make sense of the novel's "reality." By doing so, Hagedorn asks her readers to become aware of the power relations that shore up this sense of situated knowledges and exposes the staging of images and their relationship to truth. For the Filipina American Paz, the search for authentic roots is frustrated and the constructedness of authenticity opens up a question of ethics—both as a liberating modern process and as the social constraints on the terms through which readers narrate themselves and their identities. To Baudrillard's generalized sloganeering that in this moment of capitalism "We Are All Tasaday," Hagedorn deploys the absent term of "Marcos" to outline the specific conditions of possibility of her novel (Baudrillard 1994, 8). We may all be Tasaday, but we feel the effects of this regime of truth differentially. The dictatorship in fact is behind both the Tasaday phenomenon and the filming of *Apocalypse Now*. It is absolutely crucial to the understanding of currency of these events as images. The purposes to which these images are used, to whom they accrue value, how they are disseminated, and what formations and relations their exchange engenders become questions for us as readers of Hagedorn's text.

Hagedorn in fact calls attention to those who must live within the social formations of empire, by shifting narrative attention to servants, guards, the local film production crew, the food servers, and so on, and by juxtaposing national events with local ones. Those on the margins like the spectators of the filming of *Napalm Sunset,* juxtapose Zamora with the novel's heroine Rizalina in a dance of gendered gazing. At the same time, Hagedorn maintains the distance of a Filipina American subject position through the character of Paz Marlowe, just as she questions Rio's relationship to the Philippines through her cousin Pucha's undercutting of Rio's narrative authority and authenticity in *Dogeaters.* We emphasize that these are not just characters, nor even simply narrative functions or rhetoric, but possible subject positions that the novel weaves together. The subject positions generated by these juxtapositions and their situatedness are foregrounded. In other words, Hagedorn's narrative technique not only blurs the borders between fact and fiction, it also posits how these together give us a sense of borders and boundaries, how they shape our gendered subject positions from which we gaze at the world.[12] On one level, the bumping against each other of these positions allows Hagedorn to take imperialist nostalgia as a technology of identity formation and loosen the forms of authority in it. The Lacanian notion of *jouissance,* or the excess of pleasure, experienced by Hagedorn's male characters mitigates imperialist nostalgia—*jouissance* ruptures preset subject positions. The literary mode of satire and formal play she uses becomes bathetic. The multiplication of subject positions draws attention to their structuration and then allows us to follow those who negotiate the field as practice. These are distinct ways that authority is both solicited and destabilized in Hagedorn's work. On another level, this loss of imperial authority becomes a marker of the Asian American's own colonial melancholia and her inability to find a stable place to call home.

Dream Jungle is an example of Freudian dreamwork. The novel suggests that the order and meaning we find must be from some act of interpretation, an act of secondary revision where the dream images are structured to make sense of randomly produced images. The novel resists readings that wish to incorporate it smoothly into a predetermined decoding. Instead it posits stylistic excess to conjure an emotional milieu, perhaps even melodramatic, as its resistance to the imperial technologies of subjection and identification, while at the same time calling attention to those who must live within the social formations of empire. Hagedorn's work suggests that subjectivity emerges from acts of narration and interpretation and is differentially located in a social map. All such acts, however, are in turn open to uncertainty and anxiety. There is no getting over emplacement and its politics of location, and the split melancholic subject has passionate attachments to his or her own subjection. Racialized differential emplacements are not secrets that must be uncovered through symptomatic reading. Subjection and the power relations between subject positions are not hidden. The secrets, including sexual transgressions experienced by both Rizalina and Rio, examples of what we are calling intrusive intimacies, are the ways in which certain subject positions are naturalized as subaltern, and the work of ideology is hidden or at least repressed. These unmarked conditions must be exposed in order for the power of naturalized fetishizing processes to be acknowledged and possibly worked through.[13]

Erasures in the Transpacific

In a set of novels that both are and are not about "race," Indonesian author Ayu Utami tells the story of four elite women and two male activists whom the women help. As her Indonesian characters travel across the Pacific between Jakarta and New York City, Utami's novels highlight gaps and erasures that a focus on the transpacific enables. Utami's activists are hunted and tortured by the agents of Indonesia's oppressive thirty-two year New Order government but, interwoven with their fates, is the story of the elite women and the mobility that the oppressive government allowed. The first novel, *Saman*, was published in 1998 right before the end of the New Order, and the book's darker sequel, *Larung*, came out in 2001, in the period of disillusionment after the fall of the supposedly progressive post–New Order government of Abdurrahman Wahid (Utami 1998, 2001). In Utami's novels none of the women have children, and all of them have jobs. They are free to engage in cosmopolitan travel, and only one of them could be called an activist. The other women remain as feminized helpers to male activists. Transgressive sex is a strong theme in the book, as is rape, which is discussed below. Utami comments on the rapes that were commonly used for intimidation of women and men under the New Order.

Utami (2005b) states that her work is about negation and, in particular, the negation of patriarchal forms of male authority. The first novel of her two-book series ends with a premature ejaculation and the second one with a murder of one or both of the male heroes. In these two novels, the four feminine narrators create a fluid intersubjectivity that allows them to travel without losing the contours of their elite Jakartan identities. Whether they are in Jakarta or New York City, they survive through their ongoing conversations with each other. What protects the women from the melancholy isolation of Rizalina and Paz Marlowe is their ability to hear each other's voices/messages in their heads, and those messages are ones of support. Utami's activist men, lacking this intimate intersubjective support, slowly begin to blur, to lose control of themselves, their identities, and eventually their lives by the end of the second novel. Saman is often surrounded by those who help, nurse, and love him, but he does not have any interlocutors until he falls in love with Yasmin. Both Saman and Larung, the activist men whose names give the novels their respective titles, are haunted by the past. These hauntings take the form of hallucinations that both characters experience. And the hallucinations are intimately tied to the characters' mothers and/or grandmothers. The only female character who has similar hallucinations or phantasies—tied to spirit worlds of Java, Bali, and Sumatra—is Shakuntala, a bisexual dancer living on a grant in New York City.[14]

Shakuntala's phantasies of her childhood are pertinent to our discussion of race and subjectivity. Shakuntala phantasizes a male counterpart to herself who visits her, talks to her, dances with her, and makes love to her. Thus her sexual identity is split at a young age into male and female parts. At first the male part takes the form of one of a group of ogres in these phantasies, and Shakuntala sees herself as a Javanese—Indonesia's largest ethnic group—nymph.[15] These images originate in Javanese oral traditions, myths, and histories. The phantasmic ogre whom Shakuntala takes as a lover is a spice-seeker from Europe, and he has sailed as far as he could to the "East." In one phantasized verbal and physical encounter between the European ogre and Shakuntala as nymph, Utami includes an ironic description of "West" and "East."

In this country [Indonesia] people speak of your land and our land, your people and our people. We are the noble people of the East. You, the depraved of the West. Your women wear bikinis in the streets and have no regard for virginity. Your school children, boys and girls, live together out of wedlock. In this country sex belongs to adults through marriage and even if they were married at the age of eleven they were already regarded as mature. In your country people have sex on television, we have sex but not on television. We have the decent foundations of the great East. Your customs of the West are not noble. (Utami 2005a, 128)[16]

This passage and those that precede it offer readers a subtle and concise reference to various Dutch imperial formations in the Indies: the spice trade, Orientalist images the Dutch had of the Indies and its peoples, and ways in which some Indonesians today view Euro-Americans. Readers must work to find this historical depth in the horizontal flows of the transpacific. The images and references are no longer easily understood or pertinent, they are pushed to the margins of the geographic and historical space between Southeast Asia and the Americas.[17] This is one of the few references to Indonesia's colonial past other than brief mention of the shocking, at the time, marriage of Larung's grandmother to a Dutchman just before World War II. The novels, however, do explore myths and stories from the precolonial past.

Saman and *Larung* are set in the 1970s, 1980s, and 1990s, and Utami's characters, most of whom live in and around Jakarta, represent a number of Indonesia's ethnic groups: Batak, Sundanese, Javanese, Balinese, Chinese, and Javanese transmigrants to southern Sumatra. Various religious beliefs are blended into the novels: Catholicism, Islam, and Hinduism. Even more than these religious identifications, which are designed to shock when the Catholic priest who has lost his faith begins an affair with the only married one of the four main female characters, there is a deep exploration of the Javanese and Balinese spirit worlds and the magical powers they confer on older and younger practitioners from those worlds. This blend of ethnicity, religion, mysticism, and magic is another element of the situated testimonies in Utami's work. When the women and the two activist men travel, in various groupings, to New York City in the second novel, they become a group of Indonesian tourists in the United States. They do not interact with anyone except each other. The characters who reside in New York City for a time—Saman and Shakuntala—mostly befriend other foreigners or Americans from minority groups. New York becomes an extension of Jakarta in this vision of the transpacific, a cosmopolitan space where activist refugees from Indonesia's authoritarian regime can mingle with Indonesian oil-company technicians and artists like Shakuntala who is in New York on a grant from the Asian Cultural Council. Saman attends a conference at Columbia and listens to academics and activists argue over the ethics of multinational corporations like Nike in Indonesia.

Characters in the novels like Saman, Larung, and Shakuntala are trapped in their own melancholic worlds because they feel a lack of self-worth that they have inherited from their parents in the form of secrets or phantoms. Freudian melancholia is characterized as an inability to assimilate a loss and then the constant return of the loss through haunting and repetition. But Nicolas Abraham and Maria Torok's (1994) ideas of secrets, crypts, and phantoms are more useful for understanding the scenes and the characters that Utami creates. Saman carries the phantoms of his mother's spirit lover and her spirit children who take his mother's love away from him. He hides these secrets from his father. Larung carries the phantoms of his grandmother's powers, the repressed knowledge of his confused paternity, and the deaths of those close to him that he witnesses in the anticommunist mass killings of the mid-1960s. Shakuntala carries the phantoms of her *raksasa* (ogre/demon) lover whom she phantasizes, her ability to change from female to male, her seduction of her friend Laila when Laila fails to lose her virginity with her married lover. What are the messages that these secrets and phantoms contain? All the messages revolve around sexual relations. In this sense, sex is the quilting point of these two novels, and Utami uses sex to quilt over her ideological critiques of New Order repression and violence. But the sexual relationships that Utami portrays are all disturbed by the traumas inflicted by the New Order.

Laila and her married lover Sihar's relationship is unconsummated and adulterous; it exists mainly in Laila's phantasies. Cok, the promiscuous one of the four female heroines, has sexual desire that can never be satisfied, and she has numerous overlapping lovers who bring her little joy. Shakuntala's phantasmic lover is a centuries-old Dutch *raksasa*, and, as noted above, she herself has a male identity spawned by her own phantasies. It is this male identity that emerges when Shakuntala has lesbian encounters, a cop-out to some of Utami's feminist critics.[18] The relationship between Saman and Yasmin, also adulterous, is the most complex. Their sexual encounters are sadomasochistic, reenacting Saman's torture when he was imprisoned by New Order secret police. But they also reenact Yasmin's phantasies of torturing men because of the ways in which men belittle women and deny their needs. In an e-mail message—Yasmin only uses a first person voice in her e-mails to Saman—she tells Saman there is a part of her that she has always tried to deny: she wants to see his male body wounded, naked, limp. Yasmin says that what she experiences with Saman astonishes her. He lets her tie him up to the iron bed while she explores his body with her fingers. He lets her hurt him like the secret police did when they tortured him as a spy. He lets her postpone his orgasm and makes him suffer a repeated coitus interruptus. She forgets how long it has been that she has nursed the desire to hurt a man and see him suffer. Yasmin gives a Freudian interpretation of the anal stage proceeding to the phallic stage when children become obsessed with their sex organs or, in the case of women, their lack of them. She remembers being attracted to a little boy at school when she was in kindergarten and wanting to castrate him or circumcise him. She says when she was little she never associated sex with love, only with roughness, oppression, and pain. Then, as she approached the age of consent, she punished herself for her erotic fantasies as she entered the world of patriarchy. And she denied her subjectivity and allowed herself to become an object of sexual desire (Utami 2001, 155–158).[19]

> I lost my subjectivity and saw myself as a [sexual] object. I lost my femininity and became a woman. In a process I didn't understand, I began to see myself as a victim, a woman who is cursed because of her womanhood.[20]

Yasmin explains masochism to Saman through Deleuze's commentary on Leopold von Sacher-Masoch: in masochism, the superego is chased outside until it becomes part of the external world. In other words, the role of punishment and discipline is projected on another, cut off from one's own ego. At the same time, the superego becomes empty and, taking off from Deleuze, a tyrant. Masochism and humor insult power by transferring oppression into enjoyment. Both are a form of mechanical intelligence to restrain ourselves. But, Yasmin argues, Deleuze and many others only look at masochism in men. They see masochism as a male deviation because of the critical superego, the father figure, and punishment, which all appear outside of the feminine in a patriarchal world. Women are not required or even expected to turn this around—only to allow men to remain dominant—and the strongest form of this attitude is the taste for sadism of the heterosexual man. What is the difference between the idealization of women's sacrifice, polygamy, and masochism? All of them internalize injustice. Yasmin says that women safeguard themselves by internalizing Indonesian patriarchy and thus 90 percent of women become masochists. Speaking of herself, she says that she lost the sadism of her youth and became like O in *The Story of O*, a masochist who allows herself to be tortured and degraded. Yasmin complains that her husband is only interested in the physical aspects of sex rather than the psychic ones. She also thinks that because of her reputation as the "good woman and good wife" her husband does not suspect that she would enjoy or desire sexual phantasies. She and Saman are both wounded by the New Order and its prescribed gender roles. Utami also comments here on the common practice of Indonesian men of taking mistresses, second wives, or going to prostitutes. They do not suspect that their wives, the mothers of their children, could or should enjoy kinky sex (Utami 2001, 158–160).[21]

Other presentations of sexual desires in the novel include Shakuntala's substituting for Sihir, Laila's married boyfriend, to initiate Laila, a thirty-year-old virgin who has never had an orgasm, into knowledge of her sexualized body; the sexuality of Saman's mother with a spirit husband and family; the sexuality of the mentally and physically disfigured Upi, a member of the group of Javanese transmigrants in Sumatra helped by Saman, who satisfies herself with a pole, an animal, or any human willing to have sex with her. Only the psychotic Larung, whose paternity is in doubt, and who carries the secrets of his grandmother who ran off with a Dutchman in the early years of the twentieth century, is uninterested in sex—even the promiscuous Cok cannot get him to sleep with her. The theme of rape, as noted above, is threaded throughout both of the novels, but appears frequently in *Saman*: the rape of Upi; the rape and murder of various women by the Texcoil oil-rig manager Rosano; the vivid description of the rape of village leader Anson's wife, and of other women from Anson's village, by New Order thugs. The last words in the novel *Saman* are Saman's pleading with Yasmin, in an e-mail message, to rape him. Rape, that often ended in murder, was a common tool that the New Order used to humiliate, demasculinize, and depress men and women. At the end of *Larung,* Saman confuses Yasmin with his mother in his phantasies. In his foreboding dreams, through processes of displacement and condensation, his mother/lover is missing.

The only answer to these sexual abuses and deviancies that Utami presents is the bonding of the four women friends in *Saman* and *Larung.* In their fluid and overlapping subjectivity, represented in the novels by their overlapping and intertwined voices and movements, there is a promise of a future feminist agency and power that would not be activist in a masculinist sense, but would seek to find collective rather than individualistic ways to answer the problems of the postcolonial nation. The women survive at the end of *Larung,* as do Rizalina and Paz Marlowe at the end of *Dream Jungle,* but they are damaged and depressed. Melancholia is a troubled and dangerous condition, but it may be the best one can hope for in the posttraumatic world of the twenty-first century in Indonesia and possibly elsewhere.

Indonesia and its people do not blend easily into North American life. Utami's novels and the cosmopolitan spaces they depict mirror the gaps between area studies and American ethnic studies. There is a hint of reaching out to America's minorities by the Indonesian activist and ex-priest Saman when he is in New York, but the national and individual worlds remain separate. In New York, the differences among Indonesians from different ethnic groups are erased. New York remains a phantasmic space for clandestine sexual encounters that are either not consummated or are consummated in unanticipated ways. Individual failures preoccupy Utami's characters along gendered lines. The women remain unfulfilled, melancholic, and disappointed but they survive by serving as interlocutors for one another. The men, who have aspirations to serve the nation, fail completely and are themselves destroyed. Utami's comments on the potential of the nationalist project are not optimistic, but her comments on the potential for a collective and cosmopolitan women's movement leave open a space of hope for the future.

Conclusion: Questions for the Transpacific

Both Hagedorn and Utami, whose characters are situated in the space of the transpacific, suggest that women in their artistic productions give up on masculinist definitions and structurings of pleasure. Women do not fit comfortably into masculinist binaries: if men seek pleasure and satisfaction, women seem content with a kind of depressed survival or what the scholars we have cited call postcolonial melancholia. It is through a fluid class-based female intersubjectivity that Utami suggests women might be able to slowly change masculinist ideas of political activity and attachments to the nation-state. Hagedorn imagines subject positions that are arranged and juxtaposed in order to articulate the situatedness of her characters and the terrain they must negotiate and traverse in the transpacific in order to survive. In both novels, the women and some men are silenced in various ways. The language of Hagedorn's women Rizalina and Paz Marlowe and Utami's men Saman and Larung becomes demetaphorized, simplified, even as their bodies stay in motion. Hagedorn's *Dream Jungle* ends with a description of the artistic work of film director Pepito, which in turn is supplemented by an epilogue to "Zamora in the year 2000." Zamora's voice from the dead, speaking from an urn in an apartment in New York, ends the book, providing a sense of negated but still present patriarchal authority as well as a genealogy of Filipino and Filipino American hybridity. Perhaps this is the fate of area studies also: as we begin to put our subjects and ourselves more and more in motion in the transpacific, the links to our subjectivities and our politics of location become blurred as our travels change us. This was certainly true in the past as well, but now the travels have speeded up, with as many if not more people moving from Southeast Asia to the global north. The novels discussed above serve as links to the work being done in Asian American studies and in scholarship on imperial formations.

Both sets of novels address the remnants of colonial hierarchies that have left their traces on Philippine and Indonesian societies. The novels might serve as situated testimonies within literary archives. As novels, they emerge out of a specific context or "situatedness" and must be supplemented by a certain historical depth, a depth that area studies provides by researching and teaching about Southeast, East, or South Asian, to name a few, pasts. Such endeavors allow the contextual and ideological connectedness of subject formation to come more fully into view. In the case of Utami's and Hagedorn's works, this depth would illuminate the effects of empire on the formation of racialized and sexualized bodies. As the different islands of the Dutch Indies were knitted together, the Javanese came to dominate other ethnic groups and new hierarchies were created that lasted into the postcolonial period. In societies where women had a good deal of freedom and autonomy, both within and outside the family, Dutch imperial reason introduced new forms of patriarchy as well as new conditions of gendering male and female bodies. In the Philippines, Spanish and American imperial control layered the transpacific as both a space of global commerce and the terrain of thickening networks of global imperial technologies and governmentality. The postcolonial relations between the Philippines and the United States, itself manifested in Hagedorn's own diasporic status, is an integral part of *Dream Jungle* The break between the Spanish and American empires and the resultant black legend that demonized Spanish rule as feudal and backward in the Philippines is indexed by Hagedorn's treatment of the continuities in the *mestizo* Philippine upper class and their relationship to the "primitive tribes." Here the layered inheritance of subject formation tied citizenship to nationalism, with the American colonial period as the final harbinger of modern subjectivity. The arguments over various forms and privileges of citizenship that began in the early nineteenth-century Philippines and continued through the U.S. period were global in scope. This essay cannot comprehensively explore the ways in which imperial formations that were part of the global march of imperial modernity and reason left their impact on the islands, but certainly in Indonesia religion grew stronger in reaction to colonialism and women had new restrictions placed on their actions by both Islam and Christianity. Spirit beliefs, magic, and mysticism were discouraged both by colonial administrators as well as by the religious changes colonialism inspired. Religious leaders wanted to find "pure" forms of Islam, Protestant sects, or Catholicism. In the Philippines, American imperial governmentality struggled with the Catholic Church and shifted from ruling primarily through categories of religion to ones of race and ethnicity along a narrative of civilizational development.

These novels also show the ways in which subjectivity is effaced for men and women as they enter diasporic spaces and become situated differently in other social fields. No longer rooted in local cultures, the characters' subject positions in these novels begin to blur, separating these characters from what Judith Butler has called passionate attachments to modes of our own subjection.[22] Butler's idea of passionate attachments intersects with Laplanche's ideas of "afterwardsness" (*Nachträglichkeit*) in literary and area studies in that both see a potential for the future in working to change the attachments or the intrusive intimacies that individuals and groups hold and hear in their various pasts. Laplanche goes a step further and puts past and future in conversation in the present, both within and outside of psychoanalytical discourses. The messages of early childhood can be untranslated and retranslated, reinterpreted in other words so as to change the future. Understanding what those messages of the past were, understanding the subaltern situatedness of those who sent those messages, may change the ways individuals and groups feel about themselves. Rather than getting over race, gender, sexual orientation, or disability, scholars of area studies and American ethnic studies can attempt to understand how they and their various subjects and objects of study retranslate and rewrite what it means to be gendered, raced, sexed, and differently abled in the restless spaces of the transpacific. Looking through the transpacific we see what is lost by giving up a preoccupation with sites and situations that area studies and ethnic studies offer, but gain an awareness of the flows and movements that exceed fixity within structures, borders, and boundaries. It allows us to see what area studies and ethnic studies, narrowly defined, cannot explore alone but only in collaboration.

Notes to Chapter 6: Passionate Attachments to Area Studies and Asian American Studies

1. For an account of similar methodologies arising from Southeast Asia, see also Tadiar (2009).

2. See especially ch. 4. For other studies on melancholia as a likely position for twenty-first century subjects, see Khanna (2003) and See (2002).

3. For Donna Haraway, situated knowledges involve questions of partial vision and scholarly production, destabilizing a neutral masculine gaze of supposed objectivity, mastery, and power. See Haraway (1988).

4. "Diaspora discourse articulates, or bends together, both roots *and* routes to construct what Gilroy describes as alternate public spheres, forms of community consciousness and solidarity that maintain identifications outside the national time/space in order to live inside, with a difference" (Clifford 1997, 251).

5. This book was written with the idea of Southeast Asian readers in mind and was copublished by Singapore University Press.

6. Scholars of Southeast Asian Studies like Ann Stoler, Warwick Anderson, and Vicente Rafael have suggested the imperial field is where the practice of area studies takes place today. Of course, Southeast Asianists like Benedict Anderson, Ben Kerkvliet, and James Scott have done global work since the 1980s, but studies of imperial formations incorporate insights from postcolonial theories, which distinguish them from earlier global studies.

7. Lim et al.'s work follows that of Lisa Lowe who has already deconstructed the identity-based Asian American subject. See also Chuh (2003).

8. Laurie J. Sears, inspired by Donna Haraway's idea of "situated knowledges," coined the phrase "situated testimonies" as a methodology of reading literary works as part of historical and literary archives. For more on the idea of literary archives and novels as situated testimonies, see Sears (2007, 2010, 2013).

9. See, for example, Grace Kyungwon Hong's (2006) salient argument about *Dogeaters'* pastiche style as indicative of a specific moment in neocolonialism as flexible accumulation (117).

10. For a discussion of the significance of gossip in *Dogeaters,* see "Writing and History" (Lowe 1996, 97–127). For Lowe, gossip functions to undermine narrative and state authority. Here we would like to emphasize the call for a web of interlocutors that supplements our partial situated knowledges.

11. For a discussion of *mētis* as a practice of craftiness for survival that requires local and situated knowledge against empire, see Scott (1998).

12. For further discussion, see Yuval-Davis (2002).

13. Here we think of the fetish as a representation that stands in for figures of power and that imputes and expands its power over those subject to it.

14. Another one of the women, the character Laila, has fantasies, but these are very different from the phantasmic hallucinations of the three other characters mentioned above.

15. See also Utami (2001, 133–134) for Shakuntala's doubled sexual identity where she can spin out her male double who is also part of herself.

16. Translation modified and missing phrases reinserted. Cf. Utami (2005a, 135–136).

17. This loss of historical depth is a topic that the authors have discussed with Boreth Ly who finds a similar loss as he works to fit his work on Mainland Southeast Asia into the spaces of the transpacific.

18. See, for example, Bandel (2005).

19. Yasmin attributes part of her analysis here to Deleuze (1967, chs. 9–11).

20. "Aku kehilangan kesubyekan pada diriku dan menempatkan diri sebagai obyek. Aku kehilangan keperempuanku dan menjadi wanita. Dalam proses yang tak kumengerti, aku mulai menempatkan diriku sebagai si terhukum, wanita yang dikutuk karena kewanitaannya" (Utami 2001, 158).

21. For an exact statement of this male belief, see also Utami (2010, 57). The book discussed above is Deleuze's *Coldness and Cruelty* (1969), his commentary on Leopold von Sacher-Masoch's *Venus in Furs* (1870), published together as *Masochism* (Deleuze and von Sacher-Masoch 1989). See especially chs. 9–11.

22. See Butler (1997) where she makes the same point as Laplanche for the possibility of a retranslation of the wounds left by enigmatic signifiers. "This is not the same as saying that such an identity will remain always and forever rooted in its injury as long as it remains an identity, but it does imply that the possibilities of resignification will rework and unsettle the passionate attachment to subjection without which subject formation—and reformation—cannot succeed" (105).

References

Abraham, Nicolas, and Maria Torok. 1994. *The Shell and the Kernel: Renewals of Psychoanalysis.* Vol. I. Chicago: University of Chicago Press.

Anderson, Benedict. 1998. *The Spectre of Comparisons: Nationalism, Southeast Asia and the World.* London: Verso.

Bandel, Katrin. 2005. "Heteronormalitas dan Falosentrisme Ayu Utami." *Kompas,* 1 June.

Basch, Linda, Nina Glick Schiller, and Cristina Szanton-Blanc. 2000 [1994]. *Nations Unbound: Transnational Projects, Postcolonial Predicaments, and Deterritorialized Nation-States.* London: Routledge.

Baudrillard, Jean. 1994. *Simulacra and Simulation.* Ann Arbor: University of Michigan Press.

Bourdieu, Pierre, and Loïc Wacquant. 1999. "On the Cunning of Imperialist Reason." *Theory, Culture, and Society* 16 (1): 41–57.

Butler, Judith. 1997. *The Psychic Life of Power: Theories in Subjection.* Stanford, CA: Stanford University Press.

Cheng, Anne Anlin. 2000. *The Melancholy of Race: Psychoanalysis, Assimilation, and Hidden Grief.* New York: Oxford University Press.

Chow, Rey. 2006. *The Age of the World Target: Self-Referentiality in War, Theory, and Comparative Work.* Durham, NC: Duke University Press.

Chuh, Kandice. 2003. *Imagine Otherwise: On Asian Americanist Critique.* Durham, NC: Duke University Press.

Clifford, James. 1997. "Diasporas." *Routes: Travel and Translation in the Late Twentieth Century.* Cambridge, MA: Harvard University Press.

Crenshaw, Kimberlé. 1989. "Demarginalizing the Intersection of Race and Sex: A Black Feminist Critique of Antidiscrimination Doctrine, Feminist Theory and Antiracist Politics." *University of Chicago Legal Forum:* 139–167.

Deleuze, Gilles. 1989 [1967]. *Coldness and Cruelty.* In *Masochism* by Gilles Deleuze and Leopold von Sacher-Masoch, 9–142. New York: Urzone.

Deleuze, Gilles, and Leopold von Sacher-Masoch. 1989 [1967]. *Masochism.* New York: Urzone.

Dumont, Jean-Paul. 1988. "The Tasaday, Which and Whose? Toward the Political Economy of an Ethnographic Sign." *Cultural Anthropology* 3 (3): 261–275.

Hagedorn, Jessica. 1990. *Dogeaters.* New York: Pantheon Books.

———. 2003. *Dream Jungle.* New York: Penguin Books.

Haraway, Donna. 1988. "Situated Knowledges: The Science Question in Feminism and the Privilege of Partial Perspective." *Feminist Studies* 14 (3): 575–599.

Hemley, Robin. 2003. *Invented Eden: The Elusive, Disputed History of the Tasaday.* New York: Farrar, Straus and Giroux.

Hong, Grace Kyungwon. 2006. *Ruptures of American Capital: Women of Color Feminism and the Culture of Immigrant Labor.* St. Paul: University of Minnesota Press.

Khanna, Ranjana. 2003. *Dark Continents: Psychoanalysis and Colonialism.* Durham, NC: Duke University Press.

Laplanche, Jean. 1999. *Essays on Otherness,* ed. John Fletcher. New York: Routledge.

Lim, Shirley Geok-lin, et al., eds. 2006. *Transnational Asian American Literature: Sites and Transits.* Philadelphia: Temple University Press.

Lowe, Lisa. 1996. *Immigrant Acts: On Asian American Cultural Politics.* Durham, NC: Duke University Press.

Mandal, Sumit. 2004. "Transethnic Solidarities, Racialisation and Social Equality." In *The State of Malaysia: Ethnicity, Equity and Reform,* ed. Edmund Terence Gomez, 49–78. London: Routledge Curzon.

Miyoshi, Masao. 1996. "A Borderless World? From Colonialism to Transnationalism and the Decline of the Nation-State." In *Global/Local,* ed. Rob Wilson and Wimal Dissanayake, 78–106. Durham, NC: Duke University Press.

———. 1998. "'Globalization,' Culture, and the University." In *The Cultures of Globalization,* ed. Frederic Jameson and Masao Miyoshi, 247–270. Durham, NC: Duke University Press.

Sandoval, Chela. 2000. *Methodology of the Oppressed.* Minneapolis: University of Minnesota Press.

Scott, James. 1998. *Seeing Like a State.* New Haven, CT: Yale University Press.

Sears, Laurie J. 2007. "Reading Ayu Utami: Notes Toward a Study of Trauma and the Archive in Indonesia." *Indonesia* 83: 17–40.

———. 2010. "Modernity and Decadence in Fin-de-Siècle Fiction of the Dutch Empire." *Indonesia* 90: 97–124.

———. 2013. *Situated Testimonies: Dread and Enchantment in an Indonesian Literary Archive.* Honolulu: University of Hawai'i Press.

Sears, Laurie J., ed. 2007. *Knowing Southeast Asian Subjects.* Seattle: University of Washington Press.

See, Sarita. 2002. "An Open Wound: Colonial Melancholia and Contemporary Filipino/American Texts." In *Vestiges of War 1899–1999: The Philippine-American War and the Aftermath of an Imperial Dream,* ed. Angel Shaw and Luis Francia, 376–400. New York: New York University Press.

Soekarno. 1955, 17 August. Speech. In *Asia-Africa Speaks from Bandung.* Djakarta: Ministry of Foreign Affairs, 19–29. http://www.ena.lu/discours_soekarno_bandoeng_17_24_avril_1955-1-7389 (accessed 29 June 2010).

Stoler, Ann, and Carole McGranahan. 2007. "Introduction: Refiguring Imperial Terrains." In *Imperial Formations,* ed. Ann L. Stoler, Carole McGranahan, and Peter C. Perdue, 3–44. Santa Fe, NM: School for Advanced Research Press.

Tadiar, Neferti. 2009. *Things Fall Away: Philippine Historical Experience and the Makings of Globalization.* Durham, NC: Duke University Press.

Utami, Ayu. 1998. *Saman.* Jakarta: Kepustakaan Populer Gramedia.

———. 2001. *Larung.* Jakarta: Kepustakaan Populer Gramedia.

———. 2005a [1998]. *Saman: A Novel.* Trans. Pamela Allen. Jakarta: Equinox Publishing.

———. 2005b. "Writing as Negation." *Why I Write.* International Writing Program Panel. Iowa City Public Library, Iowa City, IA. 26 October. http://iwp.uiowa.edu/archives/event-docs/Utami_Why_I_write.pdf (accessed 4 July 2010).

———. 2010. *Manjali dan Cakrabirawa.* Jakarta: Kepustakaan Populer Gramedia.

von Sacher-Masoch, Leopold. 1870. *Venus in Furs.* In *Masochism* by Gilles Deleuze and Leopold von Sacher-Masoch, 143–272. New York: Urzone

Yuval-Davis, Nira. 2002. "Imagined Boundaries and Borders: A Gendered Gaze." *European Journal of Women's Studies* 9 (3): 329–344.

Part III

Transpacific Populations

7

Imaginary Languages in Translation, Imagined National Cinemas

AKIRA MIZUTA LIPPIT

In spite of the vigorous rhetoric of renewed national cinemas in East Asia, the late twentieth and early twenty-first centuries are marked by the disintegration of national cinemas throughout Asia, and the emergence of a transnational Asian cinema in its place—a phenomenon driven by inter-Asian coproduction, a greater fluidity of talent across multiple Asian cultures, and the confusion of national and nationalist politics. While the material forces that implemented an increasingly trans-Asian cinema are tangible, the immaterial or imaginary forces are equally potent: the collapse of national languages transforms certain films that might otherwise be identified as national into transnational and historical, or more accurately into anational and ahistorical works. One might take this thought a step farther: these films sometimes produce, through polyvocity, the absence of language as such. A national cinema without language; an anational cinema that emerges from this structuring absence.

Among the many examples of films that feature hybridized language are Wong Kar-wai's *2046* (2004), which includes trans-Asian Japanese pop star Kimura Takyua speaking Japanese in a Chinese-language film; Iwai Shunji's *Swallowtail* (1996), in which the native languages of a multinational cast of characters are displaced; Lee Si-myung's anti-Japanese Korean action film, *2009: Lost Memories* (2002), notable for its significant Japanese funding and bilingual performances; Kim Ki-duk's *Dream* (*Bi-mong*, 2008), with Lee Na-young and Odagiri Jo, which is acted in two languages, with all of Odagiri's lines spoken in Japanese; Pen-Ek Ratanaruang's *Last Life in the Universe* (*Ruang rak noi nid mahasan*, 2003), a hybrid Thai-Japanese gangster film; and Kore-eda Hirokazu's *Air Doll* (*Kûki ningyô*, 2009), which stars Korean actress Bae Du-na as an inflatable sex doll that comes to life. Another product of the

Asian transnational cinema is Taiwanese-Japanese actor Kaneshiro Takeshi, an international polymorphic (polyethnic) star who appears in Chinese and Japanese productions, inflected as Chinese (mainland or Hong Kong) or Japanese, depending on the needs of each film or program. Still another product is Hou Hsiao-hsien's Taiwanese history films, which reflect the multilingual realities of the colonial and immediate postcolonial eras.[1] Miike Takashi's *Sukiyaki Western Django* (2007), with a Japanese cast that acts in English, or Clint Eastwood's *Letters from Iwo Jima* (2006), an American film in Japanese or a Japanese film made in America by an American (icon), suggest further collapses of the national language in national cinemas. These and other examples of a translingual cinema reveal a trans-Asian spectrum moving from national to transnational cinemas. What are the implications of a newly configured Asian cinema that may retain its multiple nationalisms while yielding the very basis of such nationalisms, the very concept of national culture as such? What might such a nationalism without nations look like?

Although examples of mixed or hybrid languages appear throughout Asia and across the globe, the instances of hybrid Japanese-language films reveal the extent to which the pursuit of empire jeopardizes the very condition of possibility of the nation itself: the very center of the nation, its imagined language. Three examples reveal the *disarticulation* of languages at work in the imaginational cinemas of contemporary East Asia.

Iwai Shunji's *Swallowtail*, set in a fictional near future, renames a trans-Asian Tokyo as "Yen Town." Migrant workers of multiple nationalities form the city and its inhabitants, who are called similarly Yen Town. The place and its people share the same name, creating a conduit between a geography and population, a living geography or embodied site. Iwai constructs an architecture of linguistic displacement in *Swallowtail*: Caucasians speak only Japanese, while Japanese pop stars play Chinese and other Asian characters, speaking a range of languages from Chinese-accented Japanese to Japanese-accented English. During one scene, a musical audition, a Caucasian actor (in fact a well-known comic in Japan whose routine includes, among other things, a series of impersonations of famous Japanese entertainment figures) complains to the selections committee about the assumption that he speaks English because he's white.

His complaint, delivered in a fluent, unaccented, and idiomatic Japanese ("Ay donto speeku ingurisshu") is not unfamiliar in Japan, where languages and races are assumed to form an organic bond. He signals a reality in which languages are unbound from biology, but also from national ideology, revealing as an effect of colonialism the disentanglement of languages from national identities. His band, "Third Culture Kids" facilitates a visualization—

white face, Japanese idiom—of a denationalized nation, a deterritorialized nation, one might say, in which the national language has been rendered minor. The "Japanese" in *Swallowtail* speak with accents while the Third Culture Kids retain an image of the Japanese language. Language is visualized in this scene, imagined in the bodies of deterritorialized Japanese, of a deterritorialized Japan no longer distinguishable from its Yen Town inhabitants.

Language plays a similarly disorienting role in Kore-eda Hirokazu's *Air Doll*. Kore-eda's decision to cast Korean actress Bae Du-na as the lead character in a film about a sex doll that acquires a heart or soul ("kokoro wo motte shimatta") raises specters of Japanese colonialism and the legacy of sexual slavery.[2] As Youngmin Choe has said, Kore-eda "cannot be unaware of the implications, yet chooses not to thematize them in the film" (Choe 2010). A film that at once discloses and forecloses Japanese war crimes, *Air Doll* is similarly a film about Japan, about the state of Japan and of Japaneseness (of an abject loneliness), while transcending or universalizing Japan into the realm of the human condition, and the task of becoming human.

An early scene in *Air Doll* shows a newly mobile and embodied Nozomi ("desire") dressed in a maid's fetish outfit beginning to learn everyday human greetings and practices. What is unclear in this scene, given the extradiegetic knowledge of Bae's nationality, is the extent to which she is learning to be Japanese as opposed to learning to be human. Nozomi learns to send children off to school, to separate "burnable" from "nonburnable" garbage (a corporeal divide that will ultimately separate her plastic body from those of fleshly human beings), and—following the lead of an eccentric neighborhood woman—to thank the neighborhood's workers. (She is in fact here being misled, since these greetings appear excessive and out of the ordinary.) Throughout the scene, Nozomi's language is marked less as Korean-accented than as stilted or tentative: if her language sounds unnatural, it is an effect of her fragile relation to humanity rather than her nonnative tongue. (In a later scene, after Nozomi has imitated a phrase uttered earlier by her "owner," Junichi, her quasi-boyfriend, asks her where she learned to speak with an Osaka dialect.) Nozomi's language, like her body, is malleable. The way she walks, in short hops, reveals an equally tentative relationship to her body, to its mobility, underscoring the delicate embodiment she has achieved at this stage of her life.

Complicating an otherwise Pinocchio-esque story is Kore-eda's refusal to deemphasize the sexual dimension of this film, in particular the ways in which multiple male characters, multiple Japanese male characters one is compelled to add, use Nozomi's body for sexual pleasure. Nozomi herself repeats a refrain throughout the film: "I am an air doll, a substitute object for others to fulfill their sexual desires." Although Nozomi's body is a figure for *the* body—for her own as well as others' bodies, a substitute (*fuyôhin*), a figure for figures—her language is literal, ametaphorical: when others describe themselves as "empty," she assumes that they are, like her, filled with air. Her language is an extension of her body—formal, corporeal, figural only to the extent that it refers to her body as an originary substitute. Nozomi accepts and even embraces her raison d'être, an ontology that renders her a being whose existence is based on responding to the other's sexual desire, the other's sex. In *Air Doll*, the lines that separate Nozomi's language from her body; her neighborhood and nation from the place of her origin in a factory; her quasi-Japaneseness from her quasi-humanity; and her destiny with the nonburnable garbage from the burnable bodies of human beings vanish, evoking the image in its place of a Japanless Japan. Like the audition sequence from *Swallowtail*, Nozomi's tenuous relation to her language and her body, enhanced by the fact that a Korean woman is playing a nonhuman character in a Japanese film, breaks the natural relations assumed to exist between a national body and its national language. Bae Du-na's presence in the film calls into question the naturalness of all the bodies around her, of the language that each speaks, and ultimately perhaps, the Japaneseness of any Japanese person. Kore-eda, who claims to have never even considered casting a Japanese actress for the role of Nozomi, effects in *Air Doll* a film that no longer appears Japanese, a film whose language has been deterritorialized, disarticulated, deconstructed into a series of removable, transposable, disposable body parts.

The transposition of bodies, affects, and languages in Kim Ki-duk's *Dream* goes farthest perhaps in decoupling national languages from national bodies and the national cinemas they inhabit. The film, about a man whose dreams are acted out by a complete stranger, a woman he's never met, features two Asian stars, Korean actress Lee Na-young and Japanese actor Odagiri Jo. (Odagari also plays a small part in *Air Doll* as Nozomi's creator, a Geppetto figure to whom Nozomi returns at one point in the film. Odagiri's character greets her by saying, "welcome home" ["okaeri"]. To which she responds, "I'm home" ["tadaima"]. The "home" that the dollmaker refers to is the factory where Nozomi was created, but it also resonates ambiguously with the sense of home lost in the empire of Japan and of human beings.) In *Dream*, the ambiguously named Jin (which could sound Korean or Japanese, and in Japanese is a homophone for "person"), played by Odagiri, delivers all of his lines in Japanese. Ran, played by Lee Na-young, speaks in Korean throughout, as do all the other characters in *Dream*. Their communication, frequently intimate, takes place telepathically in one sense, and through a transcendental, pre-Babelian "pure language" in another.

The multilingualism of Kim's paranormal thriller evokes the colonial era, but like *Air Doll*, makes no explicit reference to what nonetheless appears to function as a referent. Within the diegesis, Jin is Korean; only the spectator has access to his difference. The naturalization of Japanese as Korean—and the integration of the two languages into one, as if each was a related dialect of one centralized language—returns to a colonial moment but also reverses it. It is not only an inversion of power, but a deterritorialization of language, a perversion of the logic of languages, of Korean and Japanese. Japanese becomes indistinguishable from Korean—no one notices. Japanese is absorbed into Korean until it disappears. Jin is a Korean who speaks an imperceptible Japanese. The non–Japanese-speaking Korean audiences are asked to read subtitles, to follow a Korean character whose idiom is Japanese. The language (difference) disappears into the murmur of subtitles, which opens onto a third language or space of language.

By weaving together two languages, which at one time represented hierarchies of power and identity, Kim produces an imaginary language that visualizes the spectral space of its own communication. In *Dream,* communication takes place between two strangers in dreams, in the quasi-visual space of dreams where, according to Freud, languages and words operate materially and graphically as well as symbolically.[3] In dreams, words become objects as well as signs, images of signs. The fact that two languages are fused into one in *Dream* works in contrast to the fantastic communication that moves between Jin's and Ran's unconscious. The language that binds them is imagined, imaginary, composed of images they transpose from one psyche to another, one body to another, from the inside to the outside world.

The imagined languages of imagined communities or nations are not imaginary because they are false. They may be illusory projections, but they are imaginary because they generate images, because they transform language into a series of signs or images that dismantle the relationship between national languages and nations. And when this relation collapses, the entire organization of the national body disperses into a series of hybrid bodies, into a series of inter- or transnational cyborgs, dolls, phantoms, only ever part-human or part-national at any given moment. One might imagine an Asian national cinema in such a state of perpetual disassembly: a contemporary Asian cinema that has moved from the vernacular literacy that Benedict Anderson imagines through the rise of print capitalism to the "quasi-literacy" that Derrida names as an effect of the audiovisual media.[4] In his conversation with Bernard Stiegler, on and about television, Derrida speaks of the diminished literacy the technical media induce:

We are by and large in a state of quasi-literacy with respect to the image. Just as literacy and mastery of language, of spoken or of written discourse, have never been universally shared (it goes without saying that there have always been, not only people who can read and people who can't, but among those who can, a great diversity of competencies, abilities, etc.) so today, with respect to what is happening with the image, we might say, by analogy, that the vast majority of consumers are in a state analogous to these diverse modalities of relative literacy (Derrida and Stiegler 2002, 59).

Derrida's inscription of literacy by analogy, of an analogical or analog literacy, brings the question of images, the history of images and their consumption, into alignment with the history of language and the "diverse modalities of relative literacy" they engender. His qualification of image literacy as a quasi- or partial literacy is revealing. He situates the current state of media literacy on the side of neither fluency nor illiteracy, but within an interstitial literacy, a half-literacy that renders one, as a consumer of images, both literate and illiterate at once, understanding some of what images convey without full comprehension or competency. The "quasi-literacy" may not be a contemporary historical phenomenon only; which is to say the partial literacy that Derrida locates may not be an effect of the evolution of new literacies that are still, today, immature. Rather, media literacy may be essentially a quasi-literacy, a condition of literacy that always remains partial to the hybrid literacies of image cultures. For the audiovisual media may be only quasi-literate, only in part linguistic, only ever quasi-lingual in nature. If so, then media literacy would always require not a full literacy but a quasi-literacy, a transliteracy not only between languages but between media, between language and media. Quasi-literacy as the condition of media fluency, media flow. A quasi-literacy that calls for a supplementary translation, a quasi-translation that leaves the text suspended between two languages, two media, two states of articulation.

What kind of nation or nationalism can be founded on such quasi-literate states? Can the audiovisual media form new nationalisms along the lines Anderson imagines in the late eighteenth and nineteenth centuries? And would media archivization of the past resemble by way of analogy the eighteenth- and nineteenth-century drives to translate that Anderson describes? What would the relation between translation and archivization mean for the foundation of nations and nationalisms between the era of the book and that of audiovisual media? Alain Resnais and Marguerite Duras's 1959 collaboration *Hiroshima mon amour* brings the questions of national identity, national trauma, and the literacies of both into focus. Begun as a Franco-Japanese documentary intended to commemorate the fifteenth anniversary of the atomic bombing of Hiroshima, the work was already envisioned as a translation of Resnais's searching exposé of French complicity in the Holocaust, *Night and Fog (Nuit et brouillard*, 1955). It also involves the exclusion of a key national figure, the United States. (The signifier of the United States does appear in several key moments in the film, perhaps most notably when the scene moves to a café named "Casablanca."[5]) Resnais came close to abandoning the project until his French producer convinced author Marguerite Duras to write the script, following Resnais's comment that he needed her. As a result of Duras's intervention, the film turned from documentary to fiction, becoming a documentary folded into a fiction, a fiction framed by a document, a documented fiction. The film traces a brief love affair between a French actress (Emmanuel Riva) who has come to Japan to shoot an antiwar film about Hiroshima and a Japanese architect (Okada Eiji), whom she meets while there. During their encounter, she recalls an earlier episode in her life, a quasi-trauma that took place in her village, Nevers, during the war. As a young woman, she fell in love with a German soldier in occupied France; he was killed and she was ostracized, confined in a basement and then exiled to Paris after the end of the war. She tells and relives this past event in the present, through her Japanese lover who channels, transfers, translates the unspeakable loss that has left her at a loss for words, suspended in her loss since the end of the war.

At work throughout Resnais and Duras's transformed film is a sustained dialectical difference: "He" and "She," men and women, the named and the nameless (those who name and those who are named), "Hiroshima" and "Nevers," Japan and France, architecture and acting, documentary and fiction. The two characters never receive proper names, although they give each other as names the names of their respective cities, Hiroshima and Nevers. Of the proper name and its untranslatability, Derrida says, "A proper name as such remains forever untranslatable, a fact that may lead one to conclude that it does not strictly belong, for the same reason as the other words, to the language, to the system of language, be it translated or translating" (1985a, 171).[6] As such "Hiroshima" and "Nevers" remain outside of language, outside of the system of language, untranslatable, as Derrida says; their names are proper to the untranslatability of the places they name. It is the untranslatable dimension of the film that drives its dialectic, which operates throughout the film, in virtually every aspect of the film, without language. The film turns around questions of sexual difference and the imaginary languages of individual and national trauma. Resnais's imagined documentary on Hiroshima is replaced, displaced by another site of trauma, the one that "She" (Emmanuelle Riva) describes in Nevers. As a young woman in occupied France, "She" fell into a secret and prohibited love (another dialectic opens up between Germany and France, inter-European). Her German lover was eventually killed by a French sniper, and she was kept in seclusion to hide and inscribe her shame for betraying her nation. "She" suffers from loss, from the loss of her German lover, but also the doubled loss she experiences when she begins, day by day, to forget him. "I am starting to forget you." Her amnesia is interrupted in Hiroshima, in her encounter with "He" (Okada Eiji), with him, "Hiroshima," whose twitching hand in the morning jolts her memory, and reactivates the nervous amnesia that conceals her trauma. From Hiroshima to Nevers and back, the dialectical economy of *Hiroshima mon amour* moves by transference, through substitution, names, and proper names for affects that move from one country to another, one body to another without any ruptures in language. Things stand for other things in an economy of deferral; one for another becomes the primary mode of communication between the two principal characters. Ultimately the transferential economy of *Hiroshima mon amour* comes to replace the possibility of translation, which never takes place in the film. There is, throughout *Hiroshima mon amour*, no space of translation, no occasion for it, with the exception of a quasi-comical scene at the train station when an old woman inquires about the two and "He" is forced to speak Japanese for the first time in the film, a language that no longer sounds native to him—another Japanese, the other's Japanese, a French quasi-Japanese.

For, despite the complex play of difference—sexual, political, cultural, and national—that drives the interactive economy of *Hiroshima mon amour*, in one crucial register difference never intervenes: language. "He" and "She" speak in French, idiomatic French, Duras's French. Not only do "He" and "She" speak French, they speak the same French. "Tu n'as vu rien à Hiroshima." In the register of language, all of the differences, all difference itself collapses into a universal language: love, sympathy, Esperanto. Is this the fantasy of what Walter Benjamin calls "pure language" (*reine Sprache*)? He says, "All suprahistorical kinship of languages rests in the intention underlying each language as a whole—an intention, however, which no single language can attain by itself but which is realized only by the totality of their intentions supplementing each other: pure language" (Benjamin 1968, 74). A synthetic language achieved or rather imagined, Benjamin argues, in translation, in *translatability*. Is Resnais and Duras's French such a language, supplemented, supplementary, imagined as the "pure language" spoken between two people who share no language? A language, French, at the end of translation, beyond translation and translatability? Is it a French that has incorporated Japanese, a French spoken by speakers with traces of Japanese, a suprahistorical language at the end of French and Japanese? But what if the French here were also not French, but another, different French? (Derrida says: "Translation can do everything except mark this linguistic difference inscribed in the language, this difference of language systems inscribed in a single tongue. At best it can get everything across except this: the fact that there are, in one linguistic system, perhaps several languages or tongues" [Derrida 1985b, 100].[7]) A quasi-French, spoken between two people, imagined only as one language, the language of a trauma that erases language? Is his francophony a quasi-francophony, their shared francophony a fantasy like everything else between them? In this case, an imaginary French spoken only here in the space of an improbable encounter between those two unnamed characters in Resnais and Duras's detour. What if this French that elides, even negates, translation, the necessity for translation—that imagines a world without translation and love without translators—itself needed translation? What if this French were already a translation and at the same time, a French whose translation to come, as Benjamin says, was already anticipated?

Such a translation before and after the fact, in fact exists. Suwa Nobuhiro's *H Story* (2002), a narrative feature about a failed remake of *Hiroshima mon amour*, appears to be, or to turn into during the course of the film, a documentary about a failed remake of Resnais and Duras's film. It translates the failure embedded in the original into a narrative about failure, making visible what vanishes into the first minutes of the original: the footage that Resnais shot for a documentary he never completed. *H Story* becomes a documentary about a failed narrative film, an inversion of Resnais's failed documentary. Suwa's film turns to the original, returns to it, and transforms the universal and universalizing language of the original from a transferential language without language to a language that comes into being only in its ultimately failed translatability. Suwa's "remake" features Béatrice Dalle in the role played by Emmanuelle Riva; his purported objective is to reshoot the original scene by scene, shot by shot, line by line. During the shooting of the remake, Dalle rebels against the ventriloquism and mimicry and refuses to continue. At this point the film breaks down, and Dalle disappears with another of the film's actors, Machida Kou. They end up in the same shopping arcades that Emmanuelle Riva and Okada Eiji roam in the original, and the film concludes in failure inside the Atomic Bomb Dome where the two have spent the night. *H Story* is not only a translation of *Hiroshima mon amour*, it is a film about translation, a film about the incommensurability of language and of languages. "All translation," Benjamin says, "is only a somewhat provisional way of coming to terms with the foreignness of languages" (1968, 75). What happens to language, to national languages and the nationalisms they make possible when specific languages become untranslatable? When the foreignness of language, of my language, our language, remains insurmountable? Although Suwa is himself from Hiroshima, it is a far less nationalist film than *Hiroshima mon amour;* his is a film that in contrast to Resnais and Duras's original removes Hiroshima from the space of language, leaving it instead as a series of traces within many languages. (Whereas

"Hiroshima" in Resnais and Duras's language names the Japanese man, his body, or national body [kokutai].) Suwa never claims Hiroshima, the place, word, or initial as his own. In this sense, Suwa's disavowal of nationalism in *H Story* renders him an ideal translator, according to Benjamin. "Our translators," says Benjamin, "have a far greater reverence for the usage of their own language than for the spirit of the foreign works . . . The basic error of the translator is that he preserves the state in which his own language happens to be instead of allowing his language to be powerfully affected by the foreign tongue" (1968, 80–81). Suwa's language seems to be given over to a foreign tongue almost entirely. He is lost inside this translation, without "fixed boundaries," as Trinh T. Minh-ha says: "In the politics of constructing identity and meaning, language as translation is necessarily a process whereby the self loses its fixed boundaries" (Trinh and McDonald 1992, 133).[8] In this sense, it is not meaning that is lost in translation, it is the subject, the translator who yields to the other's foreign tongue. And in this moment, everything is lost, including the humanity of the subject itself.

Suwa's withdrawal in *H Story,* the withdrawal of his discourse into history, a history without subjectivity, a history without an "I," renders him a translator, according to a logic of translation developed by Naoki Sakai. Following Émile Benveniste's distinction between "discourse," which produces and is produced by a singular subject (of enunciation) and "history," which effects a narrative through the withdrawal of the discursive subject, the "I," Sakai describes the depersonalization of the translator as subject in acts of translation:

> The translator cannot be designated either as "I" or as "you" straightforwardly: she disrupts the attempt to appropriate the relation of the addresser and the addressee into the *personal* relation of the first person vis-à-vis second person. To follow the determination of "person" as espoused by Émile Benveniste—that is, that only those directly addressing and addressed in what he calls "discourse" as distinct from "story" or "history" can be called persons, and those that are referred to or talked about in the capacity of "he," "she," or "they" in "story" or "history" cannot be "persons." (Sakai 1997, 12–13, original emphasis)[9]

"He" or "she" cannot be persons in a historical enunciation, while no translator can address or be addressed in the first or second person pronouns. The third person replaces the subject in history, while the first person translator recedes in the translation, a vanishing "I" from the subject of enunciation. The two sides of history (discourse and story) describe the dialectic of translation that moves between *Hiroshima mon amour* and *H Story*: the imaginary "homolingualism" of the former is replaced by the defiant untranslatability of the latter.

Sakai's term "homolingualism" refers to the shared idiom of two speakers, even if their languages are different, as in the case of the otherwise nameless "He" and "She" in *Hiroshima mon amour*.[10] On the other side of history, translation itself gives rise to untranslatability. Sakai says, "It is translation that gives birth to the untranslatable" (1997, 14). He adds: "The translatable and untranslatable are both posterior to translation as *repetition*. Untranslatability does not exist before translation: translation is the a priori of the untranslatable" (Sakai 1997, 5, original emphasis). Untranslatability as such, according to Sakai, exists as an effect of translation; translation creates as an aftereffect and condition of translation, untranslatability. The dialectic of language that moves between *Hiroshima mon amour* and *H Story* involves the disappearance of the subjects of history—"He" and "She" in *Hiroshima mon amour*—into the story, into history itself, while the subject of translation, the translator, vanishes from history, from the title or name of history (*H Story*). This is also what happened to hundreds of thousands at Hiroshima who on August 6, 1945, vanished in a flash into the shadows of history, leaving traces of themselves, and of a language to remember them by. What is left between an imagined and imaginary homolingualism in one and the aporias of language and translation in the other is a representation, an image, an imagined language and the imaginary nations they name.

Sakai emphasizes this aspect of translation: translations do not produce unities between languages. Rather, they "articulate" the two (or more) languages as if they were "autonomous and closed entities," rendering a *representation* of languages and translatability. What translations engender are representations. Sakai says,

> Strictly speaking, it is not because two different language unities are given that we have to translate (or interpret) one text into another; it is because translation articulates languages so that we may postulate the two unities of the translating and translated languages as if they were autonomous and closed entities through a certain *representation of translation*. (Sakai 1997, 2, original emphasis)

Translations articulate two languages into a representation of language, of communicability, of translatability and untranslatability, of an image of the nation and of nations. In this sense, Suwa's disavowal of a national language, of the articulation of Hiroshima as a national and nationalist signifier, replaces the idea of a national language with a representation, with what Paul de Man calls a "disarticulation" of the original language in translation. *H Story* unleashes the destructive force of language itself, the atomic force of "pure language." "Translation," says de Man, "to the extent that *it disarticulates the original*, to the extent that it is pure language and is only concerned with language, gets drawn into what he [Benjamin] calls the bottomless depth, something essentially destructive, which is in language itself" (de Man 1986, 84, emphasis added). What Suwa achieves in *H Story* is the destruction—the disarticulation—of Japanese as a national language, creating in its place the representation of a Japanese language, an imaginary Japanese language estranged from the national body. This is also what Gilles Deleuze and Félix Guattari call in another context but to the same effect, the "deterritorialization" of language.[11]

H Story undoes nationalism by failing to produce a national language, by disarticulating or deterritorializing it, losing Japanese in translation: Suwa allows the French word for Hiroshima to replace the authenticity of the same Japanese word. "Hiroshima" in Japanese is translated by "Hiroshima" in French or quasi-French. The signifier "Hiroshima" in Suwa's film refers neither to a place, a historical event, or any signified dimension of the sign Hiroshima. It is an estranged signifier that refers only, in the context of the film and its diegesis, to another film. Suwa's signifier refers only to a sign that signifies the limits of signification. His Hiroshima, his Japanese, disappears in translation and re-emerges in the quasi-Japanese of the other. As subject, as translator, Suwa loses himself in the language of another, a language other than his own, the Japanese spoken by another, by the other. Of the suffering that translation effects, the estrangement of the subject from his or her own language, de Man says,

> What translation does, by reference to the fiction or hypothesis of a pure language devoid of the burden of meaning, is that it implies—in bringing to light what Benjamin calls "die Wehen des eigenen"—the suffering of what one thinks of as one's own—the suffering of the original language. We think we are at ease in our own language, we feel a coziness, a familiarity, a shelter in the language we call our own, in which we think we are not alienated. What the translation reveals is that this alienation is at its strongest in our relation to our own original language, that the original language within which we are engaged is disarticulated in a way which imposes upon us a particular alienation, a particular suffering. (de Man 1986, 84)

The suffering that one feels in language, one's own language, is originary; translation makes the suffering visible, the alienation of language visible to oneself. As Sakai says, "It is translation that gives birth to the untranslatable." The untranslatable suffering of originary language, of an originary self brought into being, born in translation, is rendered in translation, turned from the untranslatable origin into a *representation of untranslatability*. All translations are, according to Benjamin, Derrida, Sakai, and de Man, representations of a profoundly disarticulated and powerfully alienated self. No language, originary or national, is proper to anyone. Translations make this condition clear. Suwa understands this.

If the untranslatable trauma of Hiroshima is replaced in Resnais's film by Nevers (displaced or reimagined in an imaginary topography elsewhere), then in order to return to Hiroshima, Suwa substitutes, through translation, the trauma of Nevers with the film itself, *Hiroshima mon amour*. The referent of Suwa's Hiroshima is not the actuality of Hiroshima, the authenticity of a place, of its taking place in the place that it names, but rather the film that takes the name of Hiroshima, that takes the place of Hiroshima, and that names the place of the name of Hiroshima. By tracing Hiroshima to the name of a film, Suwa undoes the film (his as well as "hers"), undoes the original detour (which was in fact always only a turn) and arrives at Hiroshima in the last scene, in the very interior of the Hiroshima named as a referent in the original, inside the Dome. Suwa ends with a view of Hiroshima from the inside out, a view of the outside that situates Hiroshima elsewhere, in a flash that exposes and over-exposes the film into pure white radiation. Suwa's "Hiroshima" is in fact a translation of Resnais and Duras's "Hiroshima." It represents an intra-phonic or homophonic translation.

H Story begins in its title with a translation, with the return to a language erased in Hiroshima (mon amour). It is itself a language of erasure. "H Story" suggests a contraction of Hiroshima to the letter H; it also points to a missing letter, "I," which would complete the title as "history," suturing the two words into one. A missing subject or "I," which would make the story *his* story, his as opposed to hers, an I-novel or *shishôsetsu*, with a particular point of view or "eye." The missing "I" can also be heard in Japanese as a missing "ai," or love: "History without "I," "ai," or "love" (*Ai ga nai hisutorî* [history without love]). Suwa's English title and ambiguity of a missing letter suggests a translation between English and Japanese in addition to the French-Japanese translations that suffuse the film, both the original and the remake. "H Story" can also be read as "The Story of H," a play by Suwa perhaps on Pauline Réage's 1954 erotic novel *Histoire d'O* (The Story of O). "H," which means sexual perversion *and* intercourse in Japanese, is a ubiquitous word in the Japanese vernacular, is at once a quasi-acronym ("H" for *hentai*); a naturalized foreign word or *gairaigo* (the Roman letter "H"); a verb—*H wo suru* means "to do 'H'"; and a noun meaning "pervert." "H" is a Japanese word in translation that is perhaps *untranslatable*. Paul de Man notes in his reading of Benjamin that the translatable and untranslatable are one and the same, which render the economies of H and translation, its translation uncanny.[12] *H Story* then is also the story of sex or of perversion. The Japanese "H" is an uncanny word, since it means one thing (sexual intercourse) and its opposite (sexual perversion). It functions as an explicit and opaque term that both overexposes and underexposes the object it names. To be "H" is to be revealed and withheld in a tangled economy of sexual identification. The strange dynamic of this metonymic word/letter signals simultaneously normal and abnormal, casual and obsessive, sexualities. (The H is already at work in the original: the Japanese title of *Hiroshima mon amour* is *Nijû yojikan no jôji* [twenty-four-hour love affair], a perverse although not inaccurate translation of the French title.)

The turn from Hiroshima to H in Suwa's film, the ambiguous contraction of Hiroshima into a letter or perhaps some other signifier (hydrogen or H bomb, for example), signals a series of turns that takes place between genders; in the spaces of eros and sexual encounters; between cultures and languages; between film and literature; between cinema and language; and between films and filmmakers. The shift from France to Japan in this film, and the way that shift is registered, suggests a number of possibilities for thinking about Hiroshima, the representation of Hiroshima, and the limits of both Hiroshima and representation. The attempt at an exact shot-for-shot remake ends in failure, is destined, one might say, for failure yet the failure arrives, as it were, at the point of Resnais's own failed film: in failing at the remake—the shooting collapses and the film becomes at one point a documentary, which reproduces in reverse the failure that constitutes Resnais's point of departure—Suwa completes the remake, the repetition and translation of Resnais and Duras's film. Had the film succeeded as imagined, what would it have achieved? A project, perhaps, like Pierre Menard's radical rewriting, word for word, of Cervantes's *Don Quixote* in Borges's story: neither reinscription, interpretation, nor translation, but the original work itself.[13]

Between *Hiroshima mon amour* and *H Story*—reiterations, revisions, translations, and transformations—between transference and translation, between the absence of translation and the paralysis of a translated untranslatability, or posttranslatability, one feels the effects of an ekphrasis in reverse. Not the description of visual materials in language, but the production of a visuality from the elements of language. This image or imaginary language is neither a transference nor translation, but, as Sakai says, a "representation of translation." For "translation," says Derrida, "is neither an image nor a copy," it is neither "representative" nor "reproductive."[14] Translations are themselves neither, but the representation of translation, of the transposition of one language to another, produces a representation, an image of language, perhaps the image of an elusive, illusory *pure language* that takes place between two languages, takes the place of any two or more languages, and appears not as the representation of one language in another, but as the representation of the movement from one language to another.

After Béatrice Dalle's rebellion, her refusal to ventriloquize the untranslatable lines of Duras's "She," *H Story* turns in on itself, against itself, becoming what appears to be now the documentary of a failed fiction; a film about the return of *Hiroshima mon amour* to its documentary origins. The film features scenes of Suwa's struggles to finish the film, interviews with the actors on Dalle's situation, and ultimately Suwa's decision to shut down production. One significant feature of Suwa's film is his inclusion of documentary footage of the aftermath of Hiroshima's bombing in color. Color 16 mm footage taken by U.S. and Japanese cinematographers in the days following August 6 exists. Their inclusion here draws attention to the black and white anachrony of Resnais and Duras's film: footage from 1945 appears in color while 1959 appears in black and white,[15] as if time is reversing or undoing itself between the two films, the distant past more recent than the recent past. Toward the film's end, Dalle and Machida Kou, who have fled the set and Suwa's failed remake, return to the same covered shopping alleys where Okada and Riva find themselves toward the end of *Hiroshima mon amour*. The intensity of their dialogue in the original is replaced in *H Story* by the quasi-comedic force of complete incommunicability between Dalle and Machida. If Okada and Riva suffer from the impossibility of their union in the original, Dalle and Machida appear resigned, even at ease with the impossibility of basic communication in the remake.

The imaginary French, a quasi- or universal French idiom spoken by "He" and "She" in *Hiroshima mon amour*, disintegrates into a series of disjointed monologues in *H Story*, addressed between Dalle and Machida at times, readdressed at others, and misaddressed entirely at yet other times. The disarticulation of the original produces a translation in the remake of absolute incommunicability. In the alley, Machida says to a stray dog, "I may never see you again." Machida's address to the dog, which Dalle is present for but cannot understand, comes to the viewer like a quasi-translation of a line from the original. It arrives like a deflected line, a detour through failed affect, which brings the question of imaginary languages and their translations to the very threshold of the human world. Machida's address to the dog, a quasi-translation of a line between "He" and "She" in the original, underscores de Man's point about the essential inhumanity of language. "That there is a non-human aspect of language," says de Man, "is a perennial awareness from which we cannot escape, because language does things which are so radically out of our control that they cannot be assimilated to the human at all" (de Man 1986, 101). The reference of language, made clear in its translations, is the nonhuman space that enfolds all human life: translations expose the hidden dimensions of such non- or inhuman being that is there always, nonetheless. The shot ends with Machida and Dalle walking toward the camera and out of the frame, the camera lingering on the dog, the nonhuman and failed translator of Suwa's remake.

If language originates, as de Man suggests, in the nonhuman realms of representation, then the originary translation, the first and primal translation, is not the movement from one language to another, even from a sacred language to a vernacular one, but rather the entry into language itself, from non-language to language, from the nonhuman languages to the human ones: the first translation is marked by the transition from radical singularity or solitude, from total alienation to repetition and language. It is only from the entry into language, into translatability and the loss of the proper name as proper that the individual comes into being, belatedly and after the fact. The suffering that de Man highlights in Benjamin's essay on translation is the trace of this originary translation, the movement into language and the human condition. Nozomi in *Air Doll* understands this perfectly. She embodies it. And Jin and Ran in *Dream* perform this affective, telepathic translation from psyche to body, unconscious to conscious, Japanese to Korean in the form of an invisible, secret translation that erases the interaction of national languages, replacing them with radically imaginary languages forged upon the traces of languages that no longer exist, anywhere. Here, elsewhere, national languages and cinemas, along with the nationalist imaginations they effect, are rendered imaginary, imaginational, imaginationalist fantasies.

Notes to Chapter 7: Imaginary Languages in Translation, Imagined National Cinemas

1. In response to an earlier presentation of this material, Dudley Andrew pointed out that heterogeneity of languages within national cinemas is not at all uncommon in many postcolonial countries, throughout West Africa for example. In those cases, the postcolonial state becomes itself the referent of the multilingualism; the nation defined in this instance by the multiplicity of languages. Hou Hsiao-hsien's Taiwan trilogy—*A City of Sadness* (1989), *The Puppetmaster* (1993), and *Good Men, Good Women* (1995)—reflects the multiplicity of languages as the effect of multiple colonial occupations in Taiwan. Characters speak to each other in different languages, with differing accents, and sometimes through translators. In some instances characters begin the sentence in one language and finish it another, or freely intersperse words from one language into another. There is in these films by Hou no single national language, only national languages, everything always in flux, in translation. The linguistic fluidity that Hou inscribes, however, has its referent in history. By contrast to Hou's Taiwanese trilogy, Kore-eda's *Air Doll* silences the sound of Korean, while Kim's *Dream* juxtaposes two distinct languages with no mediation. In both cases, language never refers to the postcolonial states of Japan and South Korea, although the specters of empire appear to haunt both films.

2. Bae Du-na, a veteran actor in the Korean cinema—Bong Joon-ho's *Barking Dogs Never Bite* (2000) and *The Host* (2006), Jeong Jae-eun's *Take Care of My Cat* (2001), and Park Chan-Wook's *Sympathy for Mr. Vengeance* (2002), among others—has also appeared in Japanese-language films, most notably Yamashita Nobuhiro's *Linda Linda Linda* (2005), in which she plays the lead vocalist of an all-girl rock band, although here she is a Korean exchange student whose limited Japanese is inscribed diegetically. In one scene, a Japanese suitor speaks to Son (Bae Du-na) in Korean, while she responds in Japanese; in another scene, a dream sequence, a fellow band member, Kei (Kashii Yu), responds to Son's Korean lines appropriately in Japanese, producing a conversational exchange between differing languages not unlike those effected in Kim's *Dream*.

3. In his reading of the effects of a critical mistranslation in Freud's work, "On the History of a Mistranslation and the Psychoanalytic Movement," Alan Bass emphasizes Freud's identification with translators and his comparison of psychoanalytic insight to acts of translation. "Freud often compared his initial discoveries to triumphs of translation," Bass writes. "During the 1890s he frequently maintained that he had found the means to translate hysterical symptoms and dreams into ordinary language, thereby claiming for science what had once been considered incomprehensible or trivial" (Bass 1985, 102). With regard to Kim's *Dream*, dreams may be here the translation machine, the vehicle or medium for disparate languages that synthesizes Japanese and Korean into a single Korean language, a form of secondary revision that keeps the spectator asleep in the film, like the characters Kim depicts.

4. Anderson narrates the rise of vernacular languages as national languages and the significance of translation to this process: "From this point on [the eighteenth century] the old sacred languages—Latin, Greek, and Hebrew—were forced to mingle on equal ontological footing with a motley plebian crowd of vernacular rivals, in a movement which complemented their earlier demotion in the market-place by print-capitalism. If all languages now shared a common (intra-) mundane status, then all were in principle equally worthy of study and admiration. But by who? Logically, since now none belonged to God, by their new owners: each language's native speakers—and readers" (1983, 70–71). Vernacular languages became interchangeable with sacred languages as well as with other vernacular languages. The totality of any specific vernacular language was measured by the translations of classical texts it could produce: the greater the number, the greater the language, and by extension the nation it founded. "By the middle of the eighteenth century," says Anderson, "the prodigious labors of German, French and English scholars had not only made available in handy printed form virtually the entire extant corpus of the Greek classics, along with the necessary philological and lexicographic adjuncts, but in dozens of books were recreating a glittering, and firmly pagan, ancient Hellenic civilization" (72). According to Anderson's account, the standardization of vernacular languages as national languages required the acts of translation that allowed other worlds—past worlds as well as alternate worlds, elsewhere—to open up inside the nation's readers, inside the nation's language which became itself a vessel for the appearance of the world as such. And as such, for the very condition of possibility of nationalism.

5. Other references to the United States and to English appear in the demonstrators' signs during the film shoot, when a waiter or host approaches Emmanuelle Riva's

character by speaking to her in English, and in the name of her village of origin, which gives her in turn her name: Nevers. The word can be heard in English as "never." The only place where French is spoken, where France exists, is between the two of them, "He" and She," as if it were a private, intimate French shared only between two people here and in the world. It is an imaginary French reminiscent of the Japanese that Chris Marker imagines himself to understand on Japanese television in *Sans Soleil* (1983), which turns out to be a broadcast about French poet Gérard de Nerval, or the many Japanese languages that Roland Barthes dreams of in *The Empire of Signs* (1970).

6. If the proper name begins outside of language and its systems, then it works its way into language through translation: not the translation from language into another, Derrida says, but through its translation *into* language as such. "One would be tempted to say *first* that a proper name, in the proper sense, does not properly belong to the language; it does not belong there, *although and because* its call makes the language possible (what would language be without the possibility of calling by a proper name?); consequently it can properly inscribe itself in language only by allowing itself to be translated therein, in other words, *interpreted* by its semantic equivalent: from this moment it can no longer be taken as proper name" (Derrida 1985a, 172, original emphasis). By entering language, proper names lose their singularity and cease being proper names.

7. Derrida further qualifies the frequency with which multiple languages appear within a single linguistic system: "Sometimes—I would even say always—several tongues" (1985b, 100).

8. "A disturbing yet potentially empowering practice of difference," she adds (Trinh and McDonald 1992, 133).

9. Sakai explains this elision of the first person subjectivity of the translator: "Supposedly it is not the translator who in translation is speaking or writing for the addressee. 'I' uttered by the translator does not designate the translator herself but the original addresser as the subject of the original enunciation. And if by 'I' the translator indicates the subject of the secondary and translational enunciation, she will then have to designate the original addresser as 'he' or 'she'" (Sakai 1997, 12).

10. Sakai describes homolingualism as "a regime of someone relating herself or himself to others in enunciation whereby the addresser adopts the position representative of a putatively homogeneous language society and relates to the general addressees, who are also representative of an equally homogeneous language community. Let me note that by the homolingual address I do not imply the social condition of conversation in which both the addresser and the addressee belong to the same language community; they believe themselves to belong to different languages yet could still address themselves homolingually" (1997, 3–4). Two speakers who speak different languages, according to Sakai, could still relate to one another homolingually. In this sense, Sakai's homolingualism is an imaginary language, a shared imaginary language.

11. In their study of Franz Kafka, Gilles Deleuze and Félix Guattari develop the notion of a "minor literature," which "doesn't come from a minor language; it is rather that which a minority constructs within a major language" (Gilles Deleuze and Félix Guattari, *Franz Kafka: Toward a Minor Literature,* trans. Dana Polan [Minneapolis: University of Minnesota Press, 1986], 16). For Deleuze and Guattari, the "deterritorial-

ization of language" that defines a minor literature comes from the creation of new languages within (major) languages, forcing the writer "to be a stranger," they say, within [one's] own language" (26). This minor literature deterritorializes the nation, the state language, producing a pack or horde of nomads. "How many people today live in a language that is not their own? Or no longer, or not yet, even know their own and know poorly the major language they are forced to serve? This is the problem of immigrants, and especially of their children, the problem of minorities, the problem of a minor literature, but also a problem for all of us: how to tear a minor literature away from its own language, allowing it to challenge the language and making it follow a sober revolutionary path? How to become a nomad and an immigrant and a gypsy in relation to one's own language?" (19).

12. In his seminar on Benjamin's "The Task of the Translator," de Man relates a story about the translation and mistranslation of Benjamin's own text. de Man recounts that in a seminar in French on Benjamin's essay, Derrida used Maurice de Gandillac's French translation of the German original, which included a mistranslation of the word "translatable" (*schlechthin*) as "untranslatable" (*intraduisable*). Noting Gandillac's mistake, de Man continues with this story: "What adds some comedy to this particular instance is that Jacques Derrida was doing a seminar with this particular text in Paris, using the French—Derrida's German is pretty good but he prefers to use the French, and when you are a philosopher in France you take Gandillac more or less seriously. So Derrida was basing part of his reading on the 'intraduisable,' on the untranslatability, until somebody in his seminar (so I'm told) pointed out to him that the correct word was 'translatable.' I'm sure that Derrida could explain that it was the same . . . and I mean that in a positive sense, it *is* the same, but still, it is not the same without some additional explanation" (de Man 1986, 80, original emphasis). Derrida confirms this. In "Des Tours de Babel," on the limits of translation, Derrida says: "Here we touch—at a point no doubt infinitely small—the limit of translation. The pure untranslatable and the pure translatable here pass one into the other—and it is the truth" (Derrida 1985a, 190).

13. Borges describes Pierre Menard's project thus: "He did not want to compose another *Quixote*—which is easy—but *the Quixote itself*. Needless to say, he never contemplated a mechanical transcription of the original; he did not propose to copy it. His admirable intention was to produce a few pages which would coincide—word for word and line for line—with those of Miguel de Cervantes" (Borges 1964, 39, original emphasis). Suwa's proposed remake resembles, at least at the outset, Menard's imaginary translation of the *Quixote*; both projects are themselves Quixotic. The result of Menard's rewriting produces a translation of Cervantes not unlike those imagined by Benjamin: "Cervantes' text and Menard's are verbally identical, but the second is almost infinitely richer. (More ambiguous, his detractors will say, but ambiguity is richness.)" (Borges 1964, 42).

14. Derrida 1985a, 180.

15. Color film stock was used widely in the United States from the mid-1950s onward. Although color stock was available throughout the world, for financial and aesthetic reasons, it took several more years into the 1960s for color films to become the standard elsewhere, in Europe and Asia, for example.

References

Anderson, Benedict. 1983. *Imagined Communities: Reflections on the Origin and Spread of Nationalism.* London: Verso.

Barthes, Roland. 1982 [1970]. *The Empire of Signs.* Trans. Richard Howard. New York: Hill and Wang.

Bass, Alan. 1985. "On the History of a Mistranslation and the Psychoanalytic Movement." In *Difference in Translation,* ed. and trans. Joseph F. Graham, 102–141. Ithaca, NY: Cornell University Press.

Benjamin, Walter. 1968. "The Task of the Translator." In *Illuminations: Essays and Reflections,* ed. Hannah Arendt, trans. Harry Zohn, 69–82. New York: Schocken.

Borges, Jorge Luis. 1964. "Pierre Menard, Author of the *Quixote.*" In *Labyrinths: Selected Stories and Other Writings,* trans. James E. Irby, 36–44. New York: New Directions.

Choe, Youngmin. 2010. Panel discussion. "Contemporary Japanese Cinema: Outside, Elsewhere, In the World . . ." University of Southern California, Los Angeles, CA, 20 February.

de Man, Paul. 1986. "'Conclusions': Walter Benjamin's 'The Task of the Translator.'" In *The Resistance to Theory,* 73–105. Minneapolis: University of Minnesota Press.

Deleuze, Gilles, and Félix Guattari. 1986. *Franz Kafka: Toward a Minor Literature.* Trans. Dana Polan. Minneapolis: University of Minnesota Press.

Derrida, Jacques. 1985a. "Des Tours de Babel." In *Difference in Translation,* ed. Joseph F. Graham, 165–248. Ithaca, NY: Cornell University Press.

———. 1985b. "Roundtable on Autobiography." In *The Ear of the Other: Otobiography, Transference, Translation,* ed. Christie V. McDonald, trans. Peggy Kamuf, 39–90. New York: Schocken.

Derrida, Jacques, and Bernard Stiegler. 2002. *Echographies of Television.* Trans. Jennifer Bajorek. Cambridge, UK: Polity.

Réage, Pauline. 1954. *Histoire d'O* (The Story of O). Paris: Chez Jean-Jacques Pauvert.

Sakai, Naoki. 1997. *Translation and Subjectivity: On "Japan" and Cultural Nationalism.* Minneapolis: University of Minnesota Press.

Trinh, T. Minh-ha, with Scott McDonald. 1992. "Film as Translation: A Net with No Fisherman." In *Framer Framed,* 111–136. New York: Routledge.

8

Militarized Refuge

A Critical Rereading of Vietnamese Flight to the United States

YẾN LÊ ESPIRITU

In the spring of 1975, as the North Vietnamese Army encircled Saigon, U.S. aircraft carriers airlifted approximately 125,000 Vietnamese citizens out of the city. The most frequently used route for these airlifted refugees was from Vietnam to Clark Air Force Base (AFB) in the Philippines to Andersen AFB on Guam to Marine Corps Base Camp Pendleton in California; over 41 percent traveled it (Liu et al. 1979, 80). About 19 percent went from Vietnam to Guam and then on to Camp Pendleton; another 32 percent traveled to Camp Pendleton, making stops in the Philippines, Guam, or Wake Island. Although these refugee flights have been widely covered by the media and scholars alike, few have analyzed the colonial and militarized nature of these routes. With the Department of Defense coordinating transportation, and the Joint Chiefs of Staff-Pacific Command in charge of the military moves necessary for the evacuation, Vietnamese were airlifted from Saigon on U.S. military aircraft, transferred to U.S. military bases in the Philippines, Guam, and also Thailand, Wake Island, and Hawaiʻi, and delivered to yet another set of military bases throughout the United States: Camp Pendleton in California, Fort Chaffee in Arkansas, Eglin AFB in Florida, and Fort Indiantown Gap in Pennsylvania. That few have interrogated these military connections speaks to the power of the myth of U.S. "rescue and liberation" to make in/un-visible the militarized nature of these evacuations.

This chapter challenges the "rescue and liberation" narrative of what has been dubbed "the largest humanitarian airlift in history" (Jolly 2010) by exposing the militarized nature of the U.S. refugee resettlement effort. In April 1975, it was the U.S. continuing military presence on the Philippines and Guam, its former and current colonial territories respectively, that made possible the quick conversion of these islands into refugee-receiving centers. I trace the most-traveled refugee route via military aircraft—from Vietnam to the Philippines to Guam and then to California, which routed the refugees through U.S. military bases—as a critical lens through which to map, both discursively and materially, the transpacific *displacement* brought about by the legacy of U.S. colonial and military expansion into the Asia-Pacific region. I make two related arguments: the first about military colonialism, which contends that it is the region's (neo)colonial dependence on the United States that turned the Philippines and Guam into the "ideal" receiving centers of U.S. rescuing project; the second about militarized refuge, which emphasizes the mutually constitutive nature of the concepts "refugees" and "refuge" and shows how both emerge out of, and in turn bolster, U.S. militarism.

Transpacific Displacement and Critical Refugee Studies

U.S. scholarship has largely separated the Vietnam War and Vietnamese refugees into different fields of study. This decoupling obscures the aggressive roles that the U.S. government, military, and corporations have played in generating the Vietnamese exodus; it also reduces the specificities of their flight to a conventional story of voluntary immigration and ethnic assimilation. Most refugee studies have fixated on refugee adjustment, with successful adjustment defined as the achievement of economic self-sufficiency (Espiritu 2006, 341). This hyperfocus on the refugees' needs and achievements has located the *problem* within the bodies and minds of the refugees, rather than in the global historical conditions that produce massive displacements and movements of refugees to the United States and elsewhere. Since at least World War II, transpacific displacement/migration to the United States "has been the product of specific economic, colonial, political, military, and/or ideological ties between the United States and other countries . . . as well as of war" (Ngai 2005, 10). Indeed, all of the nation-states from which the largest numbers of U.S. refugees originate— El Salvador, Cuba, Guatemala, Vietnam, Laos, Cambodia, and Somalia—have been deeply disrupted by U.S. "counterinsurgency" actions, anticommunist insurgencies, terrorism counteraction, and peacekeeping operations. And yet, in the U.S. academy, popular media, and published autobiographies and memoirs, Vietnamese flight to the United States is most often portrayed as a matter of desperate individuals fleeing political persecution and/or economic depression, or simply fleeing "the Communists," completely discounting the aggressive roles that the U.S. government, military, and corporations have played in generating this exodus in the first place. This "willed forgetfulness of the American imaginary . . . write[s] out the specificities of forced migration and the legacy of the American/Vietnam War" (Palumbo-Liu 1999, 235), enabling the people of the United States to remake themselves from military aggressors into magnanimous rescuers.

Elsewhere, I have argued that the narrative of the "good refugee," constructed as successful and anticommunist, has been key in enabling the United States to turn the Vietnam War into a "good war"—that the war, no matter the human costs, was ultimately necessary, moral, and successful (Espiritu 2006, 340). But the good war narrative requires the production not only of the good refugee, but also of the good *refuge*. The making of the "good refuge" was launched in April 1975, as U.S. media turned U.S. defeat, the fall of Saigon, into a feat of heroism by extolling and sensationalizing the United States' last-ditch efforts to evacuate frantic Vietnamese out of Saigon and to resettle them on various military bases. As I will argue below, the "good refuge" narrative became solidified with images of Americans caring for shell-shocked Vietnamese in the various refugee camps in Asia.

Studies of refugee camps constitute the bulk of early scholarship on Vietnamese refugees, as researchers repeatedly portray refugees as passive objects of sympathy that suffer not only the trauma of forced departure but also the boredom, uncertainty, despair, and helplessness induced by camp life (Harding and Looney 1977; Chan and Loveridge 1987). However well-intentioned, this crisis model, which fixates on the refugees' purported fragile psychosocial and emotional state, discursively constructs Vietnamese as "passive, immobilized and pathetic" (DuBois 1993, 5). Catchphrases used to characterize the refugees' journey such as "no-man's-land," "midway-to-nowhere," "transition to nowhere," "the limbo state," and "halfway to nowhere," all further underscore the refugees' perceived learned helplessness and demoralized mental state (Kunz 1983, 133; Liu et al. 1979; Morrison and Moos 1982). Popular oral history collections that detail the refugees' traumatic escape and prolonged stay in refugee camps, all done in the name of "helping" the refugees to "express themselves in their own terms," further reinscribe the refugees as only victims in the U.S. imaginary (Freeman 1989, 10, 291–352).

Importantly, studies of refugee camps often pair the construct of Vietnamese refugees as passive objects of sympathy with a plea for the West to "assume an *active* role in caring, counseling, or intervening" (DuBois 1993, 4). An example of one such call to action:

The immediate moral responsibility of the Western world to relieve the increasing intensity of the sufferings of thousands of Indochinese refugees in transit camps in Hong Kong as well as those in the other major countries of first asylum in Southeast Asia, cannot be overexaggerated. Any further delay on the part of the western countries . . . will certainly allow an experience in transit to degenerate into one of "no exit." (Chan and Loveridge 1987, 757)

Such calls to action naturalize and buttress the United States' self-appointed role as rescuers, whose magnanimity promises swift deliverance of the refugees from a bleak life of "no exit" to one of boundless possibilities. Not only does this construct racialize and feminize the Vietnamese as only passive recipients of such generosity, it also precludes any critical examination of the U.S. role in creating and sustaining the refugee "crisis" (Palumbo-Liu 1999, 235). In all, the military's alleged role in *solving* the refugee crisis enables the United States to transform itself from violent aggressor in Vietnam to benevolent rescuer of its people, a feat that helped to recuperate its status as the mighty and moral leader of the Asia-Pacific region, its defeat in Vietnam notwithstanding.

Military Colonialism: About Islands

As was mentioned above, in 1975, about 92 percent of the first-wave Vietnamese refugees who fled to the United States trekked through the Philippines, Guam, or Wake Island—all islands, all with prominent U.S. military bases (Liu et al. 1979, 80). Not mere happenstance, these stopovers followed the dictates of a "militarized organizing logic" (Shigematsu and Camacho 2010, xvii) that reflected—and revealed—the layering of past colonial and ongoing militarization practices on these islands. Since the Spanish–American War in 1898, the United States had colonized islands—Cuba and Puerto Rico in the Caribbean, and Guam, eastern Samoa, Wake Island, Hawai'i, and the Philippines in the Pacific—and transformed them into strategic sites for advancing American economic and military interests. Throughout these islands, the United States established coal stations, communication lines, and naval harbors, wreaking havoc on the local population, economy, and ecology in the process (Shigematsu and Camacho 2010, xx). Calling attention to the connections between colonialism and militarization, Robert Harkavy reports that from the nineteenth century until and beyond World War II, most overseas bases throughout the world were "automatically provided by colonial control and were an important aspect and purpose of imperial domination" (Harkavey 1982, 17).

The Philippines: America's "First Vietnam"

In 1898, in the aftermath of the Spanish–American War, the United States brutally took possession of the Philippines over native opposition and uprising, thereby extending its "Manifest Destiny" to Pacific Asia. Linking U.S. war in the Philippines to that in Vietnam, Luzviminda Francisco dubs U.S. imperial aggression in the Philippines the "first Vietnam" in order to dispute the contention that the United States' violent war in Vietnam is an "aberration" of American foreign policy (Francisco 1973, 2). It was during the Philippine-American War (1899–1902), which resulted in the death of about a million Filipinos, the violent destruction of the nationalist forces, and the United States' territorial annexation of the Philippines, that the United States established its first military bases in the Philippines. For the next century, the Philippines hosted—often unwillingly—some of the United States' largest overseas air force and naval bases. As a consequence, the Philippines has been key to U.S. power projection capabilities in the Pacific Basin, serving as its prime military outpost and stepping stone to China and the Asian mainland (Kimlick 1990).

Established as a direct consequence of the U.S. colonial occupation of the Philippines, Clark AFB was initially a U.S. Cavalry post, Fort Stotsenberg, until the creation of the Air Force in 1947. From 1903 to 1979, Clark remained a "virtual territor[y] of the United States,"[1] providing a vital "umbrella of security and surveillance to the Pacific region" (Kimlick 1990). Even after the Philippines' formal independence in 1946, the Military Bases Agreement (MBA), signed one year later, formalized the establishment of twenty-three air and naval bases in strategic parts of the Philippines, the most important of which were Clark AFB and the Subic Naval Base (Padlan 2005). Although the MBA was signed in 1947, its preliminary terms had been arranged before World War II, in effect making it an agreement between the United States and its colony, not between two sovereign states. In comparing this MBA with similar postwar military arrangements between the United States and other countries, Voltaire Garcia II concluded that "the Philippine treaty is the most onerous" and that its provisions "made the bases virtual territories of the United States." In 1951, the United States and the Philippines signed the Mutual Defense Treaty (MDT), which obligated both countries to provide joint defense against "any external armed attack in the Pacific" on either country, further entrenching U.S. military control over the Philippines (Padlan 2005). Although the MDT was purportedly about military cooperation for the good of both nations, it was in effect a colonial project, with the "American military machine (gendered masculine and racialized white) [allegedly] protecting a feminized, brown Pacific" (Gonzalez 2010, 67).

During the Cold War, Clark grew into a major American air base. At its peak, it had a permanent population of 15,000, making it the largest American base overseas (Vasquez 2001). In 1979, pressed by Filipino intellectuals and nationalists who objected to the pervasive U.S. military presence, the Philippines and the United States signed a new MBA that established Philippine sovereignty over the bases *but* still guaranteed the United States "unhampered" military use of the bases. It was not until a 1991 vote for national sovereignty by the Philippine Senate that the U.S. Air Force transferred Clark back to the Philippine government, some ninety years after the first U.S. troops landed in the Philippines.

Guam: "Where America's Day Begins"

After World War II, colonialism and militarism converged in the Pacific. Willfully aborting the decolonization movement in Micronesia, American military leaders turned the region's islands into a Pacific "base network" that would support U.S. military deployment in allied Asian nations as part of the containment of communism (Rogers 1995, 206). Once they had secured American hegemony in the Pacific, military leaders proceeded to build permanent facilities on key islands in Micronesia, primarily Guam and Kwajalein Atoll. As the largest of more than 2,000 islands scattered between Hawai'i and the Philippines, Guam's role in the geopolitics of the Pacific was transformed, from the prewar situation "in which Guam was a lonely American outpost surrounded by hostile Japanese islands, to one in which Guam was the center of an American-dominated lake that encompassed the entire western Pacific Ocean," second in importance only to Hawai'i (Rogers 1995, 207). By 1956, Andersen AFB, a 20,000-acre site located on the northern end of the island of Guam, had become Strategic Air Command's chief base in the Pacific, one of thirty-eight overseas bases that encircled the Sino–Soviet Bloc (Rogers 1995, 233).

The militarization of Guam was swift and expansive. On August 11, 1945, Admiral Nimitz informed the U.S. chief of naval operations that to convert Guam into a "Gibraltar of the Pacific" would require 75,000 acres, or 55 percent of the island (Rogers 1995, 215). About a year later, the Land Acquisition Act was passed, authorizing the Navy Department to acquire private land needed for permanent military installations on Guam (Rogers 1995, 214). By the beginning of 1950, the federal government controlled close to 60 percent of the island. Today, the U.S. military maintains jurisdiction over approximately 39,000 acres, or one-third of Guam's total land area (Bevacqua 2010, 34). Numbering about 13,000, U.S. military personnel and their family comprise close to 9 percent of Guam's current population (Broyhill 2003).

Militarized *Refuge: Resolving* Refugee Crisis

The Philippines and Guam—Pacific Stopovers

Grafting the colonial histories of the Philippines and Guam onto the history of the Vietnam War, this section illuminates how residual and ongoing effects of colonial subordination "constitute the conditions of possibility for ongoing forms of militarization" (Shigematsu and Camacho 2010, xv). Therein lies the crux of what I term "militarized refuge": it was the enormity of the military buildup in the Pacific that uniquely equipped U.S. bases there to handle the large-scale refugee rescue operation. Felix Moos and C. S. Morrison (2005, 34) describe the U.S. decision to use their military infrastructure in the Pacific as "inevitable": "An operation of this magnitude, and one requiring immediate execution, eliminated any alternative" (Moos and Morrison 2005, 34). In short, U.S. evacuation efforts were not a slapdash response to an emergency situation that arose in Vietnam in 1975, but rather part and parcel of the long-standing militarized histories and circuits that connected Vietnam, the Philippines, and Guam, dating back to 1898.

A seemingly humanitarian gesture, the United States' designation of Clark AFB as a refugee staging point was intimately linked to, and a direct outcome of, U.S. colonial subordination and militarization of the Philippines. Due to Clark AFB's prominence and proximity to Saigon, U.S. officials promptly designated it the first refugee "staging area": a temporary housing place for Vietnamese en route to the continental United States to complete the necessary screening and paperwork (Moos and Morrison 2005, 33). Flown there by military aircraft—C-141s and C-130s—more than 30,000 refugees, including over 1,500 orphans, transited through Clark AFB in spring 1975 (Vasquez 2001; Tobin et al. 1978). At its peak, in April and May, as many as 2,000 refugees at a time were housed in a "Tent City" adjacent to the base's Bamboo Bowl sports stadium (Vasquez 2001). However, as the flow of refugees surged, on April 23, President Ferdinand Marcos informed the U.S. ambassador that the Philippines would accept no more Vietnamese refugees, "thus foreclosing for all practical purposes the most promising staging base" (Moos and Morrison 2005, 33). In response, that very same day, U.S. officials moved the premier refugee-staging area from the Philippines to Guam, and ordered the local Pacific Command representative on Guam and the Commander Naval Forces Marianas to prepare to accept, shelter, and process the refugees as they were being evacuated from South Vietnam (Tobin 1975).

The United States' swift decision to designate Clark AFB a refugee-staging area, and the Philippines' equally quick refusal to accept any more refugees reflected the ambiguous nature of the MBA: while the United States had control of the bases, the Philippines had sovereignty over them. In the case of Guam, there was no such ambiguity. Since Congress passed the Organic Act in 1950, which decreed Guam as an unincorporated organized territory of the United States under the jurisdiction of the Department of the Interior, the federal government has had plenary powers—that is, full authority—over the island

(Bevacqua 2010, 34). As an island where the U.S. military controlled one-third of its territory, Guam—more specifically, its air and naval bases—became the "logical" transit camps for the processing of evacuees.

With total land area of about 200 square miles, and meager local resources, Guam was hardly an ideal location for the large-scale refugee operation. That it became *the* major refugee-staging point in the Pacific had more to do with the U.S. militarization of Guam than with U.S. humanitarianism. Directed by the Joint Chiefs of Staff Pacific Command's local area commander, Operation "New Life" was a massive undertaking, requiring the resources and manpower of all military branches on Guam, as well as from neighboring Pacific and mainland bases (Moos and Morrison 2005, 34). In all, nearly 20,000 military personnel, including the crews from visiting ships and aircrafts, were directly involved in the Guam refugee operation. Military bases, as the largest and most resourced institutions on Guam, doubled as refugee shelters: refugees were initially housed in temporary barracks on Anderson AFB, on the Naval Air Station Agana, and at the U.S. Marine Corp Camp at Asan Point, and subsequently in the hastily constructed but massive "Tent City" on Orote Point within the U.S. Naval Station, which provided tent space for about 50,000 people (Tobin 1975, 38).

At the onset of the refugee influx, the Pacific Command representatives on Guam estimated that even with the use of all military structures and all available civilian rentals, Guam could shelter a *maximum* of 13,000 people for a *short* period of time (Tobin 1975, 33). However, in all, more than 115,000 evacuees passed through Guam, a number that exceeded Guam's civilian population at that time by at least 25,000 (GlobalSecurity.org 2011c). At its peak, there were as many as 3,700 evacuees processed through and airlifted out of Andersen in any given day (Knickrehm 2010). The sheer volume of refugees overwhelmed Guam's limited resources. Locals found their access to lagoons and beaches reduced; their water supply rationed; and their travel restricted as military vehicles jammed busy roads. Children had no transportation to school because 181 school buses were used to transfer the refugees from the various air and ship terminals to the temporary military housing and campsites. Overall health conditions also deteriorated, as mosquito- and sewage-borne diseases proliferated (Mackie 1998, 57).

Not only did more refugees come than expected, they stayed longer than anticipated, thereby pushing the actual refugee population on Guam beyond an acceptable limit. Begun on April 23, Operation New Life was not officially closed until October 16, 1975, and it was not until January 15, 1976 that the last evacuee left Guam. The refugees were not supposed to linger on Guam; they were to be processed almost immediately and then sent on to the continental

United States. However, some U.S. states initially refused to accept the refugees or postponed the arrival date, in part because of lack of planning and proper facilities, but also because of adverse reaction by the public and strong opposition by state officials to the influx of refugees. As an "unincorporated territory of the United States" with second-class citizenship status, Guam had little choice but to continue housing the refugees until they could be received "properly" elsewhere (Moos and Morrison 2005, 34). That Guam had to house such a large number of refugees, even as its resources were severely stretched, bespeaks the intertwined histories of U.S. military colonialism in Guam and its war in Southeast Asia. That is, it was the militarization of the colonized island that turned it into an "ideal" dumping ground for the unwanted Vietnamese refugees, the discards of the United States' war in Vietnam.

California's Camp Pendleton—Refugees' "First U.S. Home"

From Guam, many Vietnamese refugees journeyed to the other side of the Pacific—to Marine Corps Base Camp Pendleton, a 125,000-acre amphibious training base on the Southern California coast, in San Diego County. It was here, at a U.S. military base, that the largest Vietnamese population outside of Vietnam got its start in America. Like Clark and Andersen AFBs, Camp Pendleton emerged out of a history of conquest: it is located in the traditional territory of the Juaneno, Luiseno, and Kumeyaay tribes, which had been "discovered" by Spanish padres and voyagers who traveled to Southern California in the late eighteenth century; "owned" by unscrupulous Anglo-American settlers for about a century as the California state legislature repeatedly blocked federal ratification of treaties with native communities; and ultimately "acquired" by the U.S. Marine Corps in 1942 in order to establish a West Coast base for combat training of marines (Berryman 2001, 17).[2] Camp Pendleton's prized land— its varied topography, which combines a breathtakingly beautiful seventeen-mile shoreline and "extensive, diverse inland ranges and maneuver areas," making it ideal for combat training environment (Denger n.d.; Berryman 2001, 17)—is thus "stolen land," an occupied territory like Guam (Carrico 1987). And yet, this fact remains unacknowledged. According to the official website of Marine Corps Base Camp Pendleton, "Spanish explorers, colorful politicians, herds of thundering cattle, skillful vaqueros and tough Marines have all contributed to the history of this land" ("Marine Corps Base Camp Pendleton" n.d.). Conspicuously absent in this official origin story is the account of the stolen land and the San Diego's native communities that have been made landless and destitute as a result. And yet, this buried past has continued to surface— sometimes literally. A 2001 article reported that there had been seventeen inadvertent discoveries of Native American remains and objects involving three major military projects on Camp Pendleton, including "complete burials, human bone fragments, and funerary objects" (Berryman 2001, 17).

The first military installation on the U.S. mainland to provide accommodations for Vietnamese evacuees, Camp Pendleton temporarily housed over 50,000 refugees between April and August 1975. Like other refugee centers in the Pacific, setting up the "Tent City" to house the refugees was a massive undertaking; nearly 900 marines and civilians worked for six days to erect the 958 tents and 140 Quonset huts (Jolly 2010). Heavily covered by the national and international media, Camp Pendleton's participation in the U.S. military's 1975 relocation effort, dubbed "Operation New Arrivals," was key to the United States' effort to recuperate itself after the defeat in Vietnam, its importance to the nation underscored by First Lady Betty Ford's May 21 visit to the camp to greet newly arrived Vietnamese children (Jolly 2010). For a nation still reeling from the shock of defeat and the agony of a deeply dividing war, watching images of U.S. Marines—the central players in that very war—working "around the clock to build eight tent cities and to provide water, food, clothing, medicine, electricity, power, and security for the first 18,000 refugees" (Wandering Chopsticks 2010) must have been cathartic, a step toward reclaiming their faith in America's goodness and moving beyond the extremely unpopular war. For American soldiers like Lewis Beatty, a Camp Pendleton marine with two tours in Vietnam who "helped put up tents, built latrines, hauled clothes and diapers," assisting the refugees provided a sense of redemption. Looking back on his war experiences in Vietnam thirty-five years later, Beatty confided that "we saw things that no person should ever see." Yet, the arrival of the Vietnamese and their touted assimilation into the United States had turned his sorrow into joy, enabling him to put the war behind him and to revel in their (presumed) shared experience of parenthood: "Here it was joy. In their kids, I could see my kids" (Jolly 2010).

These warm images, replayed on every anniversary of the "Fall of Saigon"—of soldiers caring for Vietnamese evacuees, of Vietnamese spouting gratitude for American generosity—tell only half-truths: they conveniently erase the fact that the majority of Americans did not welcome the refugees' arrival. A Gallup poll taken in May 1975 indicated that 54 percent of the respondents opposed the settlement of Vietnamese in the United States. In numerous letters and phone calls to public officials, many Americans urged that little or no government assistance be allocated to the refugees ("Refugees" 1975). This opposition was racially charged. In California, then-governor Jerry Brown actively opposed Vietnamese settlement, even attempting to prevent planes carrying refugees from landing at Travis AFB near Sacramento, claiming that the

Vietnamese would add to the state's already large minority population (Chapman 2010). California's Republican representative Burt Talcott exclaimed to his constituents, "Damn it, we have too many Orientals" ("Refugees" 1975). In the communities near Camp Pendleton (and the three other refugee-receiving centers), that were battling high unemployment rates, residents loudly opposed the settlement of the refugees in their neighborhoods, spurring the State Department to disperse the refugees as widely as possible all over the country in order to minimize the financial burden on any single locality ("Refugees" 1975).

The warm images also made un-visible the connection between the refugee-recovery mission and the military violence that preceded it—the fact that both were executed by the same military outfit: Camp Pendleton's 1st Marines. Indeed, the same individual, General Paul Graham, directed both combat and rescuing efforts, further eliding one into the other. In 1967, General Graham served as assistant chief of staff of the 1st Marine Division in South Vietnam, and later, as commanding officer, of the 5th Marine Regiment. In April 1975, now advanced to the rank of brigadier general, Graham, as the West Cost Marine Corps coordinator, processed over 50,000 Vietnamese and Thai refugees from Southeast Asia at Camp Pendleton. While serving in this capacity, Graham was awarded a Gold Star. Upon his retirement, Graham was presented with a personal Certificate of Appreciation from President Gerald R. Ford, for "meritorious service in the resettlement of Indo Chinese refugees in the United States, as well as the Distinguished Service Medal" ("Brigadier General" 2013). Graham's "meritorious service" in the resettlement of the refugees included setting up a tight security system in the "Tent City," making sure that "there were MPs [military police] everywhere" and "quell[ing] all the conflicts immediately. He was keeping it in total control" (Cavanaugh and Finn 2010). Graham's illustrious career, his promotions and recognitions, was thus built in part on the role that he played in executing both the violence against, and recovery of, Vietnamese bodies.

Militarized Refuge: *Producing* Refugee Crisis

The material and ideological conversion of U.S. military bases into a place of *refuge*—a place that *resolves* the refugee crisis, promising peace and protection— discursively transformed the United States from violent aggressors in Vietnam to benevolent rescuers of its people. In this section, I challenge the logic of this "makeover" by detailing the violent roles that these military bases—these purported places of refuge—played in the Vietnam War, in order to hold them accountable for the war-induced displacement of the Vietnamese people. The term *"militarized* refuge"—its intended jarring juxtaposition—exposes the hidden violence behind the humanitarian term "refuge," thereby challenging the powerful narrative of America(ns) rescuing and caring for Vietnam's "runaways" that erases the role that U.S. foreign policy and war played in inducing the "refugee crisis" in the first place.

In the Philippines, Clark AFB was the backbone of logistical support for U.S. involvement in Southeast Asia. Soon after the United States proclaimed its campaign to "contain Communism" in the late 1940s, Clark AFB became the headquarters of the 13th Air Force and played a key logistical role in support of the U.S. forces in the Korean War (1950–1953). From 1965 to 1975, as the largest overseas U.S. military base in the world, Clark AFB became the major staging base for U.S. involvement in Southeast Asia, providing crucial logistical support for the Vietnam War. Air traffic at Clark reached as high as forty transports per day, all bound for Vietnam. At the same time, in an exercise of its fledgling sovereignty, the Philippines refused to permit the United States to mount B-52 bombing runs from Clark: the aircraft had to fly from Guam but were refueled from Clark. U.S. troops at Clark also provided vital support to the war as they spent a significant portion of their alleged "temporary duty" (TDY) in Vietnam. The large number of TDY troops who were sent to Vietnam from Clark, as well as from other U.S. bases in the Pacific, was part of the Pentagon's illicit design to mislead Congress about the number of troops that were "officially" assigned to Vietnam's combat zone (Utts 2012).

While the United States could not impose its military will on the Philippines, a sovereign nation, it could and did on Guam, its unincorporated territory. When the United States was not permitted to mount B-52 bombing runs from Clark, it turned to Anderson AFB, which came to play a "legendary" role in the Vietnam War, launching devastating bombing missions over North and South Vietnam for close to a decade (Rogers 1995, 252). In this way, Guam's fate was linked to that of the Philippines' as U.S. military decisions often triangulated these two vital nodes in the Pacific base network. The two air force bases also joined efforts in providing crucial medical support for U.S. troops during the Vietnam War. Starting in November 1965, four times a week C-141 aircraft would fly from Clark into Da Nang to load casualties, return for a two-hour stop at Clark, and then fly on to Guam. The close proximity of these three sites—Vietnam, the Philippines, and Guam, linked via U.S. militarism in the Pacific—meant that injured soldiers were transferred to Guam within two or three days of injury, as flight time between Da Nang and Clark is 2 to 2½ hours and between Clark and Guam 3½ to 4 hours (U.S. Naval Hospital 2013).

Since it became operational as North Field in 1945, Andersen has continually played vital roles in U.S. wars in the Pacific, launching daily bombing missions over Japan during World War II, serving as a focal point for aircraft and material flying west during the Korean War, and supporting rotational bomber deployments from stateside bases after that war, first with B-29s, and eventually hosting B-36, B-47, B-50, B-52 and KC-97 and KC-135 units. For the next six years, Strategic Air Command would be deployed time and time again in Southeast Asia (Broyhill 2003).

Guam's involvement in the Vietnam War began in 1962, when it first served as a support base for the American advisers that President Kennedy dispatched to South Vietnam. In mid-1965, after the United States deployed ground combat units in South Vietnam, Guam's role in the war was expanded to include direct combat operations by B-52s from Andersen. A hornet's nest of intense activity, Andersen rapidly became the United States's largest base for B-52 bombers— "the eight-engine behemoths that attempted to bomb the Vietnamese communists into submission" (Thompson 2010, 62; Rogers 1995, 242). Given Guam's proximity to Vietnam, a B-52, which carries one hundred and eight 500-pound bombs, could fly from Guam to Vietnam and back without refueling (Thompson 2010, 62). On 18 June 1965, Andersen launched twenty-seven B-52s against suspected Viet Cong base operations and concentrations and supply lines, the first of thousands of conventional "iron bomb" strikes—dubbed Operation Arc Light—over North and South Vietnam, and also Cambodia and Laos. The Nixon Doctrine, announced on Guam on 25 July 1969, initiated the withdrawal of U.S. ground troops from Vietnam, but also immediately escalated the U.S. air war, with B-52 bombing missions from Guam increasing in tempo and ferocity (Rogers 1995, 243). In 1972, Andersen was the site of the most massive buildup of airpower in history, with more than 15,000 crews and over 150 B-52s lining all available flight line space—about five miles long. At its peak, Andersen housed about 165 B-52s (Rogers 1995, 252). During Operation Linebacker II (named after Nixon's favorite sport), the round-the-clock "Christmas bombing" against the cities of Hanoi and Haiphong in December 1972, bombers stationed at Andersen flew 729 sorties in 11 days. On December 18, eighty-seven B-52s were launched from Andersen in less than 2 hours. Dubbed the "11-Day War," Operation Linebacker II is credited for forcing the North Vietnamese to return to the stalled Paris peace talks, and to sign a cease-fire agreement in January 1973. The Nixon Doctrine was thus a racial project: by withdrawing American troops but intensifying the air raid, the United States prioritized American lives over Vietnamese lives, preserving the former while obliterating the latter, racialized to be dispensable, via carpet bombing.

The U.S. air war, launched from Guam, decisively disrupted life on the island. Richard Mackie, a Public Health Service officer, describes the thundering impact of the air war on everyday life:

There was no announcement. There was no warning. It just started happening. Every hour, day and night, every house . . . would almost shake off its foundation at the deafening roar of three B-52s and a refueling plane would pass a few hundred feet over our heads . . . Life became tedious, sleep was almost impossible. Conversations were continually interrupted. We found ourselves constantly gritting our teeth and staring angrily at the ceiling as each "sortie" passed overhead. Guam's main highway was jammed day and night with trucks hauling bombs from the port to the airbase. (Thompson 2010, 62–63)

As the Department of Defense's busiest training installation, California's Camp Pendleton—the refugees' first home in the United States—trains more than 40,000 active-duty and 26,000 reserve military personnel each year for combat (Denger n.d.). During the Vietnam War, marines arriving at the Camp were given fifteen intensive training days, complete with a fabricated Vietnamese jungle village with deadly booby traps, and then sent to Vietnam. As noted earlier, Camp Pendleton is also the home base of the illustrious 1st Marine Regiment, whose battalions began arriving in Vietnam in August 1965. The regiment's battalions participated in some of the most ferocious operations of the war, including Harvest Moon in December 1965, and Utah, Iowa, Cheyenne I and II, and Double Eagle in the succeeding months, and Operation Hastings in July 1966. Between January and March 1968, the 1st Marines, along with other U.S. Marine and South Vietnamese units, fought to regain control of Hue, the old imperial capital, engaging in street fighting and hand-to-hand combat, killing nearly 1,900 "enemy" in the process. The regiment was engaged in heavy fighting through the rest of the year, culminating in Operation Meade River, which "netted nearly 850 enemy killed." In 1971, the regiment was ordered back to Camp Pendleton—the last Marine infantry unit to depart Vietnam (GlobalSecurity.org 2011a).

In all, during the course of the Vietnam War, via its satellite military bases the United States dropped more explosives on Vietnam—a million tons on North Vietnam, and 4 million tons on South Vietnam—than the United States' World War II total (Turley 1987, 87). Four times as many bombs were dropped on South Vietnam as on North Vietnam because the United States' goal was to decimate the "Viet Cong" in the South in order to preserve South Vietnam as a noncommunist, pro-American country (Young 1991). The massive tonnage of bombs, along with the ground fighting provided by Marine units like Camp Pendleton's 1st Marines, displaced some 12 million people in South Vietnam—almost half the country's total population at the time—from their homes. Although there are no statistics on how many North Vietnamese were forced to flee their homes, it is likely that the percentage of the displaced there must have been even higher, as North Vietnam coped with the relentless American air war by evacuating major population centers to the countryside (Chan 1991, 56).

As such, the Pacific military bases, Clark and Andersen AFBs, and California's Marine Corps Base Camp Pendleton, credited and valorized for resettling Vietnamese refugees in 1975, were the very ones responsible for dislocating millions of Vietnamese from their homes during the course of the Vietnam War. By recognizing only the refugees fleeing Vietnam after 1975, the United States engages in the "organized forgetting" of the millions of long-term refugees who stayed in Vietnam, whose dislocation was the direct consequence of its military's "high-technology brutality" (Chan 1991, 51). Together, the hypervisibility of the former, the post-1975 refugees who left Vietnam, and the un-visibility of the latter, the internal refugees who had been displaced throughout the war, enable the United States to represent itself as a refuge-providing rather than a refugee-producing nation.

"Operation Babylift": Violence and Recovery—without a Pause

In April 2010, marking the thirty-fifth anniversary of the fall of Saigon, the Camp Pendleton Historical Society unveiled the exhibit "Images at War's End," which features a series of black and white photographs and paintings by Colonel Charles Waterhouse, depicting life at the "Tent City" refugee camp in 1975. A photograph stands out: dated May 5, 1975, it depicts two Vietnamese children walking barefoot around the camp—their bodies completely engulfed in extralong *military* jackets. Undoubtedly, the gesture was meant to be kind; the jackets intended to warm their little bodies against the morning cold. And yet, the picture encapsulates so vividly the concept of *militarized refuge*, with young Vietnamese bodies literally wrapped in U.S. protective military gear as they wander the grounds of their new home in America—a military base that housed the same 1st Marines who had waged ferocious battles in Vietnam, leaving high numbers of combat deaths in their wake. The photo symbolizes the unsettling entanglement between military acts of violence and recovery, with recovery overlaying and at times disappearing (the memory of) violence. As discussed above, Clark AFB, Andersen AFB, and Marine Corps Base Camp Pendleton were all integral to the U.S. war in Vietnam; all doubled as refugee camps.

The photo also brings to mind "Operation Babylift," the controversial U.S. emergency initiative that airlifted over 2,500 Vietnamese infants and children out of war-torn Vietnam in April 1975 (Sachs 2010, xi). In this case, the literal changeover from acts of violence to recovery occurred *without a pause*. On

April 4, 1975, a United States Air Force C-5, "which was returning to the Philippines after *delivering war material*," immediately flew to Saigon to airlift Vietnamese orphans to Clark AFB, initiating Operation Babylift (GlobalSecurity.org 2011b). In other words, the C-5 was performing two opposing missions—warring and rescuing—back to back, and yet seemingly without contradiction. In the chaotic days of the rescue mission and even long after, no one noted the irony, or what should be the incongruity, of transporting Vietnamese displaced children in the very aircraft that delivered the war material that triggered their displacement.

Operation Babylift, coined by some as "one of the most humanitarian efforts in history," was hastily arranged and executed. On April 3, 1975, in an effort to reposition the United States as a do-gooder in Vietnam, President Gerald Ford pledged $2 million to airlift the children from orphanages to new homes in the United States and granted all parolee status. The majority of the flights were military cargo planes, ill-equipped to carry passengers, especially infants and young children. On some flights, the babies were placed in temporary cribs, empty crates, or cardboard boxes, lined up corner to corner inside the cargo bays of Air Force planes (Manney 2006). The initial Babylift mission proved to be a disaster, for the C-5 aircraft crashed minutes after takeoff, killing 138 people, most of whom were Vietnamese children. Despite this tragic accident, however, the righteousness of the recovery mission was so self-evident that Operation Babylift resumed almost immediately.

Without a pause—that was how Operation Babylift was executed. A congressional investigation of the operation concluded that there was "a total lack of planning by federal and private agencies" (KPBS 2002). The emergency nature of the evacuation stemmed from the perceived urgency to get the children out of Vietnam at all costs, and rushed not only the transport of the young evacuees, but also the safety checks to ensure that they were bona fide orphans. When available, the children's birth records were stowed with them for the flight. But for many children swept up in the hasty evacuation from Vietnam, documentation of their family status was sketchy or incomplete at best. Bobby Nofflet, a worker with the U.S. Agency for International Development in Saigon, detailed the tumultuous days of Babylift: "There were large sheaves of papers and batches of babies. Who knew which belonged to which?" (KPBS 2002). It appears that on nearly every level, "from the original decisions about which children would be airlifted to the protocols for finalizing adoptions, Operation Babylift suffered from acute disorder and a nearly complete lack of oversight" (Sachs 2010, 190). The hasty and slipshod evacuation, even of children with uncertain family status, reflects the racialized belief that the United States is self-evidently a safer and better home than Vietnam for the children—a belief fortified by years of war and war propaganda waged in the region. As Vietnamese American journalist Tran Tuong Nhu, one of a small number of Vietnamese Americans living in San Francisco at the time who assisted with Babylift arrivals, wondered, "What is this terror Americans feel that my people will devour children?" (KPBS 2002)

Even a year after they arrived in the United States, the legal standing of hundreds of Operation Babylift children remained murky (Manney 2006). On April 29, 1975, at the urging of Tran Tuong Nhu, and on behalf of three Babylift siblings, a group of California's attorneys filed a class-action lawsuit seeking to halt the Babylift adoptions, asserting that many of the children did not appear to be orphans; that they had been taken from South Vietnam against their parents' wills; and that the U.S. government was obligated to return them to their families (Sachs 2010, 190). Because so much of the documentation was missing or fraudulent, the plaintiffs' attorneys claimed that out of the 2,242 children who had arrived in the United States, 1,511 were ineligible for adoption. The Immigration and Naturalization Service disputed this claim, but its own investigation found that over 10 percent of the evacuees—263 children—were ineligible for adoption (Sachs 2010, 207–208). After ten months of wrangling, as the case was becoming unwieldy and as no documentation was forthcoming, Judge Spencer Williams threw out the case and sealed the records (Sachs 2010, 208). Eventually, after many years and lengthy lawsuits, only twelve children were reunited with their Vietnamese parents (KPBS 2002).

As the Babylift children arrived in the United States, with their Vietnamese names imprinted on a bracelet around one wrist and the name and address of their adopted American parents on the other, the violence that brought about their orphanhood—and even their birth, as many were fathered and abandoned by American military personnel—was all but forgotten. Instead, they were celebrated as the lucky ones, bound toward a new life in America (Manney 2006). As a testament to the ideological importance of Operation Babylift for the war-weary nation, President Gerald Ford appeared on the tarmac at San Francisco International Airport and, before a horde of television cameras, welcomed to the United States the plane full of Vietnamese infants and children. The picture of Ford cradling a Vietnamese infant on board an Air Force bus shortly after carrying her off the plane in his arms—the white father protecting his brown baby—circulated widely and eventually became immortalized in a painting now housed in the President Gerald R. Ford Museum in Grand Rapids, Michigan.[3] With the arrival of the Babylift children, America became the white loving parents welcoming the arrival of their brown charges; the transition from warring to humanitarian nation was thus completed—all without a pause.

Operation Frequent Wind: About Gratitude and Ambivalence

On April 30, 2010, the USS Midway Museum in San Diego held a special ceremony at noon on its flight deck to commemorate the thirty-fifth anniversary of
Operation Frequent Wind—a widely publicized mission during which USS
Midway sailors reportedly rescued more than 3,000 Vietnamese refugees fleeing the fall of Saigon. Billed as a "remarkable rescue mission" where "untold
lives were saved,"[4] the commemoration is another salute to militarized refuge,
celebrated on the deck of the very ship that had launched tens of thousands of
combat missions that had struck military and logistics installations in North
and South Vietnam, downed a number of MiGs, and laid minefields in ports
deemed of significance to the North Vietnamese (Naval Historical Center
2009).[5] Indeed, Admiral Larry Chambers, who was captain of the ship on that
fateful day, choked up when he recounted to the packed flight deck the heroic
deeds of his crew, causing a newspaper reporter covering the commemoration
to begin her article with the following: "The USS Midway may be made of iron
and steel, but deep down it was 'all heart'" (Bharath 2010).

Named "Honoring Freedom in America," the event drew not only the
"young brave men of USS Midway,"[6] but also thousands of Vietnamese Americans, hundreds of whom credited their escape from Vietnam directly to Operation Frequent Wind (Bharath 2010). American valor and Vietnamese gratitude were the day's central themes: the daring American soldiers "who made
it all possible," and the indebted Vietnamese refugees "who were plucked to
safety" (Bharath 2010). Indeed, many Vietnamese—at the *Midway* event and
elsewhere—have ardently expressed gratitude to their American rescuers,
heaping praise on the very militarized refuge that I critique here. For instance,
when a public radio talk show host asked Dzung Le, whose family landed on
the *Midway* in 1975, to recount "what it was like to travel on this U.S. *military*
helicopter and land on this flight deck," Le responded by thanking the soldiers
of the *Midway* for their gentleness and tenderness:

> I remember, it was chaotic but, strangely enough, it's also a feeling of com-
> fort, of safety, because I knew that at the time, as we land, we are saved . . .
> One of my sister was quite ill at the time from dehydration, I guess, so the
> soldier helped carry her down there. They are very tender. And to us, we
> pretty much weighed about 100 pounds at the time for all of us, and these
> are 200 pound soldiers. They are like a gentle giant at the time, very tender.
> Very tender. (Cavanaugh and Walsh 2010)

Given the military backgrounds of many of the 1975 Vietnamese refugees,
and the long-term presence of U.S. military personnel in Vietnam, this instilled

appreciation for the American military machine and personnel—for militarized refuge—is unsurprising. But these performances of gratitude are also rooted in the material reality of Vietnamese refugee life. In view of the staggering losses that the Vietnamese had endured and the harrowing nature of their flight from Vietnam, these gestures of thanksgiving, which recall "good warm memories from the American friends here that helping us [sic]" (Cavanaugh and Walsh 2010), are to be expected and respected. At the same time, acts of gratitude make possible the forgetting of acts of military violence, and risk turning the history of military-induced refugee flight into a benign story of voluntary migration. They enable historians like Abe Shragge, when asked to comment on the proper tone for the *Midway* commemoration, to link the 1975 Operation Frequent Wind to the 1886 unveiling of the Statue of Liberty:

> I think somberness, seriousness, some joy as well that we can remember back to 1886 when we opened the Statue of Liberty to the public, that this is a nation that was created by immigrants. It was a nation that was supposed to support and nurture and welcome immigrants. And to have relived that in 1975 in this particular way under these circumstances, I think, is a very fitting tribute to a long historical process and a long heritage and tradition. (Cavanaugh and Crook 2010)

Shragge's comment encapsulates the myth of "immigrant America," a narrative of voluntary immigration that ignores the role that "U.S. world power has played in the global structures of migration" (Ngai 2005, 11).

To take seriously Vietnamese standpoints on the war and its aftermath is to critically examine the relationship between history and memory, not as facts but as narratives. Like other communities in exile, Vietnamese in the United States feel keenly the urgency to narrate unified histories, identities, and memories, which most often take the form of public denouncement of communism in Vietnam and praise of freedom in America (Espiritu 2006). As I have shown elsewhere (Espiritu 2006), the *Orange County Register* in Southern California features Vietnamese community contributors who regularly intone that "the United States is a free country where freedom is not forgotten. Vietnam is a communist country where freedom is forgotten" (Dao 2000).

In between these repetitions of thanksgiving, however, other narratives lie in wait, postponed and archived—and sometimes released (McGranahan 2006, 580). For instance, on the thirty-fifth anniversary of Operation Frequent Wind, refugees interspersed their praise for the rescue mission with laments about being uninformed of American evacuation plans, torn from loved ones, and in some cases, left behind by American rescuers—all of which constitute critiques, however muted, of the American rescue efforts (Cavanaugh and Walsh 2010).

Importantly, most refugees, even as they express gratitude for their lives in America, mourn the tattered condition of their beloved Vietnam and the fact that thirty-five years later, "millions of millions of our people [in Vietnam] are still suffering" (Cavanaugh and Walsh 2010). While this sentiment foremost indicts communism in Vietnam and validates life in America, it nevertheless reminds the public that the Vietnam War is *not* over, as Americans have repeatedly claimed, and that it has continued to exact untold tolls on Vietnamese in Vietnam and in the diaspora. At the very least, this public reminder underscores the ambivalence that many Vietnamese Americans harbor about the role of the American military in Vietnam. A 1.5 generation Vietnamese American has described this ambivalence: on the one hand, he regarded Americans in Vietnam "as crucial allies who sometimes made mistakes as they helped South Vietnam"; on the other, he "became disillusioned" with American actions:

> they talked of freedom; [but] they bombed "the hell" out of many villages as they attempted to destroy their enemy. They often did not respond to calls from South Vietnamese soldiers for air support, which resulted in the loss of many lives among those they called "allies." That hypocrisy reflected the American disrespect for Vietnamese lives. (Chan 1991, 113)

These forms of critical remembering, however irresolute and mixed with the politics of gratitude, are key to the potential formation of counternarratives on the Vietnam War and "to the imagination and rearticulation of new forms of [Vietnamese] political subjectivity, collectivity, and practice" (Lowe 1996, 158).

Conclusion

This chapter covers seemingly unrelated topics: U.S. colonialism in the Philippines, U.S. militarism in Guam, settler colonialism in California, and the Vietnam War. However, in tracing the most-traveled refugee route via military aircraft, I have knitted these different events together into a layered story of "militarized refuge"—one that connects U.S. colonialism, military expansion, and transpacific displacement. In doing this work of *critical juxtaposing,* I have treated Vietnamese refugees not as an object of study but rather as a *paradigm,* "whose function [is] to establish and make intelligible a wider set of problems" (Agamben 2002). In connecting Vietnamese displacement to that of Filipinos, Chamorros, and Native Americans, and "mak[ing] intelligible" the military colonialisms that engulf these spaces, I disrupt the U.S. myth of "rescue and liberation" that enunciates violence *and* recovery simultaneously (Yoneyama 2005, 910) and expose the hidden violence behind the humanitarian term "refuge," thereby challenging the powerful narrative of America(ns) rescuing and caring for Vietnamese that erases the role that the U.S. war played in inducing the "refugee crisis" in the first place.

Notes to Chapter 8: Militarized Refuge

1. During 1978, following negotiations that had taken place on and off since the early 1970s, the two governments agreed to establish Philippine sovereignty over the former American bases in the country and thus the Clark Air Base Command of the Armed Forces of the Philippines came into being, following the signing of a revised Military Bases Agreement on January 7, 1979.

2. Indeed, San Diego County has more Indian reservations than any other county in the United States.

3. Doc Bernie Duff declined permission to use his painting *Welcome Home* in this publication because of its critique of the Operation Babylift Project. In an e-mail correspondence, Duff (2013) stated that he had to decline permission because "I am among those people who believe that what was done during that operation was, if fact, done so as a humanitarian effort and more good has come from it than bad. I have spoken to many of the orphans, living here in the US and abroad and I agree with what was done."

4. All quotes are from USS Midway Museum (2010), a video advertisement for the thirty-fifth anniversary event.

5. It also holds the distinction of having made the first and last air-to-air kill of the Vietnam War.

6. Quotes are from USS Midway Museum (2010).

References

Agamben, Giorgio. 2002. "What Is a Paradigm?" Paper presented during a lecture at the European Graduate School, Saas-Fee, Switzerland, August.

Berryman, Stan. 2001. "NAGPRA Issues at Camp Pendleton." *Cultural Resources Magazine* 3: 17–18.

Bevacqua, Michael L. 2010. "The Exceptional Life and Death of a Chamorro Solider." In *Militarized Currents: Toward a Decolonized Future in Asia and in the Pacific,* ed. Setsu Shigematsu and Keith L. Camacho, 33–62. Minneapolis: University of Minnesota Press.

Bharath, Deepa. 2010. "Refugees 'Come Home' to the Midway after 35 Years." *Orange County Register,* 30 April. http://www.ocregister.com/articles/midway-246797 -leechambers.html (accessed May 23, 2010).

"Brigadier General Paul G. Graham—Deceased." 2013. https://slsp.manpower.usmc.mil /gosa/biographies/rptBiography.asp?PERSON_ID=705&PERSON_TYPE=General (accessed August 31, 2008).

Broyhill, Marvin T. 2003. "SAC Bases: Andersen Air Force Base." http://www.strategic -air-command.com/bases/Andersen_AFB.htm (accessed May 10, 2010).

Carrico, Richard. 1987. *Strangers in a Stolen Land: Indians of San Diego County from Prehistory to the New Deal*. Newcastle, CA: Sierra Oaks Publishing.

Cavanaugh, Maureen, and Hank Crook. 2010. "USS *Midway* Played Significant Role in Vietnam War." KPBS, 29 April. http://www./kbps.org/news/2010/apr/29/uss -midway-played-significant-role-vietnam-war/ (accessed May 10, 2010).

Cavanaugh, Maureen, and Pat Finn. 2010. "Camp Pendleton's Tent City Housed 50,000 Vietnamese Refugees." *KPBS,* 29 April. http://www.kpbs.org/news/2010/apr/29/camp -pendletons-tent-city-housed-50000-vietnamese/- (accessed May 10, 2010).

Cavanaugh, Maureen, and Natalie Walsh. 2010. "Fall of Saigon Bittersweet for Vietnamese Refugee." *KPBS,* 29 April. http://www/kbps.org/news/2010/apr/29/fall -saigon-bitter-sweet-vietnamese-refugee/ (accessed May 10, 2010).

Chan, Kwok B., and David Loveridge. 1987. "Refugees 'in Transit': Vietnamese in Refugee Camp in Hong Kong." *International Migration Review* 21 (3): 745–759.

Chan, Sucheng. 1991. *Asian Americans: An Interpretive History*. Woodbridge, CT: Twayne.

Chapman, Bruce. 2010. "As Governor, Jerry Brown was Vociferous Foe of Vietnamese Immigration." *Discovery News,* October 2. http://www.discoverynews.org/2010/10 /as_governor_jerry_brown_was_v0038831.php (accessed December 10, 2010).

Dao, Ken. 2000. "Teaching Freedom to Children Raised in a Free Country." *Orange County Register,* April 28.

Denger, Mark. n.d. "A Brief History of the U.S. Marine Corps in San Diego." http:// www.militarymuseum.org/SDMarines.html (accessed March 15, 2011).

DuBois, Thomas A. 1993. "Constructions Construed: The Representation of Southeast Asian Refugees in Academic, Popular, and Adolescent Discourse." *Amerasia Journal* 19 (3): 1–26.

Duff, Doc Bernie. 2013. E-mail correspondence with the author, April 23.

Espiritu, Yến Lê. 2006. "The 'We-Win-Even-When-We-Lose' Syndrome: U.S. Press Coverage of the Twenty-Fifth Anniversary of the 'Fall of Saigon.'" *American Quarterly* 58 (2): 329–352.

Francisco, Luzviminda. 1973. "The First Vietnam: The U.S.-Philippine War of 1899." *Bulletin of Concerned Asian Scholars* 5: 2–15.

Freeman, James. 1989. *Hearts of Sorrow: Vietnamese-American Lives*. Stanford, CA: Stanford University Press.

GlobalSecurity.org. 2011a. "1st Marine Regiment." May 7. http://www.globalsecurity .org/military/agency/usmc/1mar.htm (accessed January 28, 2014).

———. 2011b. "Clark Air Base." September 7. http://www.globalsecurity.org/military /world/philippines/clark.htm (accessed January 28, 2014).

———. 2011c. "Operation New Life." May 7. http://www.globalsecurity.org/military/ops /new_life.htm (accessed January 28, 2014).

Gonzalez, Vernadette V. 2010. "Touring Military Masculinities: U.S.-Philippines Circuits of Sacrifice and Gratitude in Corregidor and Bataan." In *Militarized Currents: Toward a Decolonized Future in Asia and in the Pacific,* ed. Setsu Shige-matsu and Keith L. Camacho, 63–90. Minneapolis: University of Minnesota Press.

Harding, Richard, and John Looney. 1977. "Problems of Southeast Asian Children in a Refugee Camp." *American Journal of Psychiatry* 134: 407–411.

Harkavy, Robert E. 1982. *Great Power Competition for Overseas Bases: The Geopolitics of Access Diplomacy*. New York: Pergamon Press.

Haulman, Daniel L. 2003. *One Hundred Years of Flight: USAF Chronology of Significant Air and Space Events, 1903–2002*. Maxwell, AL: Air University Press.

Jolly, Vik. 2010. "Pendleton Once Home for 50,000 War Refugees." *Orange County Register*, 8 April. http://www.ocregister.com/news/vietnamese-243238-pendleton -family.html (accessed May 20, 2010).

Kelly, Gail Paradise. 1977. *From Vietnam to America: A Chronicle of the Vietnamese Immigration to the United States*. Boulder, CO: Westview Press.

Kimlick, Michael F. 1990. "U.S. Bases in the Philippines." http://www.globalsecurity .org/military/library/report/1990/KMF.htm (accessed January 28, 2014).

Knickrehm, Dan. 2010. "The 43rd and Operation New Life." June 4. http://www.pope .af.mil/news/story.asp?id=123207835 (accessed January 28, 2014).

KPBS. 2002. "People and Events: Operation Babylift (1975)." http://www.pbs.org/wgbh /amex/daughter/peopleevents/e_babylift.html (accessed May 20, 2010).

Kunz, E. F. 1983. "The Refugee in Flight: Kinetic Models and Forms of Displacement." *International Migration Review* 17: 125–146.

Liu, William T., Mary Ann Lamanna, and Alice K. Murata. 1979. *Transition to Nowhere: Vietnamese Refugees in America*. Nashville: Charter House.

Lockwood, Kathleen. 2006 [1999]. "The Philippines: Allies during the Vietnam War." 12 June. http://www.historynet.com/the-philippines-allies-during-the-vietnam-war .htm/5 (accessed May 20, 2010).

Lowe, Lisa. 1996. *Immigrant Acts: On Asian American Cultural Politics*. Durham, NC: Duke University Press.

Mackie, Richard. 1998. *Operation Newlife: The Untold Story*. Concord, MA: Solution.

Manney, Kathy. 2006. "Operation Babylift: Evacuating Children Orphaned by the Vietnam War." September 13. http://www.historynet.com/operation-babylift -evacuating-children-orphaned-by-the-vietnam-war.htm (accessed May 20, 2010).

"Marine Corps Base Camp Pendleton." n.d. http://www.pendleton.marines.mil/About /HistoryandMuseums.aspx (accessed May 20, 2010).

McGranahan, Carole. 2006. "Truth, Fear, and Lies: Exile Politics and Arrested Histories of the Tibetan Resistance." *Cultural Anthropology* 20 (4): 570–600.

Moos, Feliz, and C. S. Morrison. 2005. "The Vietnamese Refugees at Our Doorstop: Political Ambiguity and Successful Improvisation." *Review of Policy Research* 1: 28–46.

Morrison, G. S., and Felix Moos. 1982. "Halfway to Nowhere: Vietnamese Refugees on Guam." In *Involuntary Migration and Resettlement: The Problems and Responses of Dislocated People*, ed. Art Hansen and Anthony Oliver-Smith. Boulder, CO: Westview Press.

Naval Historical Center. 2009. "USS Midway (CVB 41)." June 15. http://www.navy.mil /navydata/ships/carriers/histories/cv41-midway/cv41-midway.html (accessed June 12, 2009).

Ngai, Mae M. 2005. *Impossible Subjects: Illegal Aliens and the Making of Modern America*. Princeton, NJ: Princeton University Press.

Padlan, Mark. 2005. "US Militarism in the Philippines." *Peacemaking,* November 28. http://www.peacemaking.co.kr/english/news/view.php?papercode+ENGLISH& newsno=134&pubno=142 (accessed June 12, 2009).

Palumbo-Liu, David. 1999. *Asian/American: Historical Crossings of a Racial Frontier.* Stanford, CA: Stanford University Press.

"Refugees: A Cool and Wary Reception." 1975. *Time,* May 12. http://www.time.com/time /magazine/article/0,9171,917419-3,00.html (accessed June 12, 2009).

Rogers, Robert F. 1995. *Destiny's Landfall: A History of Guam.* Honolulu: University of Hawai'i Press.

Sachs, Dana. 2010. *The Life We Were Given: Operation Babylift, International Adoption, and the Children of War in Vietnam.* Boston: Beacon Press.

Shigematsu, Setsu, and Keith L. Camacho. 2010. "Introduction: Militarized Currents, Decolonizing Futures." In *Militarized Currents: Toward a Decolonized Future in Asia and the Pacific,* ed. Setsu Shigematsu and Keith L. Camacho, xv-3. Minneapolis: University of Minnesota Press.

Thompson, Larry C. 2010. *Refugee Workers in the Indochina Exodus, 1975-1982.* Jefferson, NC: McFarland.

Tobin, Thomas G. 1975. "Indo-China: Now on to Camp Fortuitous." *Time,* May 12. http://www.time.com/time/magazine/article/0,9171,917414,00.html (accessed June 12, 2009).

Tobin, Thomas G., Arthur E. Laehr, and John F. Hilgenberg. 1978. "Last Flight from Saigon." In *USAF Southeast Asia Monograph Series,* ed. Lt. Col. A. J. C. Lavalle. Vol. 4, no. 6. Washington, DC: U.S. Government Printing Office.

Turley, William S. 1987. *The Second Indochina War: A Short Political and Military History, 1954-1975.* New York: Signet.

U.S. Naval Hospital. 2013. "Command History." http://www.med.navy.mil/sites/usnhguam /information/Pages/CommandHistory.aspx (accessed March 27, 2010).

USS Midway Museum. 2010. "Operation Frequent Wind—April 30th 2010." YouTube. Posted March 29. http://www.youtube.com/watch?v=J87rgk33X84&feature=player_ embedded (accessed May 20, 2010).

Utts, Thomas C. 2012. "Gateway." http://zcap.freeyellow.com/pix3.htm (accessed September 9, 2010).

Vasquez, Tim. 2001. "Clark Air Base: History and Significant Events." http://www.clarkab .org/history/ (accessed August 31, 2010).

Vo Dang, Thanh T. 2008. "Anticommunism as Cultural Praxis: South Vietnam, War, and Refugee Memories in the Vietnamese American Community." PhD diss., University of California.

Wandering Chopsticks. 2010. "Images at War's End: Refugee and Marine Images from Col Waterhouse Collection and Marine Staff Photographs from Camp Pendleton Archives—Camp Pendleton." September 12. http://wanderingchopsticks.blogspot. com/2010/09/images-at-wars-end-camp-pendleton.html (accessed October 21, 2010).

Yoneyama, Lisa. 2005. "Liberation under Siege: U.S. Military Occupation and Japanese Women's Enfranchisement." *American Quarterly* 57 (3): 885-910.

Young, Marilyn Blatt. 1991. *The Vietnam Wars, 1945-1990.* New York: HarperCollins.

9

Special Money in the Vietnamese Diaspora

HUNG CAM THAI

In this chapter, I am concerned with the social evaluation of monetary exchanges in transnational families. That is, I address the cultural and moral meanings that surround monetary transactions between those who receive and those who send money across international borders. Although influential works in diasporic and transnational studies have looked at the nature of financial and social remittances in transnational families (Adams 1998; Adams and Page 2005; Agarwal and Horowitz 2002; Nguyen, V. C. 2009; Gamburd 2000; Hondagneu-Sotelo 2001; McKay 2003; Parreñas, R. S. 2001b; Parreñas, R. S. 2005; Wucker 2004), there is very little discussion about the cultural meanings of money and the significance of money sent and money received. This is because it is generally assumed that the use and meanings of money are universal. Simply put, money is seen as a medium of exchange on the market for the purchase of goods and services. Yet, there is no doubt that the constructions and meanings of money are diverse across cultures and societies. As Zelizer (1989) succinctly points out in her seminal work on money, "Not all dollars are equal." She argues that "culture and social structure set inevitable limits to the monetization process by introducing profound controls and restrictions on the flow and liquidity of money" (Zelizer 1989, 343). Indeed, noneconomic factors that shape and constrain the use of money include the allocation of money, the control of money, the users of money, and the sources of money. Thus, while money is a medium of exchange on the market, it is not entirely a market phenomenon. And it is not always exchangeable. Furthermore, "money is not homogenous. There are multiple monies, existing in different contexts, and not all of them are the same" (Zelizer 1989, 351). Money is social in nature and culturally specific, embedded in relations of power, interacting with differences in gender, class, and generations. When money is not simply fungible, it is therefore only appropriate for specific uses. Money received from inheritances or a wedding, for example, falls in the category of "special money"; that is, money that has social and cultural significance in its use (Zelizer 1989, 351). I suggest that remittances in the Vietnamese context are "special money," designated for specific purposes and having different meanings for senders and receivers. In many instances, it is money earmarked for the care of family members. In some cases, the act of giving money is a form of care, and in others, the money itself is used to purchase care. Thus, when this special money is used beyond the boundaries of its purpose, tensions often exist in transnational family ties, an issue that this chapter spotlights.

This chapter builds on existing research by exploring the case of the Vietnamese diaspora, suggesting that there are contemporary variants of transnational families distinguished by ethnicity, social class, generation, and composition of family ties. I restrict my analysis to the situation of low-wage Vietnamese immigrants who have recently built transnational ties with the homeland, specifically focusing on the ties of adult siblings and other assorted extended kin members. Vietnamese low-wage transnational families constitute one variation in the structural and personal organizations of family ties in global capitalism. Vietnam is a unique country relative to other high-remittance-receiving nations such as the Philippines and Mexico, having to do with the historical context of Vietnamese emigration that drives contemporary remittance flows. Unlike most Latin American and Asian countries, where the source of remittances tend to come from labor migration (Fajnzylber and Lopez 2007), which is defined as the transnational movement of individuals for the purposes of temporary or contract employment with few prospects for obtaining permanent residence in the country of destination, the vast majority of Vietnamese remittances come from the nearly 3 million *Viet Kieu*, or overseas Vietnamese, who live permanently abroad (Committee for Overseas Vietnamese 2005).[1] Over 40 percent of these *Viet Kieu* reside in the United States and they account for more than 50 percent of all remittances to Vietnam (Pham, L. T. T. 2008). Unlike labor migrants who tend to be separated from their children and spouses, since the fall of Saigon in April 1975, the Vietnamese diaspora has been made up of many transnational extended family members. From that period until the mid-1980s, when Vietnam reopened its door to the global economy, the separation of time and space meant that very little communication was made with the homeland (Thai 2008).

Based on a larger study of return migration and consumption among *Viet Kieu* throughout the diaspora, this chapter focuses on the relationship between return visits of low-wage immigrants and remittance behaviors. To be sure, although I focus on low-wage immigrants, the socioeconomic makeup of the Vietnamese diaspora is highly diverse, reflecting waves of migratory flows over the past forty years as well as the contexts of reception that immigrants face in different geographical spaces. I had not initially intended to study extended family ties, especially among those who send and receive remittances, but serendipitously stumbled on this pattern in the course of doing research on return activities—the occasional or recurring sojourns made by members of migrant communities to their homeland. I explore diverging social and economic realities of immigrants and their left-behind family members by focusing on the social dilemmas of *Viet Kieu,* who support what Robert Courtney Smith calls a "homeland remittance bourgeoisie" (Smith 2006). I follow Smith in using the term remittance bourgeoisie as a heuristic device, and not as a labeling of a specific social class, to refer to family members in the homeland who live comfortable lifestyles in large part because of their access to overseas money. Remittances play a key role in improving the daily lives of family members in the homeland. Research has shown that in Vietnam, 73 percent of all remittances are allocated for immediate consumption of goods and services, while only 14 percent are saved for household construction, and 6 percent for investment (Pfau and Long 2010).

Vietnamese low-wage immigrants in transnational families inhabit contradictory social positions through the forces of globalization. On the one hand, they work in jobs that pay low wages and involve long hours, but on the other hand, they are able to support homeland family members, who are not only able to meet daily household expenses, but also to frequently buy luxury goods relative to their social contexts. In their separation of space and time, Vietnamese transmigrants with extended kin and adult siblings back home send money because of global conditions that position many of their family members in poverty in Third World Saigon. Many of these remittance-sending family members send funds to maintain household expenses, but social factors such as consumerism and lack of communications have created disjunctures in what senders and receivers expect from the use of remittances. More often than not, as I will detail, *Viet Kieu* confront remittance dilemmas as they make homeland return visits, compelling many of them to modify their remittance behaviors over time.

Transnational family relations are frequently contested or misunderstood across space and time (Mahler 2001; Parreñas, R. S. 2001a; Parreñas, R. 2005; Schmalzbauer 2008), but return activities among immigrants potentially allow social relations to be renegotiated across national boundaries. Although a lively body of research in recent years has paid significant attention to the emergence of transnational cultures, there is currently little attention given to the role of homeland return visits within this body of research, especially to how and why return activities among overseas immigrants may produce and modify remittance behaviors (Åkesson 2009; Schmalzbauer 2008). I argue that social mobility among left-behind family members should take into account changing remittance behaviors across time, especially when migrant family members make return visits. This is because much of what we know about remittance mobility generally ignores the presence of overseas immigrants in the homeland, and the decisions that may follow their return visits in terms of remittance behaviors. How, I ask, do members of the migrant population modify remittance behaviors when they make return visits to the homeland? This focus is particularly important because remittances constitute a significant portion of economic growth in many developing countries and is especially important for immigrants who work in low-wage sectors. As the economist Michele Wucker (2004) reports, today's remittance senders are generally low-wage workers. Among immigrants in the United States, for instance, only 19 percent of immigrants who earn more than $50,000 a year send any remittances to their families in the community of origin, while 46 percent of those who earn less than $30,000 do so. Thus, those who send remittances are generally the least able to do so. They are, as Wucker succinctly puts it, "heroes of the developing world" (2004, 37).

In the following pages, I proceed by underscoring the nature of return visits as an important category of analysis. I show how many immigrants, despite struggling in the West, feel compelled to support extended family and adult siblings back home because of the vast economic divide between Vietnam and the West. Then, I demonstrate the various dilemmas faced by some family members who send money. I show how return visits are often the only times that consumptive behaviors are revealed to remittance-sending family members. Finally, I describe how some *Viet Kieu* modify their remittance behaviors following their return visits. My data reveals that *Viet Kieu* gain more clarity on how their remittances are spent only when they make homeland return visits. This helps returnees, for better or worse, modify their remittance behaviors once they understand the consumptive and leisure activities among remittance-reliant family members. The place of focus here is Saigon,[2] officially known as Ho Chi Minh City, where over 50 percent of all migrant remittances are sent in Vietnam (Nguyen D. A. 2005).

Return Activities among Immigrants in Transnational Families

In this section, I engage with research on international return visits, emphasizing the international return visits of individuals who originally migrated to industrialized countries and have returned to their homelands in less developed areas. There is a separate body of literature on internal migration patterns, including varying aspects of returns within the United States and Canada (Alexander 1998, 2005; Alexander 2006; Lee 1974; Stone 1974). There is a also an emergent body of literature on return migration between and within low-income regions, particularly with regard to political refugees and migrant laborers (Oxfeld and Long 2004). The research on international returns was relatively limited until the emergence of transnational studies because scholars had assumed for a long time that migration was a one-way process that occurred mainly through either a "rural to urban" analytical framework, viewing it through a "poor to rich nation" theoretical lens. An important observation in studies of return migration is that "migrants returning for a vacation or an extended visit without the intention of remaining at home are generally not defined as return migrants" (Oxfeld and Long 2004, 136). Indeed, *return visits* are distinct from return migration because whereas return migration situates migrants permanently back in their homeland for resettlement, return visits allow migrants to "maintain multiple, yet socially meaningful, identities in both their current place of residence and their external homeland" (Duval 2004, 51). I want to underscore this point since return migration is a challenging activity for the postwar *Viet Kieu* diaspora. It is relatively difficult for *Viet Kieu*, compared to other Asian immigrants like those from the Philippines (Espiritu 2003), to reintegrate back to the homeland, for it is difficult to buy land and properties as well as to obtain paperwork for long-term settlement. Return migration, therefore, is currently difficult and rare for the postwar *Viet Kieu* population (Long 2004), making the return visit an important social practice that enables migrants to sustain transnational family ties.

Return visits are important to consider because they serve as one measure of transnationality among contemporary migrants, some of whom are unable to legally return to their home countries and resettle. Indeed, the literature on transnationalism has not fully operationalized the nature of transnational behavior, and there are continuing debates on the extent of transnationalism (Levitt 2001; Levitt et al. 2003; Mahler 1998; Portes 2001). For instance, Pierrette Hondagneu-Sotelo and Ernestine Avila (1997) have stated that they "object to transnationalism's emphasis on circulation and indeterminance of settlement." They argue that while many immigrants return to their home countries for annual visits, "most immigrants are here to stay, regardless of their initial migration intentions" (Hondagneu-Sotelo and Avila 1997, 549–550). In the same way, Espiritu (2003) maintains that "most immigrants in the United States are here to stay regardless of their initial intentions and their continuing involvement in the political, social, and economic lives of their countries of origin" (3). Return visits could, therefore, provide some tangibility to the often abstract assertions that are being made by scholars of transnationalism. Our understanding of the reality and the extent of transnationalism could be enhanced by looking at the ways return visits are features of contemporary transnationalism that distinguishes it from historical patterns of transnational ties. Return visits ultimately bring concrete understanding to an otherwise ambivalent, if not speculative, discussion about transnational practices.

Returning from the Vietnamese Diaspora

Return visits among the postwar Vietnamese diaspora are a relatively recent development, made possible only because of recent changes in national policies by the Vietnamese government and the emergent international diplomatic relations among nation-states, particularly between the United States and Vietnam. Today, after over twenty years of economic reform started by the Vietnamese government in 1986, it is now common for the *Viet Kieu* population to return home for family visits, tourism, and other social and economic activities. Yet, except for some cursory media attention (Vietnam News 2002; Nhat 1999; Nguyen, H. 2002; Larmer 2000; Lamb 1997) and the research of one scholar (Long 2004), there has been virtually no research done on return migration or return visits among the *Viet Kieu* population. This has been mostly due to the dominant focus on the exile dimension of Vietnamese immigration history. From the mid-1970s to the early 1990s, refugee narratives defined Vietnamese migration experiences and consequently the relationship that *Viet Kieu* had with the homeland. Indeed, when one speaks of postwar Vietnamese homeland returnees, they should be understood in the context of the mass refugee migration during a specific period of political turmoil in Southeast Asia beginning in the mid-1970s. Even though there had been sporadic migration from Vietnam before this period (Pham, V. 2003), the first mass outmigration and the formation of a Vietnamese diaspora began on April 30, 1975, with the fall of Saigon and the pulling out of U.S. troops from Vietnam. These postwar Vietnamese international migrants came as refugees directly to the United States as part of the airlift effort that evacuated more than 130,000 Saigonese, who were mostly from the urban middle class (Freeman 1995). Subsequent waves of refugees and immigrants included a large number of "boat people" from diverse regions of Vietnam who spent some time in refugee camps in other Asian countries (most notably in Hong Kong, Thailand, and the Philippines) before they were sponsored by a country in the West. In more recent years, Vietnamese immigrants exit their home country mainly through family sponsorship to various parts of the diaspora (Thai 2008).

In 1986, after having no contact with most of the outside world for over a decade, the government of Vietnam adopted a new socioeconomic policy called

Doi Moi[3] (renovation) which did not end state ownership or central planning, but moved the country from complete state-sponsored socialism to partial free-market capitalism (Morley and Nishihara 1997; Ebashi 1997). In 1993, Vietnam was admitted to the Association of Southeast Asian Nations (ASEAN), but it was not until August 1995 that former U.S. president Bill Clinton reestablished full diplomatic relations with the country (Morley and Nishihara 1997). The normalization of economic and social ties by 1995 gradually increased the number of individuals from the Vietnamese diaspora who returned to Vietnam to visit family members or to vacation. Recent incentives provided by the state to the overseas population, like the ability to lease land and make investments, have created an extraordinarily important *Viet Kieu* economy, although such incentives have been slowly executed, as noted by some scholars (Thai 2008; Morley and Nishihara 1997). Remittances to Vietnam grew dramatically from only $35 million in 1991 to approximately $5 billion in 2006, accounting for about 8 percent of Vietnam's gross domestic product (World Bank 2006). In Saigon, remittances have exceeded the amount of foreign direct investment. The Vietnamese government estimates that in 2008, more than 300,000 *Viet Kieu* returned to visit, a dramatic increase from 87,000 in 1992 and 8,000 in 1988 (Thomas 1997; Carruthers 2008). Visiting *Viet Kieu* are likely to bring "pocket transfers," money migrants bring directly themselves, that dramatically increases the overall official remittance amount.

Methods

Moving beyond the rhetoric of a country reconciling with the wounds of colonialism and war that ended almost forty years ago, this project spotlights dimensions of status, power, distinctions, and respectability embedded in recent transnational social relations in global Saigon. Data analysis is derived from thirty-one months of fieldwork done in distinct intervals over a five-year period between 2003 and 2009, including nine research trips during the summers between 2003 and 2008, as well as a ten-month stint of intensive fieldwork conducted between May 2004 and March 2005. A final phase of follow-up fieldwork and interviews took place between January and June 2009. I gathered data by conducting in-depth, open-ended, tape-recorded interviews with *Viet Kieu* returnees in Saigon. Since there is no roster of people in transnational families, with the help of four full-time research assistants during the ten-month stint of fieldwork, I got to know 324 *Viet Kieu* who returned to Saigon for various reasons during that period. We began recruiting respondents through personal social networks and used snowball sampling to end up with 324 *Viet Kieu*. To avoid the problems of self-selection and systematic bias, I selected 100 potential respondents from the 324 by using a random numbers table to generate a simple random sample of respondents. From this simple random procedure, I ended up with 83 *Viet Kieu*. In addition to the *Viet Kieu*, we also interviewed 65 of their local family members, as well as 44 non-Vietnamese, non-*Viet Kieu* Westerners who were part of their social networks in Saigon.

In this chapter, I only draw on interviews with the subsample of the 83 *Viet Kieu*, with the viewpoints of their Vietnamese family members and social networks of Westerners to be reported elsewhere. To protect the anonymity of my informants, I use fictitious names throughout the chapter. The interviews with *Viet Kieu* focused on the formation of transnational ties with left-behind family members, experiences of return activities and reconnections in Vietnam, consumptive patterns, remittance behaviors, and future plans for sustaining transnational households. Of the *Viet Kieu* I interviewed, 39 were women and 44 were men. The age range was 26 to 58, with the average age being 38.6 years. Eighty-eight percent were from the core countries of the United States, Canada, France, and Australia. Sixty-one percent were American *Viet Kieu*, with French, Canadian, and Australian *Viet Kieu* representing 6, 7, and 13 percent respectively. The remaining 13 percent were from various countries of the diaspora.

The Institutionalization of Remittances in Contemporary Saigon

Remittances play a central role in the organization of transnational family ties. Vietnam is no exception to this global reality as evidenced by the fact that one out of every four Vietnamese citizens relies on remittances for their livelihood. In Saigon, the proportion of remittance-reliant individuals is estimated to be higher since over 50 percent of remittances to Vietnam are circulated in that city (Nguyen, D. A. 2005). Limited employment opportunities and a repressed economy in the homeland compel many migrant family members to send money back home, even those with precarious employment situations overseas, such as the case for the immigrants in this study who were part of the low-wage labor market. Although most studies focus on remittances sent by migrant workers to their spouses and children left behind (Schmalzbauer 2004; Parreñas, R. 2005; Parreñas, R. S. 2001b; Hondagneu-Sotelo and Avila 1997; Gamburd 2000; Åkesson 2009), very few of my respondents were in such situations. Because Vietnamese migrant workers are a recent addition to the global workforce, labor migration does not bear a strong relation to Vietnamese remittance-sending communities. This is why the majority of remittance senders in this study were sending money to adult siblings and extended relatives. In my study, I found that only 10 percent of remittances were being sent by parents or spouses, nearly

70 percent of the remittances were being sent by adult siblings, and 20 percent were being sent by other relatives like aunts, uncles, and cousins. In this section, I detail some of the reasons my informants send money to adult siblings and extended relatives, emphasizing that, over time, remittances have become an institutionalized aspect of everyday life in contemporary Vietnam. In the beginning, remittances were often sent to support daily household expenses and were typically sent once family members eased into their settlement in the West. As Tuyet, a forty-two-year-old amusement park worker from Florida, said,

> When we first got to Florida in the early 1980s, like everyone else we were struggling financially. At that time, all the Vietnamese we knew were trying to survive. Most people were on food stamps and welfare and so no one really thought about the people left in Vietnam. It was also difficult to send money back home because we could not communicate with our families in Vietnam. Both my husband and I had family back there and we still do because we could not sponsor our brothers and sisters to America. When we heard of services to send money or when we first had friends who returned to Vietnam, we sent money to our brothers and sisters. Sometimes, if someone got sick, we would send money right away, but most of the time, normally we just sent money so people can live day to day.

Researchers have noted that international remittances come in three main forms of "transfer types." The first involves money or gifts sent by migrants directly to relatives in the country of origin. The second involves "personal investment transfers," whereby senders remit regular amounts to save for their personal investments in the homeland. The third generally involves transfers for a community purpose, such as village or hometown associations. Yossi Shain and Aharon Barth (2003) suggest that the level of maturity of a specific diaspora has a lot to do with the kinds of transfers that are remitted to the homeland. In this study, I found that none of my informants were sending money to village or homeland associations. Nearly 95 percent were sending money and gifts (mostly money) to family members and the other 5 percent of the *Viet Kieu* had plans for investment in housing for their future return migration or long-term return visits. The situation is very different for Mexican migrants, as noted by David Fitzgerald (2013). He points out that many Mexican returnees invest in land and build entire communities from their earnings abroad. Moreover, diaspora capital is still very limited in helping Vietnam develop, unlike the case with China, as noted by Min Ye (2013). Individual and diaspora investments are limited because *Viet Kieu* are still in the early stages of returns, and the legal infrastructure for them to buy and build homes is not fully developed. The Vietnamese scholar Nguyen Dang Anh (2005) explains that among poor families in Vietnam most remittances are spent on household consumption, rather than on investments; he found that remittances in Vietnam generally increase household incomes of receiving families by over 50 percent. This is often not difficult to do for most *Viet Kieu* since the average monthly income in Saigon in 2005 was $1.1 Vietnamese dongs or $61 (Du 2005).

Oded Stark and Robert Lucas (1988) found that remittances are generally sent on the basis of "pure altruism," that is, the care of migrants for those relatives left behind. Indeed, like Tuyet, another respondent, Binh, a thirty-seven-year-old factory worker who migrated to Sydney, Australia, explained that he generally sent money to an adult cousin in order to support her household expenses. Like Tuyet, he also approximates the monthly income of his cousin to determine how much he remits,

> I know it is hard for people to imagine that our lives can be tough because they think that life in Australia is very comfortable. They think the government will support you if you don't make enough money. So it is hard to explain to them that even though I live in Australia and make much more money than them, I still have a lot of expenses, so I can only give them so much money. So what I try to do is I try to give them enough money to cover their expenses on a daily basis. I try to figure out how much money they make by working, and I give them about half that amount.

Binh's story also shows how remittances provide senders a sturdy basis for maintaining transnational family ties and identity to the homeland:

> I think it's going to be a few more decades before our families and friends in Vietnam can make a decent living on their own. So I think it is a responsibility for those of us who were able to leave Vietnam to help our families back home. It is not a big deal to me because I only send about $300 a month to one of my cousins [all remittance amounts are in U.S. dollars]. I leave it up to her to divide that money in whatever ways she wants, but for me, the $300 is not that much. But I know that for her, she could support at least a dozen people every month. My cousin is really the only family member I have left in Vietnam so I want to support her and I want my children in the future to go back to Vietnam and know that they still have family there. Maybe my wife and I will go back there to live when we get older, so we need to keep in touch with her.

As Binh suggested, while remittances could potentially help his family sustain transnational family ties to Vietnam, sometimes it is difficult when remittance-reliant individuals have inaccurate impressions of life in the West.

Virtually all of the respondents in my study pointed out that their family members rarely knew the details of their jobs nor were they aware of the harsh working conditions that many working-class immigrants confront in the West. As Tam, a thirty-eight-year-old female nail salon worker who migrated with her siblings to Toronto, remarked,

> When I first went to Vietnam in 1994, people were still pretty unclear about life in the West; some people actually asked me questions about how my life was like, how much money I earned and things like that. They were trying to figure it out. But I think in recent years as more and more people have access to TV and radio, they tend to only have one image of everyone's life, that everyone has a comfortable life. I guess it is all relative and it depends on who you talk to, but I am not sure that some *Viet Kieu* live more comfortable lives than those in Vietnam. I think a lot of what the Vietnamese people think is inaccurate. A lot of them have this idea that we all have office jobs, that we sit in air-conditioned rooms and that we drive fancy cars to work. There is also this idea that no one suffers financially in the West because they somehow think that if you lose your job or if you have young children, the government will just fully support you.

The relationship between popular images of Western lifestyles and *Viet Kieu*'s representation of life in the West is a paradoxical one. On the one hand, some *Viet Kieu*, like Tam, remarked that family members had inaccurate images of life in the West because of media representations. But on the other hand, many *Viet Kieu* said that they do not tell their family members about their work lives because they did not want to worry their family. Others said they felt embarrassed or that they did not want to embarrass their family members by revealing their harsh working conditions in the West. A number of studies have shown that immigrants generally do not reveal to their families the harsh realities of their lives in overseas locations, even when they struggle with jobs characterized by long hours and low pay (Thai 2006; Schmalzbauer 2004; Goldring 1998). As Trung, a thirty-three-year-old hotel worker from Montreal explained,

> I try to tell my sisters in Vietnam that working in the hotel is difficult for me, but I have to do it because I didn't do well in school and so this is the best job that I got. I have to work late hours; I have to lift a lot of heavy luggage all day long. And I don't get a lot of breaks. Even though I can describe it to them, my sisters think that my life is still way better than theirs. Well, maybe it is. But when I go back to visit, I think their life is better than mine. I mean they get to take long naps in the afternoons, and even though

they work at jobs that pay nothing, with the money I send them, they can probably live without working. The other problem is that many *Viet Kieu* when they come back, they don't tell their families about the kinds of jobs they have. They don't really talk about it. I guess it's not like when you visit for two or three weeks, all you do is sit around and complain to your family about your life in Canada. People just won't understand because if life is so hard in Canada, why would everyone in Vietnam want to leave?

As Tam and Trung suggest, the misunderstandings that family members in Vietnam have of overseas life stem partly from a lack of communication and partly from inaccurate media representations. But also note that it stems partly from a culture of migration that compels many immigrants to simply deny the realities of their economic conditions in overseas communities. This is sometimes due to migrants' sense of relative comparisons across transnational social fields. As Chi, a fifty-two-year-old restaurant worker from New York, explained,

> When I go back to Saigon, I see many poor people like my brother and two sisters. One of my sisters makes only about $40 a month working as a cleaner in a hotel and my brother makes only $70 a month as a security guard. So every month I send them each about double their monthly incomes, which they say helps them out a lot. Sometimes, when something big comes along, like when someone gets really sick I would help more. Last year, for example, my niece [sister's daughter] needed some money because she was trying to enter a school to learn English and I gave her about $800 for the tuition fees. How can we complain to them when they are making only $40 or $70 a month? Even though I make only about $1,600 a month working at a restaurant, it is still much more than how much they can ever make in Vietnam. And you know, everyone has to work. No one really knows how hard other people's jobs are, unless you have done it before. So I just don't complain to them [in Vietnam].

Dilemmas of Sending Money

While approximating monthly incomes and sending a portion of such incomes was a simple strategy many *Viet Kieu* used for determining remittance amounts, most *Viet Kieu* experienced dilemmas with remittance-reliant family members, which were often not revealed to them until they made return visits to the homeland. Among my respondents who had made at least three return visits to Vietnam since they had migrated, the majority said that they faced various dilemmas with their families concerning remittances once they started making return visits. In this section, I describe the two main interrelated dilemmas, including the problem of distribution of remittances and allocation of expenditures. Distribution has to do with apportioning money to multiple family members. Allocation, on the other hand, refers to the ways in which money is spent on specific goods and services.

Distribution

In their transnational separation, family members remit funds mainly through door-to-door remittance services such as the Hoa Phat Remittance Service and U.S. Tours Inc, both having offices all over the United States and with subsidiaries in many parts of the diaspora, including Australia, Canada, and France. These services can deliver money to Saigon in as fast as four hours, and within twenty-four hours to anywhere in Vietnam. It is easy, according to my informants, to send money directly to individual family members so long as they have a phone, preferably a mobile phone, because remittance companies can make door-to-door delivery anywhere in the city as long as they can contact the recipient. Yet, most remitters prefer to have one person in charge of remittances who distributes the money to other family members. Usually, remitters, like thirty-nine-year-old Dung, designate one family member to take charge of funds. Dung works as a seamstress in Toronto and had been sending nearly $1,800 per month back to Saigon for more than two years to support one younger sister, an older brother, and three uncles.[4]

> When I first started to send money, it was pretty hard to send each person their individual share because the banks and the remittance service centers charged a fee for each transaction so I decided that I would just put one person in charge of all the funds. It was easy to have someone get all the money and then divide it up, as I would instruct in my letter to him or her. When we send money, the remittance service center gives us a chance to write a letter to our family in Vietnam and so I did that. I have a brother and sister in Vietnam, but I also sent money to my three uncles, and sometimes to my nieces and nephews when they write and ask for something specific. But it was just convenient to have my one sister take care of all the money for me.

An important feature of sending remittances, as Dung described, is to have one person take charge of distributing money. On the receiving end, designated receivers tend to be individuals with the most access to technology, which meant that those who did not have access to telephones, preferably a mobile phone, were not generally designated receivers. This meant that the elderly and the very young were typically not designated as receivers since I generally found that those two groups were less likely to own mobile phones or have access to the Internet. As Dai, a twenty-eight-year-old mechanic from northern California, said,

> Sometimes I send money twice or three times a month because it has gotten easy to send money. I just go to the remittance center at the mall down the road from my house, fill out a form, and my family can receive the money within four hours if I ask them to rush. So it is just easier if I can have someone in Saigon with a mobile phone who I can text and make sure that they get the money in time. You know, when you send money, sometimes if the amount is large, you get nervous that your family does not receive it. Or you get anxious that they don't receive it on time. So I try to have someone I know, for me it's my brother, keep track of the money and to divide the money for me.

Both Dung and Dai found it convenient to designate one person in Saigon as the receiver of the remittances they sent. Access to advanced technology, such as the ability to send texts and e-mails, as well as the rapidity with which *Viet Kieu* can send money at remittance centers reflect the ease with which *Viet Kieu* communicate with their family members in Vietnam. Yet, among *Viet Kieu* respondents, a major problem was the issue of accurate and timely distribution of funds they sent. Over 40 percent of my informants said they encountered the problem of designated receivers not dividing funds up in the way the senders had instructed. As Cuc, a forty-seven-year-old hair stylist from Florida who had designated her thirty-five-year-old brother as the receiver, explained,

> You know you would like to trust every family member you have, especially the one you think will handle the money fairly for everyone. But it is a very sensitive issue because I can't just ask my brother, "Oh did you give the money out to everyone?" every time I send money back because when I send the money, I list out all the amounts that everyone in the family should receive. I write on the fax at the remittance center, "please give this aunt this much, that uncle that much, this niece this much." And then I call up my brother when I think he should receive the money, and I just ask him, "Did you get the money?" That's it. That's all I ask, I don't ask more, because if I ask more, I am afraid he will say that I don't trust him. It's a very sensitive issue, you know. And when you think about it, sometimes the money is not that much, and you know they are already so poor. It's already difficult for him to wait every month for the money I send.

Some informants said that sometimes the problem had existed for many years before they found out, because the separation of distance and time in addition to the issue of trust and sensitivity meant that senders generally did not find out until they returned to visit Vietnam. One sender, Vinh, a thirty-six-year-old gas station owner from Chicago, learned upon visiting Vietnam that the funds he had been sending to support four separate households were, in fact, being kept by the designated receiver.[5]

For about eight years, before I came back to Vietnam for the first time in 2003, I was sending money to my oldest brother so that he could divide the money to four people. I had another older brother, one cousin, and my grandmother who I was supporting. Each of these four people were supporting their own families with the money I sent them. I think at one point about two years ago, I started to send about $1,000 per month when my business was doing well in America. I calculated that the $1,000 I was sending each month was helping about twenty-four people. When I came back in 2003, I asked the other people [the nondesignated receivers] if they were receiving money that I was sending to the oldest brother. Some of them had received a little, but the other brother and my grandmother were not receiving anything for over four years. My brother was keeping all that money to himself for over four years. So after that, I stopped sending him money. I also made sure that I usually send money to each individual person. But it got complicated and tiring to keep all the calculations so I decided three years ago that I would just come back every year and give everyone a big chunk whenever I visited them.

Allocation

As I have shown, *Viet Kieu* remitters in transnational extended families face problems with designated receivers who do not always fulfill their role of distributing money to multiple individuals or multiple households. Another major dilemma that remittance senders face is what I call allocation, which refers to misunderstandings, disagreements, or disapproval about how remittances are spent. In other words, from a distance, most remitters were unaware of the allocations of their funds; often this became a problem when *Viet Kieu* family members return for a visit. Some remitters found out that the money they sent was allocated to goods and services that they would not have approved, including the conspicuous consumption of luxury goods. Remitters generally objected to conspicuous consumption among remittance-reliant family members because they frequently mandated that receivers spend funds on daily needs, such as food and health care. Like the problem of distribution, senders are usually not aware of what goods and services are purchased with the money they send. Nearly 80 percent of my respondents disapproved of goods their family members were buying when they made return visits. Tuyen, a thirty-six-year-old secretary from Sydney, described how she was disappointed on one visit to learn that her brother was spending money on luxury items which she did not approve of:

I have a younger brother in Vietnam who is single, and I was sending him money for about three years. Because I did not want him to work since I knew that the wages in Vietnam are very low, I sent him money so that he could go to school and just spend it on food and other necessities. I told him that he should also try to save the money for the future just in case he could never go to Australia then he could have money to start a business or do something with his life [in Saigon]. But when I came back last year, I found out that the $3,000 I sent to him was used to buy a fancy motorbike. When I came back, I asked him how he got the money to eat and use for his daily expenses, I learned from his girlfriend that he was basically starving himself, or eating at her house, while driving his fancy motorbike.

Although most—nearly 90 percent—of respondents claimed that they generally sent money for daily expenses by strategically approximating monthly incomes of their left-behind family members, nearly half of them said that they sent occasional large amounts for expensive goods like motorbikes, televisions, air conditions, and other luxury items. However, among those who sent large amounts for expensive items, many said that they often requested remittance-reliant family members to purchase goods that benefited an entire household rather than one individual. This often became a problem since it was not always clear which items benefited an entire household, and which were only enjoyed by one individual. Sang, a thirty-seven-year-old retail worker, whose parents and adult siblings were still in Vietnam and who had made at least two return visits annually in the past three years to visit them, remarked,

Four years ago when I got a big bonus at work, I sent money back to my younger brother and I asked him to buy a TV to put in my parents' house. It was at that time when they were selling those big flat screen TV in Saigon, and I knew my parents really wanted it because I had made a visit and they told me to bring one back to them. I figured I could just give my brother money to buy it for them. I thought it was good to buy it since my brother and my sisters were living with my parents and they all could watch the TV. When I came back the following year, I found out that my brother sold his old bike and used the $1,500 I sent him to upgrade to a fancier bike. He was trying to convince me that the bike was better for the whole family! [laughs]

Return Visits and Consumption in Global Saigon

A number of scholars have observed that technological advancements in globalization, while benefiting transnational families on many levels, do not always ensure constant and honest communication (Schmalzbauer 2008). This is the reality among those sending and receiving remittances in Vietnamese transnational families. As I have shown, the economic realities of migrant family members are not made known to those in the homeland, and often remittance-reliant family members do not reveal to their overseas relatives how they spend the money that are sent to them. It is clear that remittances in Vietnamese transnational families can present various problems that often do not emerge until remittance-sending individuals return to Vietnam to visit. In this section, I discuss in greater detail how return visits affect *Viet Kieu*'s perception of remittances in the homeland. Then I describe briefly how some *Viet Kieu* family members resolved the various problems they confronted as they made return visits to Saigon. As a case in point, thirty-six-year-old Trai, a department store worker from southern California, described his surprise and disappointment on making his first return visit to Vietnam:

> There is no question that I have to help my two sisters out in Vietnam because I was the only one who got to migrate to America. Because I could not sponsor them to America since they were older than twenty-one, I feel sorry for them so I just send them money every month for their expenses. A few years ago, I sent them each $2,500 so that they could renovate two of the bedrooms in the house that my parents left them when I sponsored my parents to America. When I came back for the first time in 2005, I found out that one of my sisters was using her money on fancy clothes and stuff that rich kids in Saigon are buying. She was not using the money to upgrade the house, or even for necessities. After I came back, I decided that I would not send her money from America anymore, and definitely I would not send her large amounts.

Researchers have pointed out that a consumer culture now exists in Vietnam, and has mainly been concentrated in Saigon (Taylor 2004; Earl 2004). Indeed, a common observation among respondents was that foreign influences and *Viet Kieu* remittances had made Saigon a city of consumption such that some of their family in Saigon had unrealistic expectations. Low-wage *Viet Kieu* respondents said that some of their family members were spending money on commodities that they themselves would never purchase in the West. Hien, a forty-three-year-old nail salon worker from North Carolina, who had been making annual return visits for six consecutive years when I met her, remarked,

Every year when I go back, I see that people in Saigon are spending much more money and buying a lot more stuff. I have so many nieces and nephews in Saigon and I could not believe how much they were spending on things. I don't understand how they make only $100 per month, but they can buy a $500 cell phone? I know a lot of people in Saigon have *Viet Kieu* money, but I can't afford to support my family that much! When I returned two years ago, I remember my brother asking me for a big flat screen TV. I told him, "No way! I can't even afford to have one for myself in America!"

As Hien stated, many respondents pointed to *Viet Kieu* money, that is, remittances, as the source of the rise in material culture in Vietnam. Long, a thirty-seven-year-old mechanic from Florida, explained,

Of course it is all about the *Viet Kieu* money. How else could such a poor city be opening up name brand stores like Gucci and Versace? I know so many locals who use their *Viet Kieu* money to buy luxury items. I discover this the bad way when I came back and I saw my cousin with a Gucci bag. She wrote me when I was in America asking for money so she could take English classes in order to get a job at a five-star hotel, and I thought it was a good job for her. I even had a friend in the city who could help her get a job at a hotel. But when I came back, I tested her English, and I knew right away that she did not take English classes, so I asked her what she had spent the money on. She kept telling me that she saved the money and she was waiting for the right time to take English classes. And that was like eighteen months ago that I gave her the money. So one day I saw her carrying a Gucci bag, and I knew that thing was real. I was like, "damn, let me see that bag." It was real, definitely. I knew that she had taken my money to buy that bag. I was pissed!

Given the problems most of my respondents faced over time with the remittances they were sending to their adult siblings and extended relatives, many devised new strategies for sending money. The most common strategy used among my respondents was to send money through pocket transfers rather than relying on official remittance services. This was described by Cong, a forty-two-year-old taxi driver from Hawai'i, who said he had been making visits back annually for the past four years.

Before when it was harder and more expensive to go back to Vietnam, I always used the remittance service to send money, but when flights got cheap, I began to return more. I think that was when I decided that I would just stop sending money because there were some bad experiences that created a big mess in my family about the money I spent. It's a long story, but it was basically about one cousin not dividing up the money properly and people thought that I gave money unequally to different people.

Although easy travel to Vietnam in the past ten years has made it possible for *Viet Kieu* family members to return and visit regularly, returning annually is not always possible for some informants. As Hoa, a forty-six-year-old supermarket cashier, described, relying on a designated receiver in Vietnam became a problem so she began to rely on friends and family members in the United States. Thus another alternative among those who found it costly to return regularly for the purpose of giving pocket transfers was to rely on trusted *Viet Kieu* family members and friends to deliver money to specific individuals.

When I had a bad experience two years ago with my cousin who kept more money than she should have, I decided that I would just send the money through other people I knew who were coming back to Saigon. That way, my friends from America can hand deliver the money to specific people that I ask. It's better that way because I can't go back to Vietnam every year.

Cong's and Hoa's different strategies of delivering their own remittances and relying on trusted friends and families accounted for nearly 70 percent of the ways my informants' sent money after they started to make return visits. These individuals initially used remittance services to send money, but began to rely on pocket transfers after they had become familiar with the problems they were facing in Vietnam with remittance-reliant family members.

In the most extreme and unfortunate cases, I met a few [N=4] respondents who had completely cut off ties with kin members who had unreasonable expectations for remittances or who were the cause of irresolvable problems. As a case in point, Sau, a forty-eight-year-old salesman from Toronto, explained,

Before my wife and I came back to Vietnam, we were sending small amounts of money regularly to our cousins and our aunts and uncles in Saigon. At the beginning, they were very nice to us, always treated us so well. Then after a while they asked for more and more money. Somehow, everyone just got sick more and more often and we had to give more and more money. When we returned to visit regularly, we realized that no one really was sick, and they were just asking for more money to buy stuff in the house. They got air conditioners, they got TVs and motorbikes. They were trying to live a fancy life off our money. And my wife got angry because we were working so hard in Canada and we don't save much money, but our cousins were living these comfortable lives. We were stressing out about making sure we send them money because every time they asked for money we thought it was a crisis, like someone got sick. We said we had to stop sending them money. Of course after we stopped sending money, they treated us like they don't even know us. So now my wife and our children just go to Vietnam for vacation. We just think that we don't have any family in Vietnam anymore.

Conclusion

There are two dominant models that help explain the effects of remittances on the homeland (Thai 2006). On the one hand, those adhering to the "dependency" model argue that remittances can encourage spending money on luxury goods that are not necessary for daily life—in short, they can encourage conspicuous consumption. On the other hand, those adhering to the "development" model argue that remittances help developing countries with economic growth by providing household incomes that could not otherwise be earned in the home country. Jeffrey Cohen (2001) proposes that a transnational approach to analyzing remittance allows us to "break down the contradictions of dependency and development and defines the outcomes of migration and remittance use as rooted in a series of interdependencies that emphasize production and consumption, class and ethnicity, and the individual and the community while transcending localities and national boundaries" (955). Drawing on this approach to remittance, I have focused on the relationship between remittances and return visits among low-wage Vietnamese immigrants living in various parts of the diaspora. Remittances have become an institutional dimension of contemporary Vietnamese society, especially in Saigon, where consumption and remittances are the highest in Vietnam (Taylor 2004; Pfau and Long 2010).

As Portes (2001) points out, opposing positions have developed recently regarding the relationship between migration and the socioeconomic development of sending countries. Remittances, while at the surface, could be seen as one possible advantage from developing countries, they also present multiple problems across transnational social fields, including the extraction of human capital from the developing world. My study shows that remittances play a crucial role in providing daily consumption needs, but they also cause problems. As the Vietnamese diaspora matures, remittances will likely continue to play a key role in Vietnam's development. Clearly, the economic role that *Viet Kieu* play in the homeland is significant, and the social implications are many and varied for the future development of their home country. One point that I underscore here, as noted by Portes on the relationship between migration and development, is that it is likely that remittance-reliant families in Vietnam, especially in urban centers such as Saigon, will continue to enjoy consumption and household incomes that nonremittance families will not have access to. This will contribute to the rise in income inequality in the country. On another level, the social and psychological pressures on *Viet Kieu* to sustain the needs of remittance-reliant family members will continue, as remittances become a key aspect of sustaining transnational family ties. This chapter has shown how return visits can significantly alter the form of transnational families, especially those with low-wage immigrants, and can potentially bring about enormous changes across transnational social fields. I have shown the significance of remittances among extended family members, including siblings, because this poses an important question about why and how senders remit money in situations where they may not feel as compelled to do so. That is to say, while a number of studies have shown that labor migrants send money to children and spouses to maintain household well-being, this study has shown that siblings and other extended kin send money for a number of reasons. I have established that international remittances have different social and economic meanings for those who receive and those who send. As I have shown, the value of money sent and the sacrifice it represents for senders are not always commensurate with the value placed on such money by receivers. This difference, I argue, will be at the center of tensions for transnational family members. Focusing on the relationship between remittance behaviors and return visits offers an important window onto transnational practices, class variations among families across international borders, and the social contradictions and problems transnational families confront in global capitalism.

Notes to Chapter 9: Special Money in the Vietnamese Diaspora

Financial support for this project was provided by the Haynes Foundation, the Freeman Foundation, the Dean's Office at Pomona College, and a Senior Research Fellowship at the Asia Research Institute of the National University of Singapore.

1. The term *Viet Kieu* is commonly used to mean "overseas Vietnamese," but its literal translation is "Vietnamese sojourner." See Wah (2005) and Thai (2006).

2. Although Saigon's name was changed to Ho Chi Minh City when the South surrendered to Northern Vietnamese military troops in 1975, most people I met in contemporary Vietnam still refer to the city as "Saigon," or simply "Thanh Pho" (The City). I echo their frames of reference by using the name "Saigon," and "Saigonese" to refer to the locals there.

3. Literally, "changing for the new."

4. I should note here that while Dung is a low-wage worker, she had been borrowing money from friends and credit card companies to consistently send $1,800 per month back in the previous two years.

5. Like a number of my respondents, Vinh often sent more money than he actually earned. Even though he owned his own business, the income was often unstable, and many months he would borrow money to send money back to his family members.

References

Adams, Richard. 1998. "Remittances, Investment, and Rural Asset Accumulation in Pakistan." *Economic Development and Cultural Change* 47 (1): 155–173.

Adams, Richard H., and John Page. 2005. "Do International Migration and Remittances Reduce Poverty in Developing Countries?" *World Development* 33 (10): 1645–1669.

Agarwal, Reena, and Andrew W. Horowitz. 2002. "Are International Remittances Altruism or Insurance? Evidence from Guyana Using Multiple-Migrant Households." *World Development* 30: 2033–2044.

Åkesson, Lisa. 2009. "Remittances and Inequality in Cape Verde: The Impact of Changing Family Organization." *Global Networks* 9: 381–398.

Alexander, Trent. 1998. "The Great Migration in Comparative Perspective: Interpreting the Urban Origins of Southern Black Migrants to Pittsburg." *Social Science History* 22: 349–376.

———. 2005. "'They're Never Here More Than a Year': Return Migration in the Southern Exodus, 1940–1980." *Journal of Social History* 38: 653–671.

———. 2006. "Defining the Diaspora: Appalachians in the Great Migration." *Journal of Interdisplinary History* 37: 219–247.

Carruthers, Ashley. 2008. "Saigon from the Diaspora." *Singapore Journal of Tropical Geography* 29: 68–86.

Cheal, David. 1991. *Family and the State of Theory.* Toronto: University of Toronto Press.

Cohen, Jeffrey. 2001. "Transnational Migration in Rural Oaxaca, Mexico: Dependency, Development, and the Household." *American Anthropologist* 103 (4): 954–967.

Committee for Overseas Vietnamese. 2005. *Overseas Vietnamese Community: Questions and Answers.* Hanoi: Gioi Publishing House.

Du Quang Nam. 2005. "Ho Chi Minh City Main Statistics, 1976–2005." Ho Chi Minh City: Ho Chi Minh City Statistical Office.

Duval, David Timothy. 2004. "Linking Return Visits and Return Migration among Commonwealth Eastern Caribbean Migrants in Toronto." *Global Networks* 4 (1): 51–67.

Earl, Catherine. 2004. "Leisure and Social Mobility in Ho Chi Minh City." In *Social Inequality in Vietnam and the Challenges to Reform,* ed. Taylor, 351–379.

Ebashi, Masahiko. 1997. "The Economic Take-Off." In *Vietnam Joins the World,* ed. Morley and Nishihara, 37–65.

Espiritu, Yến Lê. 2003. *Home Bound: Filipino American Lives across Cultures, Communities, and Countries.* Berkeley: University of California Press.

Fajnzylber, Pablo, and J. Humberto Lopez. 2007. "Close to Home: The Development Impact of Remittances in Latin America." Washington, DC: World Bank.

Fitzgerald, David Scott. 2013. "Immigrant Impacts in Mexico." In *How Immigrants Impace Their Homelands,* edited by Susan Eckstein and Adil Najam, 114–137. Durham, NC: Duke University Press.

Freeman, James M. 1995. *Changing Identities: Vietnamese Americans, 1975–1995.* Boston: Allyn and Bacon.

Gamburd, Michele Ruth. 2000. *The Kitchen Spoon's Handle: Transnationalism and Sri Lanka's Migrant Housemaids.* Ithaca, NY: Cornell University Press.

Gmelch, George. 1980. "Return Migration." *Annual Review of Anthropology* 9: 135–159.

Goldring, Luin. 1998. "The Power of Status in Transnational Social Fields." In *Transnationalism from Below,* ed. Michael Peter Smith and Luis Eduardo Guarnizo, 165–195. New Brunswick, NJ: Transaction.

Hondagneu-Sotelo, Pierrette. 2001. *Domestica: Immigrant Workers Cleaning and Caring in the Shadows of Affluence.* Los Angeles: University of California Press.

Hondagneu-Sotelo, Pierrette, and Ernestine Avila. 1997. "'I'm Here, but I'm There': The Meanings of Latina Transnational Motherhood." *Gender & Society* 11 (5): 548–571.

Lamb, David. 1997. "Viet Kieu: A Bridge between Two Worlds." *Los Angeles Times,* November 4, A1, A8–A9.

Larmer, Brook. 2000. "You Can Go Home Again: Returning 'Viet Kieu' Add a Strong Dash of America." *Newsweek,* November 27, 52.

Lee, Anne S. 1974. "Return Migration in the United States." *International Migration Review* 8 (2): 283–300.

Levitt, Peggy. 1998. "Social Remittances: Migration Driven Local-Level Forms of Cultural Diffusion." *International Migration Review* 32 (4): 926–948.

———. 2001. "Transnational Migration: Taking Stock and Future Directions." *Global Networks* 1 (3): 195–216.

Levitt, Peggy, Josh DeWind, and Steven Vertovec. 2003. "International Perspectives on Transnational Migration: An Introduction." *International Migration Review* 37: 565–575.

Levitt, Peggy, and Nina Glick Schiller. 2004. "Conceptualizing Simultaneity: A Transnational Social Field Perspective on Society." *International Migration Review* 38 (3): 1002–1039.

Long, Lynellyn D. 2004. "Viet Kieu on a Fast Track Back." In *Coming Home?: Refugees, Migrants, and Those Who Stayed Behind,* ed. Oxfeld and Long, 65–89.

Mahler, Sarah J. 1998. "Theoretical and Empirical Contributions toward a Research Agenda for Transnationalism." In *Transnationalism from Below,* ed. Michael Peter Smith and Luis Eduardo Guarnizo, 64–102. New Brunswick, NJ: Transaction.

———. 2001. "Transnational Relationships: The Struggle to Communicate across Borders." *Identities* 7 (4): 583–619.

McKay, Deirdre. 2003. "Cultivating New Local Futures: Remittance Economies and Land-Use Patterns in Ifugao, Phillipines." *Journal of Southeast Asian Studies* 34 (2): 285–306.

Morley, James W., and Masashi Nishihara. 1997. "Vietnam Joins the World." In *Vietnam Joins the World,* ed. Morley and Nishihara, 3–14.

Morley, James W., and Masashi Nishihara, eds. 1997. *Vietnam Joins the World.* Armonk, NY: M. E. Sharpe Press.

Nguyen Dang Anh. 2005. "Enhancing the Development Impact of Migrant Remittances and Diaspora: The Case of Vietnam." *Asia-Pacific Population Journal* 20 (3): 111–122.

Nguyen, Hong. 2002. "*Viet Kieu* Remittances Set to Top $2 Billion Target." *Vietnam Investment Review,* December 2.

Nguyen Viet Cuong. 2009. "The Impact of International and Internal Remittances on Household Welfare: Evidence from Vietnam." *Asia-Pacific Development Journal* 16 (1): 59–92.

Nhat Hong. 1999. "Hankering for 'Viet Kieu' Money." In *Vietnam Economic News*, 12.

Oxfeld, Ellen, and Lynellyn D. Long. 2004. "Introduction: An Ethnography of Return." In *Coming Home?: Refugees, Migrants, and Those Who Stayed Behind*, 1–18.

Oxfeld, Ellen, and Lynellyn D. Long, eds. 2004. *Coming Home?: Refugees, Migrants, and Those Who Stayed Behind*. Philadelphia: University of Pennsylvania Press, 2004.

Parreñas, Rhacel. (See also Parreñas, Rhacel Salazar.) 2005. "Long Distance Intimacy: Class, Gender and Intergenerational Relations between Mothers and Children in Filipino Transnational Families." *Global Networks* 5 (4): 317–336.

Parreñas, Rhacel Salazar. 2001a. "Mothering from a Distance: Emotions, Gender, and Inter-Generational Relations in Filipino Transnational Families." *Feminist Studies* 27 (2): 361–390.

———. 2001b. *Servants of Globalization: Women, Migration, and Domestic Work*. Stanford, CA: Stanford University Press.

———. 2005. *Children of Global Migration*. Stanford, CA: Stanford University Press.

Pfau, D. Wade, and Giang Thanh Long. 2010. "The Growing Role of International Remittances in the Vietnamese Economy: Evidence from the Vietnam Household Living Standard Surveys." In *Global Movements in the Asia Pacific*, ed. Pookong Kee and Hidetaka Yoshimatsu, 225–247. Singapore: World Scientific.

Pham, Lan Thi Thanh. 2008. "Access to Credit, Remittances, and Household Welfare: The Case of Vietnam." PhD diss., University of Minnesota.

Pham, Vu. 2003. "Antedating and Anchoring Vietnamese America: Toward a Vietnamese American Historiography." *Amerasia* 29 (1): 137–152.

Pham, Vu Hong. 2002. "Beyond and before Boat People: Vietnamese American History before 1975." PhD diss., Cornell University.

Portes, Alejandro. 2001. "Introduction: The Debates and Significance of Immigrant Transnationalism." *Global Networks* 1 (3): 181–193.

Schmalzbauer, Leah. 2004. "Searching for Wages and Mothering from Afar: The Case of Honduran Transnational Families." *Journal of Marriage and Family* 66: 1317–1331.

———. 2008. "Family Divided: The Class Formation of Honduran Transnational Families." *Global Networks* 8: 329–346.

Shain, Yossi, and Aharon Barth. 2003. "Diasporas and International Relations Theory." *International Organizations* 57: 449–479.

Singh, Supriya. 2006. "Towards a Sociology of Money and Family in the India Diaspora." *Contributions to Indian Sociology* 40 (3): 375–398.

Smith, Robert Courtney. 2006. *Mexican New York: Transnational Lives of New Immigrants*. Berkeley: University of California Press.

Stark, Oded, and Robert E. B. Lucas. 1988. "Migration, Remittances, and the Family." *Economic Development and Cultural Change* 36 (3): 465–481.

Stone, Leroy O. 1974. "What We Know about Migration within Canada: A Selective Review and Agenda for Future Research." *International Migration Review* 8 (2): 267–281.

Taylor, Philip. 2004. "Introduction: Social Inequality in a Socialist State." In *Social Inequality in Vietnam and the Challenges to Reform*, 1–40.

Taylor, Philip, ed. 2004. *Social Inequality in Vietnam and the Challenges to Reform*. Singapore: Institute of Southeast Asian Studies.

Thai, Hung Cam. 2006. "Money and Masculinity among Low Wage Vietnamese Immigrants in Transnational Families." *International Journal of Sociology of the Family* 32: 247–271.

——. 2008. *For Better or for Worse: Vietnamese International Marriages in the New Global Economy*. Rutgers, NJ: Rutgers University Press.

——. 2009. "The Legacy of *Doi Moi*, the Legacy of Immigration: Overseas Vietnamese Grooms Come Home to Vietnam." In *Vietnamese Families in Transition*, ed. Daniele Belanger and Magali Barbieri, 237–262. Stanford, CA: Stanford University Press.

Thomas, Mandy. 1997. "Crossing Over: The Relationship between Overseas Vietnamese and Their Homeland." *Journal of Intercultural Studies* 18 (2): 153–176.

Tran, Tini. 2000. "Business Opportunities Draw Viet Kieu Back to Vietnam." *AsianWeek* 21 (36).

Vietnam News. 2002. "First *Viet Kieu* to Receive Property Certificate." *Vietnam News*, 2.

Wah, Chan Yuk. 2005. "Vietnamese or Chinese: Viet Kieu in the Vietnam-China Borderlands." *Journal of Chinese Overseas* 1 (2): 217–232.

World Bank. 2006. "World Development Indicators." Washington, DC: World Bank.

Wucker, Michele. 2004. "Remittances: The Perpetual Migration Machine." *World Policy Journal* 21 (2): 37–46.

Ye, Min. 2013. "How Overseas Chinese Spurred the Economic "Miracle" in Their Homeland." In *How Immigrants Impace Their Homelands*, edited by Susan Eckstein and Adil Najam, 52-74. Durham: Duke University Press.

Zelizer, Viviana. 1989. "The Social Meaning of Money: 'Special Monies.'" *American Journal of Sociology* 95 (2): 342–377.

Conclusion
Living Transpacifically

YUNTE HUANG

July 25, 1991. Seeing the city of Beijing submerged beneath a sea of white clouds causes in me no particular sensation—such nonchalance, however, surprises me. I have often dreamed about this moment, sitting in an airplane, looking down on the city, or rather, the country I am leaving behind, a country where I feel all hopes have been dashed by the gunshots and bloodshed during the student protests two years ago, in which I also participated.

On one of those darkest days following the government crackdown in June 1989, I was sitting with S on a wooden bench by the campus lake, our usual spot, shaded by drooping willows, tall grasses, and wild flowers. After a long silence—it's our preferred mode of communication, a kind of lover's discourse, nonverbal and telepathic like a mental board game we would play for fun (or pain) every day, with improvised rules and no declared winner; but our silence was compounded in those days by the horror hanging in the air—she suddenly spoke about leaving the country.

She gave no explanations, only a simple and yet—I knew—strong wish. The idea of going abroad had never occurred to me, although I majored in English, planned to specialize in American poetry, and felt the country held no future for me.

Until then, my life had been one of constant expansion of vision: I had grown up in a rural village in the South, a place so small and isolated that people would be stuck forever unless they were gifted dreamers or, like in my case, had an accident which would puncture a hole in the insulated walls of provinciality.

My so-called accident occurred when I was eleven.

One night I was playing with an old, beat-up transistor radio that had belonged to my grandfather but was now left to lie around in our house. I pulled up, like my grandfather had used to do, the rusted, crooked antenna and switched to the shortwave channels. Adjusting the dial to search for a channel with bearable audibility—most channels simply buzzed either because the machine was too old or because the signals had, as often happened in the Cold War years, been scrambled by the government—I suddenly came to a spot where, after a few seconds of static, a clear, slow, and manly voice in English rang out: "This is VOA, the Voice of America, broadcasting in Special English . . ."

This encounter became a turning point in my life. In the ensuing high school years, I regularly tuned in to the daily half-hour broadcast, which began with ten minutes of the latest news followed by twenty minutes of feature programming in American culture, history, science, or short stories. My favorite was the short program called "Words and Their Stories," which introduced American idioms and their colorful etymologies. The broadcast is called Special English because its vocabulary is limited to 1,500 words, written in short and simple sentences that supposedly contain only one idea, and spoken at a slower pace, about two-thirds the speed of standard English.

Completely oblivious to the ideological agendas of VOA, a propaganda machine controlled by the U.S. State Department in the Cold War era (and also, as I now realize, at the risk of sending my parents to jail, because listening to "politically subversive" foreign radio stations was illegal at the time and parents would be held responsible for any political "crimes" committed by their pre-adult children), I had learned from the broadcasting a great deal of English and was later able to enter the top university in the country.

Her voice that day, when S spoke about going abroad, also had the magic of that old transistor radio—it opened up my world instantly. The gentle ripples on the surface of the lake, which I felt to have been caused, not by the summer breezes brushing my cheeks, but by her soft-spoken words, reminded me of the invisible shortwaves that had once traveled thousands of miles to visit me every night, carrying signals that were at first barely comprehensible, but nonetheless thoroughly tantalizing.

People often regard such moments as "awakening," but actually, or at least for me, the opposite is true: It's like falling into slumber, into dreams that cannot blossom in the hard clay of reality.

After our minds were made up—we agreed on the spot that we would both go to America—we spent the ensuing two years preparing for the English exams, taking the exams, contacting American colleges, and dealing with layers of government bureaucracy in order to get permission to leave the country, a process that inevitably involved bribes and forgeries.

Now flying above the clouds, with my old world behind me, I feel, however, neither a sense of relief nor excitement. Such a strange mental state—strange because it doesn't fit any description I have read in books about a situation like this, nor does it fit my own expectation—may have been, as I tell myself, a result of my repressed anxiety over the journey ahead.

In some ways I feel I am no stranger to this route of travel, even though this is my first trip abroad. Those radio signals, like winged angels, used to travel along this airway above the Pacific Ocean, only in the reverse direction. My journey, then, is merely to complete a circle, or to draw a bigger one.

Emerson once said that circle is "the highest emblem in the cipher of the world": "The eye is the first circle; the horizon which it forms is the second; and throughout nature this primary figure is repeated without end." But the New England sage also reminded us that behind the beautiful geometrics of ever expanding circles lies the brutal logic of destruction: "The new continents are built out of the ruins of an old planet; the new races fed out of the decomposition of the foregoing. New arts destroy the old."

Perhaps it is this fear of destruction, rather than the excitement of the new, that has made me feel numb at the moment when my beloved city for four years disappears beneath the clouds, and gone with it, the whole country.

> *edges of sedge*
> *grass sparse*
> *on red clay*
> *lay a horizon*
> *marked out*
> *vertically*
> *time zones*
> *traversed*
> *in confusion*

A day later, I land in Tuscaloosa, Alabama. I would like to make a comparison, but nothing like it exists in the People's Republic of China. Imagine, for example, leaving Manhattan and arriving in Manhattan, Kansas; or Moscow, and ending up in Moscow, Idaho. This is not to say that the experience would necessarily be unpleasant, but that one's mind boggles, and the senses gasp in the new air of change.

The Deep South, however, has its charms. Alabama, as Carl Carmer puts it, is "a land with a spell on it—not a good spell, always. Moons, red with the dust of barren hills, thin pine trunks barring horizons, festering swamps, restless yellow rivers, are all parts of a feeling—a strange certainty that above and around them hovers enchantment—an emanation of malevolence that threatens to destroy men through dark ways of its own." Carmer was a Yankee author who had taught English at the University of Alabama in the 1920s, at the height of Ku Klux Klan reign of racial terror and violence. At the time of my arrival,

Tuscaloosa may have already lost quite a bit of its malevolent luster as depicted by Carmer; nevertheless, the "Heart of Dixie" is a shock for me. Having grown up in China's homogenous society, I feel disoriented after being suddenly thrown into an environment where race, to put it mildly, matters.

I often hide out in the University library, burying myself among stacks of books, reading titles on the spines, flipping through pages, and looking for who knows what.

The first time I go to the library, however, I have something specific in mind—I'm looking for classical Chinese porn novels. In China, those are banned books, available only to high-level officials and tenured professors of Chinese literature. Pornography, it seems, is a social privilege. But not always; perhaps only classical Chinese pornography needs to be protected like family jewels. Porn novels translated from Western languages, by contrast, have been allowed to flood the market.

In college, my roommates and I were making a decent living by translating porn novels from English. The way it works is like this: a middleman would approach us, English majors, give us a book to translate, and then sell the translation to an official, state-run publisher. We would each do a chapter or two, working overnight in our dorm room, under candlelight after curfew, reading feverishly, looking up unfamiliar words in an English-Chinese dictionary, words like "cunt," "vagina," "orgasm," "cum," which made our hearts jump and palms sweat. Tantalizing words attacked the senses of budding youths across the barriers of language like candlelight attracting moths in darkness.

After we got paid, we would go out and have a feast, making toasts to each one of those beautiful words that would never be part of our college English curriculum but were now paying for our feast. "A toast to 'vagina,' hurray!" "Salute to 'BJ,' *ganbei!*" Our names as translators would of course never appear in those books or our CVs. Unlike silly moths, we didn't get burned, at least not yet. We metamorphosed.

The library, it turns out, does not have the Chinese originals of those books; there are only English translations.

I find a quiet spot in the library and sit down to read. I am quickly disappointed. Whenever the story reaches the juicy parts, the translation changes from English to Latin! I throw down the books in disgust and curse the pretentious translators.

After sex runs into a dead end in the library, my interest quickly turns to politics. I start looking for another kind of material that is also banned in China: documents related to the Tiananmen Square massacre in 1989, the event which has much to do with my being here now. On this subject the library has a decent collection: hundreds of books, thousands of images, and even half a dozen documentary videos.

Searching through the vast archive, I feel a particular hunger for connectedness: I'm looking to see if I can find myself in it.

In those tumultuous two months, when the city of Beijing was in complete chaos, with students undergoing hunger strikes on the Square, protesters swarming everywhere, S and I were also on the streets every day. Strangely, though, we never took a picture of ourselves or any of the scenes, in part for fear of leaving any evidence for the officials who would later try to hunt down every participant who could be identified in visual archives—security cameras, personal snapshots, and foreign media lenses were ubiquitous in those days.

Our good fortune in not being captured, electronically or bodily, now seems to have become a misfortune: Unable to find myself in the sea of images, I feel consigned to the oblivion of history. The evidentiary vacuum becomes especially painful for me now that our relationship is falling apart; seeing our faces together in the historical event which once brought us closer would at least provide some however ineffective consolation.

One day, while browsing through the archives in the library, my attention is caught by the following passage in a book:

> The occupation of Tiananmen Square in late May 1989 by thousands of Chinese students, workers, and other citizens stirred the imagination of millions throughout the world, but evoked far less response from the U.S. government than did the possibility of successfully concluding discussions then under way with the PRC concerning intellectual property protection. The Bush administration's professed concern about interfering in China's internal affairs, which supposedly constrained it from pushing with vigor, either publicly or privately, for a peaceful resolution of the occupation of the square, simply did not carry over to intellectual property. Instead, even as tensions mounted between hunger strikers in the square and elders of the Chinese Communist party, the U.S. government repeatedly threatened the PRC with massive and unprecedented trade sanctions if China did not promise to devise legal protection for computer software to America's liking. And so it was that as the Chinese government spent May 19 putting the finishing touches to the declaration of martial law that was to signal a tragic end to the Beijing Spring of 1989, American negotiators were busy putting their own finishing touches to a memorandum regarding computer software protection.
>
> The decisions that led the U.S. government to pay insufficient heed to the epochal events culminating on June 4, 1989, and instead to devote a

goodly portion of its available diplomatic leverage to securing promises about software, were neither inadvertent nor passing tactical errors.

I would hate to believe that my own fate is somehow inextricably tied up with some shady business interests negotiated between a country that has dashed my hopes and a country that promises to fulfill all of them. But the evidence presented in this book seems undeniable.

If the author's charge is true—that in 1989 the Bush administration promised to turn a blind eye to the impending massacre on Tiananmen Square on the condition that the Chinese government would yield to the U.S. corporate demand for protections of intellectual property—then in retrospect, I myself may have involuntarily played a small part in these larger events that seem to have sealed my own fate.

During my four years in Beijing, I spent endless hours in bookstores. At many bookstores in China at the time, there was always a room that would look like an inner chamber of a jewelry store where the owner hides rare items of dubious provenance, available for viewing and touching only by his best clients. At the entrance of the room, a sign would be posted: "NO ADMITTANCE TO FOREIGNERS." Inside that room, beyond the reach of the so-called foreigners, lay a secret world of phantasmagoria: that's where the pirated editions of Western-language books were sold.

From the viewpoint of Western countries, who have pillaged the world for centuries in the name of progress, religion, or even humanity, this room, with its piles of promiscuously imitated, cheaply reproduced, and clandestinely transacted items of piracy, symbolizes the inexcusable lawlessness and backwardness of Third World countries. But from the standpoint of the latter, piracy is like the revenge of lost innocence, or at least an attempt to chip away slightly the other's edge and use those scraps to anneal their own blades.

To me, a tiny speck in the uneven flows of global, transpacific cultural capital, the stuffy room offered the richest intellectual resources I could find at a bargain price: I bought and read with hunger the classics of Western literature and philosophy, anything from Mark Twain's *Adventures of Huckleberry Finn* to Martin Heidegger's *Being and Time,* from Herman Melville's *Moby-Dick* to Theodore Adorno's *Aesthetic Theory.* Even the textbooks for my English courses, like the Norton anthologies of British and American literature, were pirated copies purchased by my University and lent to the students.

One year, when an American editor of the Norton Anthology came to visit our class, we received advance warnings from the English Department not to bring our regular textbooks to the lecture. Then, minutes before the guest lecturer was to show up, several copies of the original editions of the anthology miraculously appeared.

The honored visitor was almost moved to tears when he saw a class of fifty students huddling over half a dozen copies of his book, as if we were a group of starved children in an African village treasuring the only copy of a textbook. Little did he know that the seeming hunger in our look was merely an expression of admiration for the beautiful cover, design, and fine paper of the original edition, which we had never seen, even though many of us had learned the book's contents almost by heart from its cheap imitation.

After the lecture, the original editions disappeared as mysteriously as they had appeared.

Up to the time of the Tiananmen massacre, the unofficial, routine Chinese response to the Western demand for better protection of intellectual property was this snickering retort: "What intellectual property? We Chinese invented paper, gun powder, compass, printing and whatnot, but we didn't even get a penny for them." Apparently, in 1989, the beneficiaries of piracy, the Chinese students who were eager to learn about the West, paid dearly, with their young blood.

When such a cruel irony finally dawns upon me, I can only think of what Milan Kundera once said, "Here the historical situation is not a background, a stage set before which human situations unfold; it is itself a human situation, a growing existential situation." The pirated editions of those books I have carried with me across the Pacific Ocean, both physically and mentally, seem to have sealed my fate the minute my hand touched them in those clandestine backrooms of Beijing bookstores.

J. Francisco Benitez

J. Francisco Benitez has recently become the ninth president of Philippine Women's University in Manila. He was formerly an assistant professor of Comparative Literature at the University of Washington. He is currently completing a manuscript on Philippine literature using Tagalog, Spanish, and English texts to explore literary subjectivity as a technology of the self in the early twentieth-century colonial Philippines. He continues to serve as Adjunct Faculty of the Comparative Literature Department and the Southeast Asia Program at the University of Washington, and his scholarly work focuses on diaspora and transnationalism, nationalism and narrative, postcolonial literature and theory, Filipino and Filipino American literature, and Philippine film.

Yến Lê Espiritu

Yến Lê Espiritu is currently a professor in the Department of Ethnic Studies at the University of California, San Diego. She is the author of three award-winning books: *Asian American Panethnicity: Bridging Institutions and Identities* (Temple University Press, 1992); *Filipino American Lives* (Temple University Press, 1995); *Asian American Women and Men: Labor, Laws, and Love* (Sage, 1997); and *Home Bound: Filipino American Lives Across Cultures, Communities, and Countries* (University of California Press, 2003). Her latest book, *Body Counts: The Vietnam War and Militarized Refuge(es)*, will be published in Fall 2014 by the University of California Press.

Janet Hoskins

Janet Hoskins is professor of Anthropology and Religion at the University of Southern California, Los Angeles. She is the author of *The Play of Time: Kodi Perspectives on Calendars, History and Exchange* (University of California Press, 1994, winner of the 1996 Benda Prize for Southeast Asian Studies), *Biographical Objects: How Things Tell the Story of People's Lives* (Routledge, 1998), and is a contributing editor of *Headhunting and the Social Imagination in Southeast Asia* (Stanford University Press, 1996), *Anthropology as a Search for the Subject: The Space Between One Self and Another* (Donizelli, 1999), and *Fragments from Forests and Libraries* (Carolina Academic Press, 2000). After two decades doing ethnographic research in Eastern Indonesia, she moved to studying transnational Vietnamese religion, and recently completed *The Divine Eye and the Diaspora: Vietnamese Syncretism Becomes Transpacific Caodaism* (University of Hawaiʻi Press, 2015). From 2011–2013 she was president of the Society for the Anthropology of Religion, an official section of the American Anthropological Association.

Yunte Huang

Yunte Huang is professor of English at the University of California, Santa Barbara. He is the author of *Transpacific Imaginations: History, Literature, Counterpoetics* (Harvard University Press, 2008), and *Transpacific Displacement: Ethnography, Translation, and Intertextual Travel in Twentieth-Century American Literature* (University of California Press, 2002). His most recent book, *Charlie Chan: The Untold Story of the Honorable Detective and His Rendezvous with American History* (W. W. Norton, 2010), won the Edgar Award and was a finalist for the National Book Critics Circle Award.

Heonik Kwon

Heonik Kwon is professorial senior research fellow at Trinity College, University of Cambridge, and previously taught social anthropology in the London School of Economics. He has conducted fieldwork in indigenous Siberia, central Vietnam, and, more recently, in Korea. He is the author of the prizewinning *After the Massacre* (University of California Press, 2006) and *Ghosts of War in Vietnam* (Cambridge University Press, 2008). His other publications include *The Other Cold War* (Columbia University Press, 2010) and *North Korea: Beyond Charismatic Politics* (Rowman and Littlefield, 2012, coauthored). His forthcoming book explores intimate histories of the Korean War.

Weiqiang Lin

Weiqiang Lin is a doctoral candidate at Royal Holloway, University of London, and has experience both in academia and government service. His research interests converge around issues of mobilities, in particular air transport, urban transport, migration, and transnationalism in the Asian context. In 2010 he won the Wang Gungwu Medal and Prize for best Master's thesis at the National University of Singapore. He has published in a diverse range of edited volumes and peer-reviewed journals in recent years, including *cultural geographies, Geoforum, Political Geography,* and *Mobilities*. His most immediate lines of flight in the future will see him explore various sociocultural aspects of airspace-making in Southeast Asia, and the consequent transnational mobilities that result from them.

Akira Mizuta Lippit

Akira Mizuta Lippit teaches film and literature at the University of Southern California. His teaching and research focus on the history and theory of cinema, world literature, and critical theory; Japanese film and culture; and visual cultural studies. His published work reflects these areas and includes three books: *Ex-Cinema: From a Theory of Experimental Film and Video* (University of California Press, 2012), *Atomic Light (Shadow Optics)* (University of Minnesota Press, 2005), and *Electric Animal: Toward a Rhetoric of Wildlife* (University of Minnesota Press, 2000). Lippit is presently finishing a book-length study on contemporary Japanese cinema, which looks at the relationship of late twentieth- and early twenty-first-century Japanese culture to the concept of the world.

Nancy C. Lutkehaus

Nancy Lutkehaus's research interests include gender and political economy, art and anthropology, the history of anthropology, and visual anthropology. Her ethnographic research has focused on Pacific Island cultures. She is author of *Zaria's Fire: Engendered Moments in Manam Ethnography* (Carolina Academic Press, 1995) and *Margaret Mead: The Making of an American Icon* (Princeton University Press, 2008), and the co-edited volumes *Sepik Heritage: Tradition and Change in Papua New Guinea* (Carolina Academic Press, 1990), *Gender Rituals: Female Initiation in Melanesia* (Routledge, 1995), *Gendered Missions: Women and Men in Missionary Discourse and Practice* (University of Michigan Press, 1999). She was a scholar at the Getty Research Institute where she started her current project, "The Met Goes Primitive": *The Western Transformation of Artifacts into "Primitive Art,"* presented in 2013 as the Jensen Memorial Lectures at the Frobenius Institute, Frankfurt, Germany.

Viet Thanh Nguyen

Viet Thanh Nguyen is an associate professor of English and American Studies and Ethnicity at the University of Southern California. He is the author of *Race and Resistance: Literature and Politics in Asian America* (Oxford University Press, 2002). He has held residencies, fellowships, and scholarships at the Fine Arts Work Center, the Djerassi Resident Artists Program, the Bread Loaf Writers' Conference, the Radcliffe Institute for Advanced Study, and the American Council of Learned Societies. He is currently working on a comparative study of American and Vietnamese memories and representations of the American War in Vietnam, focusing on the literary and visual arts. Grove/Atlantic will publish his novel *The Sympathizer* in 2015.

John Carlos Rowe

John Carlos Rowe is University of Southern California (USC) Associates' Professor of the Humanities. He is the author of nine books, including *Literary Culture and U.S. Imperialism: From the Revolution to World War II* (Oxford University Press, 2000), *Afterlives of Modernism: Liberalism, Transnationalism, and Political Critique* (University Press of New England, 2011), and *The Cultural Politics of the New American Studies* (Open Humanities Press, 2012), available in open access from www.openhumanitiespress.org, as well as nine edited volumes, including *A Concise Companion to American Studies* (Wiley-Blackwells, 2010). His area of specialization is the cultural history of U.S. imperialism.

Laurie J. Sears

Laurie J. Sears is the author and editor of books and articles about history, literature, and the politics of empire in twentieth-century Indonesia. Her publications include *Shadows of Empire: Colonial Discourse and Javanese Tales* (Duke University Press, 1996), which won the Harry Benda Book Award of the Association for Asian Studies in 1999. She is also the editor of *Fantasizing the Feminine in Indonesia* (Duke University Press, 1996) and *Knowing Southeast Asian Subjects* (University of Washington Press, 2007). She is a professor in the University of Washington History Department where she teaches critical historiographies, feminist methodologies, and Indonesian histories. Her latest book, *Situated Testimonies: Dread and Enchantment in an Indonesian Literary Archive* (University of Hawai'i Press, 2013) looks at psychoanalysis as a transnational discourse of desire in colonial and postcolonial Indonesia.

Hung Cam Thai

Hung Cam Thai is associate professor of Sociology and Asian American Studies at Pomona College in the Claremont University Consortium, where he is also president of the Pacific Basin Institute and chair of Sociology. His first book, *For Better or for Worse: Vietnamese International Marriages in the New Global Economy* (Rutgers University Press, 2008), is a study of international marriages linking women in Vietnam and overseas Vietnamese men living in the diaspora. His second book, *Insufficient Funds: Money in Low Wage Transnational Families* (Stanford University Press, 2013) examines how and why transnational families in the Vietnamese diaspora spend, receive, and give money. An award-winning teacher, he is a recipient of fellowships from the Haynes Foundation, Hewlett Foundation, National University of Singapore, and the Institute of East Asian Studies at Berkeley. He is currently writing a book about how people evaluate each other along lines of financial and moral worth in contemporary Vietnam.

Biao Xiang

Biao Xiang is a lecturer in Social Anthropology at the University of Oxford. He is the author of *The Intermediary Trap* (Princeton University Press, forthcoming); *Global "Body Shopping"* (Princeton University Press, 2007, winner of the 2008 Anthony Leeds Prize; Chinese edition by Peking University Press, 2012); *Transcending Boundaries* (Chinese edition by Sanlian Press 2000; English edition by Brill Academic Publishers, 2005), *Return: Nationalizing Transnational Mobility in Asia* (co-edited with Brenda Yeoh and Mika Toyota, Duke University Press, 2013) and over forty articles in both English and Chinese. He was awarded the 2012 William L. Holland Prize for outstanding article in *Pacific Affairs*.

Brenda S. A. Yeoh

Brenda S. A. Yeoh is Provost's Chair Professor in the Department of Geography, as well as dean of the Faculty of Arts and Social Sciences, at the National University of Singapore (NUS). She is also the research leader of the Asian Migration Cluster at the Asia Research Institute, NUS. Her research interests focus on the geographies of migration and include key themes such as cosmopolitanism and highly skilled talent migration; gender, social reproduction, and care migration; migration, national identity, and citizenship issues; globalizing universities and international student mobilities; and cultural politics, family dynamics, and international marriage migrants. She has published widely in these fields. Her latest book titles include *The Cultural Politics of Talent Migration in East Asia* (Routledge, 2012, with Shirlena Huang); *Migration and Diversity in Asian Contexts* (ISEAS Press, 2012, with Lai Ah Eng and Francis Collins); and *Return: Nationalizing Transnational Mobility in Asia* (Duke University Press, 2013, with Biao Xiang and Mika Toyota).

California, 32, 43, 64, 109–129, 140, 211, 219; Camp Pendleton, 201–202, 209–211; 214–216, 220; Monterey Park, 45–46

Camacho, Keith, 9

Cambodia, 7–8, 10, 109, 118, 153, 162, 202, 213

Canada, 2, 33, 43, 45, 47, 51, 54, 97, 137, 147, 229, 236–237, 243

capital: capitalism, 1–33, 46, 49–50, 77, 85–99, 102, 148, 154, 158, 164, 185, 197n. 4, 231, 226, 245; cultural capital, 53; East Asian capitalism, 88–89; Euro-American capitalism, 44–45; free trade and capitalism, 16, 139; capitalism as justified by heteronormativity, 16

Cartier, Carolyn L., 47

Chakrabarty, Dipesh, 17, 73–74, 76–78, 80

Chatterjee, Partha, 74

Chen, Kuan-Hsing, 21–22, 34n. 9, 35n. 15

Cheng, Anne Anlin: *The Melancholy of Race*, 152. *See also* race, melancholia and

China, 1–33, 43, 55–56, 58, 64, 109, 111, 117, 121, 134–148, 158, 164, 205, 233, 252–255; bombing of embassy in Belgrade, 95–96; Central Committee, 94; Chimerica, 86, 102 n. 3; cross-Strait crisis, 95; Cultural Revolution, 92–93; G2, 86, 102n. 3; human rights record of, 95–96; nationalism, 85–97; and the Pacific Paradox, 29, 85–103; Twelve-Characters Approach, 97–98

China Can Say No, 86

Chinatowns (North American), 45

Chinn, Thomas, 45

Chiou, Pauline, 49

Cho, Grace, 34 n. 8

Chuh, Kandice, 174n. 7

cinema, 15, 31, 181–199

Clifford, James, 174n. 4

Cold War, 6, 18, 64–81, 95, 142, 144, 153, 162, 251; Asian Cold War, 65; as bipolar conflict, 81; post-, 20; cf. the "long peace," 67; racial inequality as a "Cold War liability," 70; transpacific Cold War, 29, 64–91

colonialism, 8–9, 13, 20–21, 27, 32; military, neocolonialism, 14, 21, 32 161; and religion, 173; settler colonialism, 23, 220; and sexual slavery, 183

comfort women, 15. *See also* colonialism, and sexual slavery

communism, 7, 66, 70–71, 77–79, 87–88, 94, 206, 219–220; Chinese Communist Party, 254; containment of, 7, 70, 212–214

Confucianism, 5–6; neo-Confucianism, 88–89

Connery, Chris, 7

Conradson, David, 53

Conwell, Donna, 130n. 13

cosmopolitanism, 3, 13–14, 25–26, 31, 49, 52, 153, 155–156, 159, 166, 168, 171; armored, 14; elite nomadism, 26

Coughlan, James E., 47

Covarrubias, Miguel, 30, 109–129; artworks: *Clark Gable vs. Edward, Prince of Wales* (1939), 114; *Harlem Dancers* (photo, n.d.), 115; *Island of Bali* (1937), 115; *Negro Drawings* (1927), 113; "Pageant of the Pacific" murals, 109–129; *The Prince of Wales and Other Famous Americans* (1925), 113; books: *The Eagle, the Jaguar and the Serpent: Indian Art of the Americas* (1954), 117; *Indian Art of Mexico and Central America* (1957), 117; Guggenheim fellowship, 115, 118; marriage to Rosa Cowen, 114, 130n. 11

Cuba, 26, 145, 202–204; Guantanamo Bay, 145

Cumings, Bruce, 7–8, 64–65, 81

decolonization, 134–148

Deleuze, Gilles, 169–170, 175nn. 19, 21, 198n. 11; and Guattari, 192; and Parnet, 44

Deng, Xiaoping, 92

De Young Museum, 110, 128

minorities (cont.)
  literature, 198–199n. 11; minor
  transnationalism, 11
Mitchell, Timothy, 5
Miyoshi, Masao, 16, 34n. 12, 154
mobility, 3, 25, 45–49, 85–90; of Asian
  versus white migrants, 52–53; astronaut
  families, 46; capital and, 45–46; dual
  and flexible citizenship, vii, 46–47;
  elitism and, 155; exile, vii; Guangzhou
  Overseas Students Fair, 98–99;
  intraregional flows, 53; neoliberalism,
  101–102; overseas working conditions,
  234–236; regulation, 53; return visits,
  229
money: allocation of, 239–241; as
  culturally specific, 225; distribution of,
  237–239; remittances, 28, 32, 53–54,
  225–245; special money, 226; transfer
  types, 233
Montenegro, Roberto, 117
Mrazek, Rudolf, 26
Mullen, Bill, 34n. 7

Nandy, Ashis, 5
nations: and *guojia,* 92; as imagined
  communities, 31; indigenous, 47; regions
  and regionalism, 6–7. *See also*
  Anderson, Benedict
Native Americans, 110, 139–141, 146–147,
  209–210, 220
neoliberalism, 13–14, 85; transpacific, 101
neostatism. *See* statism
Neuhaus, Eugen, 121, 127, 130n. 16,
  131n. 30
New Zealand, 2, 33
Nguyen, Viet Thanh, vii–viii, 1–33, 34n.
  13, 81
Nonini, Donald, 53
North Atlantic Treaty Organization
  (NATO), 86

Obama, Barack Hussein, 109, 111, 129nn.
  1, 2, 145
Oceania, 9

oceans: oceanic thinking, 136–138; Oceans
  Connect, 149n. 1; transoceanic, 42
Okihiro, Gary, 140
Oles, James 130n. 12
Olson, James S., 71
Olympics (Beijing), 86–87
Ong, Aihwa, 45–50, 90–91
Orientalism, 4–33, 17, 135–136, 167–168;
  self-orientalizing, 88
Orozoco, Jose Clemente, 112
Osgood, Robert E., 72

Pacific, vii; as "American lake," 86;
  counter-Pacific space, 86; economic
  development of, 3; as imperial fantasy,
  3; insular communities, neglect of,
  135–136; the "Pacific century," viii;
  Pacific Unity as artistic style, 109;
  paradox, 29, 85–102; Spanish Pacific, 33
Pacific Asia, 6, 55–56
Pacific Basin, 2, 42, 44–45; representa-
  tions of, 123–125
Pacific Islands, 23, 33; Alliance of Small
  Island States (AOSIS); 148; marginal-
  ization of, 143–145; Pacific Islanders, 33
Pacific Rim, 2, 7, 42, 44–45, 47–48, 85–91,
  109; America's Pacific Rim, 44;
  asymmetrical understanding of, 58;
  discourse, 7; reconceived in oceanic
  terms, 137; as trope, 2
Palat, Ravi, 44
Palumbo-Liu, David, 10
Pan-Asianism, 5–6
Parreñas, Rhacel, 11, 15
Perez, Craig Santos, 135
Pfau, D. Wade, 47
Philippines, 7, 9, 26, 32, 153–174; as
  America's "First Vietnam," 204–206;
  Filipino diaspora, 51, 153–174; Filipinos,
  50; healthcare workers, 141–142;
  Marcos regime, 159–162; Philippine-
  American War, 141–142; Spanish
  colonization, 164; as U.S. client-state,
  141
Pollock, Sheldon, 80

postcolonialism, 29, 68–69, 134–148; charge of presentism, 134
Portes, Alejandro, 41
power: soft power vs. crude power, 88–89
Prashad, Vijay, 34n. 7
Pratt, Gerry, 50–51
Preston, Valerie, 47
provincializing, 17

queer studies: lesbianism, 169; queer diasporas, 16; queerness, 16. *See also* feminist studies; gender studies; sexuality

race, 111–112, 159–174, 252–253; affinities based on color, 123; black Americans in Harlem, 113–114; Chineseness, 96–97; hybridity, 172; internment of Japanese-Americans, 128; intersectionality, 151; marginalization, 160; melancholia and, 31, 151–174; mixed-bloods, 68; racial inequality as a "Cold War liability," 70; segregation, 70
Rafael, Vicente, 174n. 6
Ratanaruang, Pen-Ek: *Last Life in the Universe* (*Ru-ang rak noi nid mahasan*, 2003), 181
Reaves, Wendy Wick, 130nn. 9, 10
remittances. *See* money
River Elegy (He Shang), 85, 88–89, 97
Rivera, Diego, 112, 129nn. 5, 8
Roberts, Randy, 71
Robinson, Geoffrey, 71
Rogers, Alisdair, 45
Rowe, John Carlos, 17, 28, 30, 134–148; scholarly state apparatus, 17, 21
Ryang, Sonia, 79
Rydell, Robert, 111

Saénz, Moisés, 117
Said, Edward, 4–33; *Culture and Imperialism*, 128; *Orientalism*, 4–5
Sakai, Naoki, 15, 192, 198nn. 9, 10
San Juan, E., Jr., 77
Scott, James, 174nn. 6, 11

See, Sarita, 174n. 2
Sears, Laurie J., 28, 30–31, 151–174, 174n. 8
Seoul War Memorial, 14
sexuality, 151–174, 181–196; and the body, 159–174, 183–184; masochism, 169–170; and pornography, 253; sadomasochism, 169–170; sex workers, 142, 161; sexual orientation, 159–174; as transgression, 166–174. *See also* gender studies; queer studies
Shigematsu, Setsu, 9
Shih, Shu-mei, 11
signifiers: enigmatic, 31
simultaneity, 46
Siu, Lok, 11
Soco, Maria Andrea, 52
Southeast Asia, 20; *Knowing Southeast Asian Subjects*, 155–157; Southeast Asian studies, vii, 20, 151–174
Soviet Union, 7
spatiality: production of, 6; transpacific, 45–49
Spivak, Gayatri, 13
Spoonley, Paul, 52
Stackpole, Ralph, 119
Stahl, Charles, 56
statism, 89; neostatism, 29, 89, 103n. 4; state capacity, 93
Stoler, Ann, 68, 174n. 6
Sukiyaki Western Django (2007), 182
Swallowtail (1996), 181–182

Tadiar, Nefertiti, 15, 174n. 1
Taiwan, 9–10, 14, 18, 21, 43, 46, 55, 86, 95; and China, 85–86, 182, 196n. 1
Tamayo, Rufino, 112
Taoism, 5
terror, 67
Thai, Hung Cam, 28, 32, 245n. 1
Thailand, 7, 109, 181, 201, 230
Tiananmen Square, 33, 93, 250–251, 253–256
tourism, 9, 23
transcolonial imagination, 140
translocalism, 3

transnationalism: 41–58; accumulation, 98–101; dimensions of, 75; and the transpacific, 5, 151–174

transpacific, vii–viii; 85–97, 135, 153–174; crossings, 53; displacement, vii–viii; migration, 42–45; neoliberalism, 101–102; routes, 136–137; studies, 2–33; subjectivities, 49–53; vis-á-vis the transatlantic, 3, 64–65

Trans-Pacific Partnership (TPP), 2, 16, 23

Trask, Haunani-Kay, 9

Trinh, T. Minh-ha, 198n. 8

Tsing, Anna, 26

Tsuda, Takeyuki, 49

Twain, Mark, 140, 255

2046 (2004), 181

Unhappy China, 86–87

United States, 14; and American exceptionalism, 31; Census Bureau, 43; China-U.S. competition, 85–97; expansionism and Manifest Destiny, 138; humanitarianism of, 220–221; military, 30, 32; as a Pacific nation, 109; Truman Doctrine, 72

University of Southern California, vii–viii

Urry, J., 25

USS Midway Museum, 218–219, 221n. 6

Utami, Ayu, 31, 166–174, 175nn. 15, 16, 20, 21

Vanity Fair, 113, 123

Vietnam, 7–8, 14, 32; low-wage immigrants, 226–245; and moves toward free-market capitalism, 231; Operation Babylift, 215–218; Operation Frequent Wind, 218–220; Parisian Vietnamese, 78–79; red blood lines, 70; refugees from, 202; Viet Hoa, 47; *Viet Kieu*, 226–245; Vietnam War, 32, 66–68, 109, 202–220; Vietnamese communities: *See* diaspora studies (Vietnamese)

Viswanathan, Gauri, 5

Von Eschen, Penny, 34n. 7

Wade, Peter, 71

Wagnleitner, Reinhold, 72

Wah, Chan Yuk, 245n. 1

Wang, Gung Wu, 55

Wang, Hui, 4, 6, 9, 17–18, 33n. 4, 34n. 14; politics of imagining Asia, 4

Wang, Shaoguang, 93

Waters, Johanna L., 47

Westad, Odd Arne, 75

Wigen, Kären, 5, 137, 147

Wilbur, Ray Lyman, 131nn. 19, 22, 28, 31

Wilkins, Thomas, 42

Williams, Adriana, 130n. 7, 131n. 21

Wilson, Rob, 42, 57, 85, 134–135; oppositional localism, 3; translocalism, 3

Wing, Hong Chui, 43

women. *See* feminist studies; gender studies; sexuality

Wong, Bernard, 45

Wong, Kar-wai, 181

Wong, Tai-Chee, 55

Woo, Jung-En, 14

Wright, Richard, 8

Xiang, Biao, 28–29, 85–102

Ybarra-Frausto, Tomas, 131n. 26

Yeoh, Brenda S. A., 28, 41–59

Yin, Xiao-Huang, 43

Yoo, Hyon Joo, 15

Young China Association, 92

Yun, Taik-Lim, 71

Yuval-Davis, Nira, 174n. 12

Zhao, Suisheng, 87

Zweig, David, 56